GOVERNANCE IN POST-CONFLICT SOCIETIES

This book explores the problem of states that fail, leading to conflict and war, and how to rebuild them. Focusing on governance as critical to post-conflict reconstruction, the contributors illustrate the connections among the core functions that governance fulfills in any society: assuring security, achieving effective provision of public goods and services, and generating legitimacy. This volume brings together chapters by scholars and practitioners studying and working on governance issues from a variety of perspectives. Divided into three sections, this volume opens by taking a fresh look at the historical record on nation-building, constitutional design in deeply divided societies, the dynamics of elections, and governance of the security sector. It then explores the range of actors involved in governance reconstruction and highlights the evolving role of the US military, the influence of multinational firms, the importance of the civil service, and the potential impact of Internet-based diasporas. Finally, it looks at local governance, highlighting the subnational state–society structures and relations in fragile and post-conflict states, and draws on case studies from Latin America, Africa, and Afghanistan.

This book will be of much interest to students of international public administration, global governance, post-conflict reconstruction, foreign policy and international relations in general, as well as to practitioners in the field.

Derick W. Brinkerhoff is Senior Fellow in International Public Management with RTI International, and has an associate faculty appointment at George Washington University's School of Public Policy and Public Administration.

CONTEMPORARY SECURITY STUDIES

NATO'S SECRET ARMIES
Operation Gladio and terrorism in Western Europe
Daniele Ganser

THE US, NATO AND MILITARY BURDEN-SHARING
Peter Kent Forster and Stephen J. Cimbala

RUSSIAN GOVERNANCE IN THE TWENTY-FIRST
CENTURY
Geo-strategy, geopolitics and new governance
Irina Isakova

THE FOREIGN OFFICE AND FINLAND 1938–1940
Diplomatic sideshow
Craig Gerrard

RETHINKING THE NATURE OF WAR
Edited by Isabelle Duyvesteyn and Jan Angstrom

PERCEPTION AND REALITY IN THE MODERN YUGOSLAV
CONFLICT
Myth, falsehood and deceit 1991–1995
Brendan O'Shea

THE POLITICAL ECONOMY OF PEACEBUILDING IN
POST-DAYTON BOSNIA
Tim Donais

THE DISTRACTED EAGLE
The rift between America and Old Europe
Peter H. Merkl

NATO AND WEAPONS OF MASS DESTRUCTION
Regional alliance, global threats
Eric R. Terzuolo

EUROPEANISATION OF NATIONAL SECURITY IDENTITY
The EU and the changing security identities of the Nordic states
Pernille Rieker

INTERNATIONAL CONFLICT PREVENTION AND PEACE-
BUILDING
Sustaining the peace in post conflict societies
Edited by T. David Mason and James D. Meernik

CONTROLLING THE WEAPONS OF WAR
Politics, persuasion, and the prohibition of inhumanity
Brian Rappert

CHANGING TRANSATLANTIC SECURITY RELATIONS
Do the U.S., the EU and Russia form a new strategic triangle?
Edited by Jan Hallenberg and Håkan Karlsson

THEORETICAL ROOTS OF US FOREIGN POLICY
Machiavelli and American unilateralism
Thomas M. Kane

CORPORATE SOLDIERS AND INTERNATIONAL SECURITY
The rise of private military companies
Christopher Kinsey

TRANSFORMING EUROPEAN MILITARIES
Coalition operations and the technology gap
Gordon Adams and Guy Ben-Ari

GLOBALIZATION AND CONFLICT
National security in a 'new' strategic era
Edited by Robert G. Patman

MILITARY FORCES IN 21ST CENTURY PEACE OPERATIONS
No job for a soldier?
James V. Arbuckle

THE POLITICAL ROAD TO WAR WITH IRAQ
Bush, 9/11 and the drive to overthrow Saddam
Nick Ritchie and Paul Rogers

BOSNIAN SECURITY AFTER DAYTON
New perspectives
Edited by Michael A. Innes

KENNEDY, JOHNSON AND NATO
Britain, America and the dynamics of alliance, 1962–68
Andrew Priest

SMALL ARMS AND SECURITY
New emerging international norms
Denise Garcia

THE UNITED STATES AND EUROPE
Beyond the Neo-Conservative divide?
Edited by John Baylis and Jon Roper

RUSSIA, NATO AND COOPERATIVE SECURITY
Bridging the gap
Lionel Ponsard

INTERNATIONAL LAW AND INTERNATIONAL RELATIONS
Bridging theory and practice
*Edited by Tom Biersteker, Peter Spiro, Chandra Lekha Sriram and
Veronica Raffo*

DETERRING INTERNATIONAL TERRORISM AND ROGUE
STATES
US national security policy after 9/11
James H. Lebovic

VIETNAM IN IRAQ
Tactics, lessons, legacies and ghosts
Edited by John Dumbrell and David Ryan

UNDERSTANDING VICTORY AND DEFEAT IN CONTEMPORARY
WAR
Edited by Jan Angstrom and Isabelle Duyvesteyn

PROPAGANDA AND INFORMATION WARFARE IN THE TWENTY-
FIRST CENTURY
Altered images and deception operations
Scot Macdonald

GOVERNANCE IN POST-CONFLICT SOCIETIES
Rebuilding fragile states
Edited by Derick W. Brinkerhoff

GOVERNANCE IN POST-CONFLICT SOCIETIES

Rebuilding fragile states

Edited by Derick W. Brinkerhoff

Routledge
Taylor & Francis Group

LONDON AND NEW YORK

First published 2007
by Routledge
2 Park Square, Milton Park, Abingdon, Oxon, OX14 4RN

Simultaneously published in the USA and Canada
by Routledge
270 Madison Ave, New York NY 10016

Routledge is an imprint of the Taylor & Francis Group, an informa business

Transferred to Digital Printing 2007

© 2007 selection and editorial matter, Derick W. Brinkerhoff; individual
chapters, the contributors

Typeset in Times by Wearset Ltd, Boldon, Tyne and Wear

British Library Cataloguing in Publication Data
A catalogue record for this book is available from the British Library

Library of Congress Cataloging in Publication Data
A catalog record for this book has been requested

ISBN10: 0-415-77150-1 (hbk)
ISBN10: 0-203-96512-4 (ebk)
ISBN10: 0-415-46324-6 (pbk)

ISBN13: 978-0-415-77150-4 (hbk)
ISBN13: 978-0-203-96512-2 (ebk)
ISBN13: 978-0-415-46324-9 (pbk)

CONTENTS

CONTENTS

ILLUSTRATIONS

Figures

Tables

CONTRIBUTORS

Nicole Ball is a Senior Fellow at the Center for International Policy in Washington, DC, and a Visiting Senior Research Scholar at the Center for International Development and Conflict Management, University of Maryland. For much of her career, she has worked on security and development. Since 1998, she has consulted for the U.K., U.S., German, and Dutch governments, UNDP, the OECD Development Assistance Committee, and the World Bank on various aspects of security in developing countries and fragile/failed states. She holds an MA in International Relations from the University of Sussex.

Eric Bjornlund is a lawyer who has designed and directed democracy and governance programs in more than twenty-five countries. He is a co-founder of Democracy International. He worked for more than a decade for the National Democratic Institute for International Affairs, served as Field Office Director in Indonesia for the Carter Center, and was a Fellow at the Woodrow Wilson International Center for Scholars. He holds an MPA from the Kennedy School of Government, Harvard University, and a JD from Columbia University.

Harry Blair is Associate Department Chair, Senior Research Scholar and Lecturer in the Department of Political Science at Yale University. His research interests currently focus on democratization in developing countries, particularly on civil society, and decentralization. He has been a frequent consultant to USAID on democracy and governance issues. Previously he taught at Bucknell, Colgate, Cornell, and Rutgers universities. He has published widely, and holds a Ph.D. from Duke University.

Gary Bland is Director of the Center for Democratic Governance at RTI International. He has written extensively on decentralization, local elections, and Latin American politics. Previous positions include: consultant on decentralization and local government in Latin America with the Woodrow Wilson Center, the Inter-American Development Bank, and the World Bank, and Democracy Fellow in the U.S. Agency for International Development's Center for Democracy and Governance. He has also been an adjunct professor of comparative public policy at Georgetown University. He holds a Ph.D. from Johns Hopkins University's School of Advanced International Studies.

Derick W. Brinkerhoff is Senior Fellow in International Public Management with RTI International, and has a faculty associate appointment at George Washington University's School of Public Policy and Public Administration. His research focuses on post-conflict societies, democratic governance, decentralization, and citizen participation. Among his previous positions have been Principal Social Scientist at Abt Associates; Associate Director for Research, International Development Management Center, University of Maryland, College Park; Resident Adviser, Ministry of Planning, Haiti; and Senior Management Specialist in USAID's Office of Rural and Institutional Development. He has published extensively, including six books and numerous book chapters and articles. He holds an Ed.D. in social policy and administration from Harvard University and a MAdmin. from the University of California, Riverside.

Jennifer M. Brinkerhoff is Associate Professor of Public Administration and International Affairs, School of Public Policy and Public Administration, George Washington University. Her research interests include international development management, government–NGO relations, and diasporas as transnational policy actors. She has done consulting and research assignments with the Asian Development Bank, the US Agency for International Development, and the World Bank. She holds a Ph.D. in public administration from the University of Southern California. She is the author of two books and over twenty-five articles and book chapters.

Glenn Cowan is a founding principal of Democracy International. He has been an adviser to the National Democratic Institute, USAID, UN, the Carter Center, and the OAS in democracy promotion and elections in thirty-five countries. He was a senior staff member in the 1980 Carter and 1984 Mondale presidential campaigns. He is currently an elected town council member in Kensington, Maryland. He holds a BA in political science from Rutgers College, and did graduate work at the School of Public and International Affairs, University of Pittsburgh.

Joshua B. Forrest is Director of the Kerr Institute of African History, Culture and Politics, at La Roche College in Pittsburgh, where he teaches courses in comparative public policy, political science, and history. His research focuses on the development of subnationalist movements in Africa, the evolution of rural civil society in Africa, and the public management of rural resources. He taught previously at the University of Vermont. He holds a Ph.D. in political science and African studies from the University of Wisconsin, Madison.

William Gallery is a Program Assistant for Democracy International. Previously, he worked for the Florida Democratic Party in the 2004 presidential campaign. He holds a BA from Harvard University.

Arthur A. Goldsmith is a Professor at the University of Massachusetts, where he teaches in the College of Management and is Senior Fellow at the John W. McCormack Graduate School of Policy Studies, Center for Democracy and Development. During the 2004 to 2005 academic year he was a Senior Research Fellow at the International Security Program and the Program on Intrastate Conflict at the Belfer Center for Science and International Affairs, Harvard University. He has published widely on comparative public administration and has been a consultant to international agencies. He holds a Ph.D. in political science from Cornell University and an MBA from Boston University.

Virginia Haufler is an Associate Professor in the Department of Government and Politics, and an Associate of the Harrison Program on the Future Global Agenda and of the Center for International Development and Conflict Management, University of Maryland, College Park. Her current research focuses on the role of the private sector in world politics, and multinational corporations and conflict prevention in the developing world. From 1999 to 2000, she was a Senior Associate at the Carnegie Endowment for International Peace. She is a consultant to industry, non-profits, and international organizations.

Aliza Belman Inbal is currently working as a senior consultant and task manager for the World Bank's Independent Evaluation Group while pursuing doctoral studies in post-conflict development at George Washington University, School of Public Policy and Public Administration. Prior to returning to academia, she held a variety of positions at MASHAV, Israel's Center for International Cooperation; she served in Kinshasa, coordinated aid to Central Asia, and was Head of the Middle Eastern Desk. She holds an M.Phil. in International Relations from the University of Cambridge.

Hanna Lerner is a faculty member at the Mandel Leadership Institute in Jerusalem, where she has coordinated an in-service professional development program on social policy studies for senior civil servants in the Ministry of Labor and Welfare. She holds a Ph.D. and an M.Phil., both in political science, from Columbia University, and an MA in philosophy from Tel-Aviv University.

Sarah Lister is Regional Governance Adviser, East Asia, for Oxfam. Her current work focuses on governance, the politics of post-conflict reconstruction, local government reform, political representation of marginalized groups, and the role of civil society in policy processes. Previously, she was Senior Researcher for Political Economy and Governance at the Afghanistan Research and Evaluation Unit in Kabul; Research Fellow in Governance, Institute of Development Studies, University of Sussex; and consultant to the World Bank, DFID, the Overseas Development Institute, and international NGOs. She holds M.Sc. and Ph.D. degrees from the London School of Economics.

Susan Merrill is a Foreign Service Officer (retd) with the U.S. Agency for International Development, where she served for over twenty years. She represented USAID at the U.S. Army War College's Peacekeeping and Stabilization Operations Institute. She was a policy study Task Force Leader, Acting Mission Director in Cambodia, Director of the Center for Development Information and Evaluation, and Director of the Office of Evaluation. Her overseas posts included Jamaica, El Salvador, Nicaragua, and Liberia. She holds an MS in Foreign Service and an MA in Economics, both from Georgetown University.

Tammy S. Schultz is a Research Fellow at the Peacekeeping and Stability Operations Institute, U.S. Army War College. She conducts research and training on security, terrorism, and military preparedness for post-conflict reconstruction and stabilization. She also conducts training at the State Department and is an Adjunct Professor at Georgetown University's Security Studies Program. She holds a Ph.D. from Georgetown University and an MA in International Relations from Victoria University in New Zealand. She was a Brookings Institution Research Fellow from 2003 to 2004.

Andrew Wilder was, until April 2005, the founding Director of the Afghanistan Research and Evaluation Unit. Previously, he served as the Director of Save the Children's Pakistan/Afghanistan field office for six years. From 1989 to 1992 he was Coordinator of the International Rescue Committee's cross-border Rural Assistance Program in Afghanistan, and from 1986 to 1987 started up Mercy Corps' Afghan assistance program in Balochistan and southwest Afghanistan. He has written and published widely on politics in Pakistan and Afghanistan. He was born in Pakistan, and has spent more than thirty years there and in Afghanistan. He holds MA and Ph.D. degrees from the Fletcher School of Law and Diplomacy at Tufts University.

FOREWORD

Transitions from conflict are among life's most perilous journeys. Once societies have unraveled into violence and neighbors are preying on each other, trust is destroyed and the confidence to build a community is undermined. How then do we move ahead?

The endeavor is worthy of our best efforts. War, with millions of lives lost and human potential thwarted, is the tragedy of every era. Advancing peaceful, democratic change has consumed American national security and international efforts, and the breakdown of civilizations in localized conflicts has required the United States, along with its allies, to send soldiers to fight in six countries in the past fifteen years and the United Nations to have peacekeeping forces in almost twenty nations during the same time.

Successes have been too few for anyone to make great claims. Wars have a way of hanging on, and some estimates say that 50 percent of conflicts return within five years. Often, outside assistance is too brief and caught up in familiar approaches that do not match the reality on the ground. Soldiers are sent when robust policing is required, diplomats continue high-minded dialogue when focused action plans are needed, humanitarians offer life-saving aid when the process of rebuilding should start, and development experts assess and review when modest daily progress would suffice.

In the midst of chaos it is unwise to be too formulaic. Recent experiences have shown the dangers of underestimating the challenges, poor planning, overly institutionalized approaches, decision-making without follow-through and interventionist hubris. Through triumphs and tragedies and the daily efforts of thousands of dedicated civilians and soldiers, much has been learned.

This collection takes a fresh look at post-conflict reconstruction, focusing on governance. A broad array of contributions offers clear analytic and operational insights.

The scene-setting introduction addresses the deficits in security, legitimacy, and effectiveness and the book begins with a look at the nation-building record. There is then an examination of today's efforts to establish viable and authentic government, restore security and services, and create a favorable climate for economic progress. Part I looks at key institutions that provide for

xvi

state–society relations: constitutions, political parties and elections, and the security sector.

The actors involved in governance reconstruction are the focus of Part II. Chapters examine the shifts in policy, doctrine, and training that are taking place within the US Army; the important role of the private sector; civil service renewal and reform as an essential effectiveness element; and the efforts of diaspora groups to influence policies and programs in their native lands through new information technologies. Part III looks at local governance building with analysis of cases in Latin America, Africa, and Afghanistan.

By bringing together academics and practitioners, this volume helps us to understand the complexities of rebuilding governance in failed and fragile states. New light is shed on the emerging integration of diplomacy, development, and defense. Numerous helpful reminders are shared: avoid excessive transformation ambitions that overwhelm weak institutions; make progress on a few fronts and build on the local level; recognize the interconnections between the various dimensions of governance; and realize that service delivery is central to citizens' perceptions of state legitimacy.

Improving our practices so that the damage of conflict is mitigated is at the heart of this book. We have made sincere efforts for some time. Now we must be measured by the progress of freedoms in the conflict-prone world. This collection should help to advance that cause.

Frederick D. Barton
Senior Adviser and Co-Director of the Post-Conflict Reconstruction Project
Center for Strategic and International Studies, Washington, DC

PREFACE

The role of state failure in the outbreak of conflict and war has put a spotlight on the importance of sound governance in mitigating conflict, establishing peace, and moving toward a society that provides citizens with security, effective services, and legitimate institutions. The complexity of governance reform and reconstruction in failed states has challenged the foreign policy and international development communities. While the knowledge and experience base is growing, gaps in understanding and practical application remain. The purpose of this book is to explore questions of rebuilding governance in post-conflict societies from new interdisciplinary perspectives and to examine how current approaches to governance reconstruction might be modified. The overarching thesis of the book is that rebuilding governance depends upon filling three interconnected gaps that arise in failed and failing states: deficits in legitimacy, effectiveness, and security.

The core of the volume assembles a selected set of revised papers originally presented at a conference held in May 2005, jointly sponsored by RTI International (Research Triangle Institute), George Washington University's School of Public Policy and Public Administration, and George Washington University's Institute of Global and International Studies. Several additional contributors, some of whom were invited to participate in the conference but were not able to attend, expand coverage of the topic. The contributors and I hope that the book is helpful to practitioners, policy-makers, and academics with interests in post-conflict reconstruction, fragile states, and governance. Edited volumes are by their nature collective efforts, and I would like to thank my contributors, without whom this book would not be possible; and Andrew Humphrys, Editor, Military and Strategic Studies, at Routledge, for his support. I also acknowledge the support of the Fellow Program at RTI International and of Ronald Johnson, Executive Vice President, International Development Group, RTI International.

Derick W. Brinkerhoff
Senior Fellow in International Public Management,
RTI International, Washington, DC

ACKNOWLEDGMENTS

Earlier versions of two of the chapters included in this volume were previously published in an issue of *Public Administration and Development*, Vol. 25, No. 1, 2005, copyright John Wiley and Sons, Limited, and are reproduced here with permission. These are:

Nicole Ball, "Strengthening democratic governance of the security sector in conflict-affected countries," pp. 25–39.
Sarah Lister and Andrew Wilder, "Strengthening subnational administration in Afghanistan: technical reform or state-building?," pp. 39–49.

1

INTRODUCTION – GOVERNANCE CHALLENGES IN FRAGILE STATES

Re-establishing security, rebuilding effectiveness, and reconstituting legitimacy

Derick W. Brinkerhoff

It has become commonplace to observe that we live in a globalized world. Issues, problems, and people that once seemed remote now appear on our doorstep, both the virtual one created by today's instant communication and the physical, territorial one. Global and local dynamics interconnect, creating a world characterized by what Rosenau (2003) terms "distant proximities." Globalizing forces penetrate down to the local level through a variety of pathways, and local forces diffuse upward to the global level. For instance, lack of access to economic opportunities leads individuals in poor local communities to migrate to other countries in search of a better life; the aggregation of these individuals into vast transnational flows of people has global impacts. Localized political instability can engender social tensions, ethnic conflict, and dislocation. In some cases, these pressures in weak and fragile states lead to collapse, creating negative spill-overs for their immediate neighbors, and opening up a haven for illicit activities, such as the drug and arms trade or terrorism, which affect nations and people who are geographically removed from those troubled localities.

The problem of fragile states that fail, leading to conflict and war, and how to rebuild them in the post-conflict period, is the topic addressed by the contributors to this volume. Fragile states are not a new problem: most countries classed as poor or developing fall into the category of fragile states, and they have long been the target of international development and humanitarian assistance. In today's world of distant proximities, however, fragile states are no longer solely the concern of international assistance actors. There is a new and growing intersection among the policy, research, and programmatic agendas of the international development and humanitarian, security, and diplomatic communities that is focusing on fragile and failed states (see e.g. Carment 2003; Rice 2003; Koppell with Sharma 2003; Dombrowski 2005; Francois and Sud 2006). Particularly with the current concern over transnational terrorism, such states have been referred to as a "sleeping giant" threat that requires concerted and integrated attention (CGD 2004).

A focus on governance constitutes the integrative theme of the book. Governance concerns the rules, institutions, and processes that form the nexus of state–society relations where government and citizens interact. This domain combines public administration and state structures, politics and the exercise of power and authority, and policy-making and implementation. The quality of governance is widely acknowledged as affecting the performance of economic, social, and rights-based functions. In fragile and failed states, weak governance is recognized as a contributor to conflict and civil war, and has highlighted the importance of reformed governance in establishing peace, pursuing state reconstruction, and avoiding a descent into conflict in the first place (Brinkerhoff and Brinkerhoff 2002; Milliken and Krause 2002).

Rebuilding governance in fragile and failed states, which includes promoting more democratic forms of governance, is situated at the core of the policy and programmatic convergence mentioned above. Governance reform is inextricably entangled with the political and military objectives of the intervening countries. In the United States, these policy connections are becoming institutionalized as the actors that previously operated relatively autonomously – the State Department, the U.S. Agency for International Development (USAID), and the Department of Defense – are in the process of developing increased bureaucratic, operational, and procedural linkages.

These are turbulent times in the foreign policy community in the U.S.A. and Europe. The lessons and implications of this fusion are beginning to be explored, and feed into the current policy debates, programmatic reassessments, and bureaucratic and political realignments (see e.g. Carothers 2006; Fukuyama 2006). The contributors to this volume add their analyses and observations to this collective reflection and exchange. This first chapter reviews key terminology, presents a framework for considering post-conflict governance reconstruction, introduces the contents of the various chapters, and identifies a number of common themes that emerge from the contributions to the book.

State failure, fragility, and post-conflict

The terminology applied to failed/fragile states, conflict, and post-conflict is often imprecise.[1] In general, a failed state is characterized by: (1) breakdown of law and order where state institutions lose their monopoly on the legitimate use of force and are unable to protect their citizens, or those institutions are used to oppress and terrorize citizens; (2) weak or disintegrated capacity to respond to citizens' needs and desires, provide basic public services, assure citizens' welfare, or support normal economic activity; and, at the international level, (3) lack of a credible entity that represents the state beyond its borders (see Thurer 1999; Rotberg 2002; Francois and Sud 2006).[2]

One key issue, then, is the degree to which a given state exhibits these characteristics. The label, failed state, has been employed to describe extreme cases of collapse, such as Somalia, where civil and social authority have disintegrated. Many more countries, though, confront less drastic situations, and vary in the extent to which they have failed or risk failing to provide for the welfare of their citizens, supply basic security, or facilitate equitable economic growth. At this less extreme, opposite end of the spectrum, the state is more fragile than failed, and becomes nearly indistinguishable from the status of many, if not most, poor countries, which suffer from institutional weaknesses and capacity gaps.

No state's degree of fragility or failure is static; so another issue has to do with the trajectory that characterizes the direction and degree of change taking place. Is the state on a downward slide into a serious crisis, which could provoke collapse and the outbreak of conflict; or is it weak but recovering, with an upward trajectory toward an improved situation? Given the long time horizon for state reconstruction and for putting in place the foundations for sustainable development, anticipating and planning for ups and downs along that path is important. The record shows that countries which have experienced violent conflict face a 40 percent risk of renewed conflict within five years (Collier *et al.* 2003).

Similarly, conflict and post-conflict are relative terms as well, and subject to nuance. Post-conflict rarely means that violence and strife have ceased at a given moment in all corners of a country's territory. In practice, most post-conflict reconstruction efforts take place in situations where conflict has subsided to a greater or lesser degree, but is ongoing or recurring in some parts of the country. As Doyle and Sambanis observe, "no peace is perfect. Public violence ... never gets completely eliminated.... We should thus consider peace to be a spectrum ranging from insecure to secure" (1999: 1). The peace-building literature has evolved a more nuanced perspective on conflict, moving away from a linear conception, similar to the recognition of the artificiality of the relief-to-development continuum (see Jeong 2005). Greater understanding of conflict dynamics has led in turn to intervention designs that recognize this complexity. For example, Leatherman *et al.* (1999: 8) argue that conflict interventions need "a rehabilitative dimension oriented to the past, a resolutive dimension oriented to the present, and a preventive dimension oriented to both the present and future."

Governance definitions

Governance, as noted above, extends beyond the role and actions of public sector institutions, structures, and processes to refer to broad conceptions of how societies organize to pursue collective goals and interests. For example, Keohane and Nye (2000: 12) define governance as "the processes and institutions, both formal and informal, that guide and restrain the collective activities of a group." Some of these processes and institutions may be governmental, others may not. International donor agency definitions, while acknowledging a realm outside of government, concentrate on technical government functions and how they are administered. For example, the World Bank (2000) views governance as economic policy-making and implementation, service delivery, and accountable use of public resources and of regulatory power. The link to society comes through public participation on the policy side, such as civil society engagement in planning exercises, and public–private partnerships on the service delivery side.

Other definitions focus on state–society linkages, and address how government connects with other sectors and with citizens. USAID considers governance to "pertain to the ability of government to develop an efficient, effective, and accountable public management process that is open to citizen participation and that strengthens rather than weakens a democratic system of government."[3] DFID describes it as "how institutions, rules and systems of the state – executive, legislature, judiciary, and military – operate at central and local level and how the state relates to individual citizens, civil society and the private sector" (2001:11). The latter definitions explicitly connect the sociopolitical dimensions of governance to the more technocratic elements of macroeconomic management and public administration operational capacity, and are reflected in how governance is addressed in failed states.

A framework for rebuilding governance

In any society, the governance system fulfills a set of core functions: assuring security, achieving effectiveness, and generating legitimacy. States vary in terms of how well or how poorly their governance system fulfills these functions. The governance system may be divided into highly interconnected sub-systems that address the three functions:

1   Security governance upholds the social contract between state and citizen,[4] protects people and property, and deals with crime and illegal activity while exercising oversight of security forces to ensure legitimate application of coercive force, curbing of abuses and maintenance of the rule of law.
2   Administrative-economic governance achieves effective provision of basic services and economic opportunity through rules-driven and transparent policy-making, regulation, fiscal arrangements, partnerships, and civil service systems.
3   Political governance guides societal decision-making and public policy, and generates legitimacy through separation of powers, responsive and accountable government, representation and inclusiveness, and protection of basic rights for all citizens.

Failed/fragile states generally face deficits in fulfilling all three of these functions. The design and implementation of governance reconstruction in post-conflict states can usefully be conceptualized as targeting the governance sub-systems associated with the three: (1) re-establishing security, (2) rebuilding effectiveness, and (3) reconstituting legitimacy.

Re-establishing security

Clearly, a high-priority activity in fragile and post-conflict societies is coping with the lack of security. Without security, the other governance functions cannot be fulfilled. In post-conflict countries a key focus of establishing security is dealing with ex-combatants; this involves the classic trio of disarmament, demobilization, and reintegration. DDR connects to rebuilding effectiveness in that, without capacity to restart the economy and generate employment opportunities, reintegration will suffer, raising the possibility of crime, banditry, and re-emergence of conflict. Re-establishing security also means peacekeeping operations, often coupled with humanitarian and emergency relief, since many post-war countries have large numbers of internally displaced persons, wrecked infrastructure, and disrupted economic activity. Security is a necessary precursor to stabilization and progress toward a return to something approaching "normal" economic and political activity.

Security governance is conditioned by the status, capacity, and actions of security forces. Re-establishing security requires dealing with the police, military, and paramilitary units, and private militias through a mix of rebuilding, professionalizing, reforming, and dissolving. In the medium and long term, this governance area links closely to reconstituting legitimacy. For most post-conflict societies, civilian oversight of security forces is weak or non-existent. In addition, civil rights, judicial systems, and the operation of the courts need attention. Unaccountable, corrupt, and/or subversive security forces are major barriers to state legitimacy, impede the restoration of basic services, and often contribute to reigniting conflict (see Koppell with Sharma 2003).

Rebuilding effectiveness

Conflict and wars destroy basic infrastructure, disrupt the delivery of core services (e.g. health, education, electricity, water, sanitation), and impede the day-to-day routines associated with making a living. In the worst-case scenarios, they lead to widespread suffering, massive population dislocation, humanitarian crises, and epidemics, which overwhelm the already inadequate effectiveness of failed-state governments. The inability of fragile and post-conflict states to provide fundamental public goods and services has impacts on both the immediate prospects for tending to citizens' basic needs and restarting economic activity, and long-term prospects for assuring welfare, reducing poverty, and facilitating socioeconomic growth. Restoring (or in some cases creating) service delivery capacity and initiating economic recovery are central to governance reconstruction agendas (see e.g. UNDP 2000).

Rebuilding effectiveness has to do, first and foremost, with the functions and capacity of the public sector. Good governance in this area means, for example, a functioning civil service, basic management systems, control of corruption, adequate municipal infrastructure, widely available health care and schooling, provision of roads and transportation networks, and attention to social safety nets. Since, in most countries, effective basic services depend on more than government, the functions and capacity of the private sector and civil society are also critical.

Beyond service provision, effective economic governance is included here. Good practices involve sound macroeconomic and fiscal policy-making, efficient budget management, promotion of equitably distributed wealth-creating investment opportunities, and an adequate regulatory framework. Failing and failed states generally exhibit the opposite: policies that favor powerful elites, few budget controls and rampant corruption, cronyism and patronage arrangements that limit opportunity and siphon off public assets for private gain, and usually a combination of a punitive use of existing regulations and exemptions to benefit the favored few.

Service delivery and economic development effectiveness relate to legitimacy in that citizens tend to withdraw support from governments that cannot or will not provide basic services, limit corrupt practices, and generate some level of economic opportunity. Particularly when coupled with ethnic tensions, weak states' inability/unwillingness to do so can be an important contributing factor to state failure and the eruption of renewed conflict. This area of governance also connects to security in that if youth are in school, job opportunities are available, and families have hopes that their well-being will improve, and citizens (including demobilized combatants) are less likely to engage in crime or be recruited into insurgency.

Debates regarding rebuilding effectiveness in post-conflict states concern starting points, sequencing, and comprehensiveness; all these issues are interconnected. Where to start in helping new and weak post-conflict governments to get service delivery going, as well as which tasks should follow one another or be taken on simultaneously, are rarely clear choices. Often, donors and humanitarian NGOs take the lead in providing essential services, and responding to the immediate needs of the population trumps moving toward actions that will build government capacity to assume lead responsibility (Brinkerhoff and Brinkerhoff 2002). Yet quick-fix approaches that ignore existing local capacity and/or put off attention to institution-building are accused of creating dependency, reducing the chances for sustainability, and squandering opportunities for nascent governments to establish their legitimacy through providing services to citizens. Another starting point/sequencing issue is the choice between rebuilding/creating central-level institutions or focusing on those at subnational and local levels (see e.g. Romeo 2002).

Regarding comprehensiveness, the debate centers around the ambitiousness and appropriateness of donor models and plans for reconstructing effectiveness in weak and post-conflict states. In essence, the question here is: What constitutes "good enough" governance?[5] In many cases, the governance reform agenda advocated by the international donor community constitutes an overwhelming menu of changes deemed necessary to assure governance effectiveness (Brinkerhoff and Goldsmith 2005).

Reconstituting legitimacy

Legitimacy refers to acceptance of a governing regime as correct, appropriate, and/or right. Without a minimum degree of legitimacy, states have difficulty functioning; and loss of legitimacy in the eyes of some segment of the population is an important contributor to state failure. Reconstituting legitimacy in post-conflict states involves expanding participation and inclusiveness, reducing inequities, creating accountability, combating corruption, and introducing contestability (elections). Delivering services, which links to the effectiveness dimension, is also important for establishing legitimacy; it demonstrates government willingness and capacity to respond to citizens' needs and demands. Further, this category includes constitutional reform, re-establishment of the rule of law, and institutional design (e.g. checks and balances, allocation of functions and authorities across branches and levels of government), as well as civil society development.

Democracy is widely held to be the governance system with the strongest form of legitimacy around the world (see e.g. Diamond and Plattner 1996, UNDP 2002). Yet in numerous countries the path to democratization has proven tortuous; traditional and informal sources of power and authority vie for legitimacy, sometimes constituting an alternate "state" within a state (e.g. regional warlords in Afghanistan), or sometimes seeking legitimization through assumption of the external trappings of democracy (e.g. various former Soviet Union states in Central Asia). Experience in state reconstruction has shown that external intervention to create stable democratic societies out of the ashes of intra-state conflagration is extraordinarily difficult (see Whitehead 2002; Bermeo 2003).[6]

There is substantial debate on paths, strategies, and timetables for reconstituting legitimacy in failed and post-conflict states. Elections are a case in point. Issues concern, for example, how soon to hold them and how to organize electoral systems that lay the base for a viable political process. Fundamentally, some question whether democracy is amenable to intentional design by outsiders, no matter how well meaning (Blaug 2002; Bastian and Luckham 2003), with current debate fueled by the fluctuating fortunes of nation-building efforts in Afghanistan and Iraq. Others question the expectations that countries emerging from conflict will be able to take on the enormous number and complexity of tasks inherent in launching a democratic transition (Ottaway 2002). There is skepticism that a relatively standardized model of post-conflict democratic transition can be successfully grafted on to societies with histories and traditions that may be inhospitable to such transfers (e.g. Call and Cook 2003).

7

Contributions to the book

This volume assembles chapters by both scholars and practitioners studying and working on governance issues from a variety of disciplinary and area studies perspectives. Each of the contributors addresses one or more of the governance deficits described in the framework presented above, and seeks to illuminate the issues and challenges involved in fragile state and post-conflict governance reconstruction.

The book is divided into three sections. Part I examines established issues associated with post-conflict reconstruction, focusing on the lessons learned and implications for current governance reform in fragile and failed states. Part II explores the range of actors involved in governance reconstruction in light of the new intersection noted above, and considers the various roles they play: familiar, new, and evolving. Part III looks at local governance, highlighting the importance of subnational state–society structures and relations in fragile and post-conflict states.

Evolving perspectives on familiar issues

International intervention to assist countries following conflict and state failure and to improve governance is not a novelty. Post-conflict reconstruction, conceived of as an explicitly designed package of coordinated interventions, began with the Marshall Plan in 1945, as has been well documented (see Dobbins *et al.* 2003).[7] Attention to good governance has been a mainstay of international development assistance for many years, initially under the broad rubric of institution-building, and more recently in its current focus on democracy. The chapters in Part I begin with a look at some empirical data on nation-building and governance performance, and then turn to critical foundations of governance: constitutions, elections and political parties, and democratic governance of the security sector.

In Chapter 2, Arthur Goldsmith situates nation-building in the context of political debate in the U.S.A. and among its allies on the effectiveness of foreign aid, and looks at empirical evidence of international support and governance improvement in seventy-nine countries that had episodes of internal violence or civil war during the period 1970 to 2002. The historical data he assembles suggest that reforms in failed and fragile states have led to modest but identifiable improvements in addressing governance deficits, despite the challenges of dealing with episodes of unrest and violence. The effects of external assistance appear to be smaller than what many international donor agencies assert, but are significant enough to counteract those who would portray external help as futile and wasteful. Goldsmith observes that three factors constrain the ability of international donors to better the track record in governance reconstruction: (1) time pressures for quick results, imposed by the politics in the assistance provider countries; (2) the difficulties outsiders face in seeking to steer complex sociopolitical change processes they cannot control – and may not understand; and (3) the uncertainty that such change processes in the direction of democracy can avoid veering off into sectarianism, extremism, and the renewal of conflict.

Chapters 3 and 4 focus on two topics that are at the core of building legitimacy and that shape the contours of political governance: constitutions and elections. In Chapter 3, Aliza Inbal and Hannah Lerner look at constitution-making processes in societies with deep socio-ethnic divisions. In many post-conflict situations, an inclusive process for constitutional design is seen as a way to bridge such divisions and to establish a governance framework that can forge unity. Inbal and Lerner, however, argue that in more than a few failed and fragile states these may be unrealistic expectations for constitution-making, and efforts along this path risk creating a constitution that resolves these issues from a technical perspective, but creates a document lacking the support of key societal groups.

They propose that where agreement among societal actors may be impossible, the creative employment of ambiguity or avoidance of controversial issues can enable constitutional processes to advance even when the society is marked by deep divisions. They examine the cases of Israel and India, and discuss their relevance to some of today's post-conflict states, where divisions over religious versus secular concepts of governance and over identity questions loom large. Constitution-making in divided, post-conflict societies cannot be expected to yield a unifying "foundational moment" that establishes the framework for governance legitimacy.

Elections can be a positive force for engaging disenfranchised and marginalized constituencies into a new governance order. However, flawed elections and dysfunctional political parties undermine legitimacy, contribute to political stalemate and societal division, and can lead to renewed conflict and violence. In Chapter 4, Eric Bjornlund, Glenn Cowan, and William Gallery examine the factors that influence electoral outcomes and offer assessments of recent elections in Palestine, Iraq, Haiti, and Afghanistan. They argue that successful international intervention to support democratic governance in fragile and failed states depends upon a better understanding of the mechanics of the electoral system chosen, the political environment surrounding elections, and voter behavior. The features of the electoral system determine the representativeness of legislatures, influence incentives for coalition-building and minority opposition, support political stability, regulate access to the political arena, and affect the capacity of the legislature to exercise oversight of the executive. Support for electoral outcomes depends critically upon perceptions of fairness and respect for proper procedure. Too often, donors have been taken by surprise by the failure to anticipate outcomes that have negative consequences for improved governance and stability.

In fragile and failed states, government security forces often fail to operate according to practices that make them legitimate in the eyes of citizens, and frequently they are not the only armed actors on the scene. Nicole Ball, in

Chapter 5, notes that post-conflict intervention has often focused on strengthening the operational capacity and effectiveness of security forces, largely ignoring or downplaying issues of civilian oversight and accountability. From a governance perspective, minimizing or postponing these questions until later places the success of post-conflict reconstruction at risk. Security sector reform is highly political, frequently in ways that may not be immediately obvious. For example, powerful actors may ostensibly pursue reforms as stipulated in peace accords or agreed to with peacekeepers and donors, all the while jockeying behind the scene to gain personal advantage. Ball flags the difficulties involved in undertaking reform in the context of the enormous pressures in failed states to move quickly on numerous fronts with limited resources in situations where institutional capacity is destroyed, decayed, or needs to be built from scratch.

Actors in governance reconstruction

The chapters in Part II look selectively at the configuration of actors involved in post-conflict governance reconstruction: the military, the private sector, civil servants, and diasporas. Failed states call for military operations and civilian-led relief and reconstruction simultaneously rather than sequentially; increasingly the military has been assigned missions where they are actively engaged in the reconstruction side of post-conflict-rebuilding, not simply peacekeeping. In Chapter 6, Tammy Schultz and Susan Merrill recount the evolution of the U.S. Army's role in stability and reconstruction (S&R). Based on extensive interviews as well as written sources, they explore how the Army has adapted to shifts in focus beyond warfighting since the Vietnam era. Changes to accommodate the new S&R mission have proceeded through the elaboration of new doctrine, the preparation and implementation of new training, and the incorporation of career incentives in order to lead to new behaviors in the field.

The Army's mission, as put forward in 2005 in Department of Defense Directive 3000.05, places S&R on a par with combat operations, and lays out an end-state objective that encapsulates a functioning state ruled by democratic governance. Further, the Directive specifies that if civilian agencies lack the capacity to achieve this objective, it is the Army that must be prepared to fulfill the necessary tasks to assure success. Schultz and Merrill indicate the dilemmas the Army faces in this transformation, such as how to add preparation for this expanded mission when the training schedule is already filled with other items, and how to maintain and expand its cadre of experienced civil affairs officers at a time when resources are stretched with current deployments.

The challenge of managing international private sector actors' investment in post-conflict economies is the focus of Chapter 7. Virginia Haufler examines the role that private investors and commercial traders can play in weakening already fragile governance systems and eroding prospects for a lasting peace. Failed and post-conflict states often have natural resources that are attractive to external private investors. These resources can, to varying degrees, provide funding for combatants and rent-seeking elites; allow governments to operate without relying on revenue from citizens; fuel patronage networks, with negative consequences for transparency, accountability, and legitimacy; distort the economy, creating underinvestment in other sectors, unemployment, and vulnerability to external shocks; and exacerbate sociopolitical tensions and conflict between "have" and have-not" regions. On their part, corporations' contract negotiations held in secret undermine principles of good governance; the large sums of money generated by the contracts enable corrupt and clientelist practices; and corporations' security arrangements can have negative spill-over effects on local populations and contribute to conflict and violence.

Haufler reviews current efforts to address these problems, noting a number of transnational initiatives underway. She concludes that countering the negative effects of private investment in post-conflict settings will require a coordinated effort among corporations, governments in fragile states, transnational rights and advocacy groups, and international agencies. Despite the challenges, as illustrated by the Chad–Cameroon pipeline, private sector actors have the potential to fulfill a stabilizing role that can assist post-conflict countries to establish an economic foundation for recovery and reform.

In Chapter 8, Harry Blair looks at rebuilding and reforming the civil service, which is often ignored in the immediate post-conflict period. Fulfilling all three governance functions in the long term depends upon a viable civil service, but how to restore state capacity after prolonged periods of breakdown in public institutions and services poses significant trade-offs between short- and longer term actions. Applying a principal–agent framework that highlights the accountability and responsiveness relationship between citizens and civil servants, Blair identifies the core rebuilding and reform task as putting in place the structures, procedures, and capacity that will establish or re-establish appropriate incentives for service delivery and other key government operations. Blair discusses the challenges international donors face in providing services in the near term versus the long-range efforts required for civil service and government reform. He discusses five strategies for service delivery in terms of pluses and minuses, the role of the civil service, and the principals involved in monitoring and accountability.

Chapter 9, by Jennifer Brinkerhoff, analyzes the role that diaspora groups play to mobilize collective action that can support positive change in state-building and governance. Brinkerhoff presents three case examples of diaspora "cyber-grassroots organizations" that illustrate this role. She finds that diasporas develop hybrid identities that combine the traditional values of the homeland with liberal values acquired or strengthened by the adopted country. Collective action targeted at the homeland results in the expression of this hybrid identity, which can reinforce elements of improved governance.

Three Afghan-American organizations linked diaspora expertise to needs in Afghanistan, and have worked in cooperation with international NGOs, Afghan government ministries, and local communities on projects that have contributed to increasing service delivery effectiveness. The U.S. Copts Association promotes advocacy, action, and accountability in support of the human rights of the Coptic population in Egypt. Its efforts, while admittedly small scale, have prodded the Egyptian government to honor espoused commitments to governance principles of respect for minority rights and accountability, contributing to governance legitimacy. The third case holds implications for security. Somalinet, a large online community, provides a venue for dialogue among diaspora members on national and ethnic identity, development issues in the homeland, and assimilation into the U.S.A. The dialogue threads analyzed demonstrate the incorporation of democratic and liberal values into exchange among diaspora members, which could contribute to a reduced propensity to instigate conflict or support violence in the homeland.

Subnational governance in post-conflict societies

Part III explores the relationships among decentralization, local governance, conflict, and post-conflict reconstruction. Contributions address the distribution of power and authority between center and periphery, opportunities for citizen engagement, local versus national capacity, and ethnic and regional exclusion.

Gary Bland, in Chapter 10, surveys the decentralization experience of Colombia, Guatemala, and El Salvador, examining the role of democratic decentralization and local citizen participation in conflict mitigation. In all three countries, issues of social exclusion and non-responsiveness were drivers of citizen dissatisfaction and emergence of armed opposition to a state seen as ineffective, uncaring, and illegitimate. Policy-makers and citizens saw local governance reforms as a means of dealing with grievances and reducing conflict, thus addressing the need for the state to enhance its legitimacy and effectiveness. Bland cautions that while decentralization can be an important contributor to post-conflict reconstruction and stability, it is neither a quick fix for governance weaknesses, nor sufficient on its own to re-establish effectiveness, security, and legitimacy absent changes at other levels of government.

These same issues of state legitimacy, effectiveness, and local autonomy are analyzed in the African context by Joshua Forrest in Chapter 11. He examines the emergence of subnationalist movements as responses to policy errors made by national-level state actors: empty decentralization rhetoric with no or little substance, insufficient engagement and dialogue with local constituencies, and inequitable regional resource distribution. An analysis of Senegal's experience in dealing with twenty years of unrest and conflict in the Casamance region in the south of the country illustrates the effects of these policy errors. The Senegalese government's heavy hand in dealing with the Casamance prolonged the conflict, imposed unnecessary economic and social hardship, and contributed to instability. Forrest notes that local governance in breakaway regions of African states in some cases contains features that can promote conflict mitigation, democratic practices, and power-sharing once peace agreements are reached.

Contrary to popular perception, subnationalist movements are often multi-ethnic and alliance-based. He argues that efforts to reverse state fragility and failure in Africa must be founded on political power-sharing governance arrangements that disperse autonomy and authority to the regional and local levels.

In Chapter 12, Sarah Lister and Andrew Wilder examine the workings of local governance in Afghanistan. They contrast the limited reach and power of the formal, *de jure* state, based in Kabul and supported by the international community, with that of the informal, de facto state, where at the subnational level, regional warlords and local commanders fulfill governance functions. They document the various mechanisms by which these subnational-level actors exercise power and authority. Administrative capacity and resource gaps at the center, typical of those in many post-conflict states in the process of rebuilding, exacerbate problems of both legitimacy and effectiveness. Low salaries, paid late, encourage civil servants to engage in corrupt practices, and/or seek resources from warlords. Inadequate operating budgets hamper service delivery agencies of the formal state in meeting citizens' needs, which leads citizens to turn to the warlords for help, further discrediting the state in their eyes. The authors note that donor investments in the technical effectiveness of public administration will not yield their intended governance outcomes without a political strategy that confronts the realities of the subnational de facto state as an integral element in rebuilding formal governance in Afghanistan.

Common themes

Several common themes emerge from the chapters in this volume. These include: similarities between development and post-conflict assistance; operational challenges to linking governance's legitimacy, effectiveness, and security dimensions; the limits of intervention by external actors; and the importance of local-level governance as well as central-level state reconstruction.

Similarities between development and post-conflict assistance

The immense pressure to act quickly in failed states has led to the widespread impression that post-conflict intervention strategies share little with long-term development approaches. Yet the chapters in this book, as well as the larger literature, point to similarities between these two situations. In many respects, the development industry began as a post-conflict reconstruction enterprise with the Marshall Plan. It is not surprising, then, to find that much of what concerns development today, and how it is best achieved, yields important parallels and lessons for post-conflict governance reconstruction. Goldsmith (Chapter 2) confirms that the time requirements and slow incremental change characteristic of successful institutional building more generally also apply to post-conflict assistance, and all three constraining factors he identifies apply equally to development initiatives. Blair's (Chapter 8) discussion of capacity-building strategies also incorporates lessons from the wider development experience in making choices for post-conflict reconstruction.

Inbal and Lerner (Chapter 3) remind us that reform – whether in the context of politics "as usual" or post-conflict environments – involves a continuous negotiation among competing interests. Bjornlund *et al.* (Chapter 4) note that elections as a tool for establishing and maintaining governance legitimacy, when organized well, work in both contexts. In post-conflict settings they highlight the need to do better at anticipating potentially destabilizing outcomes. Finally, while Ball's concerns (Chapter 5) regarding citizen oversight of the military are particularly salient in post-conflict contexts, global debates around international security underscore the importance of this issue within more stable societies.

Regarding actors, Haufler's points (Chapter 7) on how corporations can undermine governance effectiveness, legitimacy, and security ring true for *rentier* states generally, though perhaps less dramatically. The civil service reform goals which Blair identifies are the staple of civil service reforms in non-conflict states. While diasporas have been relatively unnoticed in development processes to date, the types of potential governance contributions which J. Brinkerhoff (Chapter 9) identifies are arguably similar to those made by diasporas to more stable homelands, such as the Philippines and China.

Why should post-conflict reconstruction actors be concerned about similarities between post-conflict reconstruction and development? The chapters show that development experience has much to contribute to our understanding of how progress may or may not evolve even under the best scenarios and what tools are applicable in post-conflict contexts. As new roles are crafted and new actors emerge, this volume is a reminder to assess what we already know, albeit from different kinds of experiences, and to recognize that new actors will bring their existing orientations, strengths, and weaknesses to these new arenas of application. In the best of circumstances, good governance and its institutionalization is a long-haul endeavor which is viewed most usefully as a process, not a particular end-state. There are times when the exigencies of immediate response to post-conflict emergency need to take precedence, but often international actors remain in the "driver's seat" pushing preplanned reconstruction packages far beyond what is optimal for supporting the mitigation of conflict and a transition to country-led governance and local ownership. Just as with development assistance in non-conflict settings, what donors and their international partners do, with whom, and how, matters importantly in post-conflict societies.

Operational challenges to linking governance's legitimacy, effectiveness, and security dimensions

Several of the contributors highlight, in one way or another, the connections among these governance dimensions. For example, Ball's chapter brings out clearly the dangers of treating security sector reform as simply a question of professionalism and effectiveness. Without attention to oversight bodies, account-

14

ability, and human rights – all elements of the legitimacy dimension of governance – security forces can contribute to reigniting conflict and instability.
Legitimacy of the government in Afghanistan is threatened by its inability to
positively affect citizens in the provinces through service provision, leading
them to turn to warlords to meet their needs (Lister and Wilder, Chapter 12).
Bland's (Chapter 10) and Forrest's (Chapter 11) case analyses in Latin America
and Africa demonstrate how political tensions between center and periphery,
intimately related to legitimacy issues, have affected security and effectiveness.
Significantly, peace accords have either explicitly included, or laid the groundwork for, power-sharing and devolution.

A number of factors have contributed to a lack of sufficient attention to the
linkages among these three dimensions. A primary one is that the institutional missions of the major actors in post-conflict intervention emphasize one of the dimensions to the relative downplaying or exclusion of the others. The military tends to
take responsibility for the security sector; legitimacy is the key focus of diplomatic
actors (e.g. the US State Department, the UN Security Council); and effectiveness
falls to the development agencies (e.g. UNDP, USAID, DFID) and their partners
(NGOs, private firms). In post-war Iraq, for example, the separation of responsibility for reconstruction tasks was reinforced by a strong "stay in your lane"
message from the Coalition Provisional Authority (CPA): operational actors were
expected to concern themselves solely with their areas of responsibility, not the
bigger picture, which CPA leadership saw as its unique prerogative.

The templates that divide post-conflict reconstruction into linear stages have
also encouraged the separation of the three dimensions of governance. In the
past, these have discouraged the kind of integrative and comprehensive thinking
that many have advocated as necessary for effective programming and intervention (see Ball, Chapter 5).[8] As Schultz and Merrill (Chapter 6) recount, the
US Army is in the process of a "lane change" to develop a new template that
brings the military into reconstruction arenas beyond security and peacekeeping.

These shifts reflect the integration of the defense, diplomatic, and development communities, and raise another operational challenge to concerted attention to the full array of governance and reconstruction elements. The
institutional dynamics of how reconstruction efforts are organized, from structures to budget processes to policy direction, are an enduring constraint. Until
recently most development agencies and donor country governments have
organized development and reconstruction work in silos of expertise and authority rather than learning networks. Some governments have made progress in
streamlining communication and expertise sharing, as well as unifying priority-
setting, budgeting, and programming, for example, the UK's Conflict Prevention
Pools. Like most organization change efforts, the Conflict Prevention Pools have
faced the push and pull of existing loyalties and bureaucratic power structures,
which interfere with joint agendas and action (see Austin *et al.* 2004).[9]

The role of external actors

As international actors seek to intervene more effectively and rapidly to restore peace and stability, assist post-conflict countries to rebuild their economies and their governance systems, and coordinate across a range of agencies, the tendency to develop one-size-fits-all templates increases. The integration of the military into reconstruction activities of civilian actors, as Schultz and Merrill describe (Chapter 6), has provoked a shift in how civilian agencies operate. The desire to have "development doctrine" on a par with the military's has led organizations such as USAID to seek to codify strategy and programmatic principles in terminology more familiar to military partners.[10]

Doctrine and templates can facilitate preparedness, quick intervention, and coordination among external actors. They also affect prospects for the transition to longer term development; for example, favoring rapid service delivery through international NGOs to meet immediate needs leaves aside the question of how to integrate state actors. Blair (Chapter 8) illustrates how donor reconstruction strategies have an impact on the exclusion of civil servants in security, economic-administrative, and political governance. In terms of sustainable state-building and governance reconstruction, a healthy public sector is crucial. Yet the relatively short time horizon of much post-conflict assistance precludes a focus on long-term administrative reform.

From Goldsmith's synoptic, retrospective review of the results of external donors' interventions in fragile and post-conflict states, to the local perspectives in the chapters of Part III, the book's contributors highlight in various ways the tensions between the social and political forces unleashed in conflict states and the "social engineering" embodied in the templates and models of external interveners. The resources that outsiders can mobilize, and the lessons learned that are distilled in intervention templates, can convey an illusory sense of control and direction of reconstruction processes. The conclusions of many of the chapters counsel external actors to take a modest incremental approach that builds on local knowledge and the commitment of local actors to re-establish governance, and to maintain patience and funding in the face of inevitable setbacks and diversions on the path to improved state–society relations.

Two chapters point to the impacts of external actors that are not part of coordinated, predesigned interventions, yet whose actions can affect governance in post-conflict societies: Haufler on multinational corporations and J. Brinkerhoff on diasporas. These actors embody the distant proximities of today's world, and illustrate the need to expand our analytic attention beyond the borders of individual post-conflict states. The literature on "bad neighborhoods" looks at regional factors' impacts on state fragility, but Haufler and J. Brinkerhoff lead us to take account of an expanded radius of action for external actors, both geographic and virtual.

Local versus central

Rebuilding a state at the central level that citizens perceive as legitimate and effective is key to sustaining peace and creating viable governance. Yet a central state without roots that extend to the local level is inherently vulnerable and unstable. The inability to integrate regions and minorities into larger polities is a key source of state fragility, failure, and conflict across the globe. The failure to resolve this problem has repercussions for each dimension of governance. Exclusion of regions and/or minorities negatively affects the extent to which the national government is perceived as legitimate; and it exacerbates sociopolitical tensions, leading in some cases to civil war and the breakdown of security. The Latin American and African cases in Chapters 10 and 11 illustrate these effects.

Centralized governance regimes in fragile and weak states generally do poorly at equitable and inclusive resource allocation and redistribution, impacting negatively upon service delivery, economic opportunity, welfare, and ultimately legitimacy as well. Distributive mechanisms tend to operate based on patronage and clientelism, promoting economic inefficiency and heightening social and ethnic tensions. These can be exploited by those in power, both at the national level, as in Saddam Hussein's Iraq, or at the local level, as in Afghanistan (Lister and Wilder, Chapter 12).

Where the local–national governance problem has been excessive concentration of power at the center and a dominant elite, governance reform has included a focus on local governance and decentralization. The basic argument is that decentralized local governance can mitigate conflict for the following reasons. First, it can increase support for peace by transferring some degree of local autonomy, especially in settings of ethnic and inter-communal conflict. Second, it can place limits on the power of the center by shifting resources and control to other levels of government. Third, by creating multiple governance arenas, it can diminish "winner-takes-all" dynamics that can lead to the re-emergence of conflict. Fourth, strengthening local governance allows low-intensity disagreements regarding service delivery, and demonstrates that these conflicts can be managed. Fifth, local governance sets up a learning laboratory for people to acquire political and conflict resolution skills that may be used in other settings. Bland's discussion of the decentralization efforts over an extended period in Colombia, Guatemala, and El Salvador provides empirical support for these arguments.

The opposite local–national governance problem is where the national government is incapable of exerting authority throughout the national territory, and subnational entities are sufficiently powerful to resist and operate autonomously. The reform challenge in these situations is not simply to devolve central power so as to increase local autonomy, but to achieve a balanced decentralization that avoids fragmentation of the state as a coherent entity. Forrest points out that African leaders who fail to share power and authority through meaningful decentralization are courting this risk. As Lister and Wilder describe, in Afghanistan reconstruction efforts intended to create the building blocks of a formal, Weberian state are having difficulty finding a firm footing in the shifting sands of provincial governance space dominated by warlords. Attention to changed state–society relations at the local level is an important component of any nation-building exercise.

As with the need to address the interdependencies among the three governance dimensions, there are operational challenges to striking the right balance between attention to both local- and central-level capacity-building. As noted above, incentives for decentralization on the part of national actors at the center may be weak, at best. External actors may favor support to the center, as a function of ease of access, perceptions of existing capacity and appropriate starting points, and/or security considerations. Stability at the center may emerge prior to that in local areas, reinforcing ease of access and the possibility that power there may become established and entrenched before local actors are supported and are able to participate. The chapters in Part III reinforce the wisdom of looking beyond the center to the critical role of subnational levels in designing and supporting governance capacity-building.

Conclusions

Understanding, and intervening in, the dynamics of fragile and post-conflict states require a careful combination of the general (and generalizable) and the situation-specific. We have learned that the appropriate path to restored or new governance and socioeconomic development must address: (1) the nature of societal conflict and how peace has been established; (2) the conditions for a rapid restoration of security; (3) the capacity of state and non-state actors to provide priority services effectively and to transition from a war to a peace economy; (4) social and institutional arrangements that lead to inclusion, transparency, and representation of citizen interests; and (5) the roles, resources, and interests of external actors in reconstruction. In moving to models, strategies, and doctrine, it is important to base them solidly on knowledge of the particular dynamics of the country and to leave sufficient policy and operational space for flexibility and learning among all actors.

Nation-building templates risk oversimplification and conflation, and tend to discount the impact of situational, historical, and individual leadership factors. This caveat notwithstanding, analysts and practitioners have made important strides toward filling the knowledge and practice gap. No single volume can provide a comprehensive account of governance reconstruction. The chapters in this volume exemplify and contribute to the positive learning that has taken place and is ongoing. Frameworks, models, and templates are necessary for understanding and action, and the authors in this collection offer some useful food for thought in refining the governance reconstruction toolkit, particularly with respect to targets of analysis and trade-offs among immediate versus long-term intervention strategies.

Governance is about the relationships between state and society. Third parties can assist, but cannot alone repair a country's governance structure. Building or rebuilding governance systems ultimately is the responsibility of citizens and leaders in post-conflict societies. A major challenge for further developing a governance reconstruction toolkit is to develop processes and tools for bringing together local and external actors in ways that productively contribute to enhancing legitimacy, security, and effectiveness. In today's globalized world, we all benefit from solving the governance and socioeconomic development challenges in fragile and failed states.

Notes

1 The terminology and framework sections of this chapter draw upon Brinkerhoff (2005).
2 For an informative review of the literature that focuses on the dynamics of state failure, see Carment (2003).
3 From www.usaid.gov/our_work/democracy_and_governance/technical_areas/dg_office/gov.html.
4 In governance models whose political philosophical tradition derives from the eighteenth-century European Enlightenment, this equation is an implicit social contract between citizens and government whereby citizens cede their natural right of self-governance to the state in exchange for the protection and security derived from state sovereignty. Not all countries share this notion of a social contract. Many of those with a colonial legacy retain upwardly oriented governance systems with authoritarian or semi-authoritarian structures. In countries that trace their governance heritage to autocratic empires, governance was designed not as a social contract with citizens, but to enable rulers to maintain, protect, and extend their domains.
5 Grindle (2004) addresses this question in the context of poor countries and poverty reduction, not specific to post-conflict, but much of the discussion is equally relevant to the extreme case.
6 The democracy "triumphalism" of the 1990s has given way to more sober reflections on the ease or inevitability of democratic transition (see Carothers 2002, 2006).
7 Some consider the first "modern" post-conflict intervention to be the nineteenth-century U.S. reconstruction program for the South following the Civil War.
8 Perhaps the most well-elaborated framework for taking a comprehensive approach, including attention to governance, is that developed by the joint CSIS/AUSA Project on Post-Conflict Reconstruction (Center for Strategic and International Studies/Association of the U.S. Army). See the appendix in Orr (2004).
9 In the U.S.A., the State Department's Office of the Coordinator for Reconstruction and Stabilization has faced similar inter-agency turf struggles and resource allocation challenges.
10 For example, Andrew Natsios, former USAID administrator, sought explicitly to encapsulate USAID's approach to international development in doctrinal terms, largely in response to questions from senior military officers about how USAID goes about its business (see Natsios 2005).

References

Austin, G., E. Brusset, M. Chalmers, and J. Pierce (2004) "Evaluation of the Conflict Prevention Pools: Synthesis Report," London: Department for International Development, Evaluation Report EV 647, March, available at: www2.dfid.gov.uk/aboutdfid/performance/files/ev647synthesis.pdf.

Barakat, S. and M. Chard (2002) "Theories, Rhetoric and Practice: Recovering the Capacities of War-torn Societies," *Third World Quarterly* 23(5): 817–835.

Bastian, S. and R. Luckham (eds) (2003) *Can Democracy be Designed? The Politics of Institutional Choice in Conflict-torn Societies*, London: Zed Books.

Bermeo, N. (2003) "What the Democratization Literature Says – or Doesn't Say – about Postwar Democratization," *Global Governance* 9(2): 159–177.

Blaug, R. (2002) "Engineering Democracy," *Political Studies* 50: 102–116.

Brinkerhoff, D.W. (2005) "Rebuilding Governance in Failed States and Post-conflict Societies: Core Concepts and Cross-cutting Themes," *Public Administration and Development* 25(1): 3–15.

Brinkerhoff, D.W. and J.M. Brinkerhoff (2002) "Governance Reforms and Failed States: Challenges and Implications," *International Review of Administrative Sciences* 68(4): 511–531.

Brinkerhoff, D.W. and A.A. Goldsmith (2005) "Institutional Dualism and International Development: A Revisionist Interpretation of Good Governance," *Administration and Society* 37(2): 199–224.

Call, C.T. and S.E. Cook (2003) "On Democratization and Peacebuilding," *Global Governance* 9(2): 233–246.

Carment, D. (2003) "Assessing State Failure: Implications for Theory and Policy," *Third World Quarterly* 24(3): 407–427.

Carothers, T. (2002) "The End of the Transition Paradigm," *Journal of Democracy* 13(1): 5–20.

—— (2006) "The Backlash against Democracy Promotion," *Foreign Affairs* 85(2): 55–69.

CGD (Center for Global Development) (2004) "On the Brink: Weak States and US National Security," Washington, DC: CDG, Commission on Weak States and US National Security, available at: www.cgdev.org/docs/Full_Report.pdf.

Collier, P., L. Elliott, H. Hegre, A. Hoeffler, A. Reynol-Querol, and N. Sambanis (2003) *Breaking the Conflict Trap: Civil War and Development Policy*, New York: Oxford University Press, for the World Bank.

DFID (2001) *Making Government Work for Poor People: Building State Capacity*, London: Department for International Development.

Diamond, L. and M.F. Plattner (eds) (1996) *The Global Resurgence of Democracy*, Baltimore, MD: Johns Hopkins University Press.

Dobbins, J., J.G. McGinn, K. Crane, S.G. Jones, R. Lal, A. Rathmell, R. Swanger, and A. Timilsina (2003) *America's Role in Nation-building: From Germany to Iraq*, Santa Monica, CA: Rand.

Dombrowski, P. (ed.) (2005) *Guns and Butter: The Political Economy of International Security*, Boulder, CO: Lynne Rienner.

Doyle, M.W. and N. Sambanis (1999) "Building Peace: Challenges and Strategies after Civil War," World Bank: Washington, DC, available at: www.worldbank.org/research/conflict/papers/building.htm.

Francois, M. and I. Sud (2006) "Promoting Stability and Development in Fragile and Failed States," *Development Policy Review* 24(2): 141–160.

Fukuyama, F. (2006) *America at the Crossroads: Democracy, Power, and the Neoconservative Legacy*, New Haven, CT: Yale University Press.

Grindle, M.S. (2004) "Good Enough Governance: Poverty Reduction and Reform in Developing Countries," *Governance* 17(4): 525–548.

Jeong, H. (2005) *Peacebuilding in Postconflict Societies: Strategy and Process*, Boulder, CO: Lynne Rienner.

Keohane, R.O. and J.S. Nye (eds) (2000) *Governance in a Globalizing World*, Washington, DC: Brookings Institution Press.

Koppell, C. with A. Sharma (2003) *Preventing the Next Wave of Conflict: Understanding Non-Traditional Threats to Global Stability*, Report of the Non-traditional Threats Working Group, Conflict Prevention Project, Washington, DC: Woodrow Wilson International Center for Scholars.

Leatherman, J., W. DeMars, P.D. Gaffnew, and R. Vayrynen (1999) *Breaking Cycles of Violence: Conflict Prevention in Intrastate Crises*, West Hartford, CT: Kumarian Press.

Milliken, J. and K. Krause (2002) "State Failure, State Collapse, and State Reconstruction: Concepts, Lessons, and Strategies," *Development and Change* 33(5): 753–774.

Natsios, A.S. (2005) "The Nine Principles of Reconstruction and Development," *Parameters* 35(3): 4–20.

Orr, R.C. (ed.) (2004) *Winning the Peace: An American Strategy for Post-conflict Reconstruction*, Washington, DC: Center for Strategic and International Studies, CSIS Press.

Ottaway, M. (2002) "Rebuilding State Institutions in Collapsed States," *Development and Change* 33(5): 1001–1023.

Rice, S.E. (2003) "The New National Security Strategy: Focus on Failed States," Policy Brief No. 116, Washington, DC: Brookings Institution.

Romeo, L. (2002) "Local Governance Approach to Social Reintegration and Economic Recovery in Post-conflict Countries: Towards a Definition and Rationale," Discussion paper. Workshop on a Local Governance Approach to Post-conflict Recovery, October 8, New York: Institute of Public Administration and United Nations Development Program.

Rosenau, J.N. (2003) *Distant Proximities: Dynamics beyond Globalization*, Princeton, NJ: Princeton University Press.

Rotberg, R.I. (2002) "The New Nature of Nation-state Failure," *The Washington Quarterly* 25(3): 85–96.

Thurer, D. (1999) "The 'Failed State' and International Law," *International Review of the Red Cross* 836: 731–761.

UNDP (2000) *Governance Foundations for Post-conflict Situations: UNDP's Experience*, New York: United Nations Development Program, Management Development and Governance Division, Bureau for Development Policy.

—— (2002) *Deepening Democracy in a Fragmented World. Human Development Report 2002*, New York: United Nations Development Program.

Whitehead, L. (2002) *Democratization: Theory and Experience*, Oxford: Oxford University Press.

World Bank (2000) *Reforming Public Institutions and Strengthening Governance: A World Bank Strategy*, Washington, DC: World Bank, Poverty Reduction and Economic Management Network.

Part I

GOVERNANCE AND POST-CONFLICT
Perspectives on core issues

2

DOES NATION BUILDING WORK?

Reviewing the record

Arthur A. Goldsmith

Unaccountable, non-transparent, and non-participatory governance are well-recognized pitfalls in international development, but the latest U.S. *National Security Strategy* also sees them as problems of strategic concern to the United States. Any foreign state that operates by corrupt or unfair processes may fuel feelings of resentment as well as economic privation, with resultant political instability and social unrest that possibly spills across borders (U.S. President 2002, p. iv). Governance and development can thereby no longer be looked at in isolation from international security issues. The catch-phrase often used to describe this geopolitical approach to development assistance is "nation building."

Naturally, not everyone agrees that development assistance and security should be fused this way. During the 2000 U.S. political campaign, presidential candidate George W. Bush routinely dismissed nation building as an arrogant and futile exercise that did not serve the U.S. strategic interest. He called for pulling out of multinational military and development efforts in remote, unstable countries. After September 11, 2001, however, Bush did a U-turn and joined other countries in what he specifically called a nation-building exercise to establish a broad-based government in Afghanistan (White House 2001). Making no comment on the incongruity with his earlier stand, Bush explicitly drew the parallel with the Marshall Plan after World War II (White House 2002b). Bad governance and the disintegration of authority in peripheral states evidently sometimes *did* threaten the safety of the U.S. population, and might even justify pre-emptive military action to replace a system of public institutions and create new processes for public decision-making, as in Iraq in 2003.

Bush's two minds on nation building raise an important empirical issue. Even though the risk that weak or poorly governed states pose to U.S. and global security seemed palpable after 9/11, that fact, in itself, does not provide a convincing rationale for nation building. If assisting troubled societies to embrace the rule of law and inclusive institutions was beyond the international community's reach before the World Trade Center attack, the same thing was true afterward. Just how fruitless were past efforts at nation building? Is the record in reforming governance in volatile states as poor as Bush said, prior to 9/11? Alternatively, does the evidence support the more favorable prognosis for nation building implicit in the subsequent *National Security Strategy*?

The empirical case for nation building is usually based on a few case studies, often selectively chosen. During his second Presidential debate with Al Gore, for example, Bush criticized American participation in the U.N.'s humanitarian mission in Somalia in the early 1990s, which in his view broke down when it began to aim at changing the government there. He also singled out the U.S.-led, U.N.-backed intervention in Haiti as a utopian nation-building operation.[1] In making the case for "regime change" in Iraq, however, he turned to the post-war reconstruction of Germany and Japan as nation-building success stories. As the President explained to a sympathetic audience at the American Enterprise Institute shortly before the invasion:

> "Rebuilding Iraq will require a sustained commitment from many nations, including our own ... America has made and kept this kind of commitment before – in the peace that followed a world war. After defeating enemies, we ... established an atmosphere of safety, in which responsible, reform-minded local leaders could build lasting institutions of freedom."
>
> (White House 2003)

To assess past nation building systematically, we cannot rely only on stories from preferred countries; we need a comprehensive chronicle of events. We should look for empirical indications of the degree of successful nation building across a range of countries over a common time frame. Because public institutions are more constant than variable, that time frame should be measured in decades. Some of the more readily available large-*n* evidence is laid out below.

A fuzzy, often pejorative term

Before proceeding, an unambiguous definition of nation building is needed. Repeated use has not clarified the term's meaning. People have several things in mind. Most simply, nation building refers to the establishment of a common national identity within a given geographical area, based on shared language and culture. The term is associated with the modernization school of development studies of the 1950s and 1960s, but even then, it came under criticism for having a fallacious architectural or engineering connotation. Nations cannot be assembled according to plans, by a similar sequence of steps in different locations (Deutsch 1963, p. 3).

According to Reinhard Bendix (1964, p. 18), who wrote a classic text on the subject, nation building's central characteristic "is the orderly exercise of nationwide, public authority." Bendix's reference to national authority points to a parallel phenomenon called state building, or the creation of effective organs of central government. State building can diverge from nation building, since ethnic minorities are often citizens of a state without being regarded as members of the corresponding nation. For a state to function it must develop respected and effective public institutions to carry out policy within internationally recognized boundaries – which may not match a "national" territory, strictly speaking. There are historical instances in which nation building preceded state formation; for instance, Germany and Italy in the nineteenth century. More often, the state over extended time frames creates the nation, as in France, where in 1789 less than half the population spoke the French language. Nevertheless, these distinctions have faded in current foreign policy discourse. Most policy-makers today implicitly follow Bendix's lead and see nation building as more about the development of stable and viable public institutions, and less about the creation of national self-awareness. For example, the former civil affairs officer for the United Nations mission in Kosovo says nation building is simply a synonym for state building (Von Hippel 1999, fn. 2).

Nation building entered the U.S. foreign policy lexicon during the Cold War, when the phrase was used to describe such foreign aid programs as the Alliance for Progress and the Peace Corps. Drawing on an oversimplified interpretation of modernization theory, nation building's goal was to help establish unified societies in the Third World that would be a bulwark against communism (Latham 2000). The concept was sometimes linked to a sister activity labeled "institution building," which focused mainly on creating rational-legal civil service organizations (Goldsmith 1992). Following the American dbâle in Vietnam, official confidence waned about U.S. ability to influence social and political conditions in developing areas (Etzioni 2004). Still, as a practical matter, the United States continued to remain engaged in what amounted to nation-building missions all through the Cold War era and afterward (Fukuyama 2004; Rondinelli and Montgomery 2005).

With time, nation building acquired a partisan undertone, and recently conservatives have adopted the term to disparage U.S. participation in international peacekeeping. Gary Dempsey and Roger Fontaine call such interventions fool's errands in the title of their 2001 book from the Cato Institute, referring to ill-considered, fruitless undertakings. Beyond being futile, Dempsey and Fontaine argue that intervening in other countries' domestic politics may end up producing more disputes and armed confrontation. Taking away the post-conflict setting, their negative assessment of nation building echoes right-of-center criticism of foreign aid programs generally. At best, aid is a waste of resources; at worst, aid is counterproductive and destructive because it produces perverse incentives for recipient states to abuse power and develop a dependency on additional aid.

These allegations about foreign aid spurred a new approach to development in the 1990s, based on getting good governance first. To speed up economic growth and make maximum productive use of economic resources, international donors wanted low-income countries to open up their civic institutions and make market reforms before giving them financial assistance (e.g. White House 2002a, p. 22). Nation building is, in effect, a special case of the good governance strategy, applied to countries under imminent or potential threat of collapse. The underlying assumption is that changing the configuration of institutions can start a "virtuous circle" that brings together better governance, economic growth, and social stability.

Former Secretary of State Colin Powell (2005, p. 29) summarizes the U.S. government's policy toward poor nations during the early 2000s in the following terms: "We see development, democracy, and security as inextricably linked. We recognize that poverty alleviation cannot succeed without sustained economic growth, which requires that policymakers take seriously the challenge of good governance." President Bush paints the security link with bolder strokes, saying, "persistent poverty and oppression can lead to hopelessness and despair. And when governments fail to meet the most basic needs of their people, these failed states can become havens for terror" (White House 2002a).

Stripped of the derogatory connotation, therefore, nation building is generally understood today as an effort by the United States and its allies to work with a war-torn or otherwise unstable country to make over its institutional infrastructure, underpinning development and, thereby, encouraging peaceful coexistence among nations. The process stands on three legs of good governance: representative politics, efficient public management and competitive private enterprise. Some dimension of coordination within the international community is entailed. Initially there may be a military component to separate fighting groups and re-establish order, or even to overthrow the country's official leadership. The RAND Corporation, for example, defines nation building as "the use of armed force in the aftermath of a conflict to underpin an enduring transition to democracy" (Dobbins 2003, p. 16). But sending in combat troops or peacekeepers is not central to the term's meaning. Nation building is mainly about civilian expatriates helping an inoperative or threatened nation state back on to its feet by overhauling its civic institutions along democratic, capitalist lines.

One misleading side issue regarding nation building is whether or not the international community can "impose" new institutions on developing countries. This is a straw man debate, because these days no knowledgable person argues that outsiders can recast another society's governance according to a predetermined model without local say-so and assistance. Experience teaches that nation building is mainly a domestic matter, that only a nation's citizens can develop national institutions, and that external actors have no more than a supporting role to play. Speaking of the United States' capabilities, for example, even hawkish Deputy Secretary of Defense Paul Wolfowitz (2000, p. 39) admits that, "because of what is possible, we cannot engage either in promoting democracy or in nation-building simply by an exercise of will. We must proceed by interaction and indirection, not imposition."

The signs of state failure are common . . .

To consider the feasibility of nation building in a systematic way, we first need to know the number of nation states that have failed (or drawn somewhat near to failing) in recent decades, and therefore been in need of some degree of nation building. Since the appearance of Robert Kaplan's influential 1994 article "The Coming Anarchy" in the *Atlantic Monthly*, a common perception has been that state failure is a pervasive and growing problem around the globe. That year the CIA sponsored a State Failure Task Force (later renamed the Political Instability Task Force) to conduct a statistical investigation of the phenomenon. State failure refers to the collapse of the authority of the central government. The Task Force quickly recognized the obvious fact that state failure is a continuous variable rather than a binary one. While a few states do become so weakened that they cannot provide for the basic needs of their citizens, more common is the gradual erosion of authority and administrative capacity in the periphery, often accompanied by growing civil conflict. Such states may linger for years without ever succumbing or showing marked improvement. It is difficult and somewhat arbitrary to draw a line between states on the brink of collapse and those that have gone over the edge (Spanger 2000; Rotberg 2002).

According to one member of the Task Force, Robert Bates (2005, p. 6), the most important symptom of state failure is a government's inability to secure a monopoly of violence, as reflected in civil wars and armed rebellions. To establish a broad basis for cataloging states with serious domestic strife, we can turn to a complete list of major armed conflicts since World War II, maintained by another Task Force member, Monty G. Marshall (2003). From this list is selected a subset of these violent episodes covering developing and transitional or post-communist countries from 1970 (around the time when several international datasets on governance begin) to 2002. Events with a primarily international character are excluded from the list of state-threatening events. Exceptions are made for international conflicts to drive out existing foreign domination (such as Mozambique versus Portugal), and to displace another country's leadership (such as Tanzania's invasion of Uganda to oust Idi Amin). By this count, seventy-nine states faced varying prospects of failure during the period.[2] That is how many developing and transitional countries experienced one or more significant episodes of internal violence or civil warfare involving rival political groups, or the state and distinct ethnic groups.

To put the number of possibly endangered states in context, there are currently 193 independent countries in the world, including Taiwan and the Vatican. In other words, over the past three decades, close to half the world's states showed some warning signs of state failure at one point or another. The interludes of internal violence lasted for varying amounts of time. In any given year from 1970 to 2002, from twenty to forty-five endangered states were actually experiencing major internal strife. A few of these states had serial or multiple concurrent conflicts. Often, the violent events went on for many consecutive years. At other times, however, they ended quickly. These are depressing numbers, yet the recent trend is somewhat hopeful. As Figure 2.1 shows, the number of countries experiencing active internal conflicts rose steadily during the 1970s and 1980s, but has dropped sharply since the early 1990s. The current number of conflicts is about what it was in 1970.

Not all these confrontations had to be resolved through external peacekeeping, of course, and many of the sample states were never seriously put in danger. In his catalog of violent incidents, Marshall (2003) establishes a ten-point scale for assessing their magnitude and impact on societies. The scale takes account of deaths and injuries, population dislocations, harm to societal networks, impact on the physical environment, damage to the infrastructure, and diminished quality of life. Figure 2.1 shows that the average intensity of each year's acts of aggression has remained between levels "3" and "4" over the past three decades – or about half way between what Marshall labels "serious political violence" and "serious warfare." Hostilities of this degree tends to be in restricted areas and to have limited nationwide effects. Deaths range from 10,000 to 100,000. These conflicts are very destructive for the regions where they occur, but life in most of the country may go on as normal – particularly in a large country such as India or China. Some comfort may be taken in the fact that the average intensity of intrastate violence is not getting noticeably worse.

... But signs of nation building are also prevalent

Consistent with these mildly encouraging trends in worldwide domestic political violence, indications are that civic institutions in the beleaguered countries have

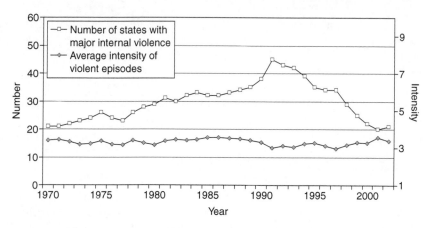

Figure 2.1 Incidence and intensity of intrastate violence, states at risk, 1970–2002 (source: Author's calculations based on Marshall (2003)).

Note
Countries may have multiple, simultaneous intrastate armed conflicts. Intensity refers to the magnitude of the violent episode on a ten-point scale (higher numbers mean greater destruction).

been marginally *gaining* strength to conduct public affairs and manage public resources. Several sources of empirical data suggest a slight quality upturn in the systems by which their governments operate. State failure, it would appear, is fortunately not always a relentless downward spiral. Nonetheless, the wished-for virtuous circle of governance, growth, and security is tenuous. At times "all good things go together" in development, but at other times they do not (Packenham 1973). Many additional factors affect the ease or difficulty of nation building, including prior experience with democracy, initial level of economic development, and ethnic homogeneity (Dobbins *et al.* 2003, p. xxv).

Democracy is spreading

The founding of democratic government institutions is one leg of nation building. Democratization is as difficult as nation building or state failure to define precisely, though most people are thinking about the spread of pluralistic national political systems under which the population is reasonably free to express its political demands and to hold rulers to account. To obtain a rough reading on changes in the degree of democratic practice in the sample of threatened or vulnerable states, we will turn to statistics assembled by Freedom House, a non-profit organization that monitors political and civil liberties around the world. Its Index of Political Freedom is plotted for each country group from 1972 to 1973 through 2003 to 2004. The results are shown in Figure 2.2.

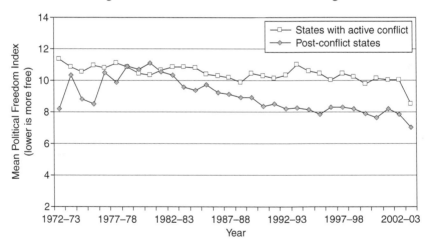

Figure 2.2 Democratic performance of states at risk, 1972–2003 (source: Author's calculations based on Freedom House (2004)).

Note
The Political Freedom Index reflects the degree to which a country has free and competitive elections, competitive autonomous parties and provisions for political opposition (2 = most freedom, 14 = least). It is based on two sets of characteristics grouped under political rights (to participate freely in the political process) and civil rights (to develop views and institutions apart from the state).

Freedom House starts with a pair of checklists, one for political rights and one for civil liberties. Each country is ranked on a pair of declining seven-point scales, from not free to free. These are combined into the summary political freedom score. The ratings can be questioned in individual cases, but overall they correlate highly with other international indexes of regime type that use different methodologies, according to Adam Przeworski and his colleagues (2000, pp. 56–57). This lends authority to the rankings. The Index of Political Freedom also has the advantage of covering more countries for more years than do rival indexes.

Figure 2.2 shows that, on average, at-risk countries experiencing active violence were consistently less democratic than were countries where violence had abated. This is not surprising given the difficulty in holding elections and maintaining the rule of law while fighting is taking place. The average democracy score for the actively violent countries was roughly constant after 1972 to 1973, with a slight movement in the direction of greater political freedom. Scores for the post-conflict states, however, showed a clear improving trend after the mid-1980s. The absolute group means still fall within what Freedom House calls the "partly free" range, but there remains a perceptible movement away from arbitrary and unrepresentative government in post-conflict states that is consistent with the goals of nation building.

Many observers question whether the sorts of changes represented by the Freedom House data are a precondition for political stability and economic prosperity, or whether democratization should come later in the nation-building process. This debate represents an overly determinative and linear perspective on development. The latest empirical scholarship denies any inherent trade-off between open political systems and economic progress, with the particular relationship depending on a country's history and tradition (e.g. Rodrik and Wacziarg 2005). In many societies, procedural representation can nurture a climate of open discussion that helps move resources to their most productive uses, thereby fostering new industries and greater productivity. Competitive politics may put constraints on leaders who are tempted to steal public resources for personal benefit. Expanding the pool of citizens represented in government decisions may induce leaders to produce the public goods that are the foundation for sustained economic growth (Bueno de Mesquita et al. 2003).

This does not mean that all countries gain from rushing ahead with free elections. The interest groups, political parties, media, and other institutions needed for systems of elected representation to work well may be missing in a partly democratized state (Zakaria 2003). Autocratic leaders may exploit the new voting machinery and use it to hold on to office, bringing about political gridlock or destructive confrontation with opposition groups. Premature elections may rend rather than reconcile ethnically split societies as they try to vote (Snyder 2000; Chua 2002). Under these conditions a political campaign may spark unrest and conflict, not resolve them. While the dangers of rapid democratization are sometimes exaggerated (Lynn-Jones 1998), it takes time before procedural political reforms open the door to substantive participation and peaceful resolution of disputes.

States appear to be making better use of the resources at their disposal

Establishing a capable state administration is the second leg of nation building. State capability concerns the capacity to deliver traditional public goods to citizens. Public goods are things that are used collectively. In the language of economics, they rank high for "non-rivalness" (one person's consumption does not limit anyone else's consumption) and "non-excludability" (no one can be prevented from consuming the good). Usually cited in the list of core public goods are public education, public health, transportation infrastructure, environmental protection and a groundwork of law by which people can resolve disputes and dispose of property. Some analysts would add civil rights as critical public goods. Rights are non-rival, in the sense that one person being treated fairly does not diminish the chance of another person being treated in the same way. They are also non-excludable. Once applied to one person the same just claims apply, in principle, to every person in the same circumstances.

Well-run nation states distribute public goods efficiently, predictably, and in the right quantities. Delivering these collective-use items entails the development of an impartial civil service and independent judiciary that draw on specialized expertise to do their jobs. When the administration and adjudication of laws are transparent and predictable, that makes government more accountable and thereby reinforces the democratic leg of nation building. Having a capable state that firms can count on also affects the third leg of nation building – the development of market institutions – by reducing uncertainty and improving the entrepreneurial and investment climate.

The international development community tends to view state capability in technocratic terms, devoid of politics. For instance, the United Nations Development Program (1997) speaks of "capacity development," of the need for developing countries to support "people-centered sustainable macroeconomic frameworks," and "critical cross-sectoral public-sector institutions responsible for systems for policy coordination, planning, economic, financial and fiscal management, and accountability."

The forging of state capacity is not the disembodied process implied by this abstract language; it takes conflict and repression. Summarizing the history of state formation in Europe, Charles Tilly (1975, p. 24) writes:

> The state-makers only imposed their will on the populace through centuries of ruthless effort. The effort took many forms: creating distinct staffs, dependent on the crown and loyal to it; making those staffs (armies and bureaucrats alike) reliable, effective instruments of policy; blending coercion, co-optation and legitimation as means of

guaranteeing the acquiescence of different segments of the population; acquiring sound information about the country, its people and its resources; promoting economic resources which would free or create resources for use by the state.

At every step there was resistance from powerful interests whose livelihoods were threatened by changes in administrative structure. We should not expect less of a struggle to fashion capable nation states in the twenty-first century.

Historically, improvements in state administrative capacity are associated with warfare, and the attendant need to raise funds and mobilize the population for the war effort. The stress forces governments to reorganize themselves and become more efficient, accountable, and legitimate. Thus we might expect to see signs of improved state capacity in countries undergoing civil unrest over the past twenty years. That is what the Bureaucratic Quality Index appears to show (see Figure 2.3).

The Bureaucratic Quality Index is an indicator of the professionalism and competence of the civil service put together by the Political Risk Services Group (unfortunately only since 1982, and with spotty country coverage). The index attempts to measure the civil service's "autonomy from political pressure," and its "strength and expertise to govern" in a consistent manner. These data are widely used in international quantitative research to track improvement or decay in national administrative capacity.

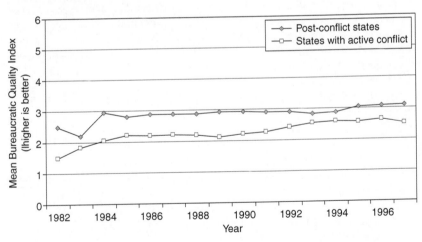

Figure 2.3 Bureaucratic performance of states at risk, 1982–1997 (source: Author's calculations based on IRIS-3 File of International Country Risk Guide Data (East Syracuse, NY: PRS Group Inc.)).

Note
Scores (0 = worst, 6 = best) indicate extent to which there is an established mechanism for recruitment and training, autonomy from political pressure and strength and expertise to govern without drastic changes in policy or interruptions in government services when governments change.

The trend line for bureaucratic quality in post-conflict states was essentially flat during the 1980s and 1990s, with a small increase in the slope toward the end of the period. States still in conflict scored lower on the index in each year. However, the group average score for this set of countries rose perceptibly, if marginally. The composition of states in conflict changed annually as internal wars ended or began, so we cannot conclude definitively that challenges to authority usually force individual states into progressively better bureaucratic performance over time – plausible though that argument may be. At a minimum, the lack of evidence for deterioration in civil service capability suggests that at-risk countries can often maintain their position on this second leg of nation building.

Many experts are uncomfortable with the Bureaucratic Quality Index because it is based on subjective evaluations and it is hard to verify or reproduce. An alternative approach is to use objective proxies that indirectly represent the capacity of the state. School enrollment as a percentage of the eligible population is sometimes taken as an indirect indicator for the state's power to mobilize its inhabitants into public institutions and secure their compliance with state rules. A similar indicator is the child rate of immunization for diphtheria, pertussis, and tetanus. States that immunize a high proportion of children implicitly demonstrate their general administrative and governance capability.

Figure 2.4 shows that enrollment and immunization rates are both rising in the at-risk states. Although the quality of the underlying data is uneven, they tend to underscore the improving pattern shown in the Bureaucratic Quality Index. The average capacity to provide schooling, health services and, by extension, other public goods seems to be heading upward in many countries in the sample.

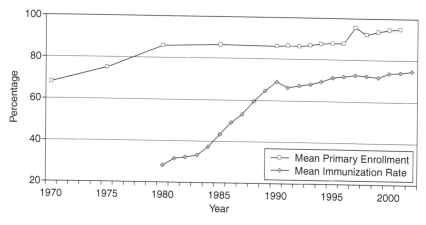

Figure 2.4 Enrollment and immunization rates of states at risk, 1970–2002 (source: Author's calculations based on World Bank (2005)).

Note

The enrollment rate is the ratio of students enrolled in primary school to the total population of children of official school age. The immunization rate is the percentage of children between the ages of twelve and twenty-three months who received DPT vaccinations before the age of one.

Markets are opening up, too

Nation building's third leg is the consolidation of a market economy. Even among threatened states today, the tendency is to let supply and demand organize economic life. While a few economic fundamentalists may believe that "in the beginning was the marketplace," even Adam Smith knew that markets do not work at their best without a public infrastructure of market-enhancing institutions. The state must enforce property rights and contracts – for the poor as well as for the rich. It must regulate business to assure the confidence and cooperation of investors, consumers, and workers, but not go too far and kill incentives to produce efficiently. The state should maintain a safety net of institutions to protect the victims of competition, without resorting to destabilizing deficit finance to pay for it. Where supportive institutions are weak or lopsided, competitive forces may break down or produce unintended adverse consequences for society.

One metric with which to measure market institutions is the Fraser Institute's Index of Economic Freedom. The summary index is based on several objective criteria intended to indicate the degree to which a nation's institutional arrangements and policies are consistent with sound money, reliance on markets, avoidance of discriminatory taxes, and freedom of international exchange. Questions have been raised about the validity of the Fraser Institute index, but it appears to measure the free enterprise institutions it claims to measure (see Snider 2000). One need not subscribe to the libertarian ideology underlying the Index of Economic Freedom to deem it a fair measure of how closely a state adheres to the capitalist norms embodied in nation building. Figure 2.5 shows that the average economic freedom scores of post-conflict countries and of ongoing conflict countries rose slightly starting in 1980. Capitalism is on the march, albeit slowly, even in threatened or unstable states.

The march of capitalism, on the other hand, has not led to robust economic growth in these countries. From 1970 to 2000, the average annual growth of GDP per capita in the shifting group of post-conflict nations was an anemic 1.7 percent. That GDP growth rate only looks good next to the average rate of change in countries with active conflicts, which was a full point lower (0.7 percent per year). There are undoubtedly diverse reasons for this disappointing economic performance, but more market-friendly governance has obviously not made up for the other factors causing slow growth among at-risk countries.[3]

The increased reliance on markets has conflicting effects on the two other legs of nation building. Sometimes the effects are favorable. The government could take advantage of budget austerity to rationalize the bureaucracy and reinforce discipline, cutting the payroll while raising salaries for a streamlined workforce. This has happened in Uganda and several other African countries (Lienert 1998). Alternatively, the government could be forced to open up the political system and create new channels of accountability between rulers and ruled. In Latin America, for example, economic liberalization undermined the capacity of

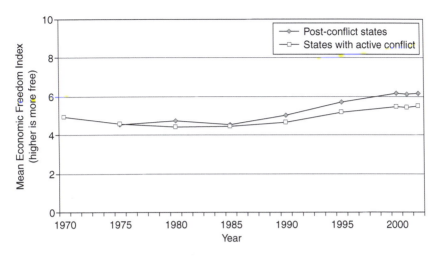

Figure 2.5 Market institution performance of states at risk, 1970–2002 (source: Author's calculations based on Gwartney and Lawson (2004)).

Note

The Economic Freedom Index (0=least freedom, 10=most freedom) comprises twenty-one components designed to identify the consistency of institutions and policies in seven major areas of economic activity.

established political parties in many countries to cultivate support by distributing particularistic benefits. As a result, the parties are, of necessity, growing more policy oriented and programmatic (Benton 2001).

However, the same set of strict economic or financial rules may also produce unfavorable outcomes for civil administration and democracy. For example, a country may adopt rules or set up organizations to ensure fiscal discipline, say, by creating a budget process that precludes deficit spending or by establishing an independent central bank to discourage expansion of the money supply. This may lead to budget austerity that erodes civil servants' work ethic and makes it difficult for them to do their jobs. Bureaucratic corruption and moonlighting grow as government workers seek to make ends meet. Lack of government services creates hardship and unrest in society. The greatest dislocations are often felt in politically sensitive urban areas, which tend to be beneficiaries of overvalued foreign exchange rates and other government subsidies. A military revolt or regional insurgency is not improbable under these circumstances, increasing the danger of state failure instead of strengthening civic institutions.

It is difficult to know in advance how the cross-cutting tensions among political, administrative, and market institutions will balance in any given country. As already suggested, many alternative pathways and sequences can lead to development. There is no single best formula for mixing democratization, civil service reform, and economic liberalization.

External involvement in nation building

Because nation building is not a predetermined or unidirectional process, local experimentation and adaptation are critical to making it work (Evans 2004). Albert Hirschman (1958, pp. 9–10) made the point years ago in his classic treatise on development:

> [T]he underdeveloped countries see only the fruits of economic progress and have little advance knowledge of the road they need to travel to obtain them.... Thus they will find out about the changes required in their own society in the course of the development processes as they make false starts and as they meet with, and overcome, successive obstacles. It is in this fashion rather than a priori that they will determine which of their institutions and character traits are backward and must be reformed or given up.

That said, poor countries can learn from the mistakes of others. The international community can accelerate improvements in governance by spreading knowledge about global "best practices," and by helping states tailor those ways of doing things to local conditions.

The best yardstick by which to measure donor support for nation building is official development assistance (ODA). Formally, ODA is defined as a net transfer in cash or kind that is administered with economic development in mind and that has a grant element of at least 25 percent. The World Bank and other agencies compile annual figures that report the actual financial disbursement of aid from all sources, less any repayments of earlier loans during the same period. The figures also include any goods or services valued at cost, including technical assistance such as the provision of experts to help with particular problems.

Official development assistance misses some international expenditure for nation building. Notably, it does not include military aid and security assistance, which may be significant at some stages of post-war reconstruction. Nor does it include the value of private charitable support for community organizations. Foreign trade and direct investment are left out, though they may be important in configuring important market institutions, such as stock exchanges or employers' associations. Finally, IMF loans are not counted as ODA, despite the fact that IMF agreements often mandate governance reforms by borrowing countries.

Little of the ODA provided over the past thirty years was self-consciously intended for nation building. Like the Marshall Plan, most ODA is aimed first at improving the economy rather than being directed at better governance per se. Democracy, bureaucratic capacity, and market institutions are often indirect byproducts of the financial assistance. Every time an international donor provides loans for a dam or a road, for example, that may enhance the national government's legitimacy and augment the local private sector's ability to trade and invest. An ODA-funded health or educational project may have the secondary consequence of persuading more citizens to accept the general validity of the governing regime. Moreover, the United States and other international donors often use development assistance as a carrot to extract changes in institutions. Working in collaboration, the donors try to convince client states that they must adopt international norms or lose access to credit.

In addition to having these indirect or incidental effects on nation building, donors also give technical assistance specifically for democracy promotion and civil service reform. The U.S. Agency for International Development, for example, has programs expressly to help judicial systems, parliaments, local governments, and electoral systems. They train local staff and help with administrative reorganization to streamline procedures and use personnel more efficiently. Promotion of democratic institutions, good governance, and the rule of law is a priority area for the European Union's aid programs. The World Bank (2002, p. 5) provides some $4.5 billion annually for public sector institution building (both stand-alone projects and technical assistance embedded in other projects). That is over half its public sector portfolio.

Figure 2.6 reports the median ODA flows from 1970 to 2002 for two groups of threatened states: the dwindling number of pre-conflict countries in the at-risk country sample (by definition there were no pre-conflict countries left by the end of the period), and the fluctuating number of states actually undergoing internal conflict in any year. To provide a common base of reference, each year's aid flows are converted to US$2000 per head of national population.

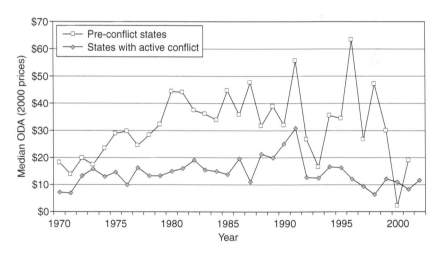

Figure 2.6 Foreign aid per capita to states at risk, 1970–2002 (source: Author's calculations based on World Bank (2005)).

Note
ODA is defined as a net transfer in cash or kind that is administered with economic development in mind and that has a grant element of at least 25 percent. Figures were converted to US$2000 using the implicit GDP deflator.

Two things should be noted about the amount of aid. One is that, as a group, sample states usually had more foreign assistance per capita before entering conflicts than they did while the conflicts were unfolding. This is hardly surprising. Countries experiencing domestic turmoil are less able to use aid, except for short-term disaster relief. Aid levels tend to fall during periods of civil unrest, but they typically jump once the fighting stops and the donors rush in to support reconstruction. After a few years of peace, aid usually begins to taper off again (Collier and Hoeffler 2004). This cycle raises the question, however, whether greater assistance at earlier points might have forestalled some internal conflicts that threatened states over the past three decades – or whether the higher volume of aid contributed to the subsequent internal conflicts, as some conservatives charge.

The other pattern worth mentioning is the relative uniformity of aid levels over time. While volume does swing up and down, for most years the median per capita foreign assistance for both groups of countries was in a fairly narrow band of $10–$40. To put that sum in perspective, annual aid flows under the Marshall Plan were the equivalent of about $100 per capita in 2000 prices (though only for five years). Again, an open question is whether increased spending might have done more to preclude the outbreak or relapse of domestic hostilities in the at-risk states – or if less spending would have been a better policy.

As noted, detractors of foreign aid and nation building assert that international development assistance is a waste of time and, worse, may actually interfere with the exercise of good governance. We will refer to this argument as the "fool's errand thesis." Taken together, the aid data and the governance indicators tend to contradict the thesis, though admittedly the data are too shaky to provide a definitive refutation. If aid were either pointless or counterproductive, as the "fool's errand thesis" says, we might expect to see massive ODA levels in the pre-conflict states coupled with declining capability and performance of governance institutions in the post-conflict states. We see neither. ODA levels are modest and declining, while governance indicators are rising slightly. These are only correlations, but they are consistent with the idea that foreign loans and technical assistance have a delayed, cumulative, but marginal benefit for governance in at-risk countries. It seems reasonable to conclude that in due course, development aid has a minor but positive net impact on public institutions in countries with internal security problems, even if the impact cannot be measured exactly or if the aid programs themselves could have been much better managed.

Policy implications

To summarize what the large-n data suggest about governance in at-risk states, state decay and failure is not the one-way process sometimes portrayed; modest positive changes in public institutions are taking place in many countries despite varying degrees of social unrest and insurgency, and foreign assistance probably has a small hand in this constructive process. Do these observations offer much encouragement that donors can do even better at reviving failed states or preventing at-risk states from sliding into turmoil and collapse? Three dilemmas suggest caution.

1. First is time. The vacuum created by a collapsed state creates urgent security needs, but that time frame is not consistent with the extended period required for setting up and legitimating a range of institutions. For instance, the bipartisan Commission on Post-conflict Reconstruction (2003) proposes a very complex, crash program for re-establishing governance in places like Iraq. History suggests that this kind of rushed approach is not realistic. It may lead to a dilution of energy so that nothing gets done well, as has happened with many conventional governance projects and programs (Grindle 2004). Then again, moving slowly on governance problems probably runs an equal risk of alienating the local population, which wants to see improvement sooner rather than later.

2. A second dilemma about nation building is due to the constrained capacity outsiders have to steer political and institutional development in directions they deem desirable. As noted above, learning and adaptation are critical to successful nation building, and every country has to work out the content and sequencing of institutional development that are right for its needs and conditions. Experimentation may go too far (or not far enough) for the aid-giving states, which are certain to want to set boundaries on what aid-receiving states do. Yet, pushing an aid recipient to follow idealized universal models may backfire or have limited staying power, especially if the local population views these efforts as foreign interference in their proper affairs.

3. A third dilemma is that no one can say for sure that the introduction of open and accountable governance in an unstable society will immunize it against large-scale religious or political extremism, as is hoped. The opposite may occur among groups that perceive themselves as left behind. Economic dislocation, combined with democratic freedoms, could let loose a local backlash against Western influence and values in some cases. Moreover, while it is true that modernized liberal democracies do not fight wars with other liberal democracies, this may not be true of the quasi-democratic states likely to emerge from contemporary nation building.

Bearing these dilemmas in mind, comparative experience since 1970 suggests three broad principles for workable nation building:

1 *Be patient.* Improved governance takes time. Make allowances for setbacks and unexpected outcomes, but also be prepared to take advantage of opportunities that come along.

2 *Be adaptable.* The sequence and content of institutional reform will probably not fit predetermined ideas. Allow experimentation about what to do first, and how to do it. Start off with problems that are do-able and that are true local priorities. Focus on outcomes more than processes, and keep an open mind regarding solutions that hold promise in a given context.

3   *Have modest expectations.* Do not attempt to do too much all at once. Try to focus on a few critical governance problems at a time, and be prepared to tolerate flawed processes and incremental progress in making institutions more open and accountable.

The new Washington consensus on the complementarities among governance, development, and international security is welcome. Nation-building assistance may eventually contribute to a safer and more prosperous world, provided that policy-makers do not err, either by trying to micromanage governance in other nation states or by withdrawing support out of frustration with the rate of improvement.

Notes

1 The United Nations does not use the term *nation building*. When the Security Council established UNOSOM II in Somalia, it never mentioned nation building by name, though it did specify the political objective of rebuilding that country's government structure. Likewise, the resolution authorizing the dispatch of the UNMIH to Haiti called for establishing a stable environment in which to hold democratic elections, rather than nation building per se. There have been forty-one United Nations peace-keeping missions since 1989.

2 A few rich countries such as Spain have had significant levels of internal violence, but they are not included in the sample. For anti-colonial wars and invasions aimed at regime change, only the country on whose territory the fighting takes place is counted as a state at risk. The sample is: Afghanistan, Albania, Algeria, Angola, Argentina, Azer-baijan, Bangladesh, Bhutan, Bosnia, Brazil, Burundi, Cambodia, Central African Republic, Chad, Chile, China, Colombia, Congo (Brazzaville), Congo (Kinshasha), Croatia, Cyprus, Djibouti, Egypt, El Salvador, Ethiopia, Georgia, Ghana, Guatemala, Guinea-Bissau, Haiti, Honduras, India, Indonesia, Iran, Iraq, Ivory Coast, Jamaica, Jordan, Kenya, South Korea, Laos, Lebanon, Lesotho, Liberia, Mali, Mauritania, Mexico, Moldova, Mozambique, Myanmar, Namibia, Nepal, Nicaragua, Niger, Nigeria, Oman, Pakistan, Panama, Papua New Guinea, Peru, Philippines, Romania, Russia, Rwanda, Senegal, Sierra Leone, Somalia, South Africa, Sri Lanka, Sudan, Syria, Tajik-istan, Thailand, Turkey, Uganda, Vietnam, Yemen, Yugoslavia, and Zimbabwe.

3 These growth rates are calculated using the Penn World Tables (Heston *et al.* 2002).

References

Bates, R.H. (2005) "Political Insecurity and State Failure in Contemporary Africa," Cambridge, MA: Harvard University Center for International Development, Working Paper No. 115.

Bendix, R. (1964) *Nation-building and Citizenship: Studies of Our Changing Social Order*, New York: Wiley.

Benton, A.L. (2001) *Patronage Games: Economic Reform, Political Institutions, and the Decline of Party Stability in Latin America*, Los Angeles: University of California, unpublished Ph.D. dissertation.

Bueno de Mesquita, B., A. Smith, R.M. Siverson, and J.D. Morrow (2003) *The Logic of Political Survival*, Cambridge, MA: MIT Press.

Chua, A. (2002) *World on Fire: How Exporting Free Market Democracy Breeds Ethnic Hatred and Global Instability*, New York: Doubleday.

Collier, P. and A. Hoeffler (2004) "Aid, Policy and Growth in Post-conflict Societies," *European Economic Review* 48 (October): 1125–1145.

Commission on Post-conflict Reconstruction (2003) *Play to Win*, Washington, DC: Center for Strategic and International Studies and the Association of the U.S. Army.

Dempsey, G.T., with R.W. Fontaine (2001) *Fool's Errands: America's Recent Encounters with Nation Building*, Washington, DC: Cato Institute.

Deutsch, K.W. (1963) "Some Problems in Nation Building," in K.W. Deutsch and W.J. Folz (eds) *Nation-building*, New York: Altherton Press.

Dobbins, J. (2003) "Nation-building: The Inescapable Responsibility of the World's Only Superpower," *Rand Review* 27 (summer): 16–27.

Dobbins, J., J.G. McGinn, K. Crane, S.G. Jones, R. Lal, A. Rathmell, R. Swanger, and A. Timilsina (2003) *America's Role in Nation-building: From Germany to Iraq*, Santa Monica, CA: RAND Corporation.

Etzioni, A. (2004) "A Self-restrained Approach to Nation-building by Foreign Powers," *International Affairs* 80 (January): 1–18.

Evans, P. (2004) "Development as Institutional Change: The Pitfalls of Monocropping and the Potentials of Deliberation," *Studies in Comparative International Development* 38 (winter): 30–52.

Freedom House (2004) *Freedom in the World 2005*, New York: Author, www.freedomhouse.org/research/survey2005.htm.

Fukuyama, F. (2004) "Nation-building 101," *Atlantic Monthly* (January/February): 159–162.

Goldsmith, A.A. (1992) "Institutions and Planned Socioeconomic Change: Four Approaches," *Public Administration Review* 52 (November/December): 582–587.

Grindle, M.S. (2004) "Good Enough Governance: Poverty Reduction and Reform in Developing Countries," *Governance* 17 (October): 525–548.

Gwartney, J. and R. Lawson (2004) *Economic Freedom of the World: 2004 Annual Report*, Vancouver, BC: Fraser Institute www.freetheworld.com/download.html.

Heston, A., R. Summers, and B. Aten (2002) *Penn World Table Version 6.1*, Philadelphia: Center for International Comparisons at the University of Pennsylvania.

Hirschman, A.O. (1958) *The Strategy of Economic Development*, New Haven, CT: Yale University Press.

Kaplan, R.D. (1994) "The Coming Anarchy," *Atlantic Monthly* (February): 44–76.

Latham, M.E. (2000) *Modernization as Ideology: American Social Science and "Nation Building" in the Kennedy Era*, Chapel Hill: University of North Carolina Press.

Lienert, I. (1998) "Civil Service Reform in Africa: Mixed Results after 10 Years," *Finance and Development* 35 (June): 42–45.

Lynn-Jones, S.M. (1998) "Why the United States Should Spread Democracy," Cambridge, MA: Harvard University Kennedy School of Government, Discussion Paper No. 98–07.

Marshall, M.G. (2003) *Major Episodes of Political Violence, 1946–2002*, Bethesda, MD: Center for Systemic Peace members.aol.com/CSPmgm/warlist.htm.

Packenham, R. (1973) *Liberal America and the Third World: Political-development Ideas in Foreign Aid and Social Science*, Princeton, NJ: Princeton University Press.

Powell, C.L. (2005) "No Country Left Behind," *Foreign Policy* (January/February): 28–35.

Przeworski, A., M.E. Alvarez, J.A. Cheibub, and F. Limongi (2000) *Democracy and Development*, Cambridge: Cambridge University Press.

Rodrik, D. and R. Wacziarg (2005) "Do Democratic Transitions Produce Bad Economic Outcomes?" Paper presented at the American Economic Association annual meetings, Philadelphia, January 7–9.

Rondinelli, D.A. and J.D. Montgomery (2005) "Regime Change and Nation Building: Can Donors Restore Governance in Post-conflict States?," *Public Administration and Development* 25 (February): 15–23.

Rotberg, R. (2002) "Failed States in a World of Terror," *Foreign Affairs* 81 (July/August): 127–140.

Snider, L.W. (2000) "Political Institutions, Disorderly Liberalization and Financial Crises: Problems of Concept Formation and Measurement," Claremont Conference on the Political Economy of Currency Crises, Claremont, California, December 1–2.

Snyder, J.L. (2000) *From Voting to Violence: Democratization and Nationalist Conflict*, New York: Norton.

Spanger, H. (2000) "Failed State or Failed Concept? Objections and Suggestions," Paper presented at Failed States Conference, Florence, Italy, April 7–10.

Tilly, C. (1975) "Reflections on the History of European State-making," in C. Tilly (ed.) *The Formation of National States in Western Europe*, Princeton, NJ: Princeton University Press.

United Nations Development Program (1997) *Capacity Development*, Technical Advisory Paper No. 2, New York: UNDP, Management Development and Governance Division, Bureau for Policy Development, July.

United States President (2002) *The National Security Strategy of the United States of America*, Washington, DC, September.

Von Hippel, K. (1999) *Democracy by Force*, Cambridge: Cambridge University Press.

White House (2001) Office of the Press Secretary, "President Holds Prime Time News Conference," October 11, www.whitehouse.gov/news/releases/2001/10/20011011-7.html.

White House (2002a) Office of the Press Secretary, "President Proposes $5 Billion Plan to Help Developing Nations," March 14, www.whitehouse.gov/news/releases/2002/03/20020314-7.html.

White House (2002b) "Remarks by the President to the George C. Marshall ROTC Award Seminar on National Security, Cameron Hall, Virginia Military Institute, Lexington, Virginia," April 17, www.whitehouse.gov/news/releases/2002/04/20020417-1.html.

White House (2003) "President Discusses the Future of Iraq, Washington Hilton Hotel, Washington, DC," February 26, www.whitehouse.gov/news/releases/2003/02/20030226-11.html.

Wolfowitz, P. (2000) "Remembering the Future," *The National Interest* (spring): 35–45.

World Bank (2002) *Reforming Public Institutions and Strengthening Governance: A World Bank Strategy Implementation Update*, Washington, DC: Author.

World Bank (2005) *World Development Indicators On-line*, Washington, DC: Author.

Zakaria, F. (2003) *The Future of Freedom: Illiberal Democracy at Home and Abroad*, New York: W.W. Norton.

3

CONSTITUTIONAL DESIGN, IDENTITY, AND LEGITIMACY IN POST-CONFLICT RECONSTRUCTION

Aliza Belman Inbal and Hanna Lerner

Post-conflict societies are almost invariably characterized by deep religious, ethnic, national, or ideological divisions. Even after formal peace has been attained, these divisions are likely to remain, often pulling societies back into conflict within a few years of cessation of hostilities. For peace to be sustained, warring parties must be persuaded that their interests will be best served by forgoing the battlefield for the halls of government. For this reason, the establishment, or re-establishment, of a system of government recognized as legitimate by diverse factions of the population is crucial for post-war stabilization. Once warring parties have accepted the government as their own and have agreed to submit societal conflicts to mutually recognized democratic mechanisms, and once interacting adversaries have been reassured that their views will be heard within the decision-making and governing process and their values reflected in its outputs, an end to violence becomes a viable possibility. This willingness to acknowledge the government as legitimate, in turn, is the first and most elemental building block upon which effective governance must be based. Without the people's agreement to accept the government as their own and its laws as binding upon them, no effective governance is possible.

In the quest for establishing legitimate government, constitutions and constitution-making processes often play a central role (CSIS and AUSA 2002: 17). From Iraq and Afghanistan to South Africa and Bosnia, constitutions have become an integral part of peacemaking and stabilization processes in deeply divided societies. This chapter will look at the interplay between constitutions, identity, and governmental legitimacy in post-conflict societies, analyzing the role that constitutions can play in reinforcing legitimacy even where differences remain or the sources of conflict remain unresolved. To do so, it will also look back in time to India and Israel: two post-conflict societies which evolved into stable, long-standing democracies despite severe societal schisms present at the countries' birth. It will analyze what role the process of constitution-making played in these societies in providing for the successful stabilization and democratization of these two societies in an attempt to provide useful lessons for current deeply divided societies engaged in the process of constitution-writing. In order to set the stage for this discussion, we will begin with a more detailed look at what legitimacy is, how it is derived, and what can and should be the role of constitutions in its generation.

Legitimacy, identity, and constitutions

There are two basic ways to generate legitimacy (Kjaer 2004: 12). *Output-oriented* legitimacy derives from the ability of governments to produce tangible results. This sort of legitimacy is a by-product of the outputs of the government in question. To the degree that governments provide needed or desired services to the people – be they social, economic and health-related services or security – the people are likely to support the government's right to govern.

Output-oriented legitimacy is inextricably linked with a second type of legitimacy, that of *input-oriented* legitimacy, derived from the consent of those who are asked to comply with the rule of law and to submit voluntarily to the government's authority. These two forms of legitimacy have a symbiotic relationship. While it is undoubtedly true that effective governmental outputs contribute to legitimacy, it is equally true that a certain degree of legitimacy is needed in order to make effective governance possible. This is a point which has been largely recognized by the international community. To quote from USAID's Fragile States Strategy, "Where legitimacy is an issue, options generally narrow.... Indeed, efforts to boost effectiveness are unlikely to succeed without legitimacy" (USAID 2005: 6).

Input-oriented legitimacy lies, first and foremost, in the "hearts and minds" of the populace; that is, in their *a priori* consent to being governed. In modern societies, such consent is expected to have formal manifestation through democratic procedures, such as participation, deliberation, and representation. However, these formal indicators of consent, to be of value, must represent a shared societal conception of what is being consented to; that is, of what the people wish to empower their government to do. If there is no common agreement on the fundamental principles that underlie the state, consent is likely to be short-lived. If citizens have vastly divergent views regarding what the government that they have consented to should or should not be able to do, then that government stands on very shaky ground. If some citizens feel that government should uphold the tenets of their religion, and others believe that it should rule according to liberal democratic norms, popular consent will be ephemeral. If some citizens believe that their government should be, first and foremost, the representative of one dominant ethnic group and others demand a more pluralist society, this too can present a problem for legitimacy. Thus, the precondition for "input-oriented" legitimacy is shared norms (Coicaud 2002: 14). This is a particularly salient issue in many present-day post-conflict and conflicted societies, such as Iraq and Afghanistan, where disputes over normative issues are often one of the main sources of societal rifts.

Constitutions, clearly, play an important role in establishing and regulating the formal mechanisms through which input-oriented legitimacy is manifest. They establish procedural rules for democratic elections and set the framework for governance by establishing the boundaries of governmental power and the relationship between the various branches of government and between the government and its citizens. In addition to establishing these institutional mechanisms, constitutions play an important role by elucidating the shared norms, goals, and values which are the ultimate source of input-oriented legitimacy. Thus, constitutions play a "foundational" role of defining the commonly held core societal values, norms, and aspirations of the people and of expressing a concept of unified peoplehood – a sense that "we the people" includes "me." While the "foundational" elements may vary from constitution to constitution, they generally include issues such as the relationship between religion and state, the fundamental rights guaranteed to all citizens, the persons defined as belonging to "the people," and the symbols of the state.

Just as input-oriented legitimacy is only possible where formal consent reflects underlying shared norms, constitutions may only reinforce legitimacy to the extent that they truly reflect public sentiment. To put it in the words of one constitutional expert, "a constitution is just a piece of paper, no better than the underlying consensus – or lack thereof – that it memorializes" (Feldman 2005: 19). For this reason, there is no blueprint constitution that may be used for all societies, and there is no utility to imposing a constitution upon a reluctant citizenry. As a result, the international community has come to put enormous emphasis on the process by which constitutions are made. Recent constitution-making processes have been accompanied by massive efforts to involve the public before, during, and after the text is finalized. Examples of such broad-based participatory processes include: Nicaragua, where 100,000 citizens took part in open town meetings as part of the constitution-writing process; Rwanda where thousands of trained facilitators were sent out to the provinces for six-month periods to educate and stimulate debate on the constitution-drafting process; and South Africa, where a massive public campaign resulted in over two million submissions from individuals, advocacy groups, professional associations, and other interests.

By including large segments of the population in the debate over the shape of the constitution, the aim is to achieve not only workable, mutually acceptable compromises but also a common sense of identity and purpose. Thus, for example, an extensive UNDP-USIP study of constitution building and peace-making asserted that the constitutional process can be "transformational" for post-conflict societies, facilitating peace and stability by "mobiliz(ing) all segments of … society and forg(ing) a collective vision of the country's future" (USIP 2005).

Constitution-making in deeply divided post-conflict societies

However, the problem of societies emerging from internal conflict is that they are very frequently characterized by deep divisions on questions of national identity, norms, and values. In such cases, engendering a successful process may not be enough to achieve a sense of collectivity and consensus. For a constitutional process to be a source of stability and unification, there must be potential for achieving workable compromises that can reinforce commonalities while reassuring all sides that their most vital concerns will be safeguarded. This may be extremely difficult to achieve in deeply divided societies. In conflicts involving competing normative perceptions of the public sphere, where the ultimate goals and character of the state are in dispute, forging a collective vision of the country's future, or even achieving mutually acceptable compromise may prove an elusive goal.

One of the more popular solutions to the problem of constitution-writing in ethnically, religious or nationally heterogeneous societies where there is no a priori sense of peoplehood is Jurgen Habermas's concept of "constitutional patriotism." Habermas argues that a common commitment to the democratic institutions of the state can in and of itself be instrumental in forging a sense of shared citizenship or peoplehood.[1] However, Habermas' solution is only relevant for societies where there is consensus on the precepts of political liberalism. As he himself acknowledges, "democratic citizenship need not be rooted in the national identity of a people. However, regardless of the diversity of different cultural forms of life, it does require that every citizen be socialized into a common political culture" (Habermas 1996: 500). Thus, constitutional patriotism is of limited utility in deeply divided societies which do not share a common political culture based on the liberalist separation between private identities/beliefs and the public sphere.

Unfortunately, modern-day fragile states tend to lack basic consensus over liberal values, suggesting that the liberal-democratic solution cannot succeed in cases like Iraq or Afghanistan, where divisions exist not only between various religious, ethnic, or national identity groups, but also concerning the role of private identities in public political life. In both societies, some of the competing factions have proven less than willing to embrace liberal democratic principles. In such deeply divided societies, those who believe that government should represent the aspirations of a dominant religious group or ethnic identity may oppose the adoption of liberal principles. This is the kind of conflict which is termed by Albert Hirschman as "either-or" or "non-divisible," as opposed to the "divisible" or "more-or-less" conflicts, which usually concern allocation of resources and products between classes, sectors, or regions (Hirschman 1994: 203). As Hirschman notes, divisible conflicts are easier to settle, as the warring parties can agree to "split the difference" or compromise. Conversely, the latter form of conflict is often characterized by an absolute unwillingness to compromise on the issues upon which the conflict is based.

These "either–or" divisions present a considerable challenge for constitution-making. Where there is no agreement even on the basic value of political liberalism, agreement on the normative aspects of the state may prove impossible. Moreover, dealing with these identity questions in the constitutional arena can easily exacerbate tensions rather than mitigate them. The process of constitution-making in post-conflict societies imports deeply rooted identity conflicts into the high-stakes arena of entrenched law. Constitutions provide the guidelines for future supreme court decisions, bind the legislature, and constrain future generations. Thus, the formalization of a written constitution is generally perceived as forcing unalterable choices regarding the state's norms and identity. In such circumstances, concessions are seen as being all the more weighty, because they may have permanent implications, and mutually acceptable compromise may thus be all the more difficult to achieve.

Hence, in post-conflict societies, we are faced with a paradox. On the one hand, we look to constitutions in order to underpin the legitimacy of the new government by providing the popularly agreed-upon structure and values by which it governs. On the other hand, by importing identity questions into the constitutional arena, we risk escalating the conflict rather than alleviating it. This paradox has troubling consequences for the chances of establishing effective governance. As discussed above, constitutions have two primary aspects: an institutional aspect, providing the framework for the conduct of government, and a foundational, or identity-related, aspect. While the institutional aspects of a constitution are essential in order to set up a stable, legitimate system of democratic governance, the foundational aspects of constitutions can easily become the deal-breaker in societies where there is no unified conception of identity. In such contexts, struggles over how to define who "we the people" are and what the values and ultimate goals of "our" state should be, can stand in the way of more procedurally oriented dialogue on how the government should best be run.

Challenges of this nature have arisen in the constitution-making process in Iraq and Afghanistan. In both cases, the debate which preceded the enactment of the constitution revealed deep divisions among the framers with regard to foundational issues. In particular, vehement debates revolved around the question of the proper relationship between the Islamic and secular character of the state. These modern-day Islamic constitutions are not, however, the first time when constitution-making processes in states emerging out of conflict have had to confront such challenges. Moreover, among the historical precedents of such cases are ones where fragile or post-conflict societies did manage to successfully establish a stable and democratic system of governance. In both India and Israel, creative solutions were found to the considerable challenge of achieving the popularly accepted consent to and agreement on the powers and procedures of government that represent the contribution of constitutions to rebuilding governance.

The Israeli and Indian constitutional solutions differ in certain fundamental aspects. Most notably, India adopted a lengthy constitution in the early years of the state, whereas Israel decided to not to adopt a written constitution at all. Nevertheless, the two countries adopted a similar constitutional approach to address a very similar problem of bitter internal conflicts over the shared norms and values of the polity as a whole. In addition, in both cases, constitutional deliberations followed violent conflict. In Israel, 1 percent of the Jewish population died in the war of independence against five Arab neighbors; in India, one million died and seventeen million were displaced during the partition between India and Pakistan. In both cases one of the most bitterly divisive issues during the constitutional discussions concerned the religious and national identity of the polity as a whole: Should the Jewish state be understood in religious or secular-national terms?[2] How to accommodate the need for Indian unity with its enormous religious, linguistic, and cultural diversity? In both cases the framers of the constitution ultimately acknowledged their inability to achieve consensus regarding the foundational issues which divided their societies. Instead, rather than forcing choices between the competing visions of the state, they transferred these controversial decisions from the constitutional sphere to future political institutions which could continue the debate over time. By employing strategies of ambiguity and avoidance, they embraced constitutional arrangements – formal and informal – which circumvented potentially explosive conflicts and facilitated the establishment of stable governments. In both cases, these solutions have impressively stood the test of time, engendering vibrant democracies despite decades of political strife and ethnic or religious tensions which have continued up until today.

Informal consociationalism in Israel

From the early days of the Jewish settlement in Mandatory Palestine, it was threatened not only by the external Arab enemies amassed upon its still-undefined borders, but also by the deep internal rifts over the role of religion in the future Jewish state. When the State of Israel was founded in 1948, Jewish Israeli society was divided between rival religious and secular conceptions of the desired nature of the Jewish state. What was at stake was "a struggle over the ultimate values rather than distributive justice, over the whole rather than the parts" (Cohen and Susser 2000). This struggle was most poignantly manifest in the discussions over the constitution.

The constitutional controversies generated by the religious–secular cleavage stem from the comprehensive nature of the Jewish religious code of law: the *Halacha*. As an autonomous system of law and procedures, the *Halacha* could feasibly comprise an alternative to the civil legal system of the state. From the perspective of many ultra-Orthodox Jews, the *Halacha* takes precedence over the law of the state whenever there is a contradiction between the two systems, and especially when civil law demands behavior that is contrary to *Halachic* rule (Horowitz and Lissak 1989: 59–60, 138). As argued in the Knesset deliberations on the constitution by Meir Levonstein, a representative of the ultra-Orthodox party Agudat-Israel, "There is no place in Israel for any constitution created by men. If it contradicts the Torah – it is inadmissible, and if it is concurrent with the Torah – it is redundant" (*Knesset Records* 1950: 744). Opposing this ultra-Orthodox perspective was that of the stolidly secular parties, who objected vehemently to the religious representatives' aspiration to establish a theocratic state. Many of them shared the position of Mapai member Efraim Tavori who declared: "As a socialist and as an atheist I an unable under any circumstances to sign on to a program which contains a religious formulation" (*Knesset Records* 1950: 774).

Thus, much like in the case of Islamic states, the nature of the *Halacha* as a comprehensive legal system meant that the problem of defining the relationship between religion and state was not merely a problem of deciding whether or not a certain religion shall have official status, as a state religion. Rather, it was a problem of defining the relationship between state and Jewish law. This problem, and the question of which law was supreme, became one of intense dispute from the early constitutional debates in the 1940s. In January 1950, when the first Knesset, which was initially elected as a constituent assembly, began formally discussing the issue of the constitution, the ardor and intractability of the religious–secular schism was immediately apparent. Consequentially, the debate did not center around the content of the constitution, but whether a written constitution should be drafted at all.

The nature of the constitutional debate in Israel reflected a deeply held fear that the drafting of a constitution could prove to be a destabilizing and incendiary exercise at a time when maximum solidarity was needed to confront the Arab enemy. This fear was poignantly expressed by Agudat Yisrael's Meir-David Levonstein:

> I would like to warn: the experience of drafting a constitution would necessarily entail a severe, vigorous uncompromising war of opinions. A war of spirit, which is defined by the gruesome concept of *Kulturkampf*. . . . Is this a convenient time for a thorough and penetrating examination of our essence and purpose? It is clear that there is no room for any compromises, any concessions or mutual agreements, since no man can compromise and concede on issues upon which his belief and soul depend.

(Knesset Records 1950: 744)

It is important to note that such warnings of the potential destabilization of the political order were not perceived as unrealistic, since they were grounded in the very delicate and fragile political order of the newly founded state. One of the most serious problems which the Israeli government faced after independence was the challenge of transforming the political culture of a voluntaristic community in the pre-sovereignty era into a society with the institutional structure of a sovereign state. Indeed, Israel's first Prime Minister, David Ben

Gurion, himself many times expressed the view that "Citizenship requires a deep mental character . . . our people does not have a character yet."[3]

During its first years, the government faced grave challenges to the state's authority. This dissent originated in the pre-state social and ideological fragmentation within the Zionist movement and outside of it. Both preceding and after the establishment of the state there were isolated instances of violence, or potential violence, of extreme national or religious groups that acted against the Jewish secular leadership in an attempt to undermine its authority. For example, in 1951, members of an organization of young zealous religious men that condemned the state's desecration of religion were arrested after planning to bomb the Knesset in protest against the draft of women into the army.[4] In addition, infighting between right-wing paramilitary factions and the Israeli defense forces was so severe that some historians have claimed that Israel had not been far from the brink of civil war in its early years.[5]

The gravity of the situation was recognized by the secular leadership of the young state, and reflected in their speeches during the Knesset debate over the adoption of a written constitution.[6] Consequently, a year and a half after the first Knesset was elected, it passed a resolution postponing the immediate enactment of a written constitution, instead deciding to construct it step by step, over the course of many years, by means of enacting individual Basic Laws which were accorded the status of higher law.[7] To be sure, there were many reasons for the decision to refrain from drafting a formal constitution at a time of independence involving political, social, and pragmatic factors. Nevertheless, clearly the inability to reach a consensus regarding the most fundamental normative principles of the state was the underlying condition which led the Knesset to avoid unequivocal majoritarian decisions, and to transfer the choices over the ultimate values of the polity to future political institutions.

In lieu of a formal constitution, the establishment of the institutions of government was achieved through conventions and the legal structure inherited from the Ottoman and the British rule. These institutional arrangements were retroactively entrenched in a series of Basic Laws which were adopted over the years.[8] Meanwhile, Israel's Declaration of Independence partially fulfilled the "foundational" aspect of the constitution, defining Israel by the arguably contradictory moniker of a "Jewish and democratic state."[9]

Since Israeli society was incapable of reaching a consensus regarding the balance between its Jewish and democratic identities, the political leaders of the young state circumvented the potentially explosive conflict over religious issues through a set of informal consociational[10] arrangements where representatives of the secular majority agreed not to threaten the core values of religious factions through majoritarian decisions on controversial issues (Horowitz and Lissak 1989; Don-Yehiya 1999: 25; Cohen and Susser 2000: 7). The Israeli consociational arrangements mandated the inclusion of religious parties in coalition partnerships, proportionality in resource allocation and the establishment of a state-funded but autonomous religious education system. In addition, a mutual veto evolved based on the principle of maintaining the status quo with regard to four issues where there would be no separation between religion and state: the observance of Jewish dietary laws and of the Sabbath in Israeli public institutions, family law, and conversions to Judaism.

The vague, unwritten quality of the consociational arrangements enabled Israeli democracy to develop despite strong social divisions. But circumventing explicit decisions on fundamental issues did not solve them. Rather, they were postponed, to be dealt with later. Even the term "status quo" itself has remained an issue of contention. Nearly all government coalition agreements have committed to upholding the status quo. And yet, as the term has never been clearly defined, its scope has remained an issue of acrimonious debate in the Knesset and the courts and among the public at large. To this day, the issue of the proper relationship between religion and state has remained one of the principal fault lines along which Israeli society is divided.

While the debate over religion and state continues to polarize Israeli society, any attempt to resolve it has proven to be even more destabilizing. In 1992, the passing of the Basic Law on Human Dignity and Liberty and the Basic Law on the Freedom of Occupation threatened to overturn the informal arrangements which had managed the relationship between religious and secular factions for over forty years. These Basic Laws were the first to deal with "foundational" issues relating to the identity of the Israeli state rather than just procedural issues regarding the functioning of governmental institutions. Both of these laws entrenched basic liberal-democratic rights that religious factions believed threatened the status quo. The opposition of the religious bloc to these laws was exacerbated by an activist Supreme Court chief justice who lauded them as a "constitutional revolution," implying that they were an important step on the way to the framing of a formal constitution (Barak 1992: 16). The suggestion that the primacy of liberal-democratic norms was being formalized in entrenched law and could be enforced in Supreme Court rulings met with severe opposition on the part of the religious camp. At the height of the struggle, the debate provoked a massive orthodox demonstration against the Supreme Court in Jerusalem in February 1999. An estimated 250,000 to 400,000 Orthodox Jews participated in what was one of Israel's largest demonstrations ever.[11]

The intensification of the religious–secular conflict in the public and the political arenas resulted in increasing institutional tensions between the judiciary and the legislature (which was, at the time, led by a coalition that included several religious parties). This escalation was reflected in several attempts by the religious parties to use the political arena to promote their struggle with the supreme court and to weaken its judicial authority in constitutional-foundational issues.[12]

The severe reaction to the attempt to take a step toward formalization of a liberal constitution in Israel makes it doubtful that Israel will be able to draft a formal constitution in the near future. It seems that the Israeli constitution will only be completed once fundamental questions over the identity of society and state are resolved. Until such time, there remains a trade-off between the degree of formalization of the basic norms of the state and the stability of the social and political system.

Constitutional ambiguity in India

India, unlike Israel, did adopt a formal constitution. Nevertheless, the case of India involves similar strategies of ambiguity and avoidance to deal with deep divisions. Religiously, culturally, and linguistically, Indian society was – and still is – one of the most diverse in the world. After the partition that created Pakistan, India was left with a Muslim minority of almost 12 percent of its population (the third largest Muslim community in the world) alongside other major religious minorities such as Christians, Sikhs, Buddhists, Jains, and Parsis. Over eighteen languages were spoken in India at the time of independence by more than one million people, and the number of dialects reached 2000. Socially and economically, the polarization among Indians was tremendous due to its rigid traditional caste system. The internal diversity of what used to be British India increased even more after independence when over 500 Princely States, most of which had monarchic traditions as well as diverse religious and ethnic backgrounds, had to be incorporated (not willingly in all cases) into the new state. In short, the problem of forging political unity amidst extensive diversity remained the main challenge of the Constituent Assembly even after partition.

The Indian framers overcame this extraordinary internal diversity by adopting a long and extremely detailed constitution, which was considered by its critics as lacking theoretical consistency and a coherent system of values and beliefs. The constitution includes provisions with potentially competing principles and perspectives, such as modernity vs. traditionalism, state intervention in religious affairs vs. separation of church and state, liberalism and individual rights vs. communitarism and special group rights, and social reform vs. social conservatism.[13] While some have seen this as a shortcoming of the constitution, others see its vagueness as its strength. The renowned scholar of Indian constitutionalism Granville Austin identifies the Constituent Assembly's ability to encompass conflicting principles as one of its most original contributions to the practice of constitution-making. He praises the Assembly's ability "to reconcile, to harmonize, and to make work without changing their context, apparently incompatible concepts – at least concepts that appear conflicting to the non-Indian, and especially to the European or American observer" (Austin 1999: 317).

Two revealing examples of the inconsistency and lack of clear decisions in the Constitution are the provisions concerning the Uniform Civil Code (namely uniformity of secular personal law) and the official language of the state. These two issues represent a fundamental controversy involving two opposing views on the identity of India: one of which aspired to unify through uniformity, and the other to maintain the religious and cultural pluralism which had characterized Indian society for generations.

Uniform Civil Code

The debate over the Uniform Civil Code lasted throughout almost the entire three years of constitutional drafting. The question was whether to entrench civic secular principles of personal law or to preserve the particular traditions of the various religions. By making all Indians answerable to the same civil law, some of the framers of the constitution wished to advance a homogeneous sense of Indian nationhood. K.M. Munshi, one of the leaders of the Congress Party, argued during the Constituent Assembly debates:

> Our first problem and most important problem is to produce national unity in this country.... There is no use clinging always to the past. We are departing from the past ... we want the whole India to be welded and united together as a single nation. Are we helping those factors which help the welding together into a single nation, or is this country to be kept up always as a series of competing communities?
>
> (*Constituent Assembly Debates*, Vol. II, 1999: 548)

However, other members of the Indian Constituent Assembly – particularly Muslims – argued against state interference in religious matters and demanded that the primacy of traditional personal laws of the religious minorities be upheld. Uniformity, claimed Moslem League representative Pocker Bahadur, during the Assembly debates, was merely a thinly disguised tyranny of the majority: "By uniform, I ask, what do you mean and which particular law, of which community are you going to take as standard?" (*CAD*, Vol. II, 1999: 545).

The debate on the Uniform Civil Code reflected fundamental disagreement on the desired role of the constitution itself. The supporters of the Uniform Civil Code wished to use the writing of the constitution to forge a source of common identity which could unify members of diverse religious and cultural groups. They wished to use the legal power and status of the constitution in order to modify religious customs and advance legal uniformity among all religious groups. On the other side was the conviction that constitutions should reflect current realities and should not impose deep social and cultural changes. Moslem League representative Naziruddin Ahmad warned against overly radical constitutional provisions, arguing that it would be too difficult, "at this stage of our society," to expect people to surrender to the state areas of their lives, such as marriage, that were previously governed only by their traditional-religious practices and institutions.

> I have no doubt that a stage will come when the civil law will be uniform. But then that time has not yet come. We believe that the power that has been given to the state to make the Civil Code uniform is in advance of the time.... What the British in 175 years failed to do

or were afraid to do, what the Muslims in the course of 500 years refrained from doing, we should not give power to the state to do all at once. I submit, sir, that we should proceed not in haste but with caution, with experience, with statesmanship and with sympathy.

(*CAD*, Vol. II, 1999: 542)

Eventually, the Indian framers created a sophisticated constitutional mechanism that included the civic-secular Uniform Civil Code in the constitution without making that code legally binding, thereby avoiding a decision between the two approaches to India's religious identity. The Uniform Civil Code was adopted as Article 44 of the constitution, which reads: "The State shall endeavour to secure for the citizens a uniform civil code throughout the territory of India." This Article was included in the Directive Principles of State Policy section of the constitution, which is non-justiciable and, as such, not enforceable by any court. The Directive Principles, including the Uniform Civil Code, were deemed by Article 37 of the constitution to be "fundamental in the governance of the country" and were intended to guide the legislature in future lawmaking as part of the reform of Indian society.

Thus, the question of whether a liberal-democratic or a religious conception of personal law was to be applied in India remained an open one after the constitution was enacted. By employing ambiguous language, the Indian constitution effectively removed the decision on this important issue from the constitutional arena, transferring it back to the political sphere. As a result, in the 1950s, the Lok Sabha (Indian Parliament) passed three bills which created a differentiation in the application of the Uniform Civil Code to different religious communities.[14] Consequently, the applicability of secular personal law to individuals in India is dependent on their religion (Galanter 1989: 155).

Even today, the ambiguous intent of the constitution still leads to heated political and legal debates in Parliament and the Supreme Court (Shankar 2002; Jacobsohn 2003). For example, in the famous Shah Bano case of 1985, the Supreme Court was forced to make tough choices between competing constitutional principles. A Muslim woman appealed to the Court for permission to settle her divorce according to the state secular law, rather then according to the traditional Muslim personal law which denied her any alimony. While the Supreme Court ruled in her favor, the Indian Parliament overturned the Court's decision by enacting a bill which limited the Court's authority to act in issues related to personal law (Pathak and Sunder Rajan 1989).

National language

The issue of whether India should have a national language provides a similar example of how the Indian Constitutive Assembly had to address fundamental issues of identity in its efforts to write a constitution. Many speakers emphasized the importance to national unity of a national language, as a "cement" to hold the various parts of India together. Other members of the Constitutive Assembly objected strongly to the subordination of their languages to that of the Hindi majority. After intense and heated debate, the Constituent Assembly could not agree upon a national language. In the compromise formula that was eventually agreed upon, while Hindi was labeled the official language, English would be used for all official purposes (Article 351). It was decided that this arrangement would hold for an "interim period" of fifteen years, during which time Hindi was to be progressively introduced into official use. However, what would happen at the end of those fifteen years was left undetermined, with the constitution providing for the establishment of a parliamentary committee to examine the issue in the future (Article 344).[15] In addition, the constitution recognized fourteen other languages for official use (Eighth Schedule of the Constitution).

Thus, the Constituent Assembly found a way to strike a balance between nationalist aspirations and pragmatic exigencies. "Instead of ceding to the linguistic nationalism of a substantial segment of the population, a pluralist compromise was engineered, which recognized the use of different languages at different levels for different purposes" (Khilnani 1999: 175). As in the case of the Uniform Civil Code, the constitutional formula regarding official language transferred the final decision to the political arena. Again, the members of the Constituent Assembly recognized the limitations of the constitutional arena to make such fundamental choices regarding the identity of the state. They preferred to adopt ambivalent formulations which did not attempt to crystallize a coherent identity and accommodated the conflicting positions.

By adopting a strategy of deliberate ambiguity, the Constituent Assembly achieved two things: first, it drafted a constitution which successfully represented the actual identity of "the people": a divided identity. Second, it left the door open to the slow and gradual emergence of united national identity, which would be crafted incrementally by the political institutions of the state.

Conclusion

The Indian and Israeli cases provide two examples of how the problem of constitution formation in divided societies was overcome when it proved impossible to agree on the most basic identity questions. In both cases, it was not elaboration and formalization of consistent, coherent definitions of national identity that made it possible to move ahead, but a conscious decision not to incorporate such definitions. What both of these cases suggest is that successful constitution-making in divided societies is not always a "moment of foundation" in which the identity of the state and the common vision of the people are defined for all future generations. Instead, the adoption of a constitution may merely be a "moment of accommodation" in which room is made for conflicting visions. In such circumstances, the constitution should not be measured by the depth of the common vision it achieves but rather by the scope of disagreement that it accommodates.

When disagreements exist on deeply held norms and values, no process may be adequate to bring about consensus. This is not to say that inclusive, participatory processes are not important in order to reinforce the legitimacy of the constitution and to build popular commitment to its precepts. However, we must be aware that processes may fall short of being "transformational" ones in which all issues are resolved and a unified people is born. Rather, we must acknowledge that in societies divided along ethnic, religious, or national lines, the resolution of these issues may take generations, if at all. Thus, while it is important that constitutional processes be inclusive and give people the sense that they are being heard and represented, it is equally important not to constrain the process by insisting that agreement be reached.

It is interesting to note that in the recent constitutions of Afghanistan and Iraq, where the most hotly debated issues involved "either–or" questions of the foundational norms and values of the state, fudging strategies similar to those employed in Israel and India were adopted in order to deal with conflicting principles of Islamic *shari'a* and liberal democracy. For example, Article 3 of the Afghan constitution includes a provision which bans laws contrary to Islam, while Article 7 of the Afghan constitution requires that the state observe the Universal Declaration of Human Rights and all covenants to which the government is a party, and Article 22 declares the legal equality of men and women, without any of the qualifications found in *shari'a*.[16] In the Iraqi case as well, contradictory provisions exist, prohibiting laws that contradict "the provisions of the judgments of Islam" while simultaneously banning laws that contravene "the principles of democracy" and the fundamental rights guaranteed by the constitution. In these cases, as in many others where "non-divisible" foundational issues of norms and values have been at issue, constitutional framers have resorted to strategies of ambiguity, avoidance, and contradictory principles in order to enable the constitutional process to go forward despite the inability to agree on the most basic, fundamental issues. What these strategies do is allow for the basic institutional structures of government to be established by way of a binding constitutional document while deferring issues which are irresolvable at the time of framing to future legislatures and judiciaries.

These strategies, however, while necessary, also carry significant dangers which must be acknowledged. Deferring contentious issues to future political institutions assumes that these institutions will have the capacity to take up the mantle of the debate. In Israel and India, the relative success of their constitutional solutions lies in the fact that both countries developed strong democratic institutions. These institutions were able to absorb the contentious issues without seriously threatening the stability of the government.

In failing, failed, or post-war states, the court system and the parliament may be ill equipped to deal with these issues. Where political structures are highly underdeveloped, and where there is little popular trust in or support for democratic institutions, there is a significant danger of opposing factions abandoning the political arena in order to try to achieve victory through violent means. In this way, unresolved disputes can act like a live grenade, quickly tossed from the constitutional arena, to the political or judicial and from there to the explosion of renewed hostilities. As Barnett Rubin has pointed out with regard to the Afghan constitution, the constitutional provisions regarding the role of Islam amounted to "a package deal that contains potential contradictions to spark future conflicts" (Rubin 2004: 15). A paradox linked to this problem is that where constitutions are not "foundational," where they do not rest on shared norms and goals, they do not provide strong input-oriented legitimacy through expression of those norms. Where there is less input-oriented legitimacy, there is more need for output-oriented legitimacy, and governmental effectiveness becomes all the more important. If governments are not capable of providing the expected outputs, they may quickly lose any semblance of legitimacy and may well collapse.

A second danger lies in the simple fact that ambiguous constitutions make for ambiguous laws and power structures. Thus, at a time when the government is trying to re-establish the rule of law, there may be significant disagreement on what that law dictates or what mechanisms the sovereign authorities may use to enforce it. In a sense, even when the institutional provisions of the constitution are clear, the power to decide on foundational issues is left "up for grabs." In this type of context, it is not clear who will decide issues left ambiguous in the constitution – the judiciary, the legislature, or the executive. This may lead to a potentially destabilizing dynamic of power struggles between the various branches of government. This was the case both in Israel and India, where a dynamic tension exists between the Supreme Court and the Knesset.

A third and final danger is that posed to minority and civil rights. An ambiguous constitution provides ambiguous protections for basic democratic rights. This problem has been poignantly illustrated in the recent death sentence conferred in Afghanistan on a convert to Christianity. Similarly, among the groups likely to suffer most from this are women, who may well be oppressed under the protected religious and cultural traditions. Thus, for example, the decision not to apply a uniform civil code to the Muslim population in India – thereby leaving decisions regarding personal law in the hands of religious authorities – affects the legal personhood of women who are those who are oppressed under religious fundamentalism. Similarly, women's rights are particularly endangered under Islamic constitutions such as the new constitution of Iraq, which indeed states that all Iraqis are equal before the law "without discrimination because of sex" yet also forbids the passing of any law that contradicts the "established rulings" of Islam (Coleman 2006: 24). This is an issue in Israel as well, where the non-separation between religion and state in the arena of personal law maintains the traditional discrimination against women by the religious authorities.

In sum, the exercise of constitution-making in deeply divided societies is a balancing act. It is a balancing act between the need for legitimate constitutions which do not try to force agreement on fundamental issues which are in dispute, and yet, on the other hand, the desire of the international community to entrench basic rights. It is a balancing act between the desire to defer controversial issues from the high-stakes constitutional arena to the political sphere and the danger that weak democratic institutions will not be able to absorb these issues. It is a balancing act between the need to clearly define legal principles as part of establishing the rule of law and the inability to push that process too far without importing irresolvable issues into the constitutional process. On all of these levels, the constitutional approach which we have presented in this chapter is essentially a range of stalling tactics, attempting to avoid having intractable issues prevent the establishment of legitimate, popularly supported governance. In doing so, it recognizes that in processes of constitution-making in deeply divided post-conflict societies, a certain amount of humility and realism is in order with regard to what constitutions can accomplish. Where it is impossible to "transform" divided societies into cohesive unities, enabling them to set up a system of governance despite ongoing differences on fundamental issues is achievement enough.

Notes

1 As Habermas (1996: 496) explains, constitutional patriotism "does not refer to the substantive generality of a popular will that would owe its unity to a prior homogeneity of descent or form of life. The consensus fought for and achieved in an association of free and equal persons ultimately rests only on the unity of a [democratic] *procedure* to which all consent."
2 Although the war of independence was between the Jewish and the Arab population in Israel, the main division, which ultimately prevented the adoption of a constitution, was between the secular and the religious sectors of the Jewish majority.
3 From Ben Gurion's archives, cited in Aaronson (1998: 17).
4 The organization was called *Brit Kanaim*, which translates into "Alliance of the Fanatics." Another example goes back to the 1920s, when ultra-Orthodox religious activists collaborated with the Arab population against the secular Zionist leadership in Mandatory Palestine. This episode ended with a political assassination of the orthodox leader Yisrael de-Han. See Horowitz and Lissak (1978).
5 The most notable example of an attempt to contest the state's governmental institutions, and particularly the state's monopolistic control over the use of violence, was the *Altalena* affair in June 1948, in which the Israeli Defense Forces fired upon and sank an armed ship brought to Israeli shores by the IZL, a right-wing paramilitary Jewish organization that opposed the partition of the land of Israel. Complete deterioration into a civil war was prevented in those years by the leader of the IZL, Menachem Begin, who decided to accept the government's authority. The government, for its part, was willing to content itself with its provisional victory and did not pursue the exclusion of these organizations from political participation (Horowitz and Lissak 1978).
6 For a detailed account of the debate see Lerner (2006, ch. 3). See also Goldberg (1993).
7 This resolution was named the "Harari Compromise," after its initiator (*Knesset Records* 1950: 1743). See also Rubinstein and Medina (1997).
8 So far, Israel has adopted eleven Basic Laws. Eight of them concern governmental issues: The Knesset, The Land, The President of the State, The State Economy, The Government, The Judiciary, The Army, and The State Comptroller. Most of these

Basic Laws reflect an existing governmental reality, which evolved from the legal structure of the Yishuv under Mandatory Palestine (see Harris 1997: 245). In addition, one Basic Law determines that Jerusalem is the capital of Israel (1980), and two additional Basic Laws concern fundamental rights: Basic Law; Human Dignity and Basic Law; Liberty and Freedom of Occupation (both adopted in 1992).

9 Among the many publications regarding the debate over the value-dualism of the state of Israel, see Mautner *et al.* (1998); Gavizon (1999); and David (2000).

10 Arend Lijphart is considered the father of the model of consociational democracy. Consociationalism, according to Arend Lijphart, allows fragmented societies to sustain a stable democratic government by employing consensual decision-making rather than majority rule and by using institutional mechanisms of power sharing such as proportionality in allocation of public funds, participation in grand coalitions, and minority veto (Lijphart 1968, 1969, 1977). As opposed to the familiar formal power sharing, or consociational, model developed by Lijphart, which stresses the formalization of compromises within a written constitution, the uniqueness of the Israeli consociational agreements in the religious sphere is that they were left vague and unformulated; see Don-Yehiya (1999).

11 Five to 8 percent of the Jewish population in Israel participated in this demonstration. Comparatively, the American proportional equivalent would be fourteen to twenty-three million protesters.

12 Two of the most controversial developments were: In 1996 the Knesset changed the Basic Law: Freedom of Occupation in order to overturn a decision of the Supreme Court regarding the importation of frozen pork meat (the Mitrael case). In 2002 the Knesset discussed (and subsequently rejected) a proposal to establish a Constitutional Council with supreme authority to review constitutional issues in place of the Supreme Court, which, the proposal asserted, did not represent the social composition of Israeli society.

13 Smith (1963), for example, argues that provisions such as Article 25, which permits extensive state intervention in religious matters in the interest of social reform, conflict with the principles of a secular state. From a different perspective, during the Constituent Assembly meetings, the constitution was criticized for failing to represent the traditional institutions and principles central to Indian practice and Hindu thought. The three provisions in the constitution that reflect the "indigenous" Hindu law – Art 47 (prohibition of alcohol), Art 48 (abolishing cow-slaughter) and Art 40 (organization of village *Panchayats*) – are all included in the non-justiciable part of the Constitution (*CAD* 1999, Vol. VII: 823). However, the lack of constitutional uniformity in questions of religion and culture is highly regarded by legal and political scholars, who argue that it should be seen as a successful attempt to craft a multi-dimensional system of values and principles corresponding to the intricate needs of Indian society. For an excellent analysis of the complex, multi-valued ethos of the Indian "contextual secularism" see Bhargava (1998, 2002).

14 The Hindu Marriage Act (1955), which outlawed polygamy and dealt with inter-caste marriage and divorce; The Hindu Adoption and Maintenance Act (1956) which concerned the adoption of girls' and wives' rights; and the Hindu Succession Act (1956) which dealt with inheritance rights of daughters.

15 In the end, after this fifteen-year period, it was decided to maintain English as the language used for all official purposes.

16 Such a provision is common in Islamic states' constitutions. Coleman (2006) analyzes the effects of such provisions on women's rights.

References

Aaronson, S. (1998) "Constitution for Israel: The British Model of David Ben-Gurion," *Politica: An Israeli Journal for Political Science and International Relations* 2: 9–30 (in Hebrew).

Austin, G. (1999) *The Indian Constitution: Cornerstone of a Nation*, New York: Oxford University Press.

Barak, A. (1992) "The Constitutional Revolution: Protected Human Rights," *Mishpat Umimshal: Law and Government in Israel* 1(1): 9–35 (in Hebrew).

Bhargava, R. (1998) *Secularism and its Critics*, New Delhi and New York: Oxford University Press.

—— (2002) "What is Indian Secularism and What is it for?" *India Review* 1: 1–32.

Center for Strategies and International Studies (CSIS) and the Association of the United States Army (AUSA) (2002) *Post Conflict Reconstruction: Task Framework*, Washington, DC: CSIS.

Cohen, A. and Susser, B. (2000) *Israel and the Politics of Jewish Identity: The Secular–Religious Impasse*, Baltimore, MD: Johns Hopkins University Press.

Coicaud, J.M. (2002) *Legitimacy and Politics*, Cambridge: Cambridge University Press.

Coleman, I. (2006) "Women, Islam, and the New Iraq," *Foreign Affairs* 85: 24–38.

Constituent Assembly Debates (*CAD*) (1999) New Delhi, Reprinted by Lok Sabha Secretariat, 12 Volumes.

David, Y. (ed.) (2000) *The State of Israel – Between Judaism and Democracy: A Compendium of Interviews and Articles*, Jerusalem: Israel Democracy Institute (in Hebrew).

Don-Yehiya, E. (1999) *Religion and Political Accommodation in Israel*, Jerusalem: Floersheimer Institute for Policy Analysis.

Feldman, N. (2005) "Agreeing to Disagree in Iraq," *New York Times*, August 30.

Galanter, M. (1989) *Law and Society in Modern India*, New Delhi and New York: Oxford University Press.

Gavizon R. (1999) *Can Israel be Both Jewish and Democratic: Tensions and Prospects*, Jerusalem: Van Leer Institute and Hakibutz Hameuchad (in Hebrew).

Goldberg, G. (1993) "When Trees are Planted There is no Need for a Constitution: On State Building and Constitution Making," *State, Government and International Relations* 38: 29–48.

Habermas, J. (1996) *Between Facts and Norms: Contributions to a Discourse Theory of Law and Democracy*, Cambridge, MA: MIT Press.

Harris, R. (1997) "The Israeli Judiciary," in Z. Zameret and H. Yavlonka (eds) *The First Decade: 1948–1958*, Jerusalem: Yad Ben-Zvi, pp. 244–262 (in Hebrew).

Hirschman, A.O. (1994) "Social Conflicts as Pillars of Democratic Market Society," *Political Theory* 22(2): 203–218.

Horowitz, D. and Lissak, M. (1978) *Origins of the Israeli Polity: Palestine under the Mandate*, Chicago, IL: University of Chicago Press.

—— (1989) *Trouble in Utopia: the Overburdened Polity of Israel*, Albany: State University of New York Press.

Jacobsohn, G. (2003) *The Wheel of Law: India's Secularism in Comparative Constitutional Context*, Princeton, NJ: Princeton University Press.

Khilnani, S. (1999) *The Idea of India*, New York: Farrar Strauss & Giroux.

Kjaer, A.M. (2004) *Governance*, Cambridge: Polity Press.

Knesset Records (1950) Jerusalem: Government of Israel, 4.

Lerner, H. (2004) "Democracy, Constitutionalism and Identity: The Anomaly of the Israeli Case," *Constellation* 11(2): 237–257.

—— (2006) *Constitution-making in Deeply Divided Societies: The Incrementalist Option*, Ph.D. dissertation, New York: Columbia University.

Lijphart, A. (1968) *The Politics of Accommodation: Pluralism and Democracy in the Netherlands*, Berkeley, CA: University of California Press.

—— (1969) "Consociational Democracy," *World Politics* 21(2): 207–225.

—— (1977) "Majority Rule versus Consociationalism in Deeply Divided Societies," *Politikon* 4: 113–127.

Mautner, M., Sagi, A., and Shamir, R. (eds) (1998) *Multiculturalism in a Democratic and Jewish State*, Tel Aviv: Ramot (in Hebrew).

Pathak, Z. and Sunder Rajan, R. (1989) "Shabano," *Signs: Journal of Women in Culture and Sociology* 14: 558–582.

Rubin, B.R. (2004) "Crafting a Constitution for Afghanistan," *Journal of Democracy* 15(3): 5–19.

Rubinstein, A. and Medina, B. (1997) *The Constitutional Law in the State of Israel* (5th edn), Jerusalem: Schocken (in Hebrew).

Shankar, S. (2002) "The War of the Worlds: Political Equality and Religious Freedom in India and Israel," Ph.D. dissertation, New York: Columbia University.

Smith, D.E. (1963) *India as a Secular State*, Princeton, NJ: Princeton University Press.

US Agency for International Development (2005) *Fragile States Strategy*, Washington, DC: USAID.

US Institute of Peace (USIP) (2005) "Iraq's Constitutional Process: Shaping a Vision for the Country's Future," Special Report No. 132, Washington, DC: USIP, February.

4

ELECTION SYSTEMS AND POLITICAL PARTIES IN POST-CONFLICT AND FRAGILE STATES

Eric Bjornlund, Glenn Cowan, and William Gallery

The dramatic global expansion of democracy and the growing acceptance of interventions to support democratic reform over the past twenty years have led to an extraordinary focus on the institution of elections. In countries around the world, elections have served to help resolve long-standing conflicts and to initiate or consolidate transitions to democracy. For states recovering from recent conflict, elections and other political arrangements are typically central to peace agreements. Fair elections have become an increasingly critical requirement for governments to have legitimacy in the eyes of the international community and their own citizens. Electoral legitimacy and outcomes, in turn, greatly affect the prospects for effective governance.

The development of inclusive, effective, and internally democratic political parties goes hand in hand with support for elections in fragile and post-conflict states. Voting is the most direct means by which citizens participate in the political process, but almost all democracies rely on political parties as the institutions that make this possible. Effective governance and genuine democracy in fragile and post-conflict states require political parties that are inclusive, transparent, accountable, and internally democratic. Parties provide critical avenues for public participation and national dialogue in post-conflict and fragile states, and effective political parties are essential to functioning democracy. Within legislatures, parties can provide a peaceful arena for public debate, political competition, and mediation of social conflicts.

Unfortunately, endemic corruption and a lack of public respect plague political parties in emerging democracies, and legislatures in countries emerging from conflict or authoritarian rule are typically weak, subordinate to the executive, and largely lacking in human, financial, and political resources. Decision-makers in some countries may even actively oppose the formation of strong parties because of their association with previous political elites. Still, the importance of political parties in directing policy-making and achieving effective governance makes it vital that transitional elections and other democrat-ization efforts are designed to allow for the development of a functioning party system.

In post-conflict states and other fragile states, the international community often becomes deeply involved in fundamental decisions about elections and political institutions. National political elites, governmental bodies, civic activists, local media, and other local actors all play critically important roles, of course, but international donors and advisers are often key de facto policy-makers. Because such countries typically lack the institutions and personnel required to organize elections, international groups often take a direct role in election administration, as did the United Nations in Cambodia in 1993 or the Organization for Security and Cooperation in Europe in Bosnia in 1996, and Kosovo in 2000 and 2001. In many post-conflict or transitional environments, the international community tends to drive the design of electoral systems, as it did for recent elections in Iraq and Afghanistan. Although national leaders and legislatures are nominally responsible for these choices, local actors tend to lack the necessary experience or knowledge of electoral systems. This also implies that in fragile states the international community plays a far greater role in deter-mining the legitimacy of elections than it does in more stable transitional or established democracies.

The international community has three main objectives for elections in post-conflict societies. The first is the transfer of power to a recognized democratic government with national and international legitimacy. The second is the intro-duction of democratic institutions and processes and the initiation of a longer process of democratization. The third is to promote reconciliation among the parties to the conflict, and to shift their struggle from a violent to a non-violent forum (Kumar 1998).

Each of these goals is linked to the broader goal of improving governance. A peaceful transfer of power is one of the key steps in improving a country's polit-ical system and establishing a new government's legitimacy in the eyes of its citizens. Developing strong, democratic institutions is crucial to creating a government that can deliver basic services and economic growth. Perhaps most importantly, the role of elections as a non-violent form of competition between different factions can significantly improve the security situation in a country and provide the atmosphere necessary for other improvements to occur.

Political parties

Genuine democracy requires competitive political parties. Parties find candid-ates, organize political competition, and seek to win elections. In opposition, they maintain pressure on incumbents to respond to public concerns. Parties also articulate positions on, and stimulate debate about, issues of public concern. They aggregate and represent local concerns and other narrow interests in the political system, which provides a structure for political participation. Political systems without free political parties can hardly be considered democratic. Indeed, in response to one-party states claiming to hold democratic elections, the UN Commission on Human Rights has specifically recognized a right to vote in "a free and fair process ... *open to multiple parties*" (UN Human Rights Commission 2000: par. 1(d)(ii)) (emphasis added).

Political parties, however, are widely held in disrepute in established and developing democracies alike. Citizens often view parties as ineffective, corrupt, and out of touch. Not infrequently, in struggling democracies, political parties are among the most undemocratic institutions. Often they become captive of strong, even autocratic personalities or function as tools of entrenched special interests. Only occasionally do parties represent the views of broad-based constituencies. Sometimes, in societies in transition, the same parties that help foster change themselves subsequently become obstacles to representative government and further reform. They can easily become part of the problem for democratic consolidation rather than part of the potential solution.

In fragile states, the barriers to successful political party and institution building are similar to the challenges posed to elections. As discussed above, a lack of government infrastructure, the threat of violence, and the existence of internally displaced persons (IDPs) all present particular problems for fragile states. For political parties, the inability to travel safely or meet with supporters can cripple their ability to effectively take part in the political process. Even in non-election years, parties or ethnic groups that are subject to discrimination or intimidation will find it difficult to organize, attract supporters, and engage in policy debates. Similarly, if members of legislatures and other political institutions are subject to threats or violence, they will be unable to do their work.

Even in states where political parties and institutions themselves are not targets of violence, unrest and instability can hinder their ability to reach large segments of the population. Techniques such as polling and constituent outreach will not be as effective if constituents are inaccessible. As a result, political parties may not adequately represent many citizens, especially IDPs.

Fragile and post-conflict states may also be especially susceptible to the development of political parties based on ethnic or religious lines. Sectarian alignments can exacerbate tensions or conflict, and so it is even more important to support inclusive parties as well as to encourage collaboration and coalitions between and among parties representing different groups.

Electoral systems greatly affect the number, nature, and constellation of political parties. Likewise, electoral systems largely determine the number and relative sizes of political parties in the legislature. The electoral system can affect the degree of internal cohesion and party discipline, the incentives for alliances between parties, and the extent to which parties are likely to appeal beyond narrow interests or ethnic identities (Reynolds *et al.* 2005a). The Single Non-transferable Vote electoral system for the 2005 legislative elections in Afghanistan, as discussed below, discouraged the emergence of strong political parties. For somewhat different reasons, the electoral system for the district-based portion of the 2006 Palestinian elections put candidates in the position of competing with other party members. This had a clear impact on the party system by rewarding the more cohesive, better organized Hamas and punishing a divided Fatah, which failed to take account of the implications of the system by limiting the number of candidates. In both cases, the party system was directly affected by the electoral system in which it operated.

Elections

Genuine democracy, of course, requires substantially more than democratic elections. Even countries that hold reasonably competitive elections may lack constitutional limits on governmental power, deprive citizens of basic rights, or lack tolerance of religious or ethnic minorities. Indeed, elections can sharpen ethnic differences or exacerbate communal tensions. In fragile or post-conflict states, the international community sometimes expects too much of elections or pushes for them to take place too soon.

Nevertheless, elections are the keystone of democracy. International declarations and norms unambiguously establish elections as the basis of legitimate government. The Universal Declaration of Human Rights, the International Covenant on Civil and Political Rights, and numerous other international instruments call for periodic elections with universal suffrage and a secret ballot. As Samuel Huntington (1991: 9) puts it, "Elections, open, free and fair, are the essence of democracy, the inescapable *sine qua non*."

Thus it is reasonable that elections remain central to strategies for promoting democratic development, including in post-conflict and fragile states. First, competitive elections can catalyze profound political change leading to greater democracy. Elections in societies in transition or crisis can be seminal events that, if successful, not only confer legitimacy on governments but can also profoundly influence institutions, power arrangements, and citizens' expectations. Second, elections provide significant new opportunities for citizen involvement in public affairs. They are an opportunity to engage civic organizations and citizens in democratic politics through voter education, election monitoring, policy research, and advocacy. They can provide an avenue for the participation of women, minorities, and disadvantaged groups, who traditionally have had less access to politics and governance. Finally, competitive elections offer a means of establishing accountability, channeling political competition, and determining leadership succession. All societies should have political institutions and processes that are capable of addressing and resolving social divisions and competition for political power through fair, peaceful means (Bjornlund 2004).

Yet, despite their importance, election results in post-conflict and transitional societies often seem to surprise the international community, even when international advisers and donors are heavily engaged in designing and supporting the electoral and political systems. The international community fails regularly to gauge accurately the effects of one or more of the factors that determine electoral outcomes in such societies, factors over which it often has significant control. The failure to anticipate unattractive political developments can create difficult and potentially untenable situations in critical countries. Elections in Afghanistan, Haiti, Iraq, and Palestine (the West Bank and Gaza) in 2005 and 2006, for example, produced unanticipated, undesired, and potentially dangerous outcomes that had real implications for the development of both political parties and governance institutions.

This continued inability to forecast election consequences, both for the immediate post-election period and for future governance, persists despite the availability of data that should permit democracy development professionals to model the range of likely political outcomes from a given set of electoral circumstances. Better forecasting of potential political results for elections in transformational or fragile states would allow political parties, policy-makers, citizens, and the international community to better prepare for what the future may bring.

The outcome of any election depends on three basic variables: (1) the electoral system, (2) the political environment, and (3) voter choice. The electoral system encompasses the legal and administrative structures for determining candidates and office holders. The electoral system directly affects – and sometimes determines – political outcomes and in turn the development of legitimate political governance. The political environment is the context in which the elections take place, including the actions of candidates and parties, and the range of protections, regulations and traditions, both legal and informal, that govern politics. Improved analysis of the political environment can provide a better sense of potential problems; it can also suggest ways to pre-empt or respond to such problems, such as through more effective voter education. Voter choice refers to the history and future of how and why the voters participate and for whom they cast their ballots. Better understanding and use of opinion polling, exit polls, and vote count verification techniques such as parallel vote tabulations (PVTs) allow earlier and more sophisticated understanding of voter preferences.

In recent elections in Afghanistan, Haiti, Iraq, and Palestine, the information available to the international community about the electoral systems, political environment, and likely voter choices, if properly analyzed, would have allowed prediction of and preparation for the eventual outcomes and the type and quality of the governments to follow. Better understanding of these three basic variables may also have enabled effective responses to improve the process or avoid especially unfortunate consequences.

Electoral systems

The electoral system in a given country defines three basic parameters: district magnitude, ballot structure, and the electoral formula for determining winning candidates (Farrell 2001; Blais and Massicotte 2002). District magnitude refers to the number of office holders who will represent a given geographical area.

Ballot structure governs how voters get to make their choices. The electoral formula is the arithmetic that determines the winners. Together, these variables substantially affect proportionality, voter participation, minority party representation, the likelihood of coalition government, the number of women and ethnic minority office holders, the prospect for genuinely representative constituencies, and the range of participating and winning candidates and parties (Farrell 2001; Norris 2004). The electoral system is often the principal independent variable in determining the constellation of a country's political parties, and the nature, effectiveness and stability of its government.

In post-conflict and transitional political environments, international experts often advise on the design of electoral systems (see Kumar (1998) for examples). But decisions about the parameters of electoral systems are too frequently a result of tactical considerations, such as how much the election will cost, how soon the election can be held, or whether the process will be simple enough. Of the three variables that affect political outcomes, electoral systems are the most amenable to outside influence. It is easier to affect electoral outcomes – meaning the broad legitimacy of the process – through changes in the electoral system than by trying to improve the political environment or influence voter choices. It may be difficult, of course, to convince a governing authority to adopt a new system. A better system may be more expensive or cause delay, or require greater diligence. But on balance, it is almost always better to start with an electoral system designed to produce a positive outcome than it is to attempt to compensate for a poorly conceived electoral system by influencing voter choices or necessary changes in the political environment.

Over the past twenty years, election and campaign professionals working in emerging democracies have developed a significant body of knowledge about the political consequences of electoral system choice (see e.g. Farrell 2001; Colomer 2004; Norris 2004; Reynolds et al. 2005a). The basic goals of electoral systems are to ensure representative legislative bodies, provide incentives for conciliation, facilitate political stability, encourage government efficiency and accountability, enable an active opposition, and permit access to the political system (Reynolds et al. 2005a). Local or international actors can pursue these objectives by designing an electoral system with full knowledge of potential outcomes. Within such a strategic framework we can predict how the electoral laws affect who can vote and hold elective and appointed positions; when, where, and for what offices elections will be held; and how these elections will be managed and monitored.

Even if the international community is not able to influence electoral design, at least it can better understand the consequences of particular electoral system choices. The body of academic literature on electoral systems is extensive and readily available to policy-makers confronted by the various permutations and combinations presented. Every possible electoral scheme has been studied, analyzed, and debated. There is no excuse for decision-makers to ever suggest they could not know that a chosen system might produce a given result.

Recent elections in Palestine, Afghanistan, and Iraq illustrate the often unintended consequences for governance of choices about an electoral system. In these cases, a lack of foresight threatened the development of a strong political party system and reduced the prospects for governance improvements, at least in the near future. The international community might have avoided these unfortunate outcomes had it urged different choices or at least could have been better prepared for the eventual results.

The 2006 Palestinian legislative elections

For the Palestinian legislative elections in January 2006, the international community failed to appreciate how the electoral system could lead to particular political outcomes. The militant group Hamas, the Islamic Resistance Movement – labeled a terrorist organization by many Western governments, and responsible for numerous violent acts against Israel and its citizens – won a large majority of seats in its first campaign for the Palestinian Legislative Council. The governing Fatah party, long dominant in Palestinian politics but widely perceived as corrupt and ineffective, lost control of the Palestinian authority for the first time.

Hamas' victory reportedly stunned Palestinians and the rest of the world. U.S. Secretary of State Condoleeza Rice said, for example, "I don't know anyone who wasn't caught off guard by Hamas's strong showing" (Weisman 2006). Secretary Rice and other world leaders and analysts commented that Hamas itself seemed to have been surprised by the strength of its showing. Some analysts argued that Hamas would have actually preferred not to have been in control of the new government (International Crisis Group 2006).

Political and electoral realities apparent even before the elections, however, should have permitted the international community to be more aware of and prepared for the possibility of a Hamas victory. The media and others failed to anticipate Hamas' victory at least in part because of a failure to understand the electoral system.

The Palestinian elections employed a mixed or parallel system that permitted voters to choose members of the legislature from two separate ballot papers: one a national party list, the other a local district list. Half of the 132 seats in the legislature were elected through the nationwide proportional representation system, and the other half were allocated to the multi-member districts. Those elected from the closed national party list were chosen by a straightforward proportional representation system designed to assign winning party members in proportion to their party's national vote percentage. The district winners were chosen using multi-member block voting. Voters were permitted to make as many choices as there were members to be elected from their district, the winners being those candidates with the highest number of votes.[1]

In the year or so leading up to the legislative elections, held after a six-month delay on January 25, 2006, opinion polls revealed the growing popularity of

Hamas. More tellingly, Hamas, which had only recently started participating in electoral politics, made large gains in local elections throughout the year, including some significant victories in cities traditionally considered Fatah strongholds. The international community, however, failed to recognize not only the extent of Hamas' growing popularity with the voters but also how the electoral system might translate this support into seats.

In the end, while Hamas won a relatively narrow plurality in the overall vote, it gained a clear majority of the legislative seats.[2] Hamas received 44.5 percent of the vote to 41.4 percent for Fatah, but took seventy-four of the 132 seats while Fatah won only forty-five. Tellingly, Fatah won twenty-eight of its seats in the national list portion of the election, only one fewer than Hamas' take from the national list. The bulk of Hamas' majority came from the local districts, where it won an overwhelming forty-five our of sixty-six seats.

Although the polls were not far off with regard to the nationwide party list voting, it should have been obvious that surveys were measuring the wrong variable. Under the Palestinian electoral system the allocation of seats at the district level would not necessarily follow the vote breakdown at the national level. Voters cast separate ballots for the district and national party list elections, and could have voted for district candidates from different parties from those they supported at the national level or for independent candidates. More significantly, the structure of a block voting system allowed a small plurality to win a large proportion of seats in a district. In Jerusalem, for example, Hamas candidates gained 34 percent of the total votes compared to 26 percent for Fatah, but won four seats compared to Fatah's two. The other 40 percent of votes went to independents, none of whom won a seat. In Tulkarem, Fatah candidates actually gained more votes than did Hamas candidates, but Fatah failed to win a seat because its votes were split among more candidates.

Hamas took full advantage of the opportunities provided by the electoral law to gain similar results in most of the local districts. Hamas never ran more candidates in a district than the number of available seats, while Fatah's vote was often split among an excess of candidates and further diluted by competition from independents. The discipline of Hamas' voters and activists allowed the party to capitalize on the opportunities provided by the block voting system. A post-election analysis indicated that Hamas and its allies ran, on average, fewer than one candidate for each available seat, compared to more than three candidates by Fatah and its affiliates (Blanc 2006). This suggests a strong awareness on the part of Hamas of the electoral system and its implications.

Ironically, this electoral system came about partly through negotiations among the different factions of Fatah. Fatah's electoral strategy suggests, however, that it was oblivious to the implications of the system it chose. Previous Palestinian elections had also used a block voting system, but Fatah's popularity at that time had overwhelmed any effect of the electoral system (Reynolds *et al.* 2005a). The surprise expressed by the governments of Israel, the United States, and other nations displayed a similar ignorance. In the end, it seems that

Hamas was the only actor to recognize the significance of the Palestinian electoral system, and the result was a political coup that left the international community scrambling to react to the new situation.

The Palestinian election is a clear example of how electoral systems can influence the development of political party systems. Heading into these elections Fatah was disorganized and split by internal conflict. Its supporters were divided among a large number of candidates, including those endorsed by the party and affiliated independents. Block voting rewards parties that are well organized and efficient, as Hamas was. The implication for future Palestinian elections is that only parties with tight control over their candidate lists and voters will succeed.

The 2005 legislative elections in Afghanistan

In contrast to its heavy involvement in the Palestinian territories at the time of the 2006 elections, the international community had relatively little involvement in choosing the electoral system or shaping the political environment in Afghanistan. Leading up to the 2005 legislative elections, it played a far more direct role. Once again, however, international donors and advisers did not understand or chose to ignore the implications of the electoral system for the outcome of the elections, and for the future political development and successful governance of the country.

The government of Afghanistan, on advice from the international community, chose a Single Non-transferable Vote (SNTV) system for elections to the new National Assembly in 2005. This simple system used multi-member districts ranging in size from two to thirty-three representatives. Each voter selected one candidate, and the candidates with the most votes were elected.[3]

Afghanistan's leaders found the SNTV attractive for several reasons. First, its simplicity made it easy to administer the balloting and vote-counting processes and to explain the process to voters who were generally poorly educated and lacked experience with voting. SNTV would also discourage the formation of strong political parties or coalitions, an important benefit to Afghanis suspicious of such groups. Because each candidate in a district was running against all other candidates, including those in his own party, parties had to be extremely well organized to avoid splitting their supporters' votes among too many candidates and to ensure that each of their candidates received enough votes to be elected. The designers of the electoral system also liked that this requirement for a high level of organization, when combined with the exclusion of political party identification on the ballot, would make it extremely difficult for any young political party in Afghanistan to gain a large number of seats (International Crisis Group 2005).

Unfortunately, other features of the SNTV system made it a poor choice. Because representatives were elected from multi-member districts, if a widely popular candidate gained a considerable proportion of the votes in a district, there would be relatively few votes remaining to be split among less popular candidates. This could allow the remaining seats to be won with a very small percentage of the vote (Rubin 2005). Moreover, because the system permitted so many candidates, many voters ended up "wasting" their votes by voting for losing candidates (Reynolds *et al.* 2005a).

Furthermore, while Afghanistan chose SNTV in part to weaken the formation of political parties, the system could actually have the opposite effect. Small parties that were able to organize their supporters could do very well at the expense of more popular, less organized parties or independent candidates. In addition, because a small number of votes can be extremely valuable, the system might encourage voter intimidation and vote buying, which would benefit the armed factions Afghanistan's new government was seeking to curtail (Rubin 2005). Finally, because a candidate could be elected with a small percentage of the vote in his district, there was little incentive to form broad coalitions or to move beyond ethnic or local interests (Farrell 2001; Reynolds *et al.* 2005a, 2005b).

The results of the elections reflected some of these shortfalls. Because party affiliations were not listed on the ballot or in official results and most candidates ran as independents, it is difficult to formally assess the effect on the development of parties or coalitions. But the absence of a role for parties in the election process necessarily limits the influence of parties in the governance of Afghanistan. Moreover, large numbers of candidates were indeed elected with very little support. In Kabul, for example, where thirty-three seats were available, more than two-thirds of the candidates elected received less than 1 percent of the vote. Only three out of the 249 candidates elected nationwide won more than 20 percent of the vote in their province, and in many provinces the candidate with the most votes won less than 5 percent of the vote.[4] News reports stated that many voters did not know who the candidates were and were confused about who to vote for, leading some to simply choose candidates whom they recognized.

As with the block voting system used in the Palestinian elections, the implications of SNTV have been widely studied and its drawbacks were well known. The International Crisis Group (2005), for example, warned, "by encouraging appeals to narrow ethnic interests rather than broad-based constituencies, the electoral system could result in the absence of workable caucuses within the new National Assembly, further raising fears about the seeds of future instability." If the international community had considered these disadvantages before the elections in Afghanistan, it could and should have pushed for a more representative, less divisive system.

As a direct result of the electoral system, few members of the National Assembly were elected with a broad base of support or with any incentive to form coherent coalitions within the Assembly to address issues of national importance. Those candidates who were elected won largely on the basis of name recognition and local or ethnic ties. This could have important implications for future governance in the country. The central government has yet to prove itself capable of delivering services or providing security to all of its citizens. The SNTV system in Afghanistan did not lead to violent conflict or widespread questions about the legitimacy of the election process. But it also did not generate a foundation for strong government and cohesive political parties that are crucial to the future stability of the country.

The 2005 parliamentary elections in Iraq

For the first post-Saddam elections in Iraq, the choice of a closed-list proportional representation system using one nationwide constituency ultimately left the Sunni population largely unrepresented in fundamental national political decision-making and may have exacerbated subsequent sectarian conflict. Unfortunately, the Sunni population, which had formed the core of support for the previous regime and was at odds with other ethnic and religious groups in Iraq, largely boycotted the elections. Given the system's use of a single national constituency, the Sunni population's failure to participate left it essentially outside the process.

In January 2005, Iraq held elections to choose a 275-member constituent assembly, charged with responsibility to write a new constitution. In selecting a nationwide proportional representation (PR) system, the Iraqi Governing Council relied heavily on advice from the UN's Electoral Assistance Division. The UN was invited to assist in developing the election system, and after consultations with a variety of stakeholders it presented the IGC with three options: (1) a system of small, multi-member majority districts, (2) a PR system using the Iraqi governorates as districts, and (3) a nationwide PR system (UN Electoral Assistance Division 2005).

The UN cited drawbacks for each of the first two systems, including the difficulty of drawing electoral districts, the unreliability of population figures on which to base representation, and the problem of dealing with displaced populations and out-of-country voters. In favor of the third option, the UN cited a variety of administrative/operational and political benefits.

The simplicity of a nationwide PR system offered significant administrative and operational advantages. A nationwide PR system would bypass the problems of drawing electoral districts and obtaining accurate census data. It would also avoid the problem of assigning displaced persons and out-of-country voters to electoral districts because they would all be voting as part of a single, nationwide district. It also simplified the logistics of voting and vote counting. The UN listed several other, more political benefits of the system. It argued that a nationwide PR system would be better for women and minorities, would encourage the formation of alliances between parties and groups, and would encourage more moderate positions.

In response to this advice, the Iraqi Governing Council adopted the national PR list system, by a vote of twenty-one to four. But leading up to the elections, there was a great deal of criticism due to the threat of a Sunni boycott. If Sunni turnout were significantly lower than for other groups, then Sunnis would be under-represented in the resulting Parliament and Shiites and Kurds would be over-represented, giving them disproportionate influence over the drafting of the new Iraqi constitution. A nationwide PR system would not produce minority representation if the minorities failed to vote. The *Christian Science Monitor* warned of the possible consequences:

> The five most violent Iraqi provinces are home to most of Iraq's Sunni Arabs, who make up about 20 percent of the country. While polling shows that nearly 80 percent of the Shiites, who make up about 60 percent of the population, and around 70 percent of the Kurds, who make up about 15 percent of the country, say they are "very likely" to vote; only about 20 percent of Sunni Arabs say the same. In practice, this will probably lead to a legislature in which both Shiite Arabs and Kurds take seats in proportion beyond their national numbers. In the short term, this will enhance Sunni fears about their place in the emerging society. Since the insurgency is led mostly by Sunni Arabs, this could lead to more violence.[5]

If all groups had turned out to vote in similar proportions, the nationwide PR system would have worked as intended, but it was obvious well before the election that this was not going to happen. Electoral authorities and the international community should have realized that in the face of a Sunni boycott, a different system was necessary to avoid serious problems. Using Iraq's governorates as districts, for example, would have still given Sunnis significant representation even with the group's low turnout because the Sunni population would have been concentrated in a few districts. No system could overcome the simple fact that those voters who show up get to vote, but a better system could have at least mitigated the consequences of the Sunni boycott and avoided some of the problems that developed subsequently.

In the event, the turnout of Sunni voters was extremely low, allowing Shiite and Kurd parties to win well over two-thirds of the seats in the Assembly. Even though Sunnis made up some 20 percent of the country's population, no party representing primarily Sunnis won more than five seats. This meant that Sunnis had almost no representation in the body responsible for drafting the new constitution. The effects of this absence on governance in Iraq were vivid. Sunnis questioned the legitimacy of the constitutional assembly from the start. The elections, rather than promoting reconciliation between different ethnic and religious groups, helped spur sectarian violence. The continued weak security situation severely impaired basic government functions. Pressure from the U.S.A. and other parts of the international community eventually forced the winning parties to include Sunni representatives in the process of drafting the constitution, but the election results laid the groundwork for a constitutional dispensation that substantially disadvantaged the Sunni minority and increased the danger of the often-raised specter of civil war.

Political environment

Beyond the electoral system, election outcomes depend on the political environment in which they take place. The local political environment includes the credibility and neutrality of electoral authorities; the fairness of the media; the extent of freedoms of speech, movement and association; the nature of the campaign; the opportunities for the opposition to compete; the readiness and needs of voters; and the relative openness of the process to women, ethnic minorities, IDPs, and other disadvantaged groups. The campaigns, strategies, and effectiveness of political leaders and parties form an important part of the political context and, of course, directly affect voter choices and thus election outcomes. The nature and effectiveness of voter education can also significantly influence voter choices and expectations.

Pre-election assessments

The international community generally has access to much information about the political environment. Even aside from intelligence and similar analyses, freely available pre-election assessments – which evaluate the prospects for meaningful, democratic elections – have become a common component of democracy development programs. International election-monitoring groups conduct such pre-election assessments for virtually every significant transitional election and make their evaluations available to policy-makers. Organizations that conduct such assessments range from those sponsored by multilateral organizations, such as the Organization for Security and Cooperation in Europe, the Organization of American States, and the European Union to nongovernmental democracy-assistance organizations such as the National Democratic Institute for International Affairs and the Carter Center to local election monitoring coalitions (Bjornlund 2004). Pre-election assessments identify potential obstacles to democratic elections and opportunities for effective assistance. They are critical to effective forecasting because factors in place long before election day often determine the quality and acceptability of the process (Bjornlund 2004).

Rarely, however, do pre-election assessments, whether from international or domestic sources, use what they have observed to inform an analysis of potential political outcomes. More typically, they have related anecdotes without any attempt to rigorously define or quantify the extent or effect of illegitimate political finance or politically motivated violence or intimidation. The best of these assessments may comment on how problems in the political environment might adversely affect minority turnout or inflate a certain party's vote, for example, but the quantitative tools do not yet exist to permit the analysis necessary to judge the specific effect of the political environment on the election. To be truly helpful to decision-makers, who need to understand the effect of the political environment as well as the electoral system and voter behavior, those assessing the electoral environment need to harden their focus and better quantify those aspects of the social and political landscape that actually affect voters' actions. Determining, for example, that a certain environmental element will hold down turnout is interesting; knowing it will likely decrease the proportion of the vote for a given candidate or party by a certain percentage provides a basis for more specific action.

At least to some degree, the limitations of pre-election assessments reflect a lack of demand. The international community has been willing to accept less rigorous pre-election analysis because it does not appear to recognize how much value could be gleaned from such efforts. Election monitoring organizations have yet to develop quantitative or other robust methods of assessing the impact of pre-election flaws (Bjornlund 2004). Perhaps a few more electoral shocks will spark some interest in a more analytical, detailed, and rigorous appraisal of the effect of the electoral environment on likely outcomes.

Voter education

Voter education programs are both a key part of the political environment and a possible tool to improve that environment. In typical transitional or post-conflict environments, many citizens have never voted in meaningful elections, lack basic information about the process, or face strong disincentives to participate. Accordingly, the international community should try to understand how voter education can affect voter behavior. Policy-makers should be in a position to better judge whether the electorate understands the process and how voters are likely to react in any given set of circumstances. Moreover, international actors often have opportunities to undertake voter education programs to counteract or ameliorate potential problems.

Electoral authorities, nongovernmental organizations (NGOs), political parties, and international groups can all conduct voter information or education campaigns. But organizations conducting voter education programs can have different priorities. Electoral authorities may emphasize the balloting process to reduce voter confusion and invalid ballots and ease the administration of the process on election day. NGOs may favor broader messages about political rights and responsibilities. Parties may focus on efforts to "get out the vote" and inform voters how to mark the ballot to support their candidates. Candidate forums can educate voters while reinforcing accountability. All of these messages may well complement each other, but some may be more important or appropriate for international assistance than others.

The nature and message of voter education efforts should be based on careful consideration of the problems to be addressed. Ideally, rigorous survey research about voter knowledge and concerns should provide the basis for voter education priorities. Unfortunately, facile approaches to voter education are common. At best, the failure to prioritize and appropriately tailor voter education messages wastes resources and misses the opportunity to improve the quality of elections. At a minimum, if analysts better evaluate the effectiveness of voter education programs, they are more likely to correctly assess the impact of such programs on voter behavior.

The 2006 presidential elections in Haiti

For the presidential election in Haiti in February 2006, the international community failed to properly assess the political environment and did not conduct effective voter education programs to make clear, among other things, how long the vote count would take and how it worked. Accordingly, it did not anticipate the dangerous public reaction to delays in the announcement of results and the apparent erosion in support of the leading candidate as later returns came in.

In February 2006, after numerous delays in the election date, Haitians voted to determine the successor to President Jean-Bertrand Aristide, who had been forced from office in 2004. The presidential electoral system was a common two-round process requiring a run-off between the top two vote getters if no candidate received more than 50 percent in the first round. Such a straightforward two-round system, though expensive, was reasonable for Haiti, which has a low rate of literacy and poor education levels.

Haiti's political and social climate historically was fragile and violent, and even the presence of UN peacekeeping forces was no guarantee of tranquility either in the lead-up to election day or the period immediately following. This known propensity for street agitation, if not actual riots, called for an extensive and competent voter education effort to combat the usual spread of rumors and discontent so common in Haiti. In this, the Haitian government, electoral authorities, civil society, media, and the international community failed.

Months before the repeatedly delayed election it was clear that former President RenéPréval, a perceived Aristide ally, was the presidential front runner. A Gallup poll in December placed his support at 37 percent, well ahead of his closest opponent, and some analysts predicted that he would gain the necessary majority to win outright in the first round (Thompson 2006a). By election day the only unknowns were whether Préval would win in the first round and, if not, who his second round opponent would be.

The calculation of whether a candidate received more than 50 percent of the votes required a defined denominator. Consistent with past practice, the election law in Haiti appeared to require that blank ballots – those indicating no choice – be included in the denominator before calculating each candidate's percentage of valid votes. (Blank ballots were different from "spoiled ballots," which were those with multiple choices or which were otherwise marked incorrectly.) Nevertheless, before the election, the election commission left some ambiguity about whether it planned to include blank ballots in the calculation. Given that uncertainty, the inclusion of blank ballots in the calculation could have been expected to cause controversy if a candidate failed to reach the first-round victory threshold because of it. Yet, electoral officials and their international advisers ignored the potential ambiguity of this calculation.

It also should have been clear that the vote count was going to take considerably longer than past practice. In addition to the presidential race, Haitians were electing members of the Senate and House of Deputies. Election officials and international advisers estimated incorrectly that it would take no more than four hours to count and tabulate the votes at each of the 9000 polling stations, each of which had 400 voters. In the actual event, the initial count of each polling station took eight to twelve hours, significantly delaying the official vote tabulation process. Prior to the election, election authorities and international advisors discussed at length the potential for and consequences of a long count. Authorities should have communicated this possibility to voters, who might then have had a more realistic sense of when to expect results.

Not only did election organizers and advisers know that logistical problems would almost certainly delay the vote count, but the logistics of the vote tabulation system, electoral history, and recent polling suggested caution about forecasts based on the early results. Early returns would come from the close-in and more accessible urban centers, which surveys and history showed to be strongholds of Préval support. The remote but significant rural vote centers would report later and were expected to be less favorably disposed to Préval. These vital facts were also missing from what limited voter education efforts there were.

Early in the vote count Préval appeared to have had a large lead due in part to the election commission's unfortunate mistake of failing to include blank but valid ballots in the denominator in the first official release of election returns. Later returns included some 4 percent blank ballots which, when combined with rural returns less favorable to the front-runner, resulted in Préval's share dropping from an initially reported 62 percent to a final 48 percent. Thus, a run-off was apparently required.

Préval's organization, knowing that the public lacked any real understanding of the process, sent its supporters to the streets in protest of alleged manipulation of the vote count. Random roadblocks paralyzed the streets of Port au Prince, and much of the country was brought to a standstill. These disruptions accentuated the discontent among both Préval supporters and others who did not trust the system (Thompson 2006b). Bowing to the threat of continued mob violence and widespread disinformation, the international community and Haitian authorities contrived effectively to remove the blank ballots from the calculation, providing Préval with the first-round victory he very likely did not win at the ballot-box. As a statement from an IFES election monitoring team put it,

> Civil unrest in the days that followed the elections resulted in a political decision being taken to change the way the blank ballots were counted (contrary to Art. 185 of the electoral decree). The result of that fundamental disregard of electoral law was the declaration of Rene Préval as winner by a narrow margin.
>
> (IFES 2006)

The danger of public misunderstanding of the process could have been avoided if those responsible had taken care to inform voters about the system. Moreover, even though he had beaten his nearest opponent by at least two to one, Préval might still have lost in a second round. In a polarized polity it is not uncommon that a first-round plurality winner will lose in a run-off against a candidate of the combined opposition. In Haiti's case we will never know.

The effects this outcome will have for Haiti's future are also unknown. A significant portion of the Haitian populace strongly supported Préval, and his victory was practically engineered by the international community. His legitimacy in the eyes of the opposition, which represents at least a strong minority, is questionable. Without their support it may be difficult for the Haitian government to rebuild its governance capabilities and to begin providing the services its citizens so desperately need.

Voter choice

Shaped by a country's electoral system and political environment, the choices of voters, of course, ultimately determine political outcomes in elections. Voter behavior in Iraq, namely the boycott by much of the Sunni population, ensured the failure of the national list proportional representation system to include all sectarian groups in the political process. The boycott interacted with the electoral system to produce an undesirable outcome.

Increasingly, even in post-conflict and transitional environments, past election results and opinion research are available that enable the international community to predict voter choices (See LeDuc *et al.* 2002). In addition, immediately after voting takes place, exit polls and vote count verification techniques such as parallel vote tabulations and quick counts not only deter fraud but also enable early knowledge of election results.

Predicting political winners in developed democracies is a highly developed art. Pollsters, pundits, bookies, journalists, and your next door neighbor have all considered views informed by opinion research, electoral history, current events, prejudice, and wishful thinking. Models based on economics, demographics, anthropology, political analysis, and the phases of the moon serve as analytical tools. Despite apparent chaotic – even incoherent – methodology, in mature democracies analysts get it right so frequently that the exceptions are news. The international community does not get surprised very often. Unfortunately and avoidably, in developing democracies analysts, media, diplomats, and others get it wrong almost as a matter of course.

Twenty years ago, as a new wave of democratic transitions began in Africa, Asia, Latin America, and the former Soviet Union, emerging democracies generally had little electoral history or solid opinion research available. None had anything approaching a democratic electoral history, and a legacy of political oppression often tainted opinions expressed in survey research so much as to make such research useless at best if not highly misleading as a guide to development policy.

The environment for systematic polling has improved considerably in developing democracies now embarking on their second or third round of post-transition elections (Singer and Scotto 2004). Not only has survey research in developing countries tended to become much more reliable, but the patterns of electoral performance are beginning to coalesce in demographic and geographic distributions. Previous election results, augmented by opinion research, often now permit reasonable predictions of voter behavior.

The international community, however, must take care to better understand the uses and limitations of survey research. To avoid erroneous conclusions, policy-makers should be aware of such issues as sampling consistency, questionnaire design and bias, methodological impediments in rural areas, the effects of conflict on sample distribution, and a whole host of other research issues. These issues can be identified and factored into margin-of-error calculations that should permit the judicious use of research even in post-conflict states.

Survey research remains at least partially an art disguised as science, particularly in developing democracies. In modern political environments, analysts can and do take survey research on faith and at best might review a short explanation of the researcher's methodology. In less mature environments, nuances in survey methods can have a considerable impact on reported results. Serious political analysts should know this, yet aside from the most cursory exploration of methodology there is almost never any critical appraisal of how these data are produced. Even simple questions are only occasionally addressed: How was the sample designed? Who were the interviewers? How were the questions ordered? Who paid for the survey? This is true even when, as is often the case in countries in which the international community plays a considerable role, the local pollsters are available and willing to share details about methodology and to discuss their analysis of the results. For whatever reason, survey research for crucial transitional elections often becomes a form of conventional wisdom, even gossip, rather than a source of the potentially significant data it might be.

In the months leading up to the January 2006 Palestinian elections, for example, opinion polls and local election results revealed the growing popularity of Hamas. By January 2006, Hamas' support had grown from a small minority to the largest single block of voters in the electorate. Yet, in addition to its failure to understand how the electoral system might translate support into seats, as discussed above, the international community still did not recognize the extent of Hamas' popularity with the voters.

Although the media reported that opinion polls showed support for Hamas increasing from around 20 percent to about 40 percent over the course of 2005, international observers nonetheless failed to appreciate the likelihood that such support would be enough to translate into a legislative majority. Two days before the elections, the *New York Times* reported that Fatah still led Hamas in Palestinian polls, though the margin seemed to be shrinking (Erlanger 2006).

In addition to past results and opinion research, any reasonable appraisal of voter choice should include an assessment of the likely legitimacy of both informal and official vote counts. Starting in the early hours after the polls have closed there will be rumors, press releases, official pronouncements, idle chatter from the media, and all other manner of supposed information about who is winning. This almost invariably contradictory information prompts a variety of reactions from different social groups, international actors, media, political parties, electoral authorities, and government officials. As one ostensibly neutral actor, the international community should be able to discern which of these "counts" is most credible and reliable. A good understanding of what should be happening and whether the authorities are conducting an accurate count is essential in formulating an effective post-election policy.

Conclusion

Although experience has shown that elections and political actors can cause or exacerbate conflict, democratic elections and effective, representative political parties are critical to improved governance in fragile or post-conflict states. Democratic elections are essential for establishing national and international legitimacy, and enabling effective governance. Electoral systems have a huge influence on the prospects for democratic elections and on political outcomes. Political parties are central to democratic governance because they are the main vehicles for political representation, for the organization of government, and for maintaining democratic accountability. They link the state and civil society, influence the executive, and formulate public policy.

International actors committed to supporting democratic outcomes and improved governance in fragile and post-conflict states often fail to anticipate the effect of electoral systems on electoral outcomes and political party development. In any given country, the electoral system, the political environment or voter behavior together drive electoral results and, thus, the prospects for system legitimacy and stable governance. Consideration of these three variables together, however, should allow the international community to better gauge and prepare for election outcomes. A sophisticated analysis of the electoral environment augmented by a detailed understanding of the electoral system narrows the range of potential outcomes, which may then be compared against what we can know about voter behavior. By analyzing these factors, the international community has the ability to model the range of likely political outcomes from a given set of electoral circumstances.

Better understanding of how electoral systems and political context drive outcomes in the context of particular voter choices will enable the international community to prepare for, if not mitigate, unattractive political outcomes. Moreover, it will enable the international donors and advisers to offer better assistance. International actors can contribute to stable, effective governance through advice on electoral system design, pre-election assessments, voter education campaigns, and analysis of voter choice. Well-designed electoral systems can lead to more stable electoral outcomes and more sustainable, effective political parties. They play critical roles in establishing the legitimacy of elections and the governments that they produce. They help determine the number, distribution, and effectiveness of political parties. The legitimacy of government and the structure of the political party system in turn directly impact upon future governance in terms of ensuring security, providing basic services, and creating economic growth. These outcomes promise to help strengthen security and to improve political governance.

Because different political outcomes may have vastly different consequences for the prospects for stable democratic development, political party development and electoral system design are strategic governance reconstruction tasks that should not be left simply to technicians to work out with their local counterparts. These are fundamentally important, strategic political decisions, not tactical or technical ones. As shown in the cases of Afghanistan, Haiti, Iraq, and Palestine, the international community has often failed to address these issues sufficiently in post-conflict and transitional elections. If international actors wish to avoid the problems they faced in these countries in the future, they must make a serious commitment to understanding the effects of the factors that determine electoral outcomes and direct the path of democratization and governance reform in post-conflict and fragile states.

Notes

1 See the website for the Central Elections Commission-Palestine for more details on the Palestinian election system, www.elections.ps/english.aspx.
2 Election results from the Central Elections Commission-Palestine website, www.elections.ps/english.aspx.
3 For a more detailed description, see the Joint Electoral Management Body (JEMB) website, www.jemb.org.
4 Election results from the JEMB website, www.jemb.org.
5 "How Iraq's Elections Will Work," *Christian Science Monitor*, January 28, 2005.

References

Bjornlund, E. (2004) *Beyond Free and Fair: Monitoring Elections and Building Democracy*, Washington, DC and Baltimore, MD: Woodrow Wilson Center Press, and Johns Hopkins University Press.
Blais, A. and L. Massicotte (2002) "Electoral Systems," in L. LeDuc, R.G. Niemi, and P. Norris (eds) *Comparing Democracies 2: New Challenges in the Study of Elections and Voting*, London: Sage.
Blanc, J. (2006) "Palestinian Election Analysis: How Hamas Won the Majority," IFES, available at: www.ifes.org/westbank-project.html?projectid=howhamaswon (accessed April 3, 2006).
Colomer, J.M. (ed.) (2004) *Handbook of Electoral System Choice*, New York: Palgrave Macmillan.
Erlanger, S. (2006) "In a Stronghold, Fatah Fights to Beat Back a Rising Hamas," *New York Times*, January 23.

Farrell, D.M. (2001) *Electoral Systems: A Comparative Introduction*, New York: Palgrave.

"How Iraq's Elections Will Work" (2005) *Christian Science Monitor*, January 28.

Huntington, S. (1991) *The Third Wave*, Norman: University of Oklahoma Press.

International Crisis Group (2005) "Afghanistan Elections: Endgame or New Beginning?" July 21, 2005, available at: www.crisisgroup.org/home/index.cfm?id=3579 (accessed April 3, 2006).

—— (2006) "Enter Hamas: The Challenges of Political Integration," January 18, 2006, available at: www.crisisgroup.org/home/index.cfm?id=3886&l=1 (accessed April 3, 2006).

IFES (2006) "IFES Reacts to Haitian Election Situation," Washington, DC: IFES, Press Release, February 21.

Kumar, K. (ed.) (1998) *Postconflict Elections, Democratization and International Assistance*, Boulder, CO: Lynne Rienner.

LeDuc, L., R.G. Niemi, and P. Norris (2002) "Introduction: Comparing Democratic Elections," in L. LeDuc, R.G. Niemi, and P. Norris (eds) *Comparing Democracies 2: New Challenges in the Study of Elections and Voting*, London: Sage.

Norris, P. (2004) *Electoral Engineering: Voting Rules and Political Behavior*, Cambridge: Cambridge University Press.

Reynolds, A., B. Reilly, and A. Ellis (eds) (2005a) *Electoral System Design: The New International IDEA Handbook*, Stockholm: International Institute for Democracy and Electoral Assistance.

Reynolds, A., L. Jones, and A. Wilder (2005) "A Guide to Parliamentary Elections in Afghanistan," Kabul: Afghanistan Research and Evaluation Unit, available at: www.areu.org.af/publications/Guide%20to%20Parliamentary%20Elections.pdf (accessed April 3, 2006).

Rubin, B.R. (2005) "The Wrong Voting System," *International Herald Tribune*, March 15.

Singer, M.M. and T.J. Scotto (2004) "Trends in Opinion Research in New Democracies: Professionalization and Quality Control?," in R. Johns (ed.) *The Encyclopedia of Public Opinion*, Santa Barbara: ABC-CLIO.

Thompson, G. (2006a) "Exiled Aristide Still Affects Haiti Voters," *New York Times*, February 5.

Thompson, G. (2006b) "Violence Flares as Top Candidate Slips in Haiti Count," *New York Times*, February 14.

United Nations Electoral Assistance Division (2005) "Iraq Electoral Fact Sheet," New York: UNEAD, available at: www.un.org/news/dh/infocus/iraq/iraq-elect-fact-sht.pdf.

United Nations Human Rights Commission (2000) *Promoting and Consolidating Democracy*, Resolution 2000/47, New York: UNHRC.

Weisman, S.R. (2006) "Rice Admits U.S. Underestimated Hamas Strength," *New York Times*, January 30.

5

DEMOCRATIC GOVERNANCE AND THE SECURITY SECTOR IN CONFLICT-AFFECTED COUNTRIES

Nicole Ball

A safe and secure environment for people, communities, and states is an essential condition for sustainable economic, political and social development, and conflict mitigation. The United Nations demonstrates the association between poor development outcomes and violent conflict in its Human Development Index, and identifies democratic governance, peace and personal security as essential ingredients for "human development in its fullest sense" (United Nations Development Programme 2002: 85). Participatory poverty assessments undertaken since the 1990s have consistently identified the lack of security as a major concern for poor people, including: (1) crime and violence, (2) civil conflict and war, (3) persecution by the police, and (4) lack of justice (Narayan *et al.* 2000: 155).

Politicized, badly managed, or ineffective security bodies and justice systems have often been a source of instability and insecurity, ranging from petty corruption to massive abuses of human rights and significant loss of life, livelihoods, and assets through violent conflict.[1] Across geographic regions, poor people complain that the police are unresponsive, corrupt, and brutal. Where the police *do* function, corrupt justice systems can significantly undermine their effectiveness. Inadequate and corrupt public security and justice systems have often led people to attempt to provide their own security. Private enterprises, wealthy citizens, and the international community are especially likely to purchase private protection. The poor are more likely to turn to "self-help" justice and security, including vigilantism.

Problems are not limited to the justice and public security sector, however. Throughout the world, armed forces are important political and economic actors and have engaged in violations of the rule of law. Rather than protecting people against external threats or internal rebellions, armed forces have protected repressive governments (including governments led by military officers). In some cases, they have even made common cause with rebels.

The existence of unprofessional and unaccountable security services derives in large measure from the failure to develop effective democratic political systems. Without democratic checks and balances, security services can all too easily be used for partisan political purposes or can intervene directly in the political process. A lack of democratic accountability can also lead to the misallocation of resources within the security sector and the hollowing out of security services. In many countries, a sizeable portion of revenue accruing to the security services forces from both budgetary and non-budgetary sources is diverted to security groups or personnel, often working closely with civilian and political elites, for private consumption (Hendrickson and Ball 2002). This corrupt activity simultaneously enriches individuals associated with the security services and impoverishes the security services themselves, leading to low salaries for the rank-and-file, inadequate operations and maintenance, and inappropriate or non-functional equipment.

There is growing appreciation that democratic governance of the security sector is critical to achieving the safe and secure environment essential for sustainable development (United Nations Development Programme 2002; Brzoska 2003; Ball and Fayemi 2004; Organisation for Economic Co-operation and Development 2005). A lack of attention to democratic security sector governance leads to tolerance of politicized security forces, war as a means of resolving disputes, flagrant disregard for the rule of law by security forces and political elites, serious human-rights abuses, budget allocations skewed toward the security forces, and diminished capacity of the security forces to carry out their constitutionally mandated tasks of protecting people and communities.

Policies and approaches of security and development donors

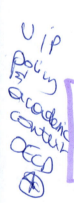

Although the linkages between security and development have long been evident to many in non-OECD countries, as well as to some academics, policy analysts and even a few policy-makers in OECD countries and multilateral organizations, mainstream development thinking has until quite recently tended to discount the impact of varying degrees of insecurity on development outcomes. Nor has much attention been paid to the impact that the security actors in developing countries have on the capacity for political, social, or economic development. During the Cold War, the major powers in both East and West provided a substantial amount of technical, financial, and material support on concessional terms to security services in allied or friendly countries, especially the military. Most of this was delivered through the donors' security and foreign ministries by security institutions or contractors. The focus was on transferring skills or weapons and other security-related equipment. While development donors sought actively to distance themselves from security-related issues, security donors paid scant attention to the quality of governance in the security sector.

Starting in the early 1990s, the strategic priorities of the major powers began to change with the breakup of the Soviet Union and the shift toward political liberalization in Eastern Europe. This shift in priorities had a number of consequences in terms of the approaches to the security sector adopted by development donors.

First, there was a significant decrease both in the volume of security assistance and the number of recipients worldwide that contributed, in some cases, to the end of long-standing conflicts. This in turn provided opportunities to examine the full range of factors affecting political and economic development, to reform public institutions, and to change élite attitudes and behaviors in both the developing and transition countries.

Second, the breakup of the bipolar world also created space for issues such as governance, poverty reduction, and conflict prevention to enter the development and security assistance agendas of OECD countries.[2] This in turn enabled the development donors to begin to discuss the linkages between security and development and the appropriate role of development assistance in strengthening security in developing and transition countries, for some modification in security assistance policies, and the beginning of a dialogue between development and security donors. Perhaps most important, the end of the Cold War created space for a discussion of the quality of development, governance, and security among local actors in the non-OECD countries themselves and for the emergence of civil society organizations and coalitions that pressed for people-centered approaches to security and the application of democratic governance principles.

Democratic security-sector governance in conflict-affected countries

Attention to democratic security sector governance is particularly important in conflict-affected countries, which typically experience significant institutional weaknesses and suffer from "the enduring legacies of undemocratic politics" (Luckham 2003:14).[3] Efforts to strengthen and restructure the state apparatus so that governments can fulfill roles critical to the efficient functioning of the economy and the political system are severely hampered by the political environment following violent conflict. That environment is characterized by a vigorous competition for power that often obscures the need to resolve critical national issues, by political leaders whose legitimacy is weak, by extreme polarization, and by a lack of consensus on the direction in which the country should move.

This situation is complicated by the low regard in which the state and political leaders from all parties and factions are often held. This disaffection derives both from past policies and behavior and from the human costs of the conflict. Conflict-affected countries generally have minimal experience of efficient, representative government. Political parties rarely offer distinct platforms or programs, serving instead as a mechanism for gaining control of the government to extract economic rents. The inability or unwillingness of political leaders to focus on substance and their tendency to view events through the lens of power politics impede the development of a national consensus on goals and priorities.

Strengthening democratic governance of the security sector in post-conflict societies presents enormous challenges. However, some guidance is emerging. This chapter explains how strengthening democratic security sector governance can be incorporated into peace-building efforts. It situates democratic security sector governance in the broader context of establishing a peaceful, secure environment for post-conflict reconstruction. It then identifies local stakeholders who affect the quality of security sector governance (positively and negatively) and who should be involved in efforts to strengthen democratic security sector governance. It also identifies the external actors that can assist local stakeholders in strengthening security sector governance. The chapter then describes the democratic security sector governance agenda and proposes five guidelines for implementing this agenda that have emerged from experience with security sector reform. It concludes by suggesting a way forward for local actors and their external partners.

Democratic security sector governance as a key element of peace-building

Although "good governance" has increasingly been recognized as central to consolidating democracy and promoting good development outcomes, very little attention was given to democratic security sector governance until the late 1990s. Yet democratic security sector governance is crucial for the success of democratic consolidation, poverty reduction, and sustainable economic and social development. It is also essential for creating a safe and secure environment for the state and its entire population.

In principle, the state commands the monopoly over the legitimate use of force. Legitimate use of force requires a legitimate state. A legitimate state is characterized by transparency, trust of the government by the governed, and accountability. A central problem confronting countries that have experienced or are in danger of experiencing major political violence is precisely that the state has lost its legitimacy in the eyes of some portion of its population. Often the state security bodies have contributed to that loss of legitimacy by their inability to protect people from violence, through their role as perpetrators of that violence, or as defenders of an unjust, repressive, and corrupt political system. Once the state has lost its legitimacy, it also begins to lose its monopoly over the means of violence, in extreme cases such as Sierra Leone even facing the mutiny of its own security forces. When state control over the monopoly of violence declines significantly, the state risks decomposition, which only further fragments the sources of violence (Luckham 2003: 11). Countries where the state has lost its monopoly over the use of violence to varying degrees in recent years include Afghanistan, Burundi, Côte d'Ivoire, Democratic Republic of Congo, Liberia, Iraq, Sierra Leone, Somalia, and Sri Lanka.

Eboe Hutchful and Robin Luckham have identified a number of challenges to civil-military relations and security sector reform following violent conflicts. These include:

- Deep physical, economic, psychological, and political scars that will take many decades to alter.
- Acceleration of decomposition and collapse of official military and security institutions.
- Establishment of covert links between official security services and paramilitaries and militias, which facilitates illegal, abusive activities that official services want to avoid.
- Difficulty in exerting democratic control over official security services when they have become factionalized and the troops cannot be controlled by their commanders.
- Complete lack of concept of democratic accountability among informal, illegal armed groups.
- Regionalization of conflicts, which complicates efforts to establish or maintain democratic accountability in one state alone (Hutchful and Luckham n.d.).

For these reasons, peace processes need to give attention both to re-creating a legitimate, as well as effective, state, and to developing democratic security sector governance. Peace processes, whether governed by peace agreements or not, generally do not give adequate attention to either objective. Peace agreements frequently contain requirements for changes in the security sector.[4] Some of these activities have the potential to strengthen democratic governance of the security sector, such as redefining the doctrines and missions of security forces to include, among other things, the primacy of civil control or reforming military and police education systems to promote human rights protection, accountability to the civil authorities, producing legislation governing the security forces, and the like. However, major overhauls of democratic security sector governance occur extremely rarely in post-conflict environments.[5] As recent experience in Afghanistan and Iraq demonstrates, most attention is focused on developing the operational capacity of security forces and the ministries charged with managing them, and on providing support for disarmament, demobilization, and reintegration programs.

In Afghanistan, the stated objective of security sector reform is to create effective and accountable security institutions. However, rebuilding the operational capacity of the army and the police service and creating special security units such as the counter-narcotics police have had far higher priority than creating the capacity for effective civil management and oversight of these bodies or ensuring that the security bodies, created are affordable (Miller and Pereito 2004; Sedra 2003, 2006). The Afghanistan Research and Evaluation Unit in Kabul noted in June 2004:

Still largely unaddressed are critical issues of good governance and the institutionalisation of civilian control over the use of force, over state resources, and over the appointment of senior government officials, as well as strengthening of governmental and non-governmental oversight.... Without a sustained commitment to ensure that the law assumes a dominant role in restricting government and security-force behaviour, government security forces may become the core areas of insecurity for the Afghan public.

(Bhatia *et al.* 2004)

Eighteen months later at the time of writing, the situation was little changed (Sedra 2006).

In many respects, one would not expect major transformations in countries that have experienced lengthy periods of major political violence, particularly those without a firm tradition of democratic governance to draw upon. In common with other forms of institutional development, moving toward democratic security sector governance may be expected to occur at a pace consistent with overall democratic consolidation and human and institutional resource capacity strengthening in each reforming country. Conflict-affected states clearly offer particular challenges in this regard, given their significant institutional and human resource deficits. Improving democratic security sector governance may even seem a second- or third-order issue for these countries, and one to be tackled once other parts of the governance framework are more firmly in place.

However, since poor democratic security sector governance has contributed in no small measure to the weaknesses in economic and political governance that led to political violence in the first place, it is impossible to strengthen overall governance without attention to the security sector. In fact, the agenda for strengthening democratic security sector governance is very much a human and institutional capacity-building agenda. By definition it recognizes that states seeking to implement the agenda do not have strong institutions or abundant human resources. At the same time, the agenda for strengthening democratic security sector governance is highly political. The issues at the core of the agenda are highly contentious and require a strategy for blunting the impact of potential spoilers as well as supporting reform-minded stakeholders.

The stakeholders

Three factors are especially important to efforts aimed at strengthening democratic security sector governance (Ball *et al.* 2003b). First, the national leadership must be committed to a significant reform process. Second, the principles, policies, laws, and structures developed during the process must be rooted in the reforming country's history, culture, legal framework, and institutions. Third, the process should be consultative, both within government and between government and civil and political society. Strengthening democratic security sector governance is thus, first and foremost, the responsibility of local actors. At the same time, appropriately designed and delivered external support (such as advice, information, analysis, financing, technical assistance, and coordination services) can significantly benefit domestic efforts to transform the security sector.

Local actors

There are five major categories of local actors that influence the quality of democratic security sector governance: (1) bodies mandated to use force; (2) justice and public security bodies; (3) civil management and oversight bodies; (4) non-state bodies; and (5) non-statutory civil society bodies. The first three groups constitute what is commonly called the security sector, as shown in Figure 5.1.[6]

Discussions about security in many post-conflict environments tend to focus on the role of the military, which is charged with protecting the state, and particularly the army. This reflects the widespread, but by no means universal, tendency to favor the military in resource allocation. It manifests the direct and indirect influence that the armed forces often exert over political life in conflict-affected states and the role they play in the genesis and conduct of the conflict.

However, providing security for states and their populations is not a task that the army or even the military can accomplish by themselves. Other bodies that are mandated to ensure the safety of the state and its citizens such as the police, the gendarmerie, civilian and military intelligence, border and coast guards, secret services and customs enforcement entities must be part of the equation. In addition, democratic governance of the security sector requires an active role for civil authorities that manage and monitor the security bodies. The security of both the state and its population will be maximized to the extent that the security bodies are subordinate to democratically elected officials. Both the executive branch and the legislature should be involved in the formulation and implementation of security policy.

The management and oversight actors tend to be the stepchildren of efforts to improve democratic security sector governance, and the needs are great. For example, formal policies and plans for implementing those policies are generally

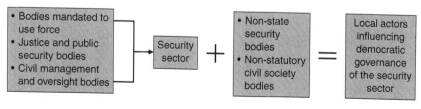

Figure 5.1 Security sector governance and local actors (source: Author).

absent in the security sector. Financial management in the sector generally does not conform to international standards. Legislatures are often unclear what their role is in making and overseeing security policy. To some extent these short-comings relate to the lack of capacity among the civil authorities, which can be remedied in the short term with technical assistance and in the medium to longer term through a variety of educational and mentoring programs. At the same time, the marginalization of these actors will not be overcome completely until the legacy of unaccountable government, executive dominance, and political involvement of some or all of the security services is adequately dealt with.

Not surprisingly, non-state security bodies are extremely important in post-conflict environments. Often the activities or even the very existence of these actors point up deficits in the formal security sector. They have proliferated since the late 1980s in Africa for several reasons that are closely related to the quality of democratic security sector governance: (1) armed conflicts that take on regional dimensions; (2) ineffective state security institutions; (3) growth of domestic and transnational crime; and (4) regime protection (see Ball and Fayemi 2004: 27–29). Some of the more common forms of non-state security organizations include the armed opposition and informal paramilitary or militia groups sponsored by the formal state security bodies, by the political élite or by neighboring states or formed by local communities for self-protection.[7]

As Figure 5.1 stresses, all of these factors need to be brought into the peace process and neutralized if democratic security sector governance is to succeed. The situation in Côe d'Ivoire in 2004 illustrates this point only too well. Militias created by political parties that first appeared in the early 1990s are now "formidable political actors who can neither be legislated nor wished away" and/or must in some way be neutralized if political violence is to end (International Crisis Group 2004: 8).

The role of civil society must also be stressed. In principle, civil society can play an important role in monitoring the development and application of security policy and the activities of security organizations, for example, through membership in community advisory/oversight boards, independent monitoring and analysis, and the dissemination of information about security policies and their implementation to a broader public. Civil society can also act as an important resource for the security community by providing a pool of knowledgable individuals to staff positions in relevant government agencies, review boards and other oversight bodies, and by providing training to members of security forces and civil oversight bodies. In many post-conflict countries, however, few civil society actors are capable of addressing security-related issues. Nor are all civil society groups democratically minded.

However, there are instances where civil society actors in conflict-affected countries have contributed to strengthening democratic security sector governance, for example, in countries as diverse as Guatemala, Sierra Leone, and South Africa.[8] With its rich associational life, South African civil society has been able to contribute in all areas mentioned above. To take just one example, the Southern African Defence and Security Management Network (SADSEM) is a key actor in developing both norms and capacity in the security sector in Southern Africa, including several conflict-affected countries. SADSEM focuses on democratic control and management of the security services, regional security cooperation, and multinational cooperation in conflict management and peace missions. It has sought to build local research and policy capacity, promote the contributions of civil society to issues of peace and security, and develop capacity within regional governments for democratic governance of security and regional security cooperation. SADSEM grew out of the first nongovernmental training program on defense and security in Africa, established by members of the Military Research Group at the University of Witwatersrand in Johannesburg in 1993 with grants from the Danish government. The Defence Management Programme was transformed into the Centre for Defence and Security Management, which is now the coordinating partner in SADSEM (Southern African Defence and Security Management Network n.d.).

External actors

Assistance intended to strengthen democratic security sector governance will be more effective to the extent that a broad range of external actors work together toward a common goal. One of the main recommendations for action contained in a policy statement approved by the Organisation of Economic Co-operation and Development's Development Assistance Committee (DAC) in April 2004 is the need to take "a whole-of-government" approach to security-related work. This requires building partnership across governmental departments and agencies to ensure that the body with the appropriate competence provides security-related support to reforming countries (OECD 2005: 12). Depending on the task at hand, this could include actors with expertise in public sector management, including the management of ministries of defense, intelligence and justice; public expenditure management; policy development and management; security affairs (defense, policing, intelligence, and regional); legislative affairs and other oversight functions such as audit; and the nongovernmental sector.

To date, the external support provided to developing countries has been financed primarily through development, defense, and justice ministries and through multilateral organizations such as UNDP or UN peacekeeping operations. Donor agencies have been seen, particularly in Europe and Canada, as a major source of funding for work intended to strengthen democratic security sector governance. All twenty-three members of the DAC and interested observers[9] endorsed the DAC SSR policy statement and paper on SSR in April 2004. Each DAC member country is at a different stage in developing national policy frameworks for SSR and is pursuing work in this area in different ways. Nonetheless, it is difficult to escape the conclusion that none of the DAC member states has yet succeeded in mainstreaming SSR, either into development work or into security-related activities. The UK has come the farthest, but even there significant gaps exist in terms of implementing the various policy frameworks that have been developed. In most other DAC countries, SSR, as defined in the DAC policy statement and paper, has barely penetrated even the development assistance ministries, let alone the foreign affairs or security-related ministries.

Security sector reform (which is not synonymous with "democratic security sector governance," although there is, in principle at least, considerable overlap) was initially championed by the UK Department for International Development (DFID) following the election of the Labour Party in 1997. The UK White Paper on International Development of November 1997 identified security as central to sustained development and poverty reduction (UK White Paper on International Development 2002: paras 3.48, 3.49, 3.52, and 3.55). In May 1998, the Secretary of State for International Development, Clare Short, announced the need for "a partnership between the development community and the military" in order to address the "inter-related issues of security, development and conflict prevention" (Short 1998). By early 1999, DFID had produced a policy note on poverty and the security sector that outlined the conditions under which development assistance could be used to engage in security sector reform and the specific criteria for DFID engagement (Short 1999; UK Department for International Development 1999).[10]

The UK was the first to adopt a whole-of-government approach to SSR by agreeing on an SSR Strategy in June 2002 (UK FCO, MOD and DFID 2002). The SSR Strategy is implemented through the UK's Global Conflict Prevention Pool, which, along with the Africa Conflict Prevention Pool (ACPP), combines the resources of several government departments to support a variety of activities intended to promote conflict reduction.[11] It created the Security Sector Development Team (SSDAT), originally known as the Defence Advisory Team (DAT). The SSDAT's institutional home is the Ministry of Defence but it draws on defense, policing, justice, intelligence, and governance expertise (UK Security Sector Development Assistance Team n.d.). The SSDAT has pioneered a facilitative approach to strengthening democratic security sector governance. It bases all activities on a detailed in-country analysis. One of its core operating principles is: "Assisting and facilitating, not doing, through the provision of processes, frameworks and methodologies in order to ensure local ownership and building increased future capacity in the customer" (Fuller 2003: para. 13).

DAC member countries that are beginning to emulate one or more aspects of the UK approach include Canada, the Netherlands, and the United States. In addition, in late 2005, the DAC Conflict Prevention and Development Cooperation Network undertook a process of developing tools to implement the DAC SSR policy statement. One of the lessons of the UK experience to date is that these new initiatives will need to address the challenge that a truly "joined-up" approach to security-related work presents.

Strengthening democratic security sector governance: constraints

The need to strengthen democratic governance of the security sector has long been evident in many developing and transition countries, including those that have experienced major political violence. Since the end of the Cold War, there have also been growing efforts in these countries to reform all or part of the security sector. Much of this activity has, however, been relatively narrowly focused on strengthening the operational capacity and effectiveness of the security forces, rather than strengthening democratic oversight and accountability mechanisms. There are at least four reasons for this. All are relevant to conflict-affected countries.

First, peace agreements frequently mandate restructuring one or more of the security bodies. Yet peace agreements rarely ensure that civil management and oversight bodies are reformed or function appropriately, or that civil society plays an oversight role. The recent trend toward severely curtailing the negotiation period of peace processes exacerbates this tendency. Nonetheless, there have been some exceptions. The Guatemala peace agreement – which is actually a series of agreements on different subjects and took several years to negotiate – is uncommonly detailed in its discussion of the security sector, and includes unusual features such as the role of the legislative branch and a provision for a civil society body to advise the president on a range of security-related issues. The latter is enshrined in Article 20 of the agreement (Agreement on the Strengthening of Civilian Power and on the Role of the Armed Forces in a Democratic Society 1996). Following a preparatory phase, the Advisory Council on Security Matters was created in June 2004.

Second, in most of these countries political elites use the security forces, particularly the military, to secure positions of power. Thus there is more interest in ensuring that security forces are able to quell incipient political unrest than in strengthening their democratic accountability.

Third, the international community often preferentially provides assistance designed to strengthen operational capability. This has particularly been the case since September 11, 2001, as the so-called "war on terror" has focused assistance on strengthening intelligence and internal security capacity in developing and transition countries. A study of forty-seven low-income, poorly performing states carried out in 2002 to 2004 found that those countries that were considered major US allies in the "war on terror" received 90 percent of the military and police aid provided by the US to that group of countries between 2000 and 2004. Ninety-three percent of the assistance to the "war on terror" subgroup went to Afghanistan and Pakistan. Much of this aid closely resembles the assistance that Washington provided to developing world allies at the height of the Cold War. That is to say, assistance to improve the accountability of the security services and their adherence to the rule of law is of essentially no concern (Ball and Isacson 2006; see also Chivers and Shanker 2005; Hendrickson 2005; and Hutchful and Fayemi 2005).

Finally, but by no means least relevant, developing and transitioning countries have limited resources to address security needs. In choosing how to invest those resources, they invariably focus on short-term security needs. A recent survey concluded that although non-OECD partner countries recognize the importance of addressing longer term issues such as improving security force professionalism and accountability, these will be sacrificed to addressing immediate security needs, such as insecurity caused by violent conflict and political unrest, organized crime, and state repression (OECD 2005). However, as Luckham (2003: 21) has correctly stressed: "Democratic accountability and the rule of law are not luxuries that can safely be postponed until order and security are restored; they are inseparable from the latter."

Strengthening democratic security sector governance: an agenda

Four main challenges must be addressed by any country seeking to strengthen democratic security sector governance. First, countries should develop a legal framework that is consistent with international law and good democratic practice, *and* ensure that it is implemented. Second, they should develop effective civil management and oversight mechanisms, *and* ensure that they function as intended. Third, governments need to develop viable security bodies that are capable of providing security for individuals, communities and the state, *and* are affordable and accountable. Fourth, governments must ensure that the institutional culture of the security forces, particularly the attitudes of the leadership, are supportive of the legal framework, international law, good democratic practice, and the functions and supremacy of civil management and oversight bodies.

To address these challenges, countries should prioritize the following tasks, which are based on principles that are increasingly accepted among reform-minded stakeholders in developing and transition countries and their external partners: (1) strengthen the professionalism of the security services; (2) develop capable and responsible civil authorities; (3) foster a capable and responsible civil society; (4) accord high priority to the rule of law; and (5) develop regional approaches to security problems.

Strengthen the professionalism of the security services

In democratic societies, professionalism has both a normative and a technical component. In the past, the tendency was to place greater emphasis on the technical aspects such as organizational, managerial and technical capabilities of security forces than on normative aspects such as respect for the rule of law, accountability to civil authorities, and rule orientation. While professional security forces are, by themselves, no guarantee that democratic civil control will be established or maintained, building the professional capacity of the security forces in both its normative and technical aspects is critical.

Develop responsible civil authorities

As in all sectors, the civil authorities in the executive and legislative branches of government should have the capacity to manage and oversee the security sector. They must also act responsibly, in accordance with democratic principles and the rule of law.

Foster a capable and responsible civil society

As noted above, civil society must be capable of monitoring security sector policies and activities and acting as a resource for the security community. In carrying out these activities, civil society must avoid the pursuit of narrow, sectarian objectives and ensure that their operations are fiscally accountable.

Accord high priority to the rule of law

Rule of law, including human rights protection, is another aspect of meeting the four challenges outlined above. Respect for the law must exist among both civilians and security force personnel. While the security forces are frequently the violators of the rule of law, their orders often come from civilian élites who seek to maintain or acquire positions of power. Similarly, all actors in the security sector need to abide by the principle of transparency, which is the cornerstone of accountable governance. Although there are legitimate reasons for some confidentiality, basic information should be accessible to both civil authorities and the public.

Develop regional approaches to security problems

Strengthening civil management and oversight of the security forces, achieving transparency in security related affairs, and attaining sustainable levels of security expenditure are challenges confronted by all states. Consequently, there is considerable potential for countries with shared problems and experiences within the same geographic area to work together to reduce tensions and enhance mutual security.12

Implementing the security sector governance agenda in conflict-affected countries

There are five guidelines that should inform all efforts to strengthen democratic security sector governance, whether undertaken by local stakeholders or external actors. These guidelines reflect lessons that are increasingly accepted among reform-minded stakeholders in developing and transition countries and their external partners.[13]

1   Local ownership of reform processes is essential.
2   The highly political nature of strengthening democratic security sector governance needs to inform reform processes.
3   The pace and content of locally owned reform processes must be shaped by conditions in the reforming country.
4   Decisions about reform strategy and programming need to be informed by a highly nuanced sense of context.
5   Situating reform efforts within a comprehensive, sector-wide framework has the potential to maximize the impact of the reforms on security and on efficient resource use.

Most of these guidelines are well known to development specialists. They are repeated here for two main reasons. The first is that they are not well known to political and security actors who have an important role to play in efforts to strengthen democratic governance of the security sectors in conflict-affected countries. The second is that despite their familiarity to development specialists, they have not yet been fully incorporated into international development programming.

Local ownership of reform processes is essential

Local ownership implies that local actors have the responsibility to take decisions on a range of policy development and implementation issues and are willing to exert the necessary leadership to do so. While the principle of national ownership is well recognized in the development arena, it is often not applied effectively in practice. In addition, peace processes involve not only development actors, but also political and security actors who are less well versed in the importance of national ownership. Whereas local ownership requires a facilitative approach aimed at helping countries identify needs and develop their own strategies for meeting them, all too often external actors are highly prescriptive and highly directive (Ball and Hendrickson 2005: 3–4, 49–52).

Local ownership is particularly difficult to achieve in post-conflict settings for two main reasons. First, peace process timetables are highly compressed, and there is a tendency to bypass government and other national actors to implement peace-related activities "on time." Second, the human and institutional capacity of post-conflict governments is generally weak, particularly in the security sector. International actors often fail to differentiate between responsibility and capacity. Local actors own a process when they have the responsibility for decisions with respect to objectives, policies, strategies, program design, and implementation modalities. If capacity is weak, as it almost always is in post-conflict environments, it can and should be strengthened. Concerns about local capacity can affect the willingness of local stakeholders to assume full responsibility for reform processes.

In the short term, capacity can be supplemented in various ways. Governments can obtain technical assistance, preferably from local or regional security specialists. South African security specialists have provided input into a range of security sector reform activities, including the drafting of white papers and legislation. The Guatemalan Advisory Council on Security Matters provides input for the government on a wide range of issues, including legislation. Expatriates can be encouraged to return, if even only for a year or two, to supplement capacity. This has happened to some extent in Afghanistan since 2001, for example. Governments can also request the secondment of individuals to fill particular positions in the bureaucracy. The government of Sierra Leone requested the secondment of a retired UK police official to fill the position of Inspector-General in the Sierra Leone Police Service.[14] In 2006, the newly elected President of Liberia, Ellen Johnson-Sirleaf, appointed a Nigerian general to head the Liberian Army.[15]

Weak capacity and the short time frame for post-conflict peace operations should not become an excuse for members of the international community to continue to exert control over activities that they support. However, because conflict-affected countries are frequently heavily dependent on external funding for the peace process, they are not in a strong position when it comes to driving processes, since they may think that by taking control they will jeopardize the delivery of assistance.

In conflict-affected countries, the transition process is typically very contentious, since it generally takes a great deal of time – a decade or more – for the animosities generated by conflict to begin to dissipate, enabling former parties to the conflict to work constructively together. For this reason, it is important to stress that national responsibility for, and leadership of, change in the security sector does not imply complete autonomy over the use of external resources provided for this purpose. Indeed, it is particularly important in post-settlement environments to ensure effective oversight of external resources.

There are some examples of good practice emerging from the donor side. The UK Security Sector Development Assistance Team, discussed above, is one. The Netherlands Ministry of Foreign Affairs commissioned a democratic security sector governance assessment framework to help partner countries determine how best to strengthen democratic governance of the security sector, although it has never attempted to implement this framework (Ball et al. 2003a).

Local stakeholders at all levels and in all relevant bodies need to accept the challenge of leadership. Without a vision of a transparent, accountable, and just state that is widely accepted throughout society, it will be impossible to generate the political will to effect a significant transformation of governance in the security sector (Ball et al. 2003b: 274–279).

A number of civil society initiatives are helping to strengthen leadership capacity, frequently supported by donor resources. Much of this has occurred in Africa. As noted above, SADSEM provides training for defense and security management and planning, and civil–military relations for government officials and civil society actors throughout Africa. Its work has been financed by a range of donor governments. Civil society organizations in Ghana, Nigeria, South

Africa, and the UK supported by foundation resources held a series of "south–south" workshops in 1999 and 2000 aimed at sharing experiences in transforming security sector governance among policy-makers, legislators, senior members of the security forces, and civil society in West and Southern Africa (CDD *et al.* 2000*)*. These "south–south" workshops were so successful that the UK SSDAT has employed the concept in Ghana, Guatemala, and Uganda.

The UK Conflict Prevention Pools have fostered the development of an African Security Sector Network, one of whose objectives is to strengthen the capacity of the civil authorities in the area of security policy formulation and execution, and are seeking to promote similar networks in Latin America and Asia. The Geneva Centre for Democratic Control of the Armed Forces, established by the Swiss government, carries out similar work in Eastern Europe and the former Soviet Union (Geneva Centre for the Democratic Control of Armed Forces n.d.) and has recently begun to liaise with the African networks. DCAF has produced several manuals that may be used for training purposes (Born *et al.* 2003; Born and Leigh 2005). The US-financed African Center for Strategic Studies engages in a number of capacity-building workshops each year. In 2005, it added a security resource management course for mid-level African officials and military personnel.

The highly political nature of strengthening democratic security sector governance needs to be factored into reform efforts

An awareness of the political context is particularly important in conflict-affected countries and especially relevant for external actors. Indeed, it is precisely due to the political nature of institutional reform that major stakeholders will resist strengthening democratic security sector governance.

It is also why improving democratic security sector governance cannot be addressed solely by technical measures. Rather, it is essential to understand critical political relationships among key actors, how and why decisions are made, and the incentives and disincentives for change.[16] Strategies need to be developed for supporting reformers and minimizing the impact of spoilers. Every reform process has its share of those who will be negatively affected by the proposed reforms and who will in consequence seek to thwart them. These will range from powerful warlords in Afghanistan or Charles Taylor in Liberia, to militia leaders such as Sam Bockerie in Sierra Leone, to militia members such as those who stand to be excluded from the DDR process in Côte d'Ivoire. They may also include members of formal security bodies in reforming countries. Identifying these individuals and developing strategies for neutralizing them is a particularly critical aspect of contextual analysis (see below), and requires looking beyond formal legislation and organizational structure to develop a picture of how local institutions actually function.

The dangers of an overly technical approach to reforming the security sector is noted by two experienced African policy analysts and civil society leaders, Eboe Hutchful and Kayode Fayemi:

> In particular, little has been put in place to enhance the capacity of civilians to make an input into strategic planning or oversight processes. Moreover, the intent behind some approaches to SSR seems, consistent with the term "reform", to be a re-engineering of often decrepit and discredited institutions and a re-centering of the state in the security system, rather than a fundamental rethinking of security, strategic concepts and frameworks, and governance institutions. The donor SSR literature is often suffused with technocratic and apolitical conceptions often derived from previous, and often unsuccessful, exercises in public sector reform. The central priority in most African countries, however, is to alter the relations of power within the security system and society at large. This is often the case in societies with a history of direct or indirect military dominance, as a necessary prelude to civil control, transformation of institutional culture, etc.
>
> (Hutchful and Fayemi 2005: 86)

The pace of locally owned reform processes must be shaped by conditions in the reforming country

Strengthening democratic security sector governance is a subset of institutional reform, and as such requires a decade or more to consolidate. Strengthening democratic security sector governance must reflect not only human and institutional capacity but also the pace of social and political change in the country in question, rather than arbitrary timetables established by the international community or funding decisions. This is particularly important for conflict-affected countries, where political and economic relations have been shaped by wartime conditions and may require substantial time to overcome these distortions.

The weaker the state, the longer the reform process is likely to take. It is extremely important, however, to make the necessary investment. There is increasing evidence that consultative processes which build consensus on both the need for change and the direction and nature of change are critical for the success of reform efforts. For these to succeed, stakeholders must be allowed adequate time to reach consensus. The highly consultative South African security sector transformation process is viewed as a model by many developing countries, both in Africa and beyond. South Africa has produced policy papers for defense, intelligence, safety and security, participation in international peace missions, and defense-related industries since 1994. Non-governmental experts have contributed to most of these, and several have been widely vetted by relevant stakeholders prior to being finalized. Such consultation lengthens the process of producing legislation, but results in a stronger product and greater buy-in on the part of key stakeholders. In addition to consultations in Cabinet and debate in the legislature, the White Paper on Safety and Security, for example, went through: (1) provincial public hearings; (2) a national hearing; (3) consultation with critical audiences; and (4) internal consultation within the South African Police Service (South Africa Department of Safety and Security 1998; Cawthra 2003).

While complete consensus on the desirability and direction of a reform process is unlikely, key stakeholders in government, the security bodies, and civil and political society need to support reform if significant changes are to occur. External actors can help increase the receptivity to change by making democratic security sector governance a regular component of policy dialogue in order to identify entry points for reform. They can ensure that the security sector is included in public sector and public expenditure management work where relevant. They can identify and support change agents within the government and the security bodies, and can support efforts to neutralize potential spoilers. They can also help civil society develop its capacity to analyze security problems and demand change, as well as to provide support for reform. Finally, external actors should explore how they can create incentives for key stakeholders to support efforts to strengthen democratic security sector governance.

External stakeholders need to approach such efforts with patience and an ability to facilitate politically sensitive discussions. Unless key stakeholders are in agreement on the way forward, it does not make sense to initiate significant work in the area of security sector governance. Rather, external actors should concentrate on developing a reform-friendly environment, through activities such as policy dialogue, support to civil society, and capacity building for reformers. Even where there is a high degree of consensus on the way forward, implementation may proceed slowly and the possibility of backsliding cannot be excluded (Cawthra and Luckham 2003: 308–309). External actors should neither become complacent themselves when reform processes appear to be moving forward, nor should they allow local stakeholders to become complacent. It is important to avoid the common mistake of assuming that good policy will, in and of itself, produce satisfactory outcomes and overlook the need for sound policy implementation.

Decisions about reform strategy and programming need to be informed by a highly nuanced sense of context

External actors, particularly the development donors, have a tendency to categorize countries according to typologies – democratizing, fragile, conflict-affected, failing, failed, and so on. These categories are of little use in identifying needs in a specific country or setting in motion a reform process. While conflict-affected countries, for example, do share certain characteristics, they do not all have exactly the same needs or capacities. Neither local stakeholders nor their external partners should assume that a particular institutional solution or sequencing of events is appropriate simply because it has been used with relative success in another conflict-affected country. Countries can and do borrow from each other. These solutions must be adapted to the context in which they are implemented (Cawthra and Luckham 2003).

Indeed, the more closely a change is related to past behavior, the more likely it is that the changes will actually be carried out. In many African countries, for example, traditional and informal institutions can contribute to a well-governed security sector. Elements of customary justice either co-exist with or have been incorporated into formal justice systems in many places. This is particularly important in rural areas where formal justice systems are often absent. In addition, informal justice mechanisms have emerged in many urban areas to support problem-solving, arbitration, and conflict resolution. Often these borrow elements from traditional law structures and procedures. Not only are these mechanisms more familiar to ordinary citizens; they are frequently far more accessible than the formal legal system (Ball and Fayemi 2004: 53–54).

It may be particularly difficult for conflict-affected countries to resist offers of inappropriate assistance and advice, or even to know what is inappropriate. Their external partners therefore bear a particular burden to ensure that the assistance they offer is appropriate to the context. Some methodologies specifically designed for the security sector are now beginning to emerge. For example, the UK uses the joint scoping mission, where representatives of different disciplines (and therefore different ministries) carry out a joint security sector reform needs assessment. This enables the UK to identify the priority issues and determine where it can provide assistance. There appears to be no documentation of the precise methodology employed as yet.

A second option, also aimed at external actors, involves developing a picture of the environment in which security-related work will occur by identifying the major characteristics of the country according to seven contextual categories: political; psychosocial; normative; institutional; societal; economic; and geopolitical. For each issue that needs to be addressed, possible forms of international assistance may be identified, but there is no means of determining priority needs or which among the possible responses is the most appropriate (Ball 2002).

A third option is to assist a country to carry out a detailed assessment of its needs and then to identify priorities. This is the approach employed by the democratic security sector governance assessment framework developed by the Clingendael Institute, which examines five possible entry points: rule of law; policy development and implementation; professionalism of the security forces; oversight; and financial management (Ball et al. 2003a). This methodology would be difficult to implement in countries in conflict, but could be used in countries that are on the road to consolidating peace.

Situating reform efforts within a comprehensive, sector-wide framework has the potential to maximize the impact of the reforms on security and efficient resource use

While no reform process can be expected to encompass all of the many actors and activities that constitute the security sector, decisions about priority needs and resource allocation should be made following a sector-wide review of a country's security environment and its broad democratic security sector governance needs. Effecting sustainable change in the security sector will almost always require a focus on one constituent element at a time (defense, public security, justice, intelligence). Within that element, there may be a focus on a specific component or process (for example, the capacity of relevant legislative committees, the courts, the defense budgeting system, and so on). However, in the absence of sector-wide assessments of security needs and governance deficits it will be difficult to identify priorities or to determine how best to sequence reform efforts.

Although experience is limited to date, evidence suggests that external actors can help reforming governments understand the components of security sector reform and how these fit together. There are two assessment mechanisms that may be useful in this process. The first is a strategic security review, which has been pioneered by the United Kingdom in Uganda (Rusoke 2003) and Sierra Leone. Regrettably, no formal methodology exists as yet and neither experience had been reviewed at the time of writing. The second is the security sector governance assessment framework commissioned by the Netherlands Foreign Ministry for use by partner countries discussed above, which had not been field-tested at the time of writing. The Conflict Prevention and Development Co-operation Network in the OECD DAC began a process in late 2005 of developing a framework to help its members implement the SSR strategy approved in April 2004. It is unclear as of writing whether this framework will assist DAC members to adopt a sector-wide approach.

There is one point that external actors must bear in mind. While it is important to have ambitious long-term objectives, it is also important to be realistic about implementation capacity. In particular, it is important to develop process-oriented benchmarks to measure progress that reflect the realities of political, human and institutional capacity on a country-by-country basis. Such benchmarks will not only assure external partners that progress is being recorded. They can also help local stakeholders avoid being overwhelmed by the enormity of the reform agenda.

Conclusion

As this chapter has shown, both external actors and domestic stakeholders have a role to play in strengthening governance in countries where there are democratic deficits in the security sector. In considering the priorities for both external and domestic stakeholders, three issues stand out.

What is necessary?

There are two complementary processes that must be undertaken to achieve democratically governed security sectors. First, the transformation agenda should be established by moving sequentially from values and principles, to goals and objectives, to doctrine and strategies, to policies and plans, and then to structures, institutions, and resources. All relevant local actors should be involved in this process: government, Parliament, the security forces, and civil and political society. The government should lead, although it is likely to need to supplement its capacity with inputs from both local and regional civil society and the international community.

This process would seek to answer questions such as: What are the values and principles that underpin security policies? How should these be translated into goals, strategies, and policies? Which institutions should be involved in developing and implementing security policy? How should these institutions function – individually and as a group – if the objective is to increase democratic accountability, transparency, and civilian control over the security forces? What is the difference between how these institutions function at present and how they should function in the future? Are the financial and human resources necessary for these institutions to operate in the desired manner available? If not, how should needs be prioritized? Can additional resources be identified?

The second process involves translating the agenda into constitutional provisions, legislation, national policies, departmental policies, and departmental plans. In order to implement the agenda, it will be necessary to rank the priorities identified by each component and to develop a series of action plans to guide implementation. These planning papers should be considered as works in progress and be updated regularly. Again, the government should lead this process, but will need to supplement its capacity. Civil society organizations and Parliament also need to development their own plans of action.

These are not easy tasks, and they are particularly challenging for conflict-affected countries. While the local stakeholders will benefit from external support in undertaking these processes, those furnishing that assistance need to bear several factors in mind. First, providing much-needed inputs to a reform process should not be confused with playing a leading role. External actors in particular must resist the temptation to drive reform processes. Second, external actors must also be prepared to proceed at a pace consistent with local capacity. In particular, conditions in conflict-affected states are likely to require that a great deal of time is devoted to preparatory work, such as confidence building and dialogue aimed at developing a constituency for reform. External actors also need to be prepared for products that vary in quality. It is likely that the first effort to determine what is necessary will not address all issues at the same level of detail. All those concerned should understand that undertaking assessments and developing priorities is an iterative process. Third, it is important to bear in mind that security sector reform must proceed in tandem with the development of basic governance capacity. While it is highly unlikely that the security sector will lead in the area of democratic governance, it is equally important that the security sector should not be excluded from efforts to enhance democratic governance capacity state-wide.

Are the resources available?

Once preliminary action plans have been produced, government, Parliament, and civil society should assess the financial, technical, and material resources necessary to begin addressing the priority issues. In some cases it may be decided that in one or more areas, assistance is required to extend the institutional assessment or further amplify the preliminary action plan. In other cases resources may be necessary to implement the action plan. It is always important, however, to be realistic in developing a wish list for external support and to try to identify those areas in which value added can be maximized.

Who is best suited to provide the necessary assistance?

With a plan of action in hand and priorities identified for external resources, it is time to approach external actors. Some of the external stakeholders may have already been involved in providing support for the assessment process. Importantly, some external actors will have very specific ideas about the types of assistance they will provide. It is often very tempting to accept offers of assistance, even if there is not a good fit with one's own priorities.

Some external stakeholders may need to be prodded into providing assistance. This is particularly likely to be the case with requests to development assistance actors for assistance in strengthening the capacity of defense ministries, improving security sector planning, or enhancing the capacity of relevant government bodies to manage the security budgeting process. While the tendency of the development agencies has in the past been to avoid involvement, they find it very difficult to ignore requests for assistance.[17] The more specific the request and the more that it is couched in language that is recognizable to them, the more likely they are to respond positively.

The reforming government needs to scrutinize each offer carefully for what it will or will not bring. Modifications to proposed assistance should be negotiated to enhance the likelihood that the assistance offered will respond to the needs of its recipient and contribute to implementing the strategic reform plan developed domestically. External actors need to understand that continuity of assistance is extremely important in conflict-affected states, and that institutional development – a long-term undertaking in the best of circumstances – takes longer than in the more developed states. It is important that external actors be prepared to commit to sustained – but not open-ended – assistance for a very long period of time.

Notes

1 The case study literature on the dynamics of conflict is extensive. For country studies see the reports of the International Crisis Group (www.crisisweb.org) and Human Rights Watch (www.hrw.org).

2 An early influence was work on democratic civil–military relations in the transition countries of Eastern Europe and the former Soviet Union that got underway in the mid-1990s. Because NATO and the EU made adherence to principles of democratic civil–military relations a condition for membership, candidate countries had an enormous incentive to begin to apply these principles. For their part, NATO and EU members had an incentive to develop the capacity to support efforts to strengthen the accountability of the armed forces in candidate countries and to improve the capacity of the civil authorities to manage the defense sector. On changes in UK military assistance, see, for example, Cottey and Forster (2004). On the EU and NATO requirements, see for example, OSCE (1994); NATO (1995); Rotfeld (1995: 275–281); and NATO (n.d.). See also Hendrickson and Karkoska (2002).

   In the early 1990s, the development donors were focusing on how much developing and transition countries were spending on the military. This was because governance had not yet embedded itself in the development agenda and, at least partly as a consequence, the rather simplistic view held sway that donors could pressure governments to change resource allocation patterns without tackling any of the deep-rooted and highly political reasons why resources are allocated as they are. It was not until the late 1990s, after governance became an accepted component of development, that the development donors began to focus on democratic governance in the security sector. For a brief review of the military expenditure approach to the security sector in developing countries, see Brzoska (2003: 5–10).

3 On the various institutional weaknesses that characterize conflict-affected countries, see Aron (2002). On the challenges of governance in conflict-affected countries, see UNDP (1999). UNDP emphasizes, *inter alia*, the importance of strengthening the legitimacy and inclusiveness of governance institutions in conflict-affected countries. On the relationship between state formation and conflict in Africa and Eurasia, see Holloway and Steadman (2002).

4 Peace processes that are not governed by peace agreements, that is, where one party is victorious, have many of the same needs, but are under less pressure to address them. Nonetheless, as Uganda's experience since the early 1990s indicates, aid-dependent countries will eventually face demands from their development partners for some degree of change in the security sector.

5 The main exception to this is South Africa since 1994. For example, see Cawthra (2003); Williams (2003); Africa (2004); Rausch (2004).

6 The OECD Development Assistance Committee includes all four in what it calls the "security system" (Organisation for Economic Co-operation and Development 2005). UNDP includes the first three in what it terms the "justice and security sector" (United Nations Development Programme n.d.).

7 See Ero (2003) on Sierra Leone, where the government relied heavily on the Civil Defence Forces to confront the Revolutionary United Front rebels as a security vacuum developed as the Sierra Leone Armed Forces (SLA) progressively collapsed, largely as a result of the politicization of the SLA.

8 In Sierra Leone, civil society tends to operate primarily in watchdog mode, while in Guatemala, watchdog activities are complemented by providing advice and input to the government. On Guatemala, see, for example, Arèalo (2002) and Arèalo and Torres (1999). On Sierra Leone, see for example, National Democratic Institute (2003).

9 The DAC is made up of twenty-two bilateral donors and the Commission of the European Communities. UNDP, World Bank, and IMF have observer status.

10 It is important to recall that DFID's SSR policy focused initially on the defense sector. DFID developed a parallel policy on safety, security, and access to justice (SSAJ) (UK DFID, 2000b). This was in direct contradiction to the new thinking on security that had emerged about a decade earlier. Now, however, the UK has adopted a broad definition of the security sector and is working to combine its approaches to SSR and SSAJ.

11 The two Conflict Prevention Pools were evaluated in 2003/2004. See Ball (2004) for the evaluation of the SSR Strategy.

12 Each of these themes emerges from the OECD regional survey (Organisation for Economic Co-operation and Development 2005). See also Ball and Fayemi (2004).

13 These lessons may be found, for example, in Washington Office on Latin America (2001); Ball (2002); Ball et al. (2003b); Cawthra and Luckham (2003); Fuller (2003); Ball and Fayemi (2004); and Organisation for Economic Co-Operation and Development (2005).

14 In this case the issue was not solely one of capacity. The government also had concerns about the political loyalty of local candidates for the position.

15 The civil society organization, African Security Sector Network, conducted the first of a series of capacity-building workshops on SSR for the Liberian government in April 2005.

16 The UK Department for International Development has developed a "drivers of change" approach in order to strengthen the effectiveness of its development assistance (UK Department for International Development 2004). Such an approach is extremely relevant in the security sector, but it is unclear whether DFID had done so to at the time of writing.

17 Historically the World Bank has had the lead in strengthening financial management and has avoided incorporating the security sector into that work. There are indications, however, that the Bank is now more prepared to respond to requests from member governments to incorporate the security sector into government-wide efforts to improve financial management. In 2004, for example, the Bank responded to a request from the government of Afghanistan to include the security sector in its ongoing review of public finance management in the country.

References

Africa, S. (2004) "The Restructuring of the Intelligence Services in South Africa: An Assessment of the Transformation Process," in C. Ferguson and J. Isima, (eds) *Providing Security for People: Enhancing Security through Police, Justice, and Intelligence Reform in Africa*, Shrivenham, UK: Global Facilitation Network for Security Sector Reform, pp. 27–40, available at: www.gfn-ssr.org/edocs/gfn060_pfsp2.pdf.

Agreement on the Strengthening of Civilian Power and on the Role of the Armed Forces in a Democratic Society (1996) Mexico City, September 19, available at: www.usip.org/library/pa/guatemala/guat_960919.html.

Aréalo, L.B. (2002) *Seguridad Democrática en Guatemala: Desafíos de la Transformación*, Guatemala City: FLACSO Guatemala.

Aréalo, L.B. and Torres, R.E. (eds) (1999) *Del Conflicto al Diálogo: El WSP en Guatemala*, Geneva and Guatemala City: UNRISD and FLACSO Guatemala.

Aron, J. (2002) *Building Institutions in Post-conflict African Economies*, Discussion Paper No. 2002/124, Helsinki: United Nations University/World Institute for Development Economics Research, available at: www.grc-exchange.org/docs/SS1.pdf.

Ball, N. (2002) "Enhancing Security Sector Governance: A Conceptual Framework for

UNDP," New York: UNDP, available at: www.undp.org/bcpr/jssr/docs/UNDP_SSR_Concept_Paper_Oct_9_2002.DOC.

Ball, N. (2004) *Evaluation of the Conflict Prevention Pools. The Security Sector Reform Strategy*, London: Department for International Development, available at: www.dfid.gov.uk/Pubs/files/ev_647a.pdf.

Ball, N. and Fayemi, K. (2004) *Security Sector Governance in Africa: A Handbook*, London and Lagos: Centre for Democracy and Development.

Ball, N. and Hendrickson, D. (2005) "Review of International Financing Arrangements for Disarmament, Demobilization and Reintegration," Stockholm: Report to Working Group 2 of the Stockholm Initiative on Disarmament, Demobilization and Reintegration, available at www.sweden.gov.se/content/1/c6/04/39/67/88c80b75.pdf.

Ball, N. and Isacson, A. (2006) "US Military and Police Assistance to Poorly Performing States," in *Short of the Goal: US Policy and Poorly Performing States*, Washington, DC: Brookings Institution Press.

Born, H. and Leigh, I. (2005) *Legal Standards for Democratic Accountability of Security and Intelligence Services: Best Practice and Procedure*, Oslo: Publishing House of the Norwegian Parliament.

Ball, N., Bouta, T., and van de Goor, L. (2003a) "Enhancing Democratic Governance of the Security Sector: An Institutional Assessment Framework," The Hague: Clingendael Institute for the Netherlands Ministry of Foreign Affairs, available at: www.clingendael.nl/cru/pdf/2003_occasional_papers/SSGAF_publicatie.pdf.

Ball, N., Fayemi, K., Olonisakin, F., Williams, R., with Rupiya, M. (2003b) "Governance in the Security Sector," in N. van de Walle, N. Ball, and V. Ramachandran (eds) *Beyond Structural Adjustment: The Institutional Context of African Development*, New York: Palgrave Macmillan, pp. 263–304.

Born, H., Fluri, P., and Johnson, A. (2003) *Parliamentary Oversight of the Security Sector: Principles, Mechanisms and Practice*, Handbook No. 5 for Parliamentarians, Geneva: Geneva Centre for the Democratic Control of Armed Forces and Inter-parliamentary Union.

Brzoska, M. (2003) *Development Donors and the Concept of Security Sector Reform*, Occasional Paper No. 4, Geneva: Geneva Centre for the Democratic Control of Armed Forces, available at: www.dcaf.ch/publications/Publications%20New/Occasional_Papers/4.pdf.

Cawthra, G. (2003) "Security Transformation in Post-Apartheid South Africa," in G. Cawthra and R. Luckham (eds) *Governing Insecurity: Democratic Control of Military and Security Establishments in Transitional Democracies*, London: Zed Books, pp. 31–56.

Cawthra, G. and Luckham, R. (2003) "Democratic Control and the Security Sector: The Scope for Transformation and its Limits," in G. Cawthra and R. Luckham (eds) *Governing Insecurity: Democratic Control of Military and Security Establishments in Transitional Democracies*, London: Zed Books, pp. 305–327.

Centre for Democracy and Development (CDD), Centre for Defence and Security Management (CDSM), Institute for Development Studies (IDS) (2000) *Roundtable on Democratic Control of Military and Security Establishments in Nigeria and South Africa. September 20–23, 2000, Johannesburg*, Lagos: CDD.

Chivers, C. and Shanker, T. (2005) "Uzbek Units Linked to Deadly Crackdown Got U.S. Training," *International Herald Tribune*, June 20.

Cottey, A. and Forster, A. (2004) *Reshaping Defence: New Roles for Military Cooperation and Assistance*, Adelphi Paper No. 365, London: IISS.

Ero, C. (2003) "Sierra Leone: The Legacies of Authoritarianism and Political Violence," in G. Cawthra and R. Luckham (eds) *Governing Insecurity: Democratic Control of Military and Security Establishments in Transitional Democracies*, London: Zed Books, pp. 232–253.

Fuller, N. (2003) *Defence Advisory Team, Annual Report 2002/03*, Swindon: Defence Advisory Team, available at: www.mod.uk/issues/cooperation/dat/.

Geneva Centre for the Democratic Control of Armed Forces (DCAF) (n.d.) available at: www.dcaf.ch (accessed October 13, 2004).

Global Facilitation Network for Security Sector Reform (n.d.) available at: www.gfn-ssr.org.

Hendrickson, D. (2005) "Overview of Regional Survey Findings and Policy Implications for Donors," in *Security System Reform and Governance*, DAC Guidelines and Reference Series, Paris: OECD, Part II, ch. 4.

Hendrickson, D. and Ball, N. (2002) *Off-budget Military Expenditure and Revenue: Issues and Policy Perspectives for Donors*, CSDG Occasional Paper No. 1, London: King's College London for the UK Department for International Development, available at: www.dfid.gov.uk/pubs/files/offbudget-military-exp.pdf.

Hendrickson, D. and Karkoska, A. (2002) "The Challenge of Security Sector Reform," in *SIPRI Yearbook 2002: Armaments, Disarmament and International Security*, Oxford: Oxford University Press, for the Stockholm International Peace Research Institute, pp. 175–201.

Holloway, D. and Steadman, S. (2002) "Civil Wars and State-building," in M. Beissinger and C. Young (eds) *Beyond State Crisis? Postcolonial Africa and Post-Soviet Eurasia in Comparative Perspective*, Washington, DC: Woodrow Wilson Center Press, pp. 161–187.

Hutchful, E. and Fayemi, K. (2005) "Security System Reform in Africa," in *Security System Reform and Governance*, DAC Guidelines and Reference Series, Paris: OECD.

Hutchful, E. and Luckham R. (n.d.) "Civil–Military Relations in Africa," Unpublished paper for the African Center for Strategic Studies, Washington, DC: U.S. National Defense University.

International Crisis Group (2004) *Côte d'Ivoire: No Peace in Sight*, ICG Africa Report No. 82, Dakar and Brussels: ICG, 12 July, available at: www.icg.org//library/documents/africa/west_africa/082_cote_d_ivoire_no_peace_in_sight.pdf.

Luckham, R. (2003) "Democratic Strategies for Security in Transition and Conflict," in G. Cawthra and R. Luckham (eds) *Governing Insecurity: Democratic Control of Military and Security Establishments in Transitional Democracies*, London: Zed Books, pp. 3–28.

Miller, L. and Perito, R. (2004) *Establishing the Rule of Law in Afghanistan*, Special Report No. 117, Washington, DC: United States Institute of Peace, available at: www.usip.org/pubs/specialreports/sr117.pdf.

Narayan, D., Chambers, R., Shah, M., and Petesch, P. (2000) *Voices of the Poor: Crying Out for Change*, New York: Oxford University Press, for the World Bank.

National Democratic Institute (2003) "Civil–Military Cooperation Workshop: Koidu Town, Kono District, January 16–18," Washington, DC: National Democratic Institute.

North Atlantic Treaty Organization (n.d.) "Membership Action Plan," Brussels: NATO, available at: www.nato.int/docu/facts/2000/nato-map.htm.

—— (1995) *Study on NATO Enlargement*, Brussels: NATO.

Organisation for Economic Co-operation and Development (2005) *Security System*

Reform and Governance, DAC Guidelines and Reference Series, Paris: OECD, available at: www.oecd.org/dac.

Organisation for Security and Cooperation in Europe (1994) "Towards a Genuine Partnership in a New Era," Budapest: OSCE, available at: www1.umn.edu/humanrto/osce/new/budapest-summit-declaration.html.

Rausch, J. (2004) "Transforming Police–Community Relations in South Africa," in C. Ferguson, and J. Isima (eds) *Providing Security for People: Enhancing Security through Police, Justice, and Intelligence Reform in Africa*, Shrivenham, UK: Global Facilitation Network for Security Sector Reform, pp. 53–58, available at: www.gfn-ssr.org/edocs/gfn060_pfsp2.pdf.

Rotfeld, A.D. (1995) "Europe: The Multilateral Security Process," in *SIPRI Yearbook 1995: Armaments, Disarmament and International Security*, Oxford: Oxford University Press.

Rusoke, R. (2003) "Defence Reform in Uganda: A Case Study," in A. Laláand A.M. Fitz-Gerald (eds) *Providing Security for People: Security Sector Reform in Africa*, GFN Paper No. 23, Shrivenham, UK: Global Facilitation Network for Security Sector Reform, pp. 23–28, available at: www.gfn-ssr.org/edocs/gfn023_book.pdf.

Sedra, M. (ed.) (2003) *Confronting Afghanistan's Security Dilemma: Reforming the Security Sector*, Brief No. 28, Bonn: Bonn International Center for Conversion, available at: www.bicc.de/publications/briefs/brief28/brief28.pdf.

—— (2006) "Security Sector Reform in Afghanistan: The Slide Toward Expediency," *International Peacekeeping* 13(1): 94–110.

Short, C. (1998) "Security, Development and Conflict Prevention," London: Speech at the Royal College of Defence Studies, May 13.

—— (1999) "Security Sector Reform and the Elimination of Poverty," London: Speech at the Centre for Defence Studies, King's College, March 9.

South Africa Department of Safety and Security (1998) *In Service of Safety*, Pretoria: Department of Safety and Security, available at: www.gov.za/whitepaper/1998/safety.htm#drafting.

Southern African Defence and Security Management Network (SADSEM) (n.d.) available at: www.sadsem.net/english/english.htm.

UK Department for International Development (1999) *Poverty and the Security Sector*, London: DFID, available at: www.dfid.gov.uk/pubs/files/poverty-security.pdf.

—— (2000a) *Security-sector Reform and the Management of Military Expenditure: High Risks for Donors, High Returns for Development*; Report on an International Symposium Sponsored by the UK Department for International Development, London, February 15–27, available at: www.gfn-ssr.org/edocs/dfid_ssr_management_expenditure_2000.pdf

—— (2000b) *Justice and Poverty Reduction: Safety, Security and Access to Justice for All*, London: DFID.

—— (2004) *Drivers of Change: Informational Note*, London: DFID, available at: www.grc-exchange.org/docs/doc59.

UK Foreign and Commonwealth Office, Ministry of Defence and Department for International Development (UK FCO, MOD and D FID) (2002) *S SR Strategy*, unpublished.

UK Security Sector Development Assistance Team (n.d.) available at: www.mod.uk/issues/cooperation/ssdat/.

UK White Paper on International Development (2002) *Eliminating World Poverty: A*

Challenge for the 21st Century, London: Presented to Parliament by the Secretary of State for International Development by Command of Her Majesty.

United Nations Development Programme (1999) *Governance Foundations for Post Conflict Situations*, New York: UNDP, available at: www.magnet.undp.org/docs/crisis/monograph.pdf.

—— (2002) *Human Development Report 2002: Deepening Democracy in a Fragmented World*, New York: UNDP.

—— (n.d.) "Justice and Security Sector Reform," available at: www.undp.org/bcpr/jssr/index.htm.

Washington Office on Latin America (2001) *From Peace to Governance: Police Reform and the International Community*, Washington, DC: WOLA, available at: www.wola.org/publications/police_reform_report.pdf.

Williams, R. (2003) "Post-conflict Security Sector Transformation: The South Africa Experience Between 1994–2002," in A. Laláand A.M. Fitz-Gerald (eds) *Providing Security for People: Security Sector Reform in Africa*, GFN Paper No. 23, Shrivenham, UK: Global Facilitation Network for Security Sector Reform, pp. 11–16, available at: www.gfn-ssr.org/edocs/gfn023_book.pdf.

Part II

ACTORS IN GOVERNANCE
RECONSTRUCTION
Old, new, and evolving roles

6

FROM BULLETS TO BALLOTS

The U.S. Army role in stability and reconstruction operations

Tammy S. Schultz and Susan Merrill

General William S. Wallace, Commander of the V Corps, recalled reaching Baghdad in April 2003, as statues of Saddam Hussein began to topple and the looting began: "There were several times I was standing on a street corner watching this looting, and it never occurred to me that we would have to replace that office furniture, or those buildings for that matter" (Wallace 2005).[1] When asked in May 2003 if he had a plan for a postwar Iraq, Wallace responded, "Well . . . we're making this up here as we go along" (Gegax 2003). In a later interview, Wallace said that he did have guidance, but the guidance was broken down geographically and into areas of responsibility rather than in terms of mission. "When you're in a pursuit," Wallace reflected, "you are not thinking about the day the shooting stops, because you still are getting shot at. And the more involved you get in the tactical combat action, the more you are intellectually distanced from the post-conflict situation" (Wallace 2005). Other accounts confirm the commanders' lack of a clear post-conflict vision. General James Mattis, Commander of the First Marine Division, said he had no guidance for post-conflict operations (Mattis 2005). The Third Infantry Division's after-action report (AAR) confirms Wallace and Mattis' stories: "Higher headquarters did not provide the Third Infantry Division (Mechanized) with a plan for Phase IV [post-conflict governance operations]. As a result, Third Infantry Division transitioned into Phase IV in the absence of guidance" (O'Hanlon 2005).[2] One could easily infer from these events that the U.S. armed forces had never performed post-conflict stabilization and transition duties before.

Yet from the U.S. frontier to multiple post-conflict stabilization missions during the 1990s, the U.S. Army was anything but a new actor to these types of missions when the Army rolled into Baghdad.[3] The U.S. soldier's rotation from warrior to peacemaker to nation-builder began with the country's birth and continues to evolve in today's operations in Afghanistan and Iraq. Before stepping into General Wallace's boots on that Iraqi street corner, understanding the U.S.

Army's approach[4] to stability and reconstruction (S&R) operations first requires appreciating how far the service had come (and how far they still had to go) since the military leadership purged training, doctrine, and education of any traces of counterinsurgency content after the Vietnam War. Despite uneven civilian strategic guidance regarding the importance and frequency of S&R operations since the end of the Cold War,[5] soldiers have deployed to a new S&R mission every two years: Panama, Somalia, Haiti, Bosnia, Kosovo, Afghanistan, and Iraq (see e.g. Crane 2001; Dobbins *et al.* 2003; Cassidy 2004). During these repeated deployments, soldiers gained invaluable experience in S&R, some of which the Army and Department of Defense (DOD) attempted to institutionalize.

This chapter examines the evolution of U.S. Army thinking from Vietnam up until the present day as the service repeatedly confronted the complexities of operating in failed and fragile states. Indeed, the U.S. Army has a long history of S&R operations (see Snyder 1947; Coles and Weinberg 1964; Utley 1978; Sandler 1998; Tevington 1998; Dobbins *et al.* 2003; Schadlow 2003; Thomas 2006). Due to a variety of factors, including an "American way of war" that stresses decisive, offensive operations (Weigley 1977), a collective amnesia regarding its rich history in S&R operations has regularly afflicted the Army. Yet, as recent operations have increasingly shown, the military is indeed an important actor not only in winning the war but winning the peace (Orr 2004). In many post-conflict environments, the U.S. Army has become a de facto government for a period and the primary instrument of U.S. foreign policy to rebuild the shattered governments of these states. Although nation building has long been seen by U.S. policy-makers as principally the mandate of civilian agencies, in reality, the "boots on the ground" have been key actors in implementing governance operations in post-conflict countries.

The analysis here examines how the Army is translating the increasing realization that it has a role in peace-building as well as warfighting into practice, and argues that the Army must continue to develop effective doctrine and training for these operations to enhance the chances for successful S&R operation.[6] Recent DOD policy decisions have increased the priority of stability operations relative to warfighting, and have mandated increased military cooperation with civilian agencies. This expanded emphasis on S&R operations, including attention to activities that contribute to rebuilding governance – not simply maintaining order and security – pose challenges to today's U.S. Army.

The long road from Vietnam to Iraq

Former Office of the Secretary of Defense (OSD) senior executive Richard L. Kugler stated, "In order to leave Vietnam behind them, the Army reconfigured themselves to be solely warfighters, and they did that brilliantly" (Kugler 2005). This section analyzes how the Army refocused solely on warfighting operations after 1976. For the Army, the Vietnam War represented the difficulties in pursuing traditional warfighting doctrine in the face of a nationalist counterinsurgency and the need to actually "govern" contested territories.[7] One year after the end of Vietnam, the Army's 1976 FM 100-5 *Operations* manual expunged all traces of counterinsurgency, suggesting the Army wanted to "flush out of the doctrine and training how to fight an insurgency" (Barry 2005).[8] The 1976 FM 100-5 focused on conventional and nuclear war, as did most army doctrine: "The Army in particular embarked upon a cycle of doctrinal renewal after Vietnam that focused on the challenges of high-intensity warfare to the virtual exclusion of contingencies at the other end of the spectrum" (Bacevich *et al.* 1988: vi–vii). Despite an increased focus during the 1980s on "low-intensity conflict" (that decade's name for S&R operations), due to fear of Soviet-supported insurgencies threatening democratic regimes, doctrine did not improve at this time for these types of missions. FM 100-5 *Operations*, published in 1982 and again in 1986, introduced the AirLand Battle concept. AirLand Battle, as the name suggests, emphasized close coordination between air and ground forces, speed of maneuver, and lethality. The doctrine, however, "concentrated on two main types of operations, offensive and defensive, with only short references to joint or combined operations" (Rose 2002: 73). In terms of applicability to S&R operations, one commentator held that the manual "embodies notions and procedures clearly aimed at European warfare alone" (Cohen 1984: 171).

S&R operations education also suffered following Vietnam. Although perhaps too little and too late, the Army did learn during the Vietnam War (Herrington 1997; Nagl 2005). But those lessons did not remain in the institutional memory or the soldiers' psyche. An Army Command and General Staff College professor traveled to the Army's John F. Kennedy Special Warfare School in North Carolina in 1987 in search of counterinsurgency materials to teach a class. "The old graybeard there told me that in 1975 he was told to get rid of all the Vietnam stuff," the professor said (Jaffe 2004). "Institutional inertia" plagued the Army War College's low intensity conflict curriculum, to include knowledge of peacekeeping, peace enforcement, and post-conflict governance (Johnson 2001: 136). The journal *Military Review* published 1400 articles between 1975 and 1989, but only forty-three of those articles dealt with low-intensity conflict topics (Cassidy 2004: 102). An Army-commissioned RAND study concluded that:

> The net effect [of purging Army doctrine of S&R concepts], while ultimately evolving into a competent operational doctrine (as evidenced by Desert Storm), was to convince a generation of soldiers that armies existed solely to fight wars and, consequently, that their energies, training, equipment, and ultimate success lay in the mainstream 'concept' of warfighting at the conventional level. [Low-intensity conflict] and related non-combat tasks were removed from the consciousness of the Army and were relegated to a corps of personnel who stepped outside the mainstream, with the knowledge that they did so at some peril to their careers.
>
> (Taw and Leicht 1992: 22)

117

Focusing the Army mindset, doctrine, and training towards warfighting alone made for a steeper learning curve during the 1990s when most were S&R operations.

The army's post-Cold War struggle to understand the mission

This disposition toward conventional conflict persisted after the Berlin Wall fell. Troops stumbled through operations in Panama (1989) and Operation Provide Comfort in Iraq (1991) using doctrine that former officers had purged of S&R content after Vietnam. Things were about to change, however. As General Sullivan, the army's Chief of Staff from 1991 through 1995, recounted, "It all started with Somalia" (Sullivan 2005). The Army deployed to Somalia using its FM 100-5 *Operations*, the manual that emphasized AirLand Battle from 1986, which the soldiers followed throughout the operation. Following the 1986 FM 100-5 *Operations*, which places "a clear emphasis on offensive operations designed to retain and make maximum use of the initiative in battle," the U.S. ground forces quickly escalated the violence in Somalia (Farrell 1995: 208). Using warfighting doctrine, when the mission met with resistance, the soldiers escalated the use of force. An appendix added to FM 3-06 *Urban Operations* in 2003 acknowledged this fact and highlighted the cost:

> Peace enforcement also requires restraint and impartiality to successfully dominate and achieve political objectives. The increased use of force resulted in increased civilian casualties, which in turn reduced the Somalis' perception of U.S. legitimacy. As a result, most moderate Somalis began to side with Aideed and his supporters.
>
> (Department of the Army 2003a: Section C-25)

Without shrouding the military operations under the operation's political objectives, the use of violence soon became divorced from the mission's underlying strategic objectives. This escalation of force ultimately undermined the legitimacy, effectiveness, and security of the U.S. operation. In addition, although the United Nations Operations in Somalia (UNSOM) had primary responsibility for nation building through creating political and administrative structures at the local, provincial, and national levels, the lack of attention to achieving political change, societal reconciliation, and institution-building undermined the success of the peace agreement. Thus, despite the temporary success of the humanitarian efforts, violence reassumed and the country was again plunged into chaos.

General Sullivan believed that the rise in S&R operations, like Somalia and Haiti, would continue: "I knew this would not be a passing moment" (Sullivan 2005). Sullivan made two moves as a direct result of Somalia to increase the Army's stability capabilities. First, in mid-1993, General Sullivan opened the U.S. Army Peacekeeping Institute (PKI), an idea that was "born out of Somalia

... I had gone to Somalia very early in the effort and was exposed to some non-governmental organizations, and it was expressed to me by people I had a lot of faith in" that working with the NGOs was hard (Sullivan 2005). The first PKI director described the institute as "a think-tank to help the senior Army leadership think through these issues" regarding S&R operations (Weinschenk 1993: 2).

Second, doctrine began to include S&R operations material again for the first time since Vietnam. Three manuals attempted to capture some of the experience the Army was gaining on the ground. In the first manual, the Army included one section on operations other than war (OOTW, which replaced the phrase "low-intensity conflict" during the 1990s) in FM 100-5 *Operation*, published in June 1993. One would have to go back to 1954 and 1962 for the last time when this capstone manual included similar topics (Johnson 2001: 155–156; Rose 2002: 72). In June 1994, a second manual called FM 100-1 *The Army* appeared, and included military operations other than war (MOOTW) as one of three operational sections. The Army's first attempt to outline an operational doctrine for peace operations came in December 1994, when the Army published a third manual entitled FM 100-23 *Peace Operations*. Although a step in the right direction, all of these manuals ultimately stressed the primacy of combat. FM 100-23 summarized the Army's approach to S&R missions best: "the philosophy used to determine *how much* and *when* training questions for operations other than war can be summed up as *just enough* and *just in time*" (Department of the Army 1994: 86; italics in original).

The idea that warriors need not train for post-conflict operations surfaced in several interviews. One interviewee gave the analogy of a fireman who trains to fight fires, but may occasionally save a cat out of a tree (Barry 2005). In other words, soldiers should train for war, but may occasionally have to pull a country back from the brink of anarchy in a post-conflict mission. With intra-state conflict growing in the 1990s, countries rarely exhibited a linear path from war to peace, and the cyclical nature of conflict required far longer and more diverse S&R operations. As more recent experience in Iraq, Afghanistan, and Bosnia has shown, the mission time from kinetic operations to post-conflict stabilization has continued to shift dramatically to the latter.[9] S&R operations also come in many different shapes and sizes. These operations include a broader array of functions – including re-establishing a national government, electoral processes, local government management, restoration of public services, and infrastructure reconstruction. The assumption that these were benign missions that required no significant training proved dangerous to the indigenous population and U.S. forces alike.

Bosnia brought the inadequacy of Army doctrine to light. As a United States Institute of Peace report found:

> The U.S. Army is a doctrine-driven institution. In Bosnia, U.S. Army doctrines were largely inadequate in an environment that forced commanders to wrestle with the political, diplomatic, and military demands

of stability operations. Almost from the inception of the IFOR operation, U.S. commanders found themselves in uncharted territory. Describing this challenge, Maj. Gen. William Nash noted that this was an "inner ear problem." Having trained for thirty years to read a battlefield, Nash observed that the general officers were now asked to read a "peace field." SFOR Commander Gen. Eric K. Shinseki posited that he had to confront a "cultural bias." Army doctrine-based training prepared him for warfighting and leadership at all levels, but "there wasn't a clear doctrine for stability operations. We are developing it, using the Bosnia experience, to define a doctrine for large stability operations. But it is this absence of doctrine for a doctrine-based institution that you walk into in this environment. There you are in a kind of roll-your-own situation."

(Olsen and Davis 1999: 2)

Having performed several post-conflict operations in the few years preceding Bosnia, the Army was in anything but "uncharted territory." The size, scope, and length of the Bosnian mission, however, meant that the operation affected a broader range of Army actors and special operations than the previous deployments to Panama, Somalia, and Haiti. Rather than attempt to further develop doctrine that stressed these were military operations other than war (MOOTW), and therefore something other than what the Army should do, the Army took doctrine in a different direction that increased the coherence between the warrior and peacekeeper.

The Army began redrafting FM 100-5 *Operations* in an attempt to move the Army past conceptualizing these S&R missions as MOOTW. The draft revision of FM 100-5 replaced MOOTW with four general categories of operations: offense, defense, stability, and support operations (Fastabend 1997, 2004). This full spectrum force construct "came straight out of Bosnia," said a member of the drafting team (Fastabend 2005). The idea of a full spectrum force argued that "'pure' operations in any of the offensive, defensive, stability, and support categories will be a rarity. Units typically implemented combinations of these categories over time and across echelons of command" (Fastabend 1997: 81–82). The willingness to make S&R doctrine relevant to the soldier on the ground demonstrated seriousness about these missions not seen in Vietnam.

Although the Army hoped to publish the new FM 100-5 in 1998, a new Army operations manual did not appear until 2001 – almost a decade after the last operations manual. The Army was struggling to define itself, and according to one officer, was asking a basic question: "Were we a combat force?" (Oliver 2005). The constant deployments to theaters that required troops to have skills other than those usually found in the warrior ethos made answering this question difficult. The chains of command, doctrine, and operating practices on the ground all served to remind the soldier that S&R was outside their perceived scope of operations. For example, in Kosovo, a group of women approached

U.S. soldiers attempting to forward a draft of a bill of rights. The list also included a "concrete request: three sewing machines.... By the next day, the document had made its way to a battalion commander at the 101st Airborne Division. 'Sewing machines! We don't do sewing machines!' " hollered the commander (Priest 2003: B1). While small-scale income-generating projects may have been outside the doctrinal and operational guidance, providing sewing machines would have had a positive and immediate impact on people's livelihoods that would have contributed to peace and stability.

As a result of the repeated deployments to Bosnia and Kosovo, the Army conducted a study analyzing whether current company and platoon training for conventional warfare applied to stability operations. The study, begun in August 1999 by the Combined Arms Center (CAC), identified 1300 jobs which soldiers at the company and platoon level would need to perform in conventional or post-conflict governance operations. The analysts took tasks from existing doctrine, the Army Universal Task List (AUTL, from which commanders create their Mission Essential Task Lists (METLs), which are task lists to which troops train), Army Training and Evaluation Program (used in training evaluations), some training tasks from the Joint Readiness Training Center (JRTC), and documents from assorted locations (e.g. the Center for Army Lessons Learned, the United Kingdom, the Army's III Corps) (Steele 2001). The study's team was to determine if stability operations tasks needed to be added to the Mission Training Plan (MTP) tasks, which would then institutionalize post-conflict training into the Army.

The study concluded that conventional and stability operations tasks matched up in 84 percent of company tasks, and in 87 percent of platoon tasks (Steele 2001). Several stability operations tasks were different from conventional operation tasks, however: control of civil disturbance operations; check-points; securing routes; conducting negotiations; conducting presence patrols; searching a building; processing confiscated documents, equipment, and material; and, operating an observation post (Steele 2001). Analysts recommended including those tasks in the MTP, but otherwise advised against significantly altering the rest of the MTPs. The study concluded, "Generic statements added to the 'conditions' and 'standards' components of relevant current MTP tasks would make most T&EOs [Training and Evaluation Outlines] usable for all Army mission sets" (Steele 2001). As one member of the study said, "The tasks that were there were about right," and it was simply necessary to add qualifiers regarding the conditions in which those tasks would be conducted for the current MTPs to apply to post-conflict operations (Banning 2005).

However, context can make a huge difference:

> [T]he particular task may be the same, but the conditions and standards are not. For example, the task of conducting a patrol is the same for both, but the conditions and standards are very different. Conducting patrols in a Peacekeeping mission is done principally as a show of force

or indicates presence, while in traditional operations stealth is paramount and detection by the enemy may prove disastrous.

(Flavin and Bankus 2004)

Given the different contexts, the Rules of Engagement (ROE, used to determine when units can use force) and Rules of Interaction (ROI, rules that govern interpersonal engagement during S&R operations) change as well. In the above example of a patrol, if a soldier reverts to his default wartime ROE allowing for maximum use of force, the entire operation could be jeopardized.

At least one study member fell into the "war is war" school, or that the best peacekeepers are good soldiers, likening the situation to a professional baseball player being able to easily play in a peewee league. The analyst did qualify these remarks, saying, "I'm not sure what would happen if they played rugby, but I suspect that if they have same command and control for the team, just the rules have changed, and [the] players could adapt" (Banning 2005). General Anthony Zinni, in speaking about Operation Iraqi Freedom, identified the potential problem with this logic: "We came to play football, but there was only one quarter of football. Then it changed to baseball, and we were still playing football" (Zinni 2005). If one expects to be a pentathlete (as the Army's Chief of Staff Peter Schoomaker often declares with regard to U.S. soldiers), two things must occur. First, the athlete must train for all sports he or she plans on playing. Second, one must be proficient enough in those sports to recognize the current game being played. As Carl von Clausewitz identified, "The first, the supreme, the most far-reaching act of judgment that the statesman and commander have to make is to establish by that test the kind of war on which they are embarking; neither mistaking it for, or trying to turn it into, something that is alien to its nature" (Clausewitz 1993: 100). The same reasoning applies to S&R operations.

At least two major flaws existed with the CAC training study. First, by relying largely on existing training materials, the study failed to adequately address the new and different requirements for stability operations. Although including some research from organizations like the Center for Army Lessons Learned, the overwhelming majority of the study's resources came from doctrine (written in 1993 and 1994), the AUTL, and the Army Training and Evaluation Program. Using old doctrine and existing tasks as the primary way to determine what S&R tasks the Army lacked was problematic at best. The "Stability and Support Operations (SASO) Study" had a second defect in that it refused to consider tasks for support operations (or, in the terminology of this book, many governance or reconstruction missions). Wrote the study's director, "Too many types of support operations exist to warrant either the development of separate Support Operations Mission Training Plans (MTPs), or even Support Operations tasks, conditions, and standards (TCS)" (Steele 2001). Conducting hurricane relief, fighting forest fires, distributing relief supplies, and containing hazardous materials were the examples given to justify this logic. One could argue just as easily, however, that a plethora of combat operation types exist (e.g. amphibious assault, airmobile assaults, desert warfare), but that does not impede training creation for these operations. More importantly, by 1999, patterns for essential reconstruction tasks had emerged from Panama, Somalia, Haiti, Bosnia, and Kosovo. Security, political, and economic vacuums bred instability that hampered stabilization efforts and reconstruction projects. Successfully performing support tasks (like turning on the electricity in Haiti during the 1994 U.S. operation) aids stabilization efforts (looting stopped in Haiti once the lights went on) (Blechman *et al.* 1997: 47). The link between legitimacy, efficiency, and security would be demonstrated yet again when the U.S. headed to Afghanistan and Iraq.

We don't do nation building

During the 2000 campaign, Bush's senior national security adviser, Condoleezza Rice, said, "Carrying out civil administration and police functions is simply going to degrade the American capability to do the things America has to do. We don't need to have the 82nd Airborne escorting kids to kindergarten" (Gordon 2000: A10). Responding to these and other remarks made by the Bush team during the campaign, the Chairman of the Joint Chiefs of Staff (CJCS), Army General Henry Shelton, said, "It is naive to think that the military will become involved in only those areas that affect our vital national interests." Shelton, however, drew "a line between what I would call nation building and what I would call sustaining a safe and secure environment." On nation building, Shelton continued, "Soldiers, per se, do not do that. . . . We can provide a safe and secure environment, but we don't do the law enforcement, we don't do the court systems, we don't get commerce going again. That is, in my definition, what you're doing when you get into nation building" ("Bush Aide Hints Police Are Better Peacekeepers Than Military" 2000). Right before the election, candidate Bush concurred with the General's sentiments on nation building, saying, "I'm worried about an opponent who uses nation building and the military in the same sentence" (Klein 2003: 25). Civilian and military leaders would undertake a long, costly journey together during the course of two Bush administrations.

Before U.S. wars in Afghanistan and Iraq put the military's role in nation building front and center, the Army published two manuals that demonstrated a shift in Army thinking regarding stability and support operations: the 1994 FM 100-1 became FM 1 *The Army*, while the 1993 FM 100-5 was renamed FM 3-0 *Operations*.[10] Unlike the 1962 Army capstone manuals that included S&R concepts, only to delete those ideas from subsequent revisions, the 2001 manuals included S&R doctrine in consecutive key manuals for the first time (Rose 2002: 77). This repetition is important since "[d]octrine is perhaps the key indicator of organizational change in the military since it influences so many aspects of military functions. An army's culture or mindset becomes institutionalized in its doctrinal manuals and its training and education programs" (Rose 2002: 58). As former Army Chief Gordon Sullivan pointed out, in addition to being a cultural indicator, doctrine can drive cultural change. In the case of S&R operations, it did both. The 1993 and 1994 manuals helped instill S&R principles into the force, and by continuing the concepts in consecutive capstone manuals, the doctrine indicated that a cultural shift was occurring.

Army culture had a way to go, however. FM 1 *The Army* pushed the full spectrum operation concept, or the idea that the Army should be able to perform offense, defense, stability, and support operations. As in previous manuals, however, a hierarchy existed in the full spectrum listing that made stability and support fall clearly behind offense and defense. As the manual stated:

> We must prepare for decisive action in all operations. But above all, we are ready to fight and win the Nation's wars – our nonnegotiable contract with the American people. The Army is, and will remain, the preeminent land warfighting force in the world. We serve as the ultimate guarantor of our way of life. Secretary of War Elihu Root wrote, at the dawn of the last century, "The real object of having an army is to prepare for war."
>
> (Department of the Army 2001a: 1)

A rather narrow definition of winning wars allowed for the offense and defense to still be prioritized: stability and support served as clean-up functions from the war effort rather than a necessary part of truly winning the nation's wars and sustaining the peace.

FM 1 at times still painted operations in strictly linear fashion: "Forces must be capable of shifting from engagement to deterrence to war to postwar reconstruction – seamlessly" (Department of the Army 2001a: 31). The idea of distinct operational phases (offense, defense, stability, and support) is at odds with both how the U.S. had approached these missions before, and the reality of most conflicts. During World War II, U.S. troops began to restore order in German towns as other troops advanced (Schadlow 2003: 90). Having a "temporal approach to war planning" allows planners to put "phase four operations" (S&R operations) on the backburner (Schadlow 2003: 91). The doctrine also assumed that offensive operations could produce "decisive victory" (Department of the Army 2001a: 31). Although the field manual notes that commanders should synchronize these missions, the operational descriptions suggest two distinct categories of missions: war (offensive and defensive) and crisis (stability and support) (Department of the Army 2001a: 31). However, in reality, as the majority of the intra-state conflicts of the 1990s (Somalia, Angola, Haiti) demonstrated, cyclical patterns of conflict or violence that require a combination of peacekeeping skills are more prevalent. Hence, actual missions would quickly blur, and enemies exploit, these artificial separations.

FM 3-0 *Operations* included many of the same concepts from FM 1, but as one Army officer said, "We would not have been anywhere today without this," pointing to his tattered copy of FM 3-0 (Oliver 2005). Each type of mission, including stability and support, received an entire chapter. As with FM 1, however, the 2001 FM 3-0 (as with the 1982, 1986, and 1993 versions) considers offensive operations as the decisive mission (Blackwell 2002: 111). FM 3-0 recognized the importance of training, calling it "the linchpin of strategic responsiveness" (Department of the Army 2001b: 3–11). Immediately after identifying the significance of training, however, the manual prohibits commanders below the three-star general corps level from incorporating S&R tasks in the METL (Department of the Army 2001b: 3–11). Instead of putting S&R mission tasks in the METL, the doctrine admonished that "units train for wartime missions and conditions first" and "commanders develop battle focused METLs" (Department of the Army 2001b: 3–11). The effect on the soldiers at the lower levels of command meant that they could not train for S&R missions until put on alert, which severely compressed training time for these operations (Cal and Hintz 2005).

As a result, for example, one soldier at Ft. Sill in Oklahoma received no S&R training before being deployed to Afghanistan, where he soon found himself heading an information operations civil-military team, holding a bag of money, and essentially serving as the mayor of three provinces – all with no formal training on how to perform those duties (Flavin 2005). Civil affairs (CA) officers in Iraq frequently found themselves in the position of playing multiple roles in a local government – mayor, local councilman, tax collector, and public works manager, with only six weeks of civil affairs training. The length of training for new civil affairs officers had been curtailed for Iraq from nine weeks to six weeks to get these officers into the field rapidly, and not all brigades were able to include CA officers due to shortages of this military occupation specialty. Thus brigade commanders, with no experience or training in local governance, also found themselves as the de facto government for their areas of operation.

Immediately after the Army published FM 3-0 in June 2001, drafting began on a new manual for S&R operations, to be named FM 3-07 *Stability Operations and Support Operations*, to replace the 1994 FM 100-23 *Peace Operations*. The manual explicitly fused combat and post-conflict operations, holding that "the characteristics that make our Army a premier warfighting organization also serve it well in conducting stability operations and support operations" (Department of the Army 2003b: 1–1). FM 3-07 also noted that "[t]he rule of law is fundamental to peace and stability," but qualified this statement by holding that "[c]ivilian organizations are responsible for civil law and order. However, Army forces may need to provide limited support" (Department of the Army 2003b: 4–26). The doctrine reflected the Army's discomfort regarding law and order missions, an important element in rebuilding governance in post-conflict societies. FM 3-07 suggested that in a case where no indigenous or International Crime Investigative Training Assistance Program (ICITAP, a U.S. Justice Department program) capability exists, the U.S. "should consider requesting civil law enforcement units from member nations of the multinational force to take the lead in these missions. This allows the military police to continue other high priority missions" (Department of the Army 2003b: 4–26). The Afghanistan and Iraq cases, however, revealed the danger of relying on other nations' or other civilian agencies' capabilities to fill security gaps.

Afghanistan: Operation Enduring Freedom (OEF)

On October 7, 2001, the United States launched Operation Enduring Freedom (OEF) in Afghanistan. A little over eleven weeks later, General Tommy Franks visited Kabul to celebrate the Afghan interim government in a ceremony on December 22, 2001. As the White House triumphantly reported, "In just weeks the military essentially destroyed al-Qaeda's grip on Afghanistan by driving the Taliban from power" (*The Global War on Terrorism: The First 100 Days* 2001: 11). Making such campaign progress in the "graveyard of empires" (Bearden 2001) should receive its due plaudits, but the months ahead showed just how far the United States and Afghanistan had to go before Afghanistan began to take steps along the path to reconstruction.

By 2003, the UN declared sixteen of Afghanistan's thirty-two provinces, which included most of the south, "too dangerous for its international staff to venture through" ("Biting the Hand That Feeds" 2003: 41). The insurgency brewing in Afghanistan deliberately began to target aid workers to slow down reconstruction efforts, a bloody reminder of the connection between security and nation building. Afghanistan was a particularly difficult nation-building challenge as many of the preconditions to a successful state were not present even before the war. The nation was fractured by twenty-three years of warfare, always had a weak central government and deep ethnic schisms that meant tribes, criminal elements, and warlords ruled the provinces. Few state institutions were functioning in 2002, and the infrastructure was crippled or destroyed during decades of conflict.

As in other missions during the 1990s, some in the U.S. military resisted the reconstruction piece of the OEF, at least at first. In reference to fighting the explosion of criminal drug networks and production, one military source said, "They just don't want to mess with that stuff.... You only have so many resources, and then they want you to start doing what is really a law-enforcement job" (Scarborough 2004: 8). The OEF coalition established the International Security Assistance Force (ISAF) to secure the Kabul region, which left "the remainder of the country to be secured by local militia, most of which came under local corps commanders and governors who were approved by the center" (Collins 2004a: 8). By 2004, ISAF's numbers reached about 8000 soldiers, with only about 20 percent of that total strength "on patrol on any given day" (Collins 2004a). The United States failed to convince other countries to expand their troop contributions. A frustrated Rumsfeld told advisers, "I'm tired of looking like the bad guy on this issue. I have no objection to spreading ISAF. We just have no troops" (Collins 2004b).

The U.S. came up with another idea to "expand the ISAF effect" without expanding ISAF itself: Provisional Reconstruction Teams (PRTs) (Collins 2004b). PRTs consist of a fifty- to hundred-person military element, and also include civilians with expertise in diplomacy, aid, agriculture, and policing (Collins 2004a: 9). Some in the military began to recognize the need for reconstruction, with the CJCS Myers saying in a November 2002 speech that "it may be time for the military to 'flip' its priorities from combat operations to 'the reconstruction piece in Afghanistan'" (Graham 2002: A20). The PRTs provided one way to focus on reconstruction as well as to extend the reach of the U.S. into the provinces, where the legitimacy and control of the new Afghan regime was in question.

The first PRT deployed to Gardez, one of the areas not considered secure, in April 2003 (Collins 2004b). Progress in Afghanistan has been slow, but in October 2004, presidential elections were successfully held. In September 2005, parliamentary elections were completed and many areas have been brought under central government control. Improvement has also occurred on the key development indicators: midwives are being trained to reduce infant and child mortality, 477 schools have been built accommodating nearly 300,000 students as well as 454 clinics to treat 340,000 patients per month, and key transportation infrastructures (roads, bridges, and highways) have been restored.

By August 2003, the Pentagon was so impressed with the PRTs that they wanted to double the number to twelve to fifteen teams (Jaffe and Cooper 2003: A4). The problem with expanding the PRT program proved to be lack of the high-demand, low-density (HDLD) military specialists required to field such effective teams.[11] A "senior Army official involved in personnel said that if the military sticks to one-year deployments for civil-affairs soldiers, it could use up its roster of these specialties as soon as [2004]" (Jaffe and Cooper 2003: A4). General Peter Schoomaker, the army's Chief of Staff as of August 2003, agreed with this assessment: "I'm going to take a little risk here, and I'm going to tell you that, intuitively, I think we need more [civil affairs personnel]. I mean, it's just that simple" (Jaffe and Cooper 2003: A4). Commanders in Afghanistan agreed, believing "they would need three times that many civil affairs teams to adequately cover all of the provinces in the 'wild wild west' of Afghanistan outside the ISAF-controlled Kabul" (Schweiss 2004: 24). HDLD units take time to recruit, train, and deploy, however. Unfortunately, not increasing the number of HDLD troops earlier meant that these types of units would not be available in the quantities needed during operations in Afghanistan and Iraq.

In addition, the lack of a clear concept of operations or guidelines for the civil–military interactions hampered efforts (Dziedzic and Seidl 2005). S&R requires as much unity of effort as warfare, yet there was little real understanding of the PRT roles, which included to: (1) help secure a safe and secure environment; (2) facilitate reconstruction efforts; and (3) assist the Afghanistan government in extending its presence and authority throughout the country. This desire for unity of effort ran directly counter to the desire of many relief agencies for clear distinctions between the military and humanitarian workers (Perito 2005). Recent reports indicate that there was and continues to be a clear lack of long-term planning for the PRTs to ultimately devolve their responsibilities to the government of Afghanistan and Afghan people (Perito 2005; USAID 2006).

Nonetheless, in late 2005, the Army agreed to expand the PRTs in Afghanistan to the entire country, and to initiate PRTs in Iraq. Recognizing the inherently difficult operating environment, the center of gravity for PRTs has begun to shift away from Kabul to Afghanistan's provinces. Since the national government's reach is limited in these areas, PRTs will continue to be one of the primary means of United States government (USG) and international assistance, as well as play a key role in stabilization of the volatile south and southeast. For the military, this has proven to be a fertile training ground for new civil affairs officers in local governance operations and operating with an inter-agency team. A recent assessment of the PRTs noted "improved stability requires activity across the full political-military spectrum" (USAID 2006).

Expanding the PRT concept requires that the military have sufficient military occupations specialties, like civil affairs, to man those PRTs. Under Chief Schoomaker, the Army unveiled plans to restructure 100,000 Army positions between FY 2004 and FY 2009. The plans called for the Army to decrease its combat assets (including field artillery, air defense, armor, and ordnance battalions) and, among other changes, to increase many HDLD units. By FY 2009, 149 MP units, nine CA units, and seven PSYOP units will be added to the force (Association of the United States Army 2005). The rebalancing initiatives also plan on taking some of the pressure off the Army National Guard and Reserves by increasing the number of HDLD specialties in the active force. By substituting HDLD units for combat occupational specialties, the Army made a strong statement regarding how far it had come since the operation in Panama. Building post-conflict governance capabilities into a force takes time, however, and these forces would not be on-line in time for the biggest stability operation the Army would undertake since the end of World War II – Iraq.

Operation Iraqi Freedom (OIF)

Secretary Rumsfeld chose Afghanistan as the model by which Iraq would be rebuilt; "some ask what lessons our experiences in Afghanistan might offer for the possibility of a post-Saddam Iraq? The President has not made a decision to use force in Iraq. But if he were to do so, that principle would hold true: Iraq belongs to the Iraqis – we do not aspire to own it or run it" (Rumsfeld 2003). At the time the U.S. launched the war against Iraq on March 19, 2003, the U.S. had 175,000 troops in the theater (Pike 2005). Chief of Staff of the Army, General Eric Shinseki, testified in February 2003 in front of the Senate Armed Services Committee that he believed the Iraq operation would take "several hundred thousand soldiers," although he qualified this response, saying that "assistance from friends and allies would be helpful" ("Army Chief: U.S. Occupying Force Could Number Hundreds of Thousands" 2003). When U.S. troops headed to war, they did so without all the help Shinseki felt was needed from the coalition of the willing.

Failure to prepare and plan jointly with civilian agencies would hamper the operations as there was a fundamental misunderstanding on the timing and scope of civilian agencies' ability to operate outside of Baghdad (Diamond 2005b; Gordon and Trainor 2006). There was also no joint understanding of the interrelationship between the local Army commanders who "owned the ground" and other USG agencies rebuilding local Iraqi institutions. Moreover, there was a gross underestimation of the need for postwar stabilization efforts, and hence the involvement of all branches of the USG (Brinkerhoff and Taddesse 2005).

All of which takes the story back to General Wallace, the V Corps' Commander, standing on a street corner in Baghdad amidst looting. General Wallace said that it would be hard to describe the simultaneity and depth of what was going on immediately after the regime fell, and how unusual that time was in his experience (Wallace 2005). For example, Wallace described how in Kuwait, when ships were being unloaded with Military Police (MP), he had to determine where he wanted those MPs to be in five or six days' time. All of this occurred during the so-called "Thunder Run" to Baghdad, so if anything went off schedule, "you've got a tactical problem on your hands" (Wallace 2005). As it turned out, six MP companies (around 2000 soldiers) were initially dispatched to Baghdad, and the looting proved difficult to stop (Barry *et al.* 2003: 34). This looting would soon become more than a tactical problem, reaching strategic proportions as America's lackluster response to the looting helped create fodder for the insurgency.

General Wallace said he did not intervene in the looting for two reasons, the first being more "ethereal" (Wallace 2005). Many of the looters targeted government buildings that represented the old regime, making the situation almost "celebratory looting" (Wallace 2005). General Wallace did not want to put his troops in the position of protecting symbols of the old regime against a people the U.S. had come to liberate. The second reason Wallace did not intervene was that "martial law was never declared, so it was not clear what authority we had to intervene" (Wallace 2005). When asked who would have declared martial law, Wallace replied, "I don't know, but that would have been a policy decision – a decision for the policymakers. But all I knew was that it wasn't done, so my authority was not clear" (Wallace 2005). Doctrinally, Wallace was correct. FM 3-0 *Operations* stated, "Often U.S. forces will not have the authority or capability to enforce civil laws in the operational area" (Department of the Army 2001b: 2–25). According to Wallace, the plan he received did not include law enforcement guidance. FM 3-0 also, however, states that "commanders seek clear law enforcement guidance from U.S. and multinational political leadership during planning for unified action" (Department of the Army 2001b: 2–25). Such guidance was not sought.

International law, however, mandates that occupying powers provide security for the population. The Hague Regulations state that "[t]he authority of the legitimate power having actually passed into the hands of the occupant, the latter shall take all steps in his power to re-establish and insure, as far as possible, public order and safety" ("Laws of War: Laws and Customs of War on Land (Hague II): July 29, 1899" 1899). Other international conventions require the provision of basic necessities such as food and medical supplies.[12] By definition, regime change means that the old government ceases to exist, so something must fill that vacuum in government. As the only large presence on the ground, that responsibility usually falls to the military (Tucker and Lamb 1996: 332; Walczak 1992: 8). A recent RAND study states:

> For the future, the U.S. military cannot assume that some other organization, either within the U.S. government or in the host country, will take responsibility for providing law, order, and security through the transition period from the end of conventional military operations until a generally secure environment has been established. Until civilian agencies can operate in a secure environment, military personnel will need to be trained and prepared to assume some responsibility for public security – including overseeing local police activities, providing short-term training, and directly suppressing criminal activity.
> (Graham and Ricks 2005: A3; Thomson 2005: 6)

Wallace recognized the cost of allowing the breakdown of law and order, saying, "We missed an opportunity for the Iraqi people to become part of the solution instead of standing on the sidelines waiting to see how things turned out" (Coon 2004). Unfortunately, many of those Iraqis did not stay on the sidelines, and an insurgency gained its strength from a disenchanted, complicit population and a disbanded, unpaid military.

In August 2002, then Secretary of State Colin Powell warned that Iraq "will crack like a goblet and it will be a problem to pick up the bits" (Gedye 2005). In fact, the problem in Iraq surpassed war damage. Decades of neglect by Saddam's regime had left public sector infrastructure in shambles, a highly autocratic central government, political power concentrated in political elites in the Baathist party, little local authority, and a security apparatus dominated by the military. As Rathmell (2005) notes, the Iraq that nation builders, both military and civilian, found on the ground was much weaker than what was anticipated. In addition, there was little social trust that could help in building a more democratic Iraq (Brinkerhoff and Mayfield 2005).

Some commanders understood the connection between stability and reconstruction, although not drawing the inevitable conclusion that the military would have to participate in reconstruction operations. General Franks recalled wondering where the civilian "wing tips" were to start civil works projects to "get the angry young men off the streets so that fewer troops" would be needed

(Gordon 2004). From where all of the "wing tips" would emerge was not clear, as civilian agencies such as the State Department or the U.S. Agency for International Development, unlike the military, do not have a surge capacity in times of war or crisis (Davidson and Schultz 2005). Nor do civilian agencies operate in a "non-permissive" environment, as the continuing insurgency made it difficult to begin normal political and economic assistance programs.

Once again, with civilian agencies' personnel and resources stretched to the limit, a failure to jointly plan S&R operations, and a non-permissive security environment where civilian agencies could not work, initial reconstruction was largely left to the organization with the capacity – the military. Even with vast military resources, there was a lack of funds initially to undertake projects and start the rebuilding effort. The Commander's Emergency Response Funds (CERPs), as well as captured Iraqi assets, were used to finance reconstruction efforts. Although relatively small in terms of the massive sums that were required to rebuild Iraq, they provided an initial source to "win the hearts and minds" of the Iraqi citizens. Yet without training and guidance on how to spend the money and determine its impact, these resources were not as effective as they could have been. For each dollar spent on reconstruction, only around 27 cents were actually made to projects that directly impacted upon Iraqis.

Tuning the car while the engine is running

Army Chief of Staff Schoomaker likened the Army's changing during wartime "to tuning a car engine while the engine is running, which is not only a complex task but dangerous as well" (Jaffe 2004: A1). Back in the United States, DOD and the Army continued to consider changes as OEF and OIF raged on. On March 14, 2004, the Pentagon released a document called the Strategic Planning Guidance (SPG, formerly the Defense Planning Guidance) that would require both the Army and the Marine Corps to examine their post-conflict capabilities. Although classified, one part of the redrafted guidance soon began circulating in unclassified briefings: "The Army and the Marine Corps will either create standing units focused on stability operations or develop the capability to rapidly assemble, within their respective Service, modular force elements that achieve the same effect as standing units." In short, the Army and Marines could either: (1) create a special purpose force (i.e. a constabulary) for post-conflict missions; or (2) continue to use general purpose forces and task-organize for these missions.

The Army's Focus Area (FA) created to address the SPG's choices quickly rejected the creation of a special purpose force, and therefore concentrated its study on how to improve the Army's general purpose force capabilities for post-conflict missions. One of the FA's primary recommendations involved adding post-conflict governance tasks to the corps' METL. The proposed METL at the corps level would read "[c]onduct stability operations and provide support to reconstruction operations" (Army Focus Area – Stability and Reconstruction

Operations 2005). The further one travels down the chain of command, the more specific the METL becomes. As noted above, previous doctrine specifically disallowed, and argued against, changing unit METLs to include post-conflict governance operations tasks, which increased the FA proposal's significance. Without post-conflict tasks in the standing METLs, troops would train for missions to which they were about to deploy with whatever time they had available. This training model – Alert, Mobilize, Train, Deploy – meant that after the unit accomplished all of the other tasks it needed to in order to deploy, little (or no) time remained to train S&R tasks. Instead of this model, troops would "Train, Alert, Deploy," which theoretically allows the forces to train across the full spectrum to include both combat and post-conflict missions (Schoomaker and Brownlee 2004). Lieutenant Colonel Donald Lisenbee, Jr., the lead Command and General Staff College student on the FA, asked, "How do you change the organizational Army to prepare for stability operations?" Answering his own question, Lisenbee said, "Put it in their METL" (Lisenbee 2005). General Wallace, now the Commanding General of the Army's Training and Doctrine Command (TRADOC), agreed that stability operations should be on every Corps' METL (Wallace 2005).

The METL's importance to the troops should not be underestimated, several soldiers interviewed advised. In his interview, General Volney "Jim" Warner, head of the Army's FA, asked: "Why do military people do what they do?" He answered, "From the time these soldiers get here, we drill into them that if you fail at your mission, the republic will die, and it is *your* fault. The *mission* matters. Money doesn't matter. Promotion matters, but on the margins. It is about the mission. I would rather die than get a U [meaning "untrained" or incomplete] on a METL and have the potential to fail at my mission" (Warner 2005). Warner cautioned, however, that simply changing the METL is not enough. The war plans would have to change as well, which requires movement on the part of the Pentagon. If the METL and the war plans did not line up, advised Warner, the result would be "a lot of 'U's," meaning untrained on the METLs. Obviously, the contents of the classified war plans may not be revealed, but Warner said the war plans have not as yet changed significantly to "push" stability and reconstruction operations (Warner 2005).

In addition to the war plans not matching up with the METLs that include post-conflict reconstruction and governance tasks, another problem exists with hoping that the METL solution will provide a quick fix to the Army's stability and reconstruction operation capabilities. There is a reason why general purpose soldiers spend most of their time training for combat missions: training for war requires a lot of time. The Deputy Director of Strategy, Plans, and Policy, General Kevin Ryan, pointed out that the infantry, armored, and artillery units must take care of their motor pool and their Strykers, do physical training, and perform myriad tasks in a normal day. Soon, said Ryan, the week is gone (Ryan 2004). FA student director Lisenbee echoed this concern, saying that with only so many hours in the day, adding more to the METL may mean something must go: "Here's another ruck in your backpack, so what's going to come out?" (Lisenbee 2005). Charles "Chuck" Barry, one of the NDU study authors, also voiced concerns over the METL solving the problem. The corps headquarters (HQ) remains a combat HQ, with post-conflict tasks just included as one more METL item. Therefore, when that HQ gears up for war, it will focus on combat (Barry 2005).[13] Finally, as General Ryan pointed out, the very fact that the METL seems a quick fix demonstrates how fast the METL can change ... including to take post-conflict operations out of the METL.

Another way that the Army attempted to tune its S&R capabilities during wartime involved the creation of a new manual on counterinsurgency – a field manual-interim (FMI), FMI 3-07.22 *Counterinsurgency Operations*, which expires after two years (Horvath 2005). The fact that the Army willingly wrote and issued the manual around a year after the insurgency began was a marked improvement from President Kennedy's struggle to include COIN concepts in Army doctrine decades earlier. FMI 3-07.22 stressed the importance of political aims, civil–military operations, and HDLD units in these types of operations. The manual identified the "American way of war" as including "mass, power, and the use of sophisticated smart weapons," but noted that many of the conflicts the country faces run counter to that mindset (Department of the Army 2004: vi).

General David McGinnis observed correctly that the Iraqi insurgency is "looking for us to be inhibited by our view of the war." He continued, "If you practice the indirect approach of [ancient Chinese military theorist] Sun Tzu, like the insurgency does, you can do it with a lot less force" (Grossman 2004: 1). For both the insurgents and the forces running the counterinsurgency, the people are the center of gravity – the population will ultimately determine the war's outcome. Accordingly, civil–military operations are the core of the counterinsurgency since these operations serve to build the indigenous government's legitimacy (Department of the Army 2004: 2–8, 3–2). More importantly, only a government chosen by the Iraq people will have the authority and support to be successful by taking the difficult and risky political and military steps necessary to defuse and defeat the growing insurgency (Diamond 2005a). The importance of civil–military operations and the initial steps toward re-establishing a legitimate government regime are critical to long-term stabilization efforts. HDLD units such as intelligence, civil affairs, and PSYOPs units are key actors in winning the population's hearts and minds, according to the FMI (Department of the Army 2004: 2–7 through 2–8, and chs 4 and 5). Demonstrating a level of commitment to improving the COIN manual that doctrinal efforts during Vietnam lacked, FMI 3-07.22 author Lieutenant Colonel Jan S. Horvath is soliciting feedback from soldiers, including those currently in the field. Should the manual produce unforeseen second or third order effects, those will be corrected in the next COIN manual produced in 2006 (Horvath 2005). In addition, Lieutenant General David Patraeus held a conference involving many leading civilian and military S&R experts at the Combined Arms Center in February 2006 to solicit feedback on the FMI draft.

Although the Army was making adjustments to how it approached S&R operations, such as adding METL tasks and FMI 3-07.22, a major Department of Defense study concluded that "DOD has not yet embraced stabilization and reconstruction operations as an explicit mission with the same seriousness as combat operations" (Defense Science Board *et al.* 2004: 45). The report stated that post-conflict operations, rather than being "lesser-included tasks of a combat mission," were instead distinct missions "with unique requirements for equipment and training" (Defense Science Board *et al.* 2004: 50). It recommended that to win the peace, traditional warriors need to be trained in nation-building tasks, cultural understanding, and economic recovery tasks.

Since 1995, the Army had begun to adapt to new types of missions, including S&R, through a structural change called modularity, which pushed the Army's organizing principle from the division to the brigade level. Modularity refers to "a force structure design methodology which establishes a means of providing force elements that are interchangeable, expandable, and tailorable to meet the changing needs of the Army" (United States Army and Training and Doctrine Command 1995, section 3-1). Each Army division contains between 10,000 and 18,000 soldiers, or three brigades of between around 3000 and 6000 soldiers. Divisions prove optimal against similarly structured opponents, like the Soviets, because they are fixed organizations that have interconnected parts within the division made up of specialists. When commanders attempted to deploy less than a division-sized force to a mission, especially when that mission required more of certain types of capabilities (such as HDLD units necessary in post-conflict governance operations), they ran into difficulties trying to mix and match various unit specialties. The Army's first modular brigade was fielded in 2004, with a proposed total of forty-two active brigade combat teams by the end of FY 2007.

Although the DSB report praised modularity, the authors warned that "modularity, in and of itself, does not ensure an effective stabilization capability" (Defense Science Board *et al.* 2004: 48). The Army would have to include "stability modules" with specific post-conflict governance capabilities. The authors went a step further, however, and called for the Army to be designated as the executive agent for post-conflict governance operations (Defense Science Board *et al.* 2004: 48). This recommendation did not mean that the Army would be the only service performing S&R operations, but that it would be the service responsible for heading the effort.

The DSB study was significant for many reasons. Among them, the report became the basis for Department of Defense Directive (DODD) 3000.05, "Military Support for Stability, Security, Transition, and Reconstruction (SSTR) Operations" (McGinn 2005). The Directive proclaims:

> Stability operations are a core U.S. military mission that the Department of Defense shall be prepared to conduct and support. They shall be given priority comparable to combat operations and be explicitly

addressed and integrated across all DoD activities including doctrine, organization, education, training, education, exercises, material, leadership, personnel, facilities, and planning.

(The Office of the Secretary of Defense 2005: 2)

The Directive is ambitious. It identifies the ultimate goal of post-conflict stability operations as being the development of "indigenous capacity for securing essential services, a viable market economy, rule of law, democratic institutions, and a robust civil society" (The Office of the Secretary of Defense 2005: 2). More importantly, the Directive does not simply pass off these tasks to civilians who may or may not have the capacity, or who may or may not be able to safely operate in the environment. Instead, the Directive identifies that "U.S. military forces shall be prepared to perform all tasks necessary to establish or maintain order when civilians cannot do so" (The Office of the Secretary of Defense 2005: 2).

The Directive mandates that regional combatant commanders, and others involved, incorporate stability operations into all phases of military planning (The Office of the Secretary of Defense 2005: 3, 9). Accordingly, the U.S. Joint Forces Command's Joint Warfighting Center (JWFC) and the State Department's Office of the Coordinator for Reconstruction and Stabilization (S/CRS) have prepared a Joint "USG Draft Planning Framework for Reconstruction, Stabilization, and Conflict Transformation." Employing the military concept of essential tasks, the document contains an Essential Task Matrix (ETM) that describes those post-conflict governance tasks which are likely to be carried out by the military and those which are the responsibility of civilian agencies, NGOs, and the host nation. The document recognizes that these tasks are "case specific," and major mission elements may change for the military depending on the situation.

Earlier drafts of DODD 3000.05 designated the Army as the Executive Agent for stability operations, as the DSB recommended, which the final draft did not include (The Assistant Secretary of Defense for the Office of Stability Operations and Low Intensity Conflict 2005: 1). Instead, the OSD's policy office was charged with implementing the Directive.[14] The fact that the Department of Defense declared that stability operations be on a par with combat operations is a significant step for an organization that had previously relegated stabilization missions to "lesser included" cases of war.

Baghdad and beyond: improving Army capacity as a post-conflict reconstruction actor

Presuming that the Army is serious about continuing to expand its post-conflict reconstruction and governance capabilities, five milestones should occur by the year 2015. First, the Army must continue adding HDLD units to its active and reserve force structure. Current service restructuring initiatives should take the

Army until FY 2009, yet as the Defense Science Board pointed out, more restructuring may be necessary. Second, the Army must continue to advance its doctrine to provide the essential mandate for these operations as well as provide operational guidance to troops. FM 3-07 *Stability Operations and Support Operations* should continue to be updated, and the Army must keep post-conflict governance concepts in its revised capstone manuals, FM 1 *The Army* and FM 3-0 *Operations*. Post-conflict concepts need to remain in the capstone manuals, and subsequent revisions must end the illusion that offensive operations are decisive. Only a combination of offense, defense, stability, and support operations working in concert provide decisive operations in today's wars.

Third, individual actors throughout DOD will have to implement the various recommendations found in DOD Decision Directive 3000.05. Since Directive 3000.05 no longer includes the proviso that the Army is the executive agent for these operations, myriad actors will need to implement a wide variety of improvements. Fourth, the Army must include stability and reconstruction tasks in the Corps' METL, actually train for post-conflict governance missions, and keep those tasks in the METL.

The fifth milestone involves the next post-conflict operation, which will undoubtedly occur before 2015, and probably sooner if history is any guide. Even with the repeated deployments during the 1990s, the services did not train or adequately plan (or disseminate those plans) for the post-conflict governance part of the mission, which resulted in short-term and problematic post-conflict reconstruction and governance results. If the Army's culture has truly changed to incorporate the importance of S&R missions, soldiers will be ready for the next post-conflict operation because of regular S&R training, S&R mission planning occurring before the operation and disseminated to the field commanders, and expanding the parameters of fighting the war to include winning the peace. The lives of those whom the U.S. intends to help, as well as American servicemen and women, rely on the soldiers' continued transformation.

Notes

1 The views expressed in this chapter do not necessarily reflect those of the U.S. Army, the Department of Defense, or other agencies of the U.S. government. Much of this chapter's research is based upon extensive interviews of over 100 civilian and military leaders conducted by Tammy Schultz, primarily while she was a Research Fellow at the Brookings Institution, an opportunity for which she is grateful. Dr Schultz also thanks all those civilian and military leaders who gave so freely of their time for this research.

2 For a different perspective on pre-war planning for post-combat operations, see Rathmell (2005).

3 For more information on the U.S. Army's rich history of stability and reconstruction operations, see Schadlow (2003) and Thomas (2006).

4 Obviously, all services participate in various ways in post-conflict reconstruction operations. This chapter focuses on the Army's contribution for three reasons. First, examining one service alone allows for more in-depth analysis. Second, the types of

operations discussed require "boots on the ground," and those boots primarily come from the Army and Marine Corps. Third, through extensive interviewing with soldiers and marines, the marines considered their service more expeditionary, making the Army the occupation (or "stay on") force.

5 All Presidential National Security Strategies since the end of the Cold War have prioritized warfighting. The only National Security Strategy to claim that warfighting assets may be sacrificed to prepare for more likely contingencies, such as post-conflict reconstruction operations, was George H.W. Bush's National Security Strategy from 1990. See United States of America and Bush (1990: 24).

6 Stability and reconstruction operations require that the country use all elements of national power – both military and civilian actors must be involved. Although this chapter focuses on the military's role in these operations, the military cannot succeed at stability and reconstruction operations alone. In addition, this chapter focuses on doctrinal and training aspects of improving the military's response to stability and reconstruction operations. We recognize that improvements must continue across the DOTMLPF (doctrine, organizations, training, materiel, leadership, personnel, and facilities) spectrum.

7 How the Army conducted the Vietnam War, and how (or if) the United States could have prevailed, is the subject of much debate. For an argument that the U.S. should have adopted a counterinsurgency strategy sooner, and why it did not, see Krepinevich (1988). Summers (1982) argues the other side of the debate – the U.S. could have won if the forces remained fighting conventionally against the right target.

8 Counterinsurgency is considered to be a subset of stability operations. In other words, not all stabilization operations are counterinsurgencies, but counterinsurgencies are a type of stability operation. One critical element that stability and counterinsurgency operations have in common is the centrality of the indigenous population's support and operational legitimacy. The Army's purging of its doctrine of counterinsurgency concepts removed critical knowledge of how to operate in these stabilization environments.

9 Whereas major combat operations used to take years, more recent wars in which the U.S. has participated last mere weeks or months. Conversely, successful stability and reconstruction operations span years.

10 The Army changed the numbering of its manuals to reflect the way the Joint Forces Command (JFCOM) numbered its publications due to the increased jointness of forces since Goldwater-Nichols (1986).

11 The types of HDLD units particularly in demand in post-conflict reconstruction operations are civil affairs, military police, psychological operations, engineers, and medics.

12 See: "Convention (IV) Relative to the Protection of Civilian Persons in Time of War, August 12, 1949." For more on the debate over responsibilities of occupying powers, see: Tucker and Lamb (1996: 322); Yoo (2004); Rosenau (1995: 122); Walczak (1992: 4–8).

13 Barry (2005) suggested putting a two-star operational HQ in each theater where the sole purpose of that HQ would be to run the post-conflict governance side of the operation.

14 National Security Policy Directive 44 (NSPD 44) determined that the Secretary of State was responsible for overall coordination of post-conflict stabilization operations, and provided the contextual framework for the military to execute a broader range of stabilization and reconstruction functions.

References

"Army Chief: U.S. Occupying Force Could Number Hundreds of Thousands" (2003) *Associated Press*, February 25.

Army Focus Area – Stability and Reconstruction Operations (2005) "PowerPoint Briefing Entitled IPR to Gen Byrnes," March 31.

Association of the United States Army (2005) "A Modular Force for the 21st Century," Institute of Land Warfare at the Association of the United States Army.

Bacevich, A.J., Hallums, J., White, R., and Young, T. (1988) *American Military Policy in Small Wars: The Case of El Salvador*, Washington, DC: Pergamon-Brassey's.

Banning, R.B.F. (2005) Interview with T.S. Schultz, May 12.

Barry, C.C. (2005) Interview with T.S. Schultz, March 29.

Barry, J., Thomas, E., Wolffe, R., Hosenball, M., and Nordland, R. (2003) "The Unbuilding of Iraq," *Newsweek*, October 6: 34.

Bearden, M. (2001) "Afghanistan, Graveyard of Empires," *Foreign Affairs* 17–30.

"Biting the Hand That Feeds" (2003) *The Economist*, October 4: 41.

Blackwell, J.A. (2002) "Professionalism and Army Doctrine: A Losing Battle?," in L.J. Matthews (ed.) *The Future of the Army Profession*, Boston: McGraw-Hill.

Blechman, B., Durch, W., Eaton, W., and Werbel, J. (1997) "Effective Transitions from Peace Operations to Sustainable Peace: Final Report," DFI.

Brinkerhoff, D.W. and Mayfield, J. (2005) "Democratic Governance in Iraq? Progress and Peril in Reforming State–Society Relations," *Public Administration and Development* 25: 59–73.

Brinkerhoff, D.W. and Taddesse, S. (2005) "Military–Civilian Cooperation in Post-War Iraq: Experience with Local Governance Reconstruction," *Lessons Learned Brief No. 7*, May, Research Triangle Park, NC: RTI International.

"Bush Aide Hints Police Are Better Peacekeepers Than Military" (2000) *New York Times*, November 17: A7.

Cal, P. and Hintz, W. (2005) Interview with T.S. Schultz, February 7.

Cassidy, R.M. (2004) *Peacekeeping in the Abyss: British and American Peacekeeping Doctrine and Practice after the Cold War*, Westport, CT: Praeger.

Clausewitz, C.V. (1993) *On War*, New York: Everyman's Library.

Cohen, E.A. (1984) "Constraints on America's Conduct of Small Wars," *International Security* 9: 151–181.

Coles, H.L. and Weinberg, A.K. (1964) *Civil Affairs: Soldiers Become Governors*, Washington, DC: Office of the Chief of Military History, Department of the Army.

Collins, J.J. (2004a) "Afghanistan: Winning a Three Block War," October 21–23.

—— (2004b) Interview with T.S. Schultz, November 10.

"Convention (IV) Relative to the Protection of Civilian Persons in Time of War, August 12, 1949" (1949) available at: www.yale.edu/lawweb/avalon/lawofwar/geneva07.htm.

Coon, C. (2004) "General: U.S. Didn't Note Post-invasion Iraq Power Shift Quickly Enough," *Stars and Stripes*, September 30.

Crane, C.C. (2001) *Landpower and Crises: Army Roles and Missions in Smaller-Scale Contingencies During the 1990s*, Carlisle Barracks, PA: Strategic Studies Institute U.S. Army War College.

Davidson, J. and Schultz, T.S. (2005) "What the Troops Really Need," *Washington Post*, December 17: A23.

Defense Science Board, Task Force on Human Resources Strategy, and Office of the Under

Secretary of Defense for Acquisition Technology and Logistics (2004) *The Defense Science Board Task Force on Transition to and from Hostilities*, Washington, DC: Office of the Under Secretary of Defense for Acquisition, Technology, and Logistics.

Department of the Army (1994) *Field Manual (FM) 100-23: Peace Operations*, Washington, DC: Headquarters of the Department of the Army.

—— (2001a) *Field Manual (FM) 1 the Army*, Washington, DC: Headquarters of the Department of the Army.

—— (2001b) *Field Manual (FM) 3-0 Operations*, Washington, DC: Headquarters of the Department of the Army.

—— (2003a) *Field Manual (FM) 3-06 Urban Operations*, Washington, DC: Headquarters of the Department of the Army.

—— (2003b) *Field Manual (FM) 3-07 Stability Operations and Support Operations*, Washington, DC: Headquarters of the Department of the Army.

—— (2004) *Field Manual-Interim (FMI) 3-07.22 Counterinsurgency Operations*, Washington, DC: Headquarters of the Department of the Army.

Diamond, L. (2005a) "It Only Looks Dead: Drafting Iraq's Constitution," *The New Republic*, August 17.

—— (2005b) *Squandered Victory: The American Occupation and the Bungled Effort to Bring Democracy to Iraq*, New York: Times Books.

Dobbins, J., McGinn, J.G., Crane, K., Jones, S.G., Lal, R., Rathmell, A., Swanger, R., and Timilsina, A. (2003) *America's Role in Nation Building: From Germany to Iraq*, Santa Monica, CA: RAND.

Dziedzic, M.J. and Seidl, M.K. (2005) "Provincial Reconstruction Teams and Military Relations with International and Nongovernmental Organizations in Afghanistan," *United States Institute of Peace Special Report* 147, September.

Farrell, T. (1995) "Sliding into War: The Somalia Imbroglio and U.S. Army Peace Operations Doctrine," *International Peacekeeping* 2: 194–214.

Fastabend, D.A. (1997) "The Categorization of Conflict," *Parameter* 27: 75–87.

—— (2004) Interview with T.S. Schultz, November 17.

—— (2005) Interview with T.S. Schultz, February 7.

Flavin, W.J. (2005) Interview with author, April 15.

Flavin, W.R. and Bankus, B.C. (2004) "Training U.S. Army Peacekeepers," *Small Wars and Insurgencies* 15: 129–139.

Gedye, R. (2005) "Powell Criticises Iraq Troop Levels and Rift with Europe," *London Daily Telegraph*, February 26.

Gegax, T.T. (2003) "Road to Anarchy," *Newsweek*, July 2.

Gordon, M. (2000) "The 2000 Campaign: The Military; Bush Would Stop U.S. Peace-keeping in Balkan Fights," *New York Times*, October 21: A1, A10.

—— (2004) "The Strategy to Secure Iraq Did Not Foresee a 2nd War," *New York Times*, October 19: A1.

Gordon, M. and Trainor, B. (2006) *Cobra II: The Inside Story of the Invasion and Occupation of Iraq*, New York: Knopf.

Graham, B. (2002) "Pentagon Plans a Redirection in Afghanistan," *Washington Post*, November 20: A1, A20.

Graham, B. and Ricks, T.E. (2005) "Pentagon Blamed for Lack of Postwar Planning in Iraq," *Washington Post*, April 1: A3.

Grossman, E.M. (2004) "Officers in Iraq: War Tactics Offer Little Prospect of Success," *Inside the Pentagon*, September 30: 1.

Herrington, S.A. (1997) *Stalking the Vietcong: Inside Operation Phoenix: A Personal Account*, Novato, CA: Presidio Press.

Horvath, J.S. (2005) Interview with T.S. Schultz, May 9.

Jaffe, G. (2004) "On Ground in Iraq, Capt. Ayers Writes His Own Playbook: Thrust into New Kind of War, Junior Officers Become Army's Leading Experts; Risky Deal with Village Sheik," *Wall Street Journal*, September 22: A1.

Jaffe, G. and Cooper, C. (2003) "Stretched Army Makes Do in Afghanistan," *Wall Street Journal*, August 1: A4.

Johnson, W.R. (2001) *Vietnam and American Doctrine for Small Wars*, Bangkok: White Lotus.

Klein, J. (2003) "It's Time for Extreme Peacekeeping," *Time*, November 24: 25.

Krepinevich, A.F., Jr. (1988) *The Army and Vietnam*, Baltimore, MD: Johns Hopkins University Press.

Kugler, R.L. (2005) Interview with T.S. Schultz, February 10.

"Laws of War: Laws and Customs of War on Land (Hague II): July 29, 1899" (1899) available at: www.yale.edu/lawweb/avalon/lawofwar/hague02.htm.

Lisenbee, D.G., Jr. (2005) Interview with T.S. Schultz, May 10.

McGinn, J.G.J. (2005) Interview with T.S. Schultz, February 8.

Mattis, J.N. (2005) Interview with T.S. Schultz, June 15.

Nagl, J.A. (2005) *Learning to Eat Soup with a Knife: Counterinsurgency Lessons from Malaya and Vietnam*, Chicago, IL: University of Chicago Press.

O'Hanlon, M.E. (2005) "Iraq without a Plan," *Policy Review*.

Oliver, G. (2005) Interview with T.S. Schultz, May 24.

Olsen, H. and Davis, J. (1999) *Training U.S. Army Officers for Peace Operations: Lessons from Bosnia*, Washington, DC: United States Institute of Peace.

Orr, R.C. (ed.) (2004) *Winning the Peace: An American Strategy for Post-conflict Reconstruction*, Washington, DC: Center for Strategic and International Studies Press.

Perito, R.M. (2005) "The U.S. Experience with Provincial Reconstruction Teams in Afghanistan: Lessons Identified," *United States Institute of Peace Special Report* 152, October.

Pike, J. (2005) "U.S. Ground Forces End Strength," available at: www.globalsecurity.org/military/ops/iraq_orbat_es.htm, October 9.

Priest, D. (2003) "Nation Building, at Its Very Corps," *Washington Post*, March 9: B1, B4.

Rathmell, A. (2005) "Planning Post-conflict Reconstruction in Iraq: What Can We Learn?" *International Affairs* 81: 1013–1038.

Rose, D.G. (2002) "FM 3-0 *Operations*: The Effect of Humanitarian Operations on U.S. Army Doctrine," *Small Wars and Insurgencies* 13: 57–82.

Rosenau, W. (1995) "Peace Operations, Emergency Law Enforcement, and Constabulary Forces," in A.H. Chayes, and G.T. Raach (eds) *Peace Operations: Developing an American Strategy*, Washington, DC: National Defense University Press.

Rumsfeld, D.H. (2003) "Beyond Nation Building," February 14.

Ryan, K. (2004) Interview with T.S. Schultz, December 15.

Sandler, S. *Glad to See Them Come and Sorry to See Them Go: A History of U.S. Army Civil Affairs and Military Government, 1775–1991*, Fort Bragg, NC: U.S. Army Special Operations Command.

Scarborough, R. (2004) "Military Resists Afghan Drug War: Some Officers Balk at Doing 'Law-Enforcement Job'," *Washington Times*, October 14: 8.

Schadlow, N. (2003) "War and the Art of Governance," *Parameters* 85–94.

Schoomaker, P.J. and Brownlee, L. (2004) "Serving a Nation at War: A Campaign Quality Army with Joint Expeditionary Capabilities," *Parameters* 4–23.

Schweiss, M.C.M. (2004) "Challenging U.S. Hegemony: The European Union's Comparative Advantage in Nation building and Democratization," March 17–29.

Snyder, M.J.M. (1947) "The Establishment and Operations of the United States Constabulary," Historical Sub-Section C-3, United States Constabulary.

Steele, W.M. (2001) "PowerPoint Presentation Entitled: Maneuver Platoon & Company Stability and Support Operations (SASO) Study," March 28.

Sullivan, G.R. (2005) Interview with T.S. Schultz, February 25.

Summers, H.G., Jr. (1982) *On Strategy: A Critical Analysis of the Vietnam War*, Novato, CA: Presidio Press.

Taw, J.M. and Leicht, R.C. (1992) "The New World Order and Army Doctrine," Santa Monica, CA: RAND.

Tevington, W.M. (1998) *The United States Constabulary: A History*, Paducah, KY: Turner Publishing Company.

The Assistant Secretary of Defense for the Office of Stability Operations and Low Intensity Conflict (2005) "Draft Department of Defense Directive Number 3000.ccE," Washington, DC: author, February 28.

The Global War on Terrorism: The First 100 Days (2001) Washington, DC: The Coalition Information Centers.

The Office of the Secretary of Defense (2005) "Department of Defense Directive Number 3000.05: Military Support for Stability, Security, Transition, and Reconstruction (SSTR) Operations," Washington, DC: Author, November 28.

Thomas, T. (2006) "Control Roaming Dogs: Governance Operations in Future Conflict," *Military Review*, January–February: 78–85.

Thomson, J.A. (2005) "Iraq: Translating Lessons into Future DoD Policies," Santa Monica, CA: RAND Corporation, February 7.

Tucker, D. and Lamb, C.J. (1996) "Peacetime Engagements," in S.C. Sarkesian and R.E. Connor (eds) *America's Armed Forces: A Handbook of Current and Future Capabilities*, Westport, CT: Greenwood Press.

United States Agency for International Development (2006) "Provincial Reconstruction Teams in Afghanistan: An Interagency Assessment," Washington, DC: USAID, Joint Forces Command, and State Department Office of the Coordinator of Reconstruction and Stabilization, Report No. PN-ADG-252, June.

United States Army and Training and Doctrine Command (1995) "Military Operations: Concept for Modularity," *TRADOC Pamphlet 525-68*, January 10.

United States of America and Bush, G. (1990) *National Security Strategy of the United States*, Washington, DC: The White House.

Utley, R.M. (1978) "The Contribution of the Frontier to the American Military Tradition," in J.P. Tate (ed.) *The American Military on the Frontier: The Proceedings of the 7th Military History Symposium, United States Air Force Academy, 30 September–1 October 1976*, Washington: Office of Air Force History, Headquarters USAF.

Walczak, C.A.M. (1992) "Conflict Termination – Transitioning from Warrior to Constable: A Primer," April 15.

Wallace, W.S. (2005) Interview with T.S. Schultz, May 10.

Warner, V.J. (2005) Interview with T.S. Schultz, May 12.

Weigley, R.F. (1977) *The American Way of War: A History of United States Military Strategy and Policy*, Bloomington: Indiana University Press.

Weinschenk, A. (1993) "Army Officials Are Preparing Report Detailing Somali Lessons," *Defense Week*, November 1: 2, 8.

Yoo, J. (2004) "Iraqi Reconstruction and the Law of Occupation," *UC Davis Journal of International Law and Policy* 11: 7–22.

Zinni, G.A.C. (2005) Interview with T.S. Schultz, January 31.

7

THE PRIVATE SECTOR AND GOVERNANCE IN POST-CONFLICT SOCIETIES

Virginia Haufler

States recovering from conflict, and seeking to prevent a reversion to violence, require the rebuilding of effective governing institutions as quickly as possible. One of the key tasks of these institutions is to rebuild the economy, which will make the reversion to conflict less likely. Policymakers need to ensure that infrastructure is rebuilt, services are provided to citizens, that there are employment opportunities – especially for ex-combatants – and that a tax base is created to support all of these tasks. But how to do this immediately following conflict, when public resources are scarce, local savings are depleted, and the post-war economy depends primarily on donor aid? Many people assume that the place to turn is to foreign investors, especially if the economy is rich in natural resources. Despite the risky environment, there will always be some foreign investors interested in entering volatile post-conflict markets.[1] However, given the dire political and security demands often facing newly installed authorities, leaders may not focus their attention right away on creating a positive investment climate, since they are preoccupied with seemingly more pressing issues (Schwartz *et al.* 2004).

This vacuum surrounding foreign investment policy in post-conflict arenas presents both opportunity and risk. The opportunity is for foreign investors to enter the country at a time when there is little regulatory oversight, and little market competition. But there is a risk that new leaders may decide to put out the welcome mat to foreign investors without developing an appropriate policy and regulatory framework. Policies and programs that unduly favor foreign investment without sufficient guidelines and regulations may undermine sound governance in ways that precipitate a return to a violent resolution of conflicts. The manner in which foreign investors enter weakly governed states can exacerbate or create conflict, and worsen problems of corruption and criminality. Peace-building missions, as Roland Paris argues, have meant both democratization and market liberalization– which in many cases "inadvertently exacerbated societal tensions or reproduced conditions that historically fueled violence in these countries" (Paris 2004: 6). Policies to attract investors must be matched by a policy framework of norms, practices, and rules.

In the following sections I explore the political economy of conflict, and the main issues raised by the role of private investors and commercial traders in post-conflict arenas. Because of my concern with the role that foreign investment can sometimes play in undermining peace and governance, the focus here is very much on the negative effects of investment. But this is not to say that all investment, or even most, can only bring ruin to a country newly emerging from war. Re-establishing the economy is a critical element of post-conflict state-building. However, I want to sound a cautionary note. Averting the potential negative effects of foreign investment in fragile states requires three interdependent groups to take positive actions. Private corporations need to be more conflict sensitive; they have tended to ignore or play down their effect on local political dynamics. Host governments need to put in place effective but not burdensome regulatory policies, particularly targeting those aspects of investment projects that tend to be the most destabilizing. And the international community needs to create norms and rules backed by international organizations and donor governments to provide a supportive environment for actions by host states and corporations, which so far the international community has failed to do (United Nations Global Compact 2005). Many of the issues raised here apply not only to countries emerging from conflict, but also to many fragile states.

The political economy of conflict

After conflict, a "normally" functioning economy that operates within the bounds of law can be difficult to re-establish. What exists is a war economy, one that has been disrupted by internal or external policy changes. A war economy can be created by policies chosen by the government itself, which may seek to militarize and close off the economy from an outside world perceived to be hostile; the extreme case of this today is North Korea. Economic activity is centralized in and directed by the state; if the state collapses, the economy does too. A similar effect occurs when a war economy is imposed from the outside by economic sanctions and deliberate attempts to isolate a particular regime from external economic resources. Economic activity often becomes centralized, but the sanctions economy also entails illegal trading and financial transactions. Illicit activities are often legitimized by the exigencies of war and by the fact that sanctions were imposed from outside the state. The economy is closed off from the world economy in some ways, but in other ways it is penetrated and shaped by regional illicit smuggling and money-laundering networks (Andreas 2005; Ballentine and Nitzschke 2005). Those who benefited from the war economy will be reluctant participants in a normalized political economy.

A completely closed war economy is increasingly rare. Typically, in the civil conflicts that dominate world politics today, state borders are porous and conflict spills across national lines. Fragile states are not able to police their own territory effectively, and policies designed to regulate flows of money, goods, and people are generally ineffective. In other cases, relatively stable states may become weakened by spill-overs from nearby regional conflicts, as has happened in much of the Balkans and the Great Lakes region of Africa. In these cases, the situation may be exacerbated when natural resource wealth becomes a source of financing for violence, arms smuggling, and the drug trade. In many post-conflict states, the weakness of governance is exacerbated by the illicit economy (Friman and Andreas 1999).

Empirical and policy-oriented research has identified a number of fundamental mechanisms by which foreign trade and investment can contribute to the political economy of conflict, by creating conditions that facilitate the eruption of violence or its continuation (Berdal and Malone 2000; Collier 2003b; Ballentine and Nitzschke 2004; Humphreys 2005). Some mechanisms are general in nature, while others are specific to the development and exploitation of natural resource wealth. The main mechanisms are: (1) the way in which resource wealth itself can be both an attractor for investors, but also undermine the rest of the economy; (2) the manner in which foreign investment enters a country, which can lead to the inequitable distribution of economic activity, often exacerbated by ethnic divisions, which can produce divisive and deadly political dynamics; (3) the way in which protection services are provided to economic actors at the project, community, and state levels can create or exacerbate political divisions and hostility, often between government and local communities; and (4) the manner in which government contracts are awarded to foreign investors and monitored afterwards can lead to corruption which undermines the legitimacy of the government, and of the project itself. These are all exacerbated by the existence of war economies.[2]

High-value natural resources have been linked to instability and conflict. There are two different types of problem that derive from natural resource wealth: the use of revenue gained from trading in high-value commodities to finance war and criminal activity by both governments and rebels; and the inequitable and too-often corrupt management and distribution of revenues from major long-term resource development, such as gas and oil projects. In a recent paper, Paul Collier describes six mechanisms by which natural resource development can contribute to conflict: (1) natural resource development projects become "honeypots," attracting new settlers into the community around the development, in addition to attracting rent-seeking by elites looking to control the new resources, and these changes can create conflict; (2) natural resource development can contribute to conflict by creating wealth for groups that control these resources, including secessionist movements that become more credible through their access to resources; (3) the revenue from natural resource development can provide rebel groups with the means to support continued conflict without depending on outside supporters; (4) the revenue from natural resource development provides governments with the means to finance government activity without depending on revenue from citizens; this autonomy often leads to less accountability and legitimacy of governing elites, which in turn can lead to a breakdown in the political system; (5) sudden extensive investment in new natural resource development can leave other economic sectors starved of funds; this collapse may cause inflation, unemployment, and a distorted macroeconomy that becomes a source of grievance for elements of the population; and (6) once an economy becomes dependent on a single commodity or sector for its revenues, it can become over-exposed to external economic shocks, which may cause significant damage to vulnerable groups that become aggrieved and willing to turn to violence (Collier 2003c). In all these cases, it is the great value of resource wealth that paradoxically leads to less national economic development and political instability.

High-value natural resources may be categorized by whether they are "lootable" or "non-lootable" resources, which have different patterns in their relationship to the outbreak of violence (Ross 2002; Ballentine and Nitzschke 2005). Lootable resources are easily obtained, often illegally, and carried from place to place. They also have the characteristic of being of high value for their size or weight. The classic case of lootable resources as a means to finance conflict is that of diamonds. Although deep-mined diamonds may be difficult to obtain and trade illegally, many areas of West Africa have alluvial diamonds, which do not require deep mining. Much of the diamond business in alluvial fields is by artisanal miners, who sell their diamonds to middlemen. These then become part of a chain of diamond sales, polishing, and marketing that stretches across the globe and spans illegal and legitimate markets and companies. At the initial stages, the diamonds can be captured by rebels or secessionist movements and used to finance the purchase of weapons and provide money for troops, facilitating the continuation of warfighting.[3] The income from diamond sales may also be captured by the governing elite, who may use it to fight rebels and prop up their own power regardless of popular support. In diamonds, there is a legitimate industry that could be further developed, and an illegitimate one that needs to be regulated or controlled to cut the link to violence.[4]

Fixed resource development ("non-lootable") such as gas and oil projects, or deep mining, typically require contracting between governments and investors to develop these national resources. That contract stipulates, among many other things, the percentage of revenue from the project that must be paid to the government as taxes and fees. These revenue payments can be a windfall to the government, allowing it to loosen fiscal controls, expand its budget, and distribute benefits through patronage to friends and relatives. If it is not managed well, resource development distorts the economy and encourages poor macroeconomic policy choices by governments.[5] Politically, it makes the government less dependent on extracting resources from the civilian population through taxes, and thus less accountable to them. In many cases, the payments become a source of competition among elites, corruption among bureaucrats, and politically directed unequal distribution among citizens. This "resource curse," as some have called it, has been associated with the outbreak of conflict (Karl 1997; Ross

1999; De Soysa 2000). The massive revenues from these projects may support authoritarian rulers by providing them with the financial means to increase the repressive capability of the state. For instance, when the deal to develop a new natural gas pipeline in Chad, discussed in more detail below, was completed, that country's corrupt ruler immediately used the signing bonus to purchase weapons. The end result is that revenues from legitimate business that have been intended for positive development goals instead produce conflict and underdevelopment. An already weakened state is particularly susceptible to the dangers of mismanaged resource development.

The potential for inequitable resource development is obvious from the fact that resources are by their nature distributed unevenly. We see in places such as Nigeria the consequences of the geographical concentration of resource wealth, where oil is located in the south and aligns with and exacerbates ethnic divisions. But trade and investment in general – not just in natural resources – affect regions within a country differently, and inhabitants may view this as inequitable. Policies designed to attract foreign investment may favor urban over rural areas, or one section of the country over another. Investment that has negative externalities, such as polluting industries, may be located in some neighborhoods and not in others. Positive forms of economic development may go into more politically favored areas, while some areas receive no investment at all. Resource development projects, often quite large, can attract people from other areas of the country into the region of development in search of jobs. This often leads to disputes between the original inhabitants and the sudden influx of newcomers.

In a post-conflict environment, these problems are exacerbated by the lack of security, which is one of the most intractable issues to face a new government. When it comes to private sector trade and investment, fixed investments face a much bigger security risk than others. Most light industry and services simply leave conflict-ridden areas, but large projects may remain in place, though in most cases they shut down at the height of violence.[6] Projects such as gas pipelines and mining operations may continue to operate despite violence, but they face threats to people and property. In many cases, foreign companies are obligated by their contracts with governments to secure protection through the use of government military or police forces. In a number of high-profile cases, particularly in Nigeria and Sudan, these very forces proved to be a threat to civilians. Government forces have used company facilities – private airports, helicopters, trucks – in order to carry out repressive operations against local communities.[7] In other cases, as in Colombia, foreign companies have tried to avoid the danger of being implicated in government human rights violations and repression by hiring private security companies.[8] In another set of high-profile incidents, such private forces also proved to be dangers to the civilian population, and were accused of corruption.[9] In all these cases, the inequity of providing security to companies and their people instead of to the local communities themselves can become a significant source of grievance.

The security situation in post-conflict situations is often fluid and unsettled. The larger security environment must be stabilized before private foreign investment is likely to become significant. Foreign investment during the early years will most often be services contracted with the government or donor governments, instead of spontaneous investment in promising entrepreneurial opportunities. Private contractors, as we see clearly in Iraq, require protection for themselves and for their operating facilities. Whether these are public or private protection services (in Iraq it is primarily private), these services will risk the same dangers as we have seen in Nigeria, Sudan, and Colombia: abuse, violence against the innocent, corruption, and dangerous mistakes. And, as in those other cases, protecting business instead of communities can easily become a source of continued political grievance. Monitoring and oversight of these contracts requires an effective government apparatus, which is also often missing in the early days of post-conflict reconstruction.

The problems with security and contracting are further complicated by the fact that much of this contracting is undertaken by foreign donor governments and international agencies, and not by the host government itself. Donors may have interests that conflict with those of the local host government. They are torn between using the post-conflict reconstruction contracts to promote their own companies, versus the need to establish a viable local commercial sector and local employment. The time pressure in trying to demonstrate progress in reconstruction in order to stabilize the political situation may work against effective, legitimate, and transparent contracting and oversight.

Rebuilding governance: the investment dimension

Rebuilding following war requires the reconstitution of the legitimacy and effectiveness of governing institutions. Brinkerhoff (Chapter 1) describes the difficult elements needed in this process: expanding participation, reducing inequity, creating accountability, combating corruption, introducing contested elections, and others. Where does foreign investment fit in this list? There are critics who argue that foreign investment has no role to play in reconstituting legitimacy, and that such investment undermines legitimacy by rewarding elites, increasing inequity, fostering corruption or patronage, and supporting authoritarian rule. Nevertheless, the majority of people around the world consider foreign companies to have a positive influence. "In 33 of 43 countries in which the question was asked, majorities think foreign companies have a generally positive influence on their countries" (Pew Research Center for the People and the Press 2003: 97). This includes majorities in every African country surveyed. But this general picture obscures the fact that different types of investment, and different specific companies, have varying effects in terms of legitimacy and governance. As noted above, the extractive sector is implicated most clearly in conflict situations.

Foreign investment can legitimize or delegitimize existing institutions and regimes depending on the way in which investment projects are embedded in society. A minimal level of legitimacy may be conferred by apparent success in terms of economic effectiveness: if the investment leads to higher levels of employment, profit that is reinvested locally, and services that are useful to the local population, then this economic success may foster community support and acceptance. The benefits of economic success, however, can easily be undermined by political dynamics. If the investment leads to increased corruption, lack of accountability by elites, and inequality that heightens grievances, then it will be difficult to establish the legitimacy of the project.

In recent years, there has been a call for the adoption of a "corporate conflict prevention" agenda. The goal is to promote practices by corporations that help reverse or mitigate some of the negative effects of investment, particularly in fragile states. Accompanying this is a call to governments and international institutions to provide a framework of incentives to foster corporate conflict sensitivity. This agenda is promoted most prominently by the United Nations Global Compact, which has held a series of policy dialogues on business in zones of conflict (United Nations Global Compact 2002, 2005). A number of governments, led by the United Kingdom, and advocacy organizations also promote this agenda, such as the conflict resolution NGO, International Alert, and the advocacy group, Global Witness. Today, there are a number of corporate conflict initiatives that range widely in character and effect, not yet embodying any coherent or centralized effort. There have been some attempts to develop a common framework on business and human rights, for instance, in the UN Human Rights Commission, but the proposed rules have not been adopted. While the issue was raised in the UN Security Council in 2005, there has not been any serious follow-up, although there is some hope that the new Peacebuilding Commission will pay attention to the corporate role in its activities. The most coherent initiatives to date have been the UN-supported Kimberly process for certifying diamonds; the Voluntary Principles for Human Rights and Security; and the UK Extractive Industries Transparency Initiative. None of these initiatives are linked to each other in an overarching framework. There are some common underlying principles, however, including transparency, respect for human rights, and a general commitment to corporate social responsibility.

Policy analysts have considered several measures regarding investment in developing countries, and these may have particular value for countries in the process of rebuilding following war. These measures concern what the private sector can do to adopt "conflict sensitive business practices"; and what governments and international organizations can do to facilitate a better public policy framework for international investment (International Alert 2005; United Nations Global Compact 2005). Most of these suggestions apply particularly to the extractive industries and their financial partners. The following section discusses the core principles found in the policy literature on this topic, and some of the main examples.

Transparency and international certification

Corporations are increasingly being pressured to be more transparent about their operations in fragile states. In the context of foreign investment, there are three main types of information that companies are encouraged to provide. The first is fairly straightforward information about the processes involved in actual business operations and long-range plans for a particular site which may affect the local community. This type of transparency is captured by the call for "dialogue" with stakeholders in a project. The second form of transparency, and the one that has garnered the most attention in recent years, is the demand to publicize information about the revenues a company draws from a particular investment, the payments and fees that go to the government, and the distribution of revenues in general. This type of transparency may also lead to calls for a revenue management system, which will be discussed separately below. Finally, the third type of transparency involves a larger framework of trade control, in which certain types of trade are deemed illegitimate, and information about legitimate traded goods is conveyed through a certification system. Certification involves both the publication of particular information, and a system of enforcement that is typically absent in the other forms of transparency.

All of these forms of transparency in the context of foreign investment are designed to enhance the legitimacy and accountability of investors, and in many cases, of the larger political system of which they are a part. Information disclosure allows interested parties to hold other actors accountable for their actions and inactions. When governing institutions are weak, transparency can be a powerful check on corruption by both public and private actors. The information may be used by citizens and consumers when they make decisions about economic, political, and social choices. Transparency can enhance trust and therefore cooperation among actors. Ideally, institutions will be strengthened by such accountability, which may enhance the prospects for reducing societal grievances and distrust (Florini 1998; Grigorescu 2003). In countries without democratic institutions, corporate transparency is often viewed as a precursor to more extensive democratic reforms.

While most of the benefits of transparency accrue to societal actors, there are also potential benefits for the ones making the disclosures. There is a "business case" to be made for companies to engage in dialogue, publish information, and support certification systems. Transparency can be a signal to others of trustworthiness and willingness to engage on issues of shared concern. Corporations that provide more information may be able to obtain wider latitude in policy choices, since providing information may reduce the suspicion with which many corporate activities are viewed. While the gulf between the private sector and the societies within which they operate can be huge, corporate transparency can enhance the ability of the private sector to negotiate with representatives of the societies in which they operate. It may also protect the "license to operate" of companies with investments in developing countries, where investment often involves direction negotiation with government agencies or government-owned companies.

The secrecy surrounding contract negotiations between governments and corporations has become particularly problematic in recent years, and especially in the context of post-conflict reconstruction. Typically, when major investments are made in developing or post-conflict countries, these require direct negotiations between government leaders and investors. They occur primarily for big projects, such as infrastructure, telecommunications, and of course the extractive industries, including oil, gas, and mining. These contracts are typically shielded from public view, and often include clauses specifying that the information contained cannot be shared. Both governments and companies have an interest in keeping the contract secret. Government elites may not want the public to understand exactly what amounts of money change hands, since that may raise questions about where it goes. They also may not want to share information about concessions made to one company in order to protect negotiating positions with other companies in the future. Company executives similarly may prefer secrecy in order to shield information from competitors and preserve a negotiating position or strategy for the future. Company executives also may simply not want to stir up trouble politically by providing too much information. Thus, both host governments and investors have been reluctant to adopt transparency as an operating principle, although this is beginning to change.

Examples of how transparency in investment can work range from very loose, voluntary initiatives, to more traditional regulatory frameworks. At the looser end are efforts to promote dialogue between foreign investors and local communities. At a micro-level, International Alert has been working for some years with oil investors in Azerbaijan to develop a more community-oriented process for investor entry (Killick 2002). Various campaigns to protect indigenous or ethnic groups endangered by investment include calls for more stakeholder involvement in planning. This kind of community involvement, limited though it is, may be viewed as a weak substitute for democratic participation in non-democratic countries. Unfortunately, too many of these efforts are not serious and constitute public relations, not public policy.

A more extensive campaign to promote more transparency is the group of NGOs organized into the Publish What You Pay (PWYP) network. The PWYP was initially funded by George Soros, extending his advocacy in favor of open societies to the extractive industries. The efforts of this campaign have been strengthened by complementary efforts by the UK government. Prime Minister Tony Blair launched the Extractive Industries Transparency Initiative (EITI), promoting transparency by both companies and host governments. Both of these efforts focus on publishing data on the revenues from extractive industry development, and support more reporting on where money comes from, and where it goes. These transparency initiatives are closely allied with anti-corruption campaigns, such as the efforts of the NGO, Transparency International. The PWYP has been gaining adherents and attempting to extend its reach and influence. The EITI has been adopted by countries with serious corruption problems, including Nigeria, Azerbaijan, and Angola, and it has the support and active participation of the World Bank. The EITI, though voluntary, establishes criteria on reporting and auditing requirements.[10] While most attention has gone to transparency in the extractive sector, the issue is relevant for a much broader range of industries, including infrastructure and finance.

Most transparency initiatives so far are voluntary in nature, with few means of enforcement. Trade control initiatives involving certification involve a deeper level of institutionalization than mere reporting. Certification systems exist already for many environmental and labor standards, but they are new to the conflict arena. Advocacy groups successfully launched a campaign against the trade in rough diamonds which was financing war in Africa, especially Sierra Leone. They called them "blood diamonds," and urged consumers to stop buying them. The industry, facing the potential loss of markets, eventually agreed to establish a certification system to provide information to consumers about the source of finished diamonds. The idea was to cut off the ability of rebels, criminals, and warlords to finance their wars by selling rough diamonds obtained from territory they held in war-torn states. The United Nations convened a larger negotiation among states, which led to widespread commitment by governments to ban the import of diamonds that are not certified. Certification is a form of transparency because it is a means of reporting information about the provenance of goods. It goes much further than mere reporting, however, since an effective system requires extensive control of trade flows on a regional or global basis. The Kimberly Process, as it is called, has a number of weaknesses, but some observers credit it with weakening the incentives for rebels to continue to fight (Smillie and Gberie 2001; LeBillon *et al.* 2002). Similar certification schemes have been proposed for other high-value natural resources, such as timber and coltan (Smillie 2005).

No systematic studies so far have analyzed the actual impact of transparency in investor–government relations on the legitimacy and stability of post-conflict regimes. Some of the advocacy in favor of transparency has an idealist flavor. The principle of corporate transparency, particularly concerning contracts and revenues between foreign investors and host governments, is not yet well established internationally, although it is gaining adherents. There is little consensus as yet on which types of transparency are most important, or at what stage in a post-conflict reconstruction process transparency provisions should be adopted. In general, I believe such principles need to be adopted from the very beginning in order to establish the framework for future investor relations. In Nigeria, the government is attempting to implement the principles of the Extractive Industries Transparency Initiative long after the initial investment contracts for oil development were signed, and those contracts include long-standing confidentiality agreements that would need to be re-negotiated.

Revenue management

The resource curse literature points to the need for government to ensure that revenues from high-value projects, such as oil and gas, are managed in ways that do not destabilize the political and economic system. This is particularly true during the process of rebuilding following war, when the need for cash is so great. In Iraq, the occupation authorities initially asserted that reconstruction would be paid for entirely from oil revenues. Current political leaders today point to the importance of oil revenues for reconstruction, although the oil sector itself requires massive investment and reconstruction in order to attain peak capacity. Under pressure to increase oil production quickly to fund reconstruction, policy-makers may be tempted to encourage investment without regard for revenue management issues. Companies are competing for lucrative production-sharing agreements, although many are hesitant to become deeply invested while the situation is still so unstable and security costs so high. This is compounded by the fact that the legal and institutional framework for governance is still in transition. The constitution is ambiguous about important elements of revenue management, state ownership, and the treatment of new versus old oil-fields (Beehner 2005). Prior to the invasion and throughout the reconstruction period, various observers have publicly worried about whether Iraqi oil revenue will be managed in a transparent way that benefits the Iraqi people (Human Rights Watch 2003; Open Society Institute 2005). The potential for destabilization is particularly high because Iraqi oil is located in regions dominated by Kurdish and Shiite populations, underlining the need for oil management to be part of broader political integration efforts (Beehner 2005).

Revenue management schemes have been used in the past to distribute oil funds in industrialized countries, such as Alaskan oil revenue in the U.S. and Norway's oil revenue, and these examples are often used as models for developing countries. One of the most significant efforts to establish an equitable, transparent, and sustainable revenue management system was developed by the World Bank for one of the poorest countries in the world. This is a project to develop natural gas resources in weakly governed and poverty-stricken Chad. It involved building a gas pipeline from the gas in Chad overland to a port in Cameroon. The Chad–Cameroon Gas Pipeline Project involved a number of major petroleum corporations led by ExxonMobil. At the time, Chad had few other options for financing the massive investments needed for this project. The World Bank required the government of Chad to agree to an extensive revenue management plan that would be embodied in domestic legislation, and not just a standard contract. Under this plan, most revenue would be directed toward development-oriented projects and overseen by a committee of "eminent persons." A percentage would be set aside for future generations, when the resource would be depleted. The intent was to reduce corruption by monitoring, oversight, and transparency regarding revenues which would ensure that the benefits would accrue to the wider population of the country, and not just elites.

The goals are to reduce poverty, promote pro-poor development, and support equitable distribution of wealth under a strengthened rule-of-law framework. This experiment has been held up as a potential source of learning for future similar projects. Unfortunately, the corrupt Chadian government has been doing everything it can to undermine the system, including recent efforts to severely modify the national law that underpins the revenue management project. In response, the World Bank at one point halted all lending operations in Chad.[11]

Some observers have argued that all major extractive industry development in fragile states, including those just emerging from war, run the risk of abetting corruption, conflict, and criminality; they should not be undertaken at all. The idea that there are "no-go" areas for resource development has been advocated by a number of human rights, development, and especially environmental groups. For instance, the World Resources Institute has called on mining companies to "make firm commitments not to develop mines in an expanded set of 'no-go' areas," citing environmental, social, and legal issues (Miranda *et al.* 2003). However, it is difficult to see how this might be enforced. Revenue management systems may provide a practical middle ground for state building following conflict.

Corporate-level management and standards

Some efforts to encourage better outcomes lie with individual corporations and their management. These are often categorized as "corporate social responsibility," and are embodied in corporate codes of conduct. Two principles guide most of the codes and management policies that are relevant for post-conflict peace building: conflict sensitivity, and "do no harm."

A number of organizations have developed guidance for companies about how to conduct a conflict impact assessment. Typically, investors exploring opportunities in politically unstable areas have conducted political risk assessments. These evaluate the risks to the investment project and to the company of factors emanating from the local environment. A conflict impact assessment evaluates the other side: the risks to the local community of the company's project. Few companies engage systematically in conflict impact assessment prior to initiating a project. Nevertheless, a number of organizations have developed guidelines and checklists to encourage companies to do this footwork before beginning a new investment (United Nations Global Compact 2004; International Alert 2005). The idea is that investors who have a more informed assessment of local conditions, and of the potential impact of the project on local dynamics, will be more likely to adopt conflict-sensitive business practices. These practices involve micro-level management decisions, including hiring policies, environmental practices, and community development and dialogue. So far, conflict impact assessments and conflict-sensitive practices are not widely or systematically practiced, so it is difficult to evaluate their impact.[12]

An important component of a corporate code of conduct involves the establishment of standards for the hiring of protection services. In the last decade, a number of corporations have been accused of complicity in crimes due to their relationship with security forces. Traditionally, when an investor needs security to protect personnel and facilities, they rely on public security forces, either police or military. But these forces themselves may not be legitimate – they may have been involved directly in human rights abuses and repression of particular groups. Some companies have been accused of knowingly assisting these security forces in these crimes, while in other cases the military may take over company assets to use for these illegitimate purposes. In order to try to avoid association with these public security forces, some companies have begun hiring private security for protection. But this too has its problems, as some private forces have been involved in corruption and accused of abuses themselves (see Avant 2005).

In an attempt to stem the foreign policy problems that arose regarding complicity, the US and UK governments convened a small group of corporate representatives, human rights and labor representatives, and others to discuss appropriate standards for companies seeking security services. They negotiated the Voluntary Principles on Human Rights and Security, concluded in 2000. These Principles provide guidance for companies, and host governments too, regarding the appropriate relationship between the private and public sector on security issues. The number of country and corporate participants has expanded beyond the initial group, and the Voluntary Principles now has regular participant meetings and a steering committee (Freeman 2005). Given the dire security needs in many post-conflict situations, there is a clear need to establish rules and norms guiding the relationship between host governments and private companies on security issues. In Iraq today, the extensive privatization of security has raised sensitive issues of accountability and control that have yet to be fully resolved. As investors begin to invest more fully in the oil sector, they will face the difficult task of rebuilding and developing oil resources in a dangerous environment. How they organize the protection of their people and assets will be a critical issue; they cannot supply protection that increases their own security at the expense of local citizens.

Changes in individual corporations' policies that address conflict prevention and peace building potentially cover a wide array of behaviors typically lumped together under the heading of corporate social responsibility. But they all address something about the relationship between a particular company and its local environment. These policies go beyond typical community development projects (clinics, schools). The goal is to address the immediate, local effects of corporate operations and ensure that policies are put in place to mitigate negative impacts. Ultimately, they are designed to increase the legitimacy of the company and its operations.

Post-conflict reconstruction, weak governments, and foreign investment

Foreign investment in post-conflict reconstruction can be a critical element in establishing a functioning market economy and in helping governments to create economic growth, jobs, and opportunities. But there are clearly conditions under which such foreign investment can be destabilizing. Resource development is sensitive, and has been linked to a host of ills.[13] Any plan for state building following war needs to address the potentially negative impact of foreign investment, particularly in the resource sector. As stated at the beginning of this chapter, three sets of actors are important to this process: the private sector, which needs to understand and mitigate its potential impact on unstable societies; the newly installed host government authorities, which cannot be so anxious to attract foreign investment that they lose sight of the need for an appropriate regulatory framework; and the international community, including donor governments and international organizations, which can facilitate action by companies and host governments by establishing a broader framework of norms, rules, and incentives. Clearly, the host governments in post-conflict situations are the weakest link. There are two ways in which the weakness of governments should be addressed: one is to rebuild the government itself and strengthen its legitimacy and capacity, as is discussed in other chapters in this volume. The other is to develop more fully the responsibilities of the private sector, and of the international community. This chapter has focused primarily on companies, which have not until now been viewed as genuine peace-building actors.

The examples given above illustrate the current state of what may be called "corporate conflict prevention practices." They include purely voluntary, company-level activities, such as conflict impact assessments. But they also include more enforceable and institutionalized efforts, including the incorporation of host governments into a larger framework of international action, such as is represented by the Kimberly Process and the Chad–Cameroon Gas Pipeline Project. All of these initiatives are still in the early stages of experimentation, and as noted above, the Chad–Cameroon Pipeline Project is hanging by a thread at the time of writing. Most initiatives are voluntary, and do not address the need for political commitment on the part of both donor governments and host governments to regulate the effects of resource development on the dynamics of conflict. There has been a proliferation of codes and standards for companies, but they cover only a handful of companies or issues, and do not have sufficient authority to be effective. Many codes are self-selecting, i.e. companies choose whether or not to adopt them. They are also self-enforcing, which means that enforcement tends to be weak or non-existent. At a broader level, the example of the Kimberly Process shows what can be accomplished when governments and corporations negotiate a regulatory framework at the international level, providing the incentives for host governments and companies to comply with high standards of conduct. However, in general, there has been little harmonization among governments in the regulation of trade and investment, reflecting collective action dilemmas among states. A recent report produced by the U.N. Global Compact argues that the international community can do much more to provide incentives to both the private sector and host governments, to encourage them to deal more directly with the negative impact of some forms of investment (UN Global Compact 2005).[14]

Rebuilding after war must include attention to the macro-level regulatory infrastructure. As Roland Paris argues, we need to pay attention to "institutionalization before liberalization" in seeking to establish sustainable liberal market democracies in post-conflict arenas (Paris 2004). This includes developing a regulatory infrastructure which minimizes risks to citizens from development and provides some central core of stability during a period of great transition. The biggest need, of course, is to re-establish security for everyone. Almost by definition, host governments are the weakest policy actors during the period of rebuilding, and yet they are the most crucial. Host governments are the main partners with many of the investors that operate in unstable regions. At the same time, in some cases, it is those very governments that bear the greatest responsibility for breakdown. How they manage their relationships with foreign investors influences their perceived legitimacy, and is a crucial element in establishing a sustainable peace.

Notes

1 The telecommunications sector has been willing to invest in countries just emerging from conflict. Around $130 million was invested in this sector in Afghanistan after the conflict there, and more than 200 companies participated in bidding on Iraqi phone licenses in 2003 (Carvalho and Melhem 2005).

2 There is an extensive debate over "greed" versus "grievance" as factors in modern civil conflict. Some of the early work included that of Keen (1998), Berdal and Malone (2000), and Collier (2000a). These can be linked to some degree to analyses of the "new wars" described by Duffield (2001) and Kaldor (1999), and critiqued by Newman (2004).

3 For excellent overviews of the role of resource flows in conflict, particularly regarding diamonds, see Smillie et al. (2000); LeBillon et al. (2002); and Humphreys (2005).

4 The policy debates over what to do about so-called conflict diamonds acknowledge the difficulty of distinguishing between legitimate and illegitimate diamonds and diamond trading. The fear is that any action against conflict diamonds might undermine legitimate markets and states with well-managed diamond sectors.

5 This is often referred to as the "Dutch disease," named after the Dutch experience with the macroeconomic pitfalls of oil resource development.

6 Most businesses flee violence, but some do not. If the violence is in a distant or inaccessible part of the country, or if the firm is not itself a target of attack, then business will continue to the extent possible. For example, the oil industry continued operating throughout the Angolan civil war because it was not a target of attack, and most of the fighting was outside the oil-producing areas (Berman 2000).

7 There are conflicting reports of the degree of direct complicity by companies in these repressive operations. In fact, the definition of complicity in cases such as these is a subject of evolving practice. See Ramasastry (2002).

8 For a thorough analysis of the global private security sector, see Avant (2005).
9 There are disputes about the exact relationship between company managers and both government and private security forces. Some within the companies defend themselves as unwitting accomplices in atrocities, while others accuse them of acting in full knowledge of the dangers of using any sort of security force in such an uncertain environment.
10 See www.eitransparency.org.
11 For more information, see the World Bank website at www.worldbank.org; the case study and research tool maintained by Columbia University at www.columbia.edu/itc/sipa/martin/chad-cam/; and a recent academic analysis in Pegg (2006).
12 Collaborative for Development Action (CDA) is attempting to develop metrics on this issue. See www.cdainc.cazzz for more information.
13 Note, however, that not all resource development in developing countries is entirely negative. For instance, most observers point to Botswana as a poor country that is dependent on diamond exports for much of its income, and yet it does not suffer all the ills seen in other diamond development states.
14 The United Nations Global Compact commissioned a report on the policy framework that could and should be developed by governments and international organizations, to which the author contributed (see United Nations Global Compact 2005).

References

Andreas, P. (2005) "Criminalizing Consequences of Sanctions: Embargo Busting and Its Legacy," *International Studies Quarterly* 49(2): 335–360.

Avant, D. (2005) *The Market for Force*, Cambridge: Cambridge University Press.

Ballentine, K. and Nitzschke, H. (2004) "The Political Economy of Civil War and Conflict Transformation," in D. Bloomfield, M. Fischer, and B. Schmelze (eds) *The Berghof Handbook for Conflict Transformation*, Berghof: Berghof Research Center for Constructive Conflict Management, pp. 1–24.

—— (eds) (2005) *Profiting from Peace: Managing the Resource Dimensions of Civil War*, Boulder, CO: Lynne Rienner.

Beehner, L. (2005) *Iraq and Oil: Revenue-sharing Among Regions*, New York: Council on Foreign Relations.

Berdal, M. and Malone, D.M. (eds) (2000) *Greed and Grievance: Economic Agendas in Civil Wars*, Boulder, CO: Lynne Rienner.

Berman, J. (2000) "Corporations and Conflict: How Managers Think About War," *Harvard International Review* Fall: 28–32.

Carvalho, A. and Melhem, S. (2005) "Attracting Investment in Post-conflict Countries: The Importance of Telecommunications," Archived Discussion, Washington, DC: World Bank.

Collier, P. (2000a) "Doing Well Out of War: An Economic Perspective," in M. Berdal and D. Malone (eds) *Greed and Grievance: Economic Agendas in Civil War*, Boulder, CO: Lynne Rienner, pp. 91–112.

Collier, P. (2003b) *Breaking the Conflict Trap: Civil War and Development Policy*, Washington, DC: World Bank.

Collier, P. (2003c) *Natural Resources, Development, and Conflict: Channels of Causation and Policy Interventions*, Unpublished ms.

De Soysa, I. (2000) "The Resource Curse: Are Civil Wars Driven by Rapacity or Paucity?," in M. Berdal and D. Malone (eds) *Greed or Grievance: Economic Agendas in Civil Wars*, Boulder, CO: Lynne Rienner, pp. 113–136.

Duffield, M. (2001) *Global Governance and the New Wars: The Merging of Development and Security*, London: Zed Books.

Florini, A. (1998) "The End of Secrecy," *Foreign Policy* 111: 50–63.

Freeman, B. (2005) "Corporate Social Responsibility – Confusion or Multi-Pronged Approach?" Congressional Human Rights Caucus Members' Briefing, Washington, DC.

Friman, R. and Andreas, P. (eds) (1999) *The Illicit Global Economy and State Power*, Lanham, MD: Rowman & Littlefield.

Grigorescu, A. (2003) "International Organizations and Government Transparency: Linking the International and Domestic Realms," *International Studies Quarterly* 47: 643–667.

Human Rights Watch (2003) *Considerations for the Management of Oil in Iraq: A Human Rights Watch Background Briefing*, Washington, DC: Human Rights Watch.

Humphreys, M. (2005) "Natural Resources, Conflict, and Conflict Resolution," *Journal of Conflict Resolution* 49(4): 508–537.

International Alert (2005) *Conflict-sensitive Business Practice: Guidance for Extractive Industries*, London: International Alert.

Kaldor, M. (1999) *New and Old Wars: Organized Violence in a Global Era*, Oxford: Polity Press.

Karl, T.L. (1997) *Oil Booms and Petro-states*, Los Angeles and San Francisco: University of California Press.

Keen, D. (1998) *The Economic Functions of Violence in Civil Wars*, Oxford: Oxford University Press, for the International Institute for Strategic Studies.

Killick, N. (2002) *Case Study No. 4: Oil and Gas Development in Azerbaijan*, London: Business Partners in Development.

LeBillon, P., Sherman, J., and Hartwell, M. (2002) *Controlling Resource Flows to Civil Wars: A Review and Analysis of Current Policies and Legal Instruments*, Bellagio, Italy: International Peace Academy Report.

Miranda, M., Burris, P., Bincang, J.F., Shearman, P., Briones, J.O, La Viñ, A., and Menard, S. (2003) *Mining and Critical Ecosystems: Mapping the Risks*, Washington, DC: World Resources Institute.

Newman, E. (2004) "The 'New Wars' Debate: A Historical Perspective is Needed," *Security Dialogue* 2: 173–189.

Open Society Institute (2005) *Iraqi Oil Wealth: Issues of Governance and Development*, London: Open Society Institute.

Paris, R. (2004) *At War's End: Building Peace after Civil Conflict*, Cambridge: Cambridge University Press.

Pegg, S. (2006) "Can Policy Intervention Beat the Resource Curse? Evidence from the Chad–Cameroon Pipeline Project," *African Affairs* 105: 1–25.

Pew Research Center for the People and the Press (2003) *Views of a Changing World, June 2003*, Washington, DC: Pew Research Center for the People and the Press.

Ramasastry, A. (2002) "Corporate Complicity: From Nuremberg to Rangoon. An Examination of Forced Labor Cases and Their Impact on the Liability of Multinational Corporations," *Berkeley Journal of International Law* 20(1): 91–159.

Ross, M.L. (1999) "The Political Economy of the Resource Curse," *World Politics* 51(2): 297–323.

—— (2002) "Oil, Drugs and Diamonds: How do Natural Resources Vary in their Impact on Civil War?," ms, Los Angeles, CA, pp. 1–36.

Schwartz, J., Hahn, S., and Bannon, I. (2004) "The Private Sector's Role in the Provision of Infrastructure in Post-conflict Countries: Patterns and Policy Options," *Social Development Papers, Conflict Prevention and Reconstruction*, Washington, DC: World Bank, pp. 1–46.

Smillie, I. (2005) "What Lessons from the Kimberly Process Certification Scheme?." in K. Ballentine and H. Nitzchke (eds) *Profiting from Peace: Managing the Resource Dimensions of Civil War*, Boulder, CO: Lynn Rienner, pp. 47–68.

Smillie, I. and Gberie, L. (2001) "Dirty Diamonds and Civil Society," Partnership Africa Canada, Fourth CIVICUS World Assembly, Vancouver, BC.

Smillie, I., Gberie, L., and Hazleton, R. (2000) *The Heart of the Matter: Sierra Leone, Diamonds, and Human Security*, Ottawa, Ont: Partnership Africa Canada.

United Nations Global Compact (2002) *Dialogue on Business in Zones of Conflict: Rapporteur's Report*, New York: United Nations, pp. 1–5.

—— (2004) *Business Guide to Conflict Impact Assessment*, New York: United Nations.

—— (2005) *Enabling Economies of Peace: Public Policy for Conflict-sensitive Business*, New York: United Nations.

8

REBUILDING AND REFORMING CIVIL SERVICES IN POST-CONFLICT SOCIETIES

Harry Blair

The bottom line of the social contract between a modern state and its citizens holds that the state must secure the life and limb of its citizens, who in turn must give their first civic loyalty to the state.[1] In violent conflict both sides generally fail in these obligations, whether through inability or unwillingness to fulfill them, and it can take many years to reweave the social contract. It stands to reason, then, that the primary donor strategic objective in the post-conflict state has generally been to combine stability with an anti-poverty-oriented development program. The primary path to that objective has been to rebuild (or build) a state that is accountable to its citizenry, or in other words a democratic governance system. Very prominent among the institutions involved in that process should be the civil service, as the main agent delivering the state's obligations to the citizenry and encouraging the latter to accord legitimacy to the state. Surprisingly, though, while the international donor community has in recent years devoted much attention to the general problem of post-conflict reconstruction, it has given relatively little consideration to rebuilding and reforming civil services.[2] This chapter is intended to address this deficit.

The chapter opens by defining "civil service" and locating the post-conflict state within the general rubric of fragile state systems by employing several typologies and key concepts, in particular the "principal–agent" problem in terms of the civil service as agent. A second section explores a number of approaches to monitoring and accountability in post-conflict bureaucracies. The third and final section discusses these approaches as strategy options for donors.

Definitions and typologies

Civil service

Definitions of "civil service" have varied from the British colonial concept of a small professional cadre of elite managers serving as the "steel frame" of empire (the Indian Civil Service) to an all-inclusive term covering everyone on any kind of government payroll. For simplicity's sake, I will employ the World Bank's definition of civil servants as "those personnel (outside public enterprises) whose salaries are supported by the central government's wage bill" (World Bank 1999: 1). This would include all "line ministry" (e.g. health, education, agriculture) employees as well as military and police personnel.[3]

Core state functions

In his introductory chapter to this volume, Brinkerhoff lists three core functions a state must undertake if it is to be a sustainable enterprise: assuring security; achieving effectiveness; and generating legitimacy. All three functions are dependent on a civil service. Security needs an operational police power and justice system; effectiveness as used here means delivery of essential services like water, health, sanitation, electricity, and education; and legitimacy requires a state to provide political governance that citizens are willing to accept as valid. In this chapter, our main interest centers on service delivery.

State legitimacy and accountability

For a state to be sustainable over time and promote development that will benefit the population as a whole, it must be accountable to its citizenry. The World Bank posits that there are two basic routes to accountability, as shown in Figure 8.1.[4] In the "short route" citizens/consumers deal directly with the providers (private firms, NGOs, INGOs, international public agencies, the state) in acquiring services by purchase or – especially in the early days of post-conflict assistance – by relief distribution. In the "long route," consumers exercise "voice" (participation in the political process) to influence the state (i.e. the legislature or the executive directing the bureaucracy) to offer services through arrangements (a "compact") with providers.

The short route is the most direct one, and, when the state can maintain the necessary operating conditions (property and contract rights, monitoring quality standards, e.g. for medicines), it provides the best way to distribute the goods and services that can be allocated through a market. For the services that cannot be allocated through a market – particularly those enumerated above as the "core state functions" – the long route is the preferred one, because it allows the citizenry to set the rules of behavior through representative government. And even when a market-managed short route is best, the long route must function to assure that the short route will be maintained in good working order.

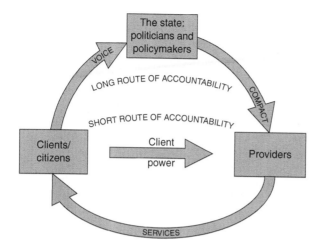

Figure 8.1 The long and short routes to accountability for service delivery (source: Adapted from World Bank (2004: 49)).

The central role of a civil service is to keep the right side of the long route operating and maintain the conditions for a smoothly functioning short route, as indicated in Figure 8.2. This role can be a large one, where various echelons of the civil service draw up the rules to implement the broad policies determined by the political leaders, operate the organizations to deliver services, and finally provide

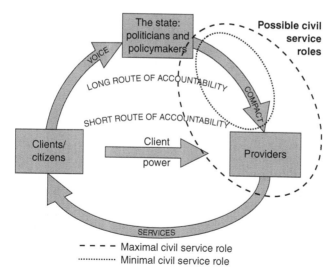

Figure 8.2 The long and short routes to accountability for service delivery: civil service roles (source: Adapted from World Bank (2004: 49)).

the services to consumers. Examples would be policing, public education, or a public sector railroad. The civil service role could also be quite minimalist – though nonetheless essential – as in overseeing a private sector pharmaceutical industry, and ensuring that drugs in the pharmacopoeia are up to standard.

The principal–agent problem

Over the past couple of decades, a leading paradigm for analyzing organizational behavior has been the "principal–agent" concept. In this approach, the principal (e.g. a municipal council) sets the goal (solid waste disposal) and assigns an agent (sanitation workers) to carry out the task. Agents are assumed to be individual utility maximizers who – given the opportunity – will use any opportunity to benefit themselves rather than the principal, by shirking, rent-seeking, offering goods of deceptively low quality, and so on. The principal's task, accordingly, is to shape the agent's incentive structure so as to align the latter's interests with his own (e.g. through close monitoring, piecework pay, soliciting consumer complaints).

The long and short routes illustrated in Figures 8.1 and 8.2 easily lend themselves to a principal–agent interpretation.[5] The first principal here is the citizenry, which through the long route exercises control of the state as its agent by exercising "voice." The state, in turn, acts as principal in its "compacting" relationship with providers. In the short route, the citizen/principal uses the provider directly as his agent.

A key assumption in principal–agent analysis is "methodological individualism" – the idea that each agent inherently maximizes his/her own individual self-interest, which of course does not necessarily coincide with the interests of the principal (or those of the organization, which may differ from the principal's, e.g. in a turf battle between bureaucratic agencies). The remedy for the principal, according to public choice theory, the dominant analytic perspective at present, is to impose transparency and monitoring to keep the agent in line. An older solution, as Fukuyama (2004: 61ff.) points out, is for the principal to encourage group norms that inspire agents to cooperate in common cause, as with an athletics team or a military unit.

The principal–agent approach faces two problems in a developing country context, even in normal times. First, methodological individualism is to a very large extent the product of Western development over the past two centuries. The prevailing orientation in many, perhaps most, developing countries with their neo-patrimonial cultures is one that may be described as "methodological clientism,"[6] in which individuals' basic motivation is not so much for self as for the kinship group – nuclear and extended family, then, in wider circles, community, caste, and tribe – while their *modus operandi* is to work not as part of an achievement-oriented organization but as a client serving a patron who will advance their interests in return for loyalty and support.[7] Not that self is unimportant (as anyone who has witnessed the lifestyles of developing country elites can testify), but patronage and its handmaiden corruption are at least as important in societal terms and arguably more so.

The second problem stems from degree of discretion and transaction intensity involved in providing services of all types, as shown in Figure 3.[8] In providing a service, the agent has a degree of *discretion* that can be quite narrow (e.g. inoculating children in a health campaign or serving school lunches) or very wide (deciding how much to emphasize preventive vs. curative medicine at health clinics or teaching primary school students). The former are easy to monitor and to gauge outputs and outcomes for. The latter are difficult in terms of either task (who can tell what is the real trade-off between preventive and curative efforts at village level or how much the pupils have actually learned in terms of useful life skills?). The range involved constitutes the vertical dimension of Figure 8.3.

The horizontal dimension captures the *frequency* of transactions involved. Some activities involve only a few decisions (though each one may be exceedingly complex), as in setting interest rates at the central bank or determining the national health strategy, while others require dozens or even hundreds of decisions daily, as with the policeman on the beat or the primary schoolteacher in class. Earlier efforts at civil service reform wanted to move activities upward and to the right (Figure 8.3); that is, to reduce discretion and increase the services provided, or in other words to routinize procedures by training and make them more available to the public by making the bureaucracy more efficient. This is the "Weberian imperative" in the figure, for which the extreme form would be Taylorism in the upper righthand corner.[9]

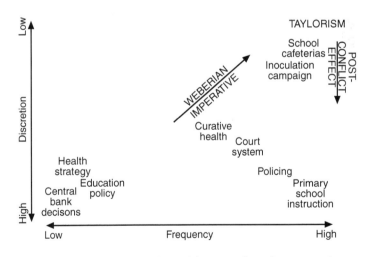

Figure 8.3 Transaction discretion and frequency for various sectors (source: Author).

The post-conflict difference

In fragile states generally, and in post-conflict states especially, the long route is beset by difficulties citizens face in exercising voice vis-àvis the state and by problems of patronage and corruption in the compact arrangements between the state and providers. A weakened bureaucracy is less able to offer services to begin with (transactions decrease) and the scope for discretion grows as monitoring becomes less feasible. Even the most routinized procedure, if available at all, becomes snared in even more corruption and patronage, as individuals with their families seek desperately to become clients in order to grasp at any hint of available public service. In terms of Figure 8.3, things move downward and to the left. As a consequence, state capacity drops sharply.

The donor community and post-conflict assistance

Into the post-conflict situation come the donors, generally with large initial aid flows at the outset, which are critical in providing first relief and then reconstruction, especially inasmuch as private investment flows – whether from within the country or without – are typically at low ebb in the immediate post-conflict environment. In the immediate post-conflict period, official development assistance zooms up, drops gradually for a couple of years, and then falls precipitously as donors lose focus, other world crises emerge, and funds are diverted elsewhere.[10] Private investment funding takes an almost opposite course, timid at first (except for some quick-return opportunities such as cell-phone systems), and then gradually picking up tempo as conditions normalize and investments seem more secure. The strategy implication for donors is that the immediate post-conflict period offers a brief policy window in which they can use the leverage of their assistance to press for civil service (and other) reforms. After just a few years, however, private investors have become the major players and will have begun using their resources to affect host government policies, displacing the donor community as the primary change agent.

Donors in the immediate post-conflict environment, facing a mandate to provide first relief and then essential services, find themselves making a choice between working through the institutions in place before and during conflict, or setting up ad hoc structures to do the job. Given the decrepitude if not outright absence of state institutions (certainly in the initial post-conflict phases), choosing the second option becomes the obvious choice. These alternatives may seem like the long and the short routes of Figure 8.1, and the choice taken may appear to embrace the short route but it in fact constitutes a third answer to the challenge of service provision by replacing both accountability routes with the donors themselves, as shown in Figure 8.4. For the donors have now become the principals, with their ad hoc providers acting as the agents, both within the state apparatus and as direct providers (hence the two funding arrows in Figure 8.4). Consumers have little power over providers, who are now accountable to the donors.[11]

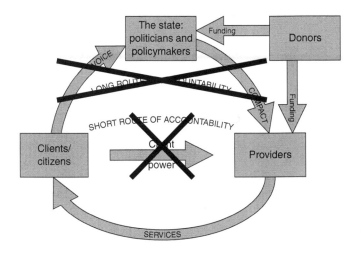

Figure 8.4 Post-conflict accountability for service delivery (source: Adapted from
World Bank (2004: 49)).

Donors know that they must start immediately on building in-country capacity to deliver services, and in general there are at least four distinct ways to do
this (Mckechnie 2003):

- build capacity *directly* by investing in government institutions;
- build *temporary* capacity by hiring from diaspora or foreign nationals;
- buy capacity by *contracting out* to the private sector or NGOs (domestic or
  more likely foreign);
- bypass weak government altogether and have *donors* do it themselves.

The first option amounts to reconstructing (if the previous state was democratic)
or constructing (if it was not) the long route of Figure 8.1. The other three ways
comprise variants on the short route. In some areas, notably the first and third of
the "core state functions" noted earlier, donors have no choice. These functions
– security/justice, and political governance – must be provided by the state.[12] In
anything other than the shortest of terms, the long route is the only route to take
in offering them. Only the second function – "essential services" – presents a
choice between the two routes.

This "essential services" function comprises the overwhelming majority of
what the state is obligated to provide for its citizens – health, education, transport, energy – taking up the largest portion of the budget and the highest proportion of civil service employees at all levels, and it is here that donors can choose
from among the several options listed above. Immediate efforts in the health
sector (e.g. combating epidemics, cleaning up polluted drinking-water), transportation (repairing main roads and bridges), energy (reconstructing the electric

grid), communications (restoring the telephone system), even agriculture (re-establishing seed distribution networks) can be jump-started by donor-supported contractors, NGOs, or even donors directly (e.g. army engineers replacing damaged bridges). Some monitoring will be required, of course, to ensure that funds are properly spent, but initially donors can perform that function as well.

To sum up the discussion so far, the post-conflict situation tends to be characterized by:

- A host of immediate needs in all sectors, from security to food supply to health.
- A population desperate for assistance, especially in basic needs such as potable water and emergency medical treatment, and to a large extent more than willing to abandon Weberian expectations for engagement in patron–client modalities for service allocation.
- A civil service woefully short of skilled personnel, equipment, even basic necessities such as lighting, paper, and pencils.
- A prostrate economy with little employment or liquid assets.
- A rapid increase in discretion allowed to service providers, who can turn their ability to allot a scarce supply of needed services among many anxious supplicants into rent-seeking opportunities.
- Rapidly escalating levels of corruption as citizens pursue all possible avenues to obtain scarce services; whatever had been allocated according to Weberian bureaucratic norms (with perhaps a small bribe, such as an electrical hook-up or a vehicle registration) has now become subject to intense competition and much more serious venality.

In such circumstances, it is scarcely surprising that donors come quickly to rely on outside providers to get essential services back up and running, or even indeed that a post-conflict country finds itself with what amounts to a "second civil service" of NGOs and contractors performing the tasks that the original civil service had once undertaken.[13] Further downsides ensue:

- The "second civil service" comes at a much higher price than the first, as expatriates will not provide their expertise without high pay checks and living costs.
- Seeking to hold down expenses, donors hire local expertise wherever it can be found, but that often means raiding what is left of the already decimated first civil service, thus further weakening it.
- What accountability exists can only be exercised by the donors, as indicated in Figure 8.4. The long route is inoperative altogether, and even the short route only functions sporadically, for desperate citizens are in no position to exercise any accountability against providers.
- Everyone knows that the first civil service urgently needs thoroughgoing reform, and many understand that any serious reform is best done (and most likely only done) at the very outset of the post-conflict period, before things

become locked in; but this is clearly a long-term task, while services must be provided in the immediate present, so reform is all too likely to be relegated to the back burner.

- In the meantime, as the first civil service slowly comes back to life, the discretion its members can exercise becomes if anything wider amid the confusion attendant upon restoring some kind of normality. The potential for corruption continues to grow.

The basic challenge, then, is how to reduce discretion among service providers involved with high-volume transactions, not necessarily to Weberian standards (that would be impossible anyhow for so many inherently high-discretion functions like primary schoolteaching), but at least to a position where services are in fact provided, rent-seeking is reduced to an acceptable level (it would be utopian to think it could be removed altogether), and providers are accountable in some workable fashion. Donors have a number of strategies for facing the challenge, both for providing services and assuring accountability, which will now be taken up.

Approaches to monitoring and accountability in service delivery

Before agent/providers can be held to standards for their work and rent-seeking can be reduced, there has to be some way(s) for principals to ascertain what they have done and failed to do – in short, monitoring. Francis Fukuyama (2004: 59ff.) offers a number of options for monitoring, whether the principal is a donor or the host country government. With some additions, they are presented here in order of monitoring difficulty, beginning with the easiest, as shown in Figure 8.5, first for service delivery mechanisms, as shown in Table 8.1, and then for accountability mechanisms, as indicated in Table 8.2.

Figure 8.5 Monitoring and accountability dimensions for service delivery (source: Author).

Table 8.1 Post-conflict service delivery mechanisms

Strategy	Advantages	Drawbacks	Civil service role	Monitoring principals
Contracting out ("outsourcing" to foreigners)	Quick start-up Quality work Least corruption	Most expensive No host-country capacity built Dependency Unaccountable to state or citizenry	Marginalized by "second civil service"	Donors
Domestic NGOs	Quality work Cheaper than foreigners Flexible work force Less corruption	More expensive than state provision Cannot cover entire need	Marginalization as above	Donors, then accountability mechanisms shown in Table 8.2
Private sector competition	Consumer choice ensures quality and affordability Market as monitor	Market failures Imperfect consumer knowledge Insider privatization sell-offs	Minimal involvement Easily corrupted	Market
Devolution	Services tailored High flexibility Citizen control Shorter route to accountability	Local elites become principals Corruption localized Increasing inequality between localities	Local expansion Fragmentation of career services Opposition to decentralization	Local citizens
Line bureaucracy	Experience in place Incremental expansion feasible	Bad habits endure Serious reform more difficult later on	Main service delivery agency	Accountability mechanisms shown in Table 8.2

Source: Author.

Service delivery and monitoring

Contracting out to foreigners

Donors can engage foreign private firms and/or NGOs to provide services, making contracts with reliable organizations that can maintain high levels of accountability for what they do. Intimately familiar with international standards, they can get their operations quickly up to speed, keep reliable records, do their own self-monitoring, manage honest procurement processes, and in general adhere to a high degree of probity.

Of course, these same foreign contractors are also extremely costly, generally do nothing to build up host-country government capacity (in fact they often undermine it by hiring away the more able civil servants), and tend to create dependency among both beneficiary populations and host country governments. And while as agents they are accountable to donors as principals, they can never become accountable to the state, which could never afford to pay their costs. The civil service remains at the margins, superseded by this "second civil service" of foreign providers.

Domestic NGOs

Although they will take longer to gear up to an acceptable level, domestic non-governmental organizations have many advantages. They can also do quality work (if perhaps not as professionally), and can do it at lower cost than foreign contractors. They are generally less prone to corruption than the civil service, and at the same time are more flexible, since their employees have no rights to tenure or due process, and in the uncertain post-war situation they are anxious to hold on to their jobs, however temporary. In many ways they are a good follow-on to foreign contractors, as donors begin to phase down their assistance budgets.

However, they tend to be more expensive than the civil service, and like foreign contractors they tend to marginalize it, perhaps more so in that they may stay on for long periods delivering services that in the pre-conflict era had been provided by the bureaucracy. While NGOs can be very effective, they cannot really cover more than a fraction of a country's total service needs.[14] Monitoring is likely to be the province of donors, at least at the beginning when outsiders are paying the bills, though the host-country government may be expected to take on a larger role over time.

Competition

Some services can be privatized, either in part or completely, so that the consumer becomes the direct principal and the market does the monitoring. Private transportation companies can be invited to compete against government bus operators, and private schools can be certified to enable competition with public schools. With the buses, riders can decide whether to ride public or private transport, thus forcing the two to compete with each other. With the schools, things are not so straightforward. Public schools are generally free, while private operators run on tuition fees, so the competition is less than fair, though in many countries the cost of books, supplies, and uniforms for public schools makes up part of the difference, and the need to pay schoolteachers extra (as well as illegal) fees for private instruction to supplement deficient public schools' classes will make up more. In the United States, experimental voucher systems introduced in the 1990s award parents a stipend for each child, which may be spent in either public or private schools, further leveling the playing field, but this kind of scheme would be difficult to manage in most developing country settings, to say nothing of post-conflict situations. A bolder kind of competition can be induced by privatizing a whole sector, as with bus lines or a government airline. In these cases, the market may be relied upon to do the monitoring, with firms offering superior service and flourishing, while those providing inferior service will decline. The World Bank's short route to accountability is all that is needed.[15]

The bureaucracy will face large-scale lay-offs in the privatized sectors, and the reaction of retrenched civil servants may be intense and even violent. Those that remain will be charged with monitoring the newly privatized activities to make sure they are up to an acceptable standard (e.g. non-polluting buses, safe airplanes, achieving pupils). Naturally, such an assignment will also provide opportunity for rent-seeking abuses, whereby state inspectors take bribes in return for issuing bogus certificates of compliance.

Sometimes the market can monitor effectively, but as always there is the risk of market failure of one sort or another. Will one competitor attain a monopoly position which may then be exploited to public disadvantage? Will two or three competitors collude to form an oligopoly that does the same thing?[16] Will the consuming public have the knowledge to differentiate among providers (presumably it can with public transport, but likely not among illiterate parents choosing between schools). A second problem comes all too often with the initial privatization effort itself. Public assets can be sold off for a song to cabals of insiders, who then have little incentive to husband their cheaply acquired possessions, instead salvaging what is immediately worthwhile and ignoring or abandoning the rest. Services do not get provided as they had been, and accountability disappears altogether. The civil service has little more role than with the outsourcing option. At best it will monitor service delivery on behalf of the state (e.g. ensuring that private bus fleets maintain clean-air standards, overseeing adherence to education test standards), but corruption comes easily with such assignments, and aside from some rent-seeking opportunities, the civil service is not likely to have a large role to play.

Devolution

Decentralization, if properly done, moves both responsibility and resources for service provision to lower levels of governance.[17] Local government institutions become the principals, while decentralized civil service personnel become the agents. Services can be tailored to local conditions in ways that centralized management could never accomplish, and the providers can be held accountable for what they do by representative local councils. The whole loop of the long route is shortened and made manageable.

At the same time, however, devolution has to face the question of just who are the principals. Are agents really accountable to representatives of an engaged public exercising its voice in determining public policy? Or have local elites managed to seize control of the new machinery, turning it into another avenue for exercising patronage? Can corruption be brought under control, or will it merely move along somewhat different channels? There are further questions as well. Will devolution lead to unacceptable regional inequalities, as some localities inevitably do better than others over time, thus increasing possibilities for renewed conflict? The total number of civil servants will probably expand as local government units take on more tasks in responding to citizen demand for public services. But the civil service cadres, now cut off from their mother line ministries and their previous career tracks, find themselves fragmented and reporting to local councils. Hopes for eventual promotion to the capital city (and in many cases the higher levels of graft that come with higher ranks) are dashed. How will they react to such reverses and with what consequences?

Line bureaucracy

This option represents a return to the status quo ante for most countries. The civil service continues to deliver (or recovers its position in delivering) essential services in health, education, infrastructure provision, and so on. Once the security situation has become normalized, the civil service can draw upon its experience and expertise, and quickly take over from whatever contractors or NGOs may have provided in interim services. If expansion is called for, incremental hiring can bring in new groups that have to be accommodated in a peace accord or de facto settlement, and the bureaucracy can expand to take on new tasks as needed (e.g. an environmental protection agency).

The downside, of course, is that all the bad habits – corruption, ineffectiveness, shirking – will return as well. The answer, of course, is thoroughgoing civil service reform, but from the donor standpoint, reforming the bureaucracy will probably be more difficult than any of the first three options listed here. Contracting, privatizing, and even devolution will seem simpler.

Service delivery and accountability

The options shown in Table 8.2 are not service delivery agencies but rather "long route" accountability mechanisms ensuring that service delivery takes place at an acceptable level of quality for the four methods discussed above.

Civil society

When it works, competition forces agents to monitor each other in the interest of their principals, who are consuming the services provided. Civil society takes a different route, in effect organizing principals by bringing them together to promote their interests vis-àvis providers. Parents put pressure on a school system by forming a parents' association. Water users do the same with respect to the agency managing an irrigation system. Neighborhood groups press for better waste collection, water delivery, and police protection.

Success for civil society advocacy depends on a suitable enabling environment to guarantee the right of association, autonomy from state control, and so on. It also depends on a free media so that citizens can gain and share information about what the state is doing and not doing. Its main attraction for donors in the context of monitoring and accountability for service delivery, however, is its relatively low cost and its central role in democratization generally. Generally there are at least some civil society organizations (CSOs) already on the scene, or at least groups that can become CSOs with a little training, so program expenses are not large and the preparation time is not lengthy. In addition, civil society operates on a continuous basis as a democratic engine, constantly demanding accountability to the citizenry. It is not subject to an electoral cycle

Table 8.2 Post-conflict service delivery accountability mechanisms

Strategy	Advantages	Drawbacks	Civil service role
Civil society	Citizens become principals Low donor cost Easy programming	Dependent on enabling environment, media Elite CSO bias "Demosclerosis"	Kept in line by CSO monitors
Constitutional structures	Legitimacy – ideal longroute to accountability Monitoring by representative bodies and rule of law	Costly Long maturation Flagging donor interest over time Difficult to get right constitutional formula	Subject to executive direction, legislative and judicial oversight
Bureaucratic worker norms	Self-monitoring professionalism Less need for the long route	Social capital needed Very long time frame Moral economy possibly neo-patrimonial	Legitimacy through probity

Source: Author.

or to the long delays characteristic of court systems. Thus it is easy to see why post-conflict donors find civil society an attractive strategy option.

But will CSOs represent the society as a whole? Donors do tend to emphasize poor and marginal elements in their civil society programming, it is true, but how representative are the CSOs they assist? Do women's organizations advocate for women generally, or are they more active on behalf of elite women (who usually form the core leadership of such groups)? One can ask the same question of ethnic minority CSOs, professional groups, or small farmers. One can pose these questions differently to ask whether CSOs will help minimize discretion on the part of civil servants (or service deliverers of whatever stripe) and steer them toward Weberian norms of behavior, or will they tend to steer them more toward satisfying the interests of their own groups – perhaps even the interests of elites within their groups – at the expense of the public interest? In other words, will they produce more gridlock and "demosclerosis" than realization of the public good?[18]

CSOs could serve as a system's main monitoring agency under any of the approaches outlined in Table 8.1 except foreign outsourcing. In all the others, accountability is domestic, so CSOs could conceivably take on a watchdog role with respect to competition, devolution, constitutional structures, or worker norms. But it is when the state itself is the main delivery agent that civil society assumes its most effective role as a monitor of civil service performance and as a force demanding accountability. The private sector is often too opaque for civil society to observe well, and devolution so fragments service delivery that it is difficult for civil society to spread itself thinly enough to monitor effectively. But with line bureaucracy and the constitutional structures discussed below, civil society can exercise a critical monitoring role.

Constitutional structures

Elections, representative legislative bodies, and legal systems do not themselves deliver services, but they comprise the main political (as opposed to civil society) structures for monitoring delivery and the ultimate institutions through which citizens can exercise accountability. Voters collectively can eject from office those who fail to provide satisfactorily for service delivery and individually can bring legal proceedings to compel performance. This is, after all, the essence of the long route to accountability.

Setting up electoral structures has by now become something of a production line industry among donors in recent years, and, all things considered, quality control has been impressive. Even in countries with virtually no electoral experience, it has been possible to set up and run reasonably free and fair post-conflict elections, as in Mozambique, although the results may not always be to the donors' liking. In states with some electoral history, these processes have by now become almost routine, as is attested to by many success stories in election assistance. It is what comes after a free and fair election that has caused so much difficulty. Legislatures that demand accountability from the executive on behalf of the citizenry and courts that enforce it have taken much longer and have proven much harder to attain than running elections. Furthermore, not only does this kind of institution-building take much longer, it is also much more expensive and takes a much higher level of political will to secure. If donors, political elites, and civil society can stay the course in keeping structural development on track, the long route to accountability will be realized, and the civil service will become subject to executive direction, legislative rule-setting, and judicial oversight. Combined with effective civil service monitoring, this is a very good formula indeed for accountability, but the time requirements tend to be too great for this path to fit into the post-conflict repertoire in most countries. Exceptions would be countries such as Croatia or Serbia where much of the constitutional infrastructure is already in place and can be reconstructed.

Worker norms

Whereas principal–agent thinking assumes agents are inherently individualistic self-seekers at the expense of their principals whenever possible and thus need monitoring, Fukuyama (2004: 63ff.) looks elsewhere, wondering why it is that in many institutions' agents do not shirk wherever they can but instead seem to act according to some kind of group norm of behavior. Why don't professors all go to sleep on the job once they have tenure? Why does professional pride so often induce workers to do more than is necessary? Why do policemen take more risks than is necessary? In the extreme case, why do soldiers sacrifice themselves for their comrades? His answer is that: (1) social capital produces a moral order that acts as a filter in determining behavior in many organizations, and (2) in successful organizations, leadership reinforces the group norms.

To the extent that they function, worker norms are the best monitor of all, since they amount to self-monitoring. And they exact the highest standards of accountability since they are self-enforcing, and the civil service attains legitimacy through professional probity and elã. But these norms assume social capital, and in fact they assume social capital of a particular kind that cements one's interest with that of co-workers and professional colleagues. Other, more common kinds of social capital strengthen ties with one's family, community, tribe, or kinship group.[19] The first can (and does) makes for a public-oriented moral order, while the second promotes what may be termed a familistic moral order. The latter type of course is the one commonly found in post-conflict societies and leads agents to steer their behavior even further from Weberian standards than mere individual greed. Indeed, it can make "methodological individualism" look like beneficence. It does generate a kind of long route to accountability, but this perverse neo-patrimonial path leads from particular familial (or caste/kinship) groups through patronage to the state and back down through the providers to the clients and consumers as indicated in Figure 8.1. Accountability is there, but only in distorted form and only to those tied into the reigning patron–client network.

How can that first type of social capital be built in a civil service? It has happened, as with the Cornwallis reforms in India at the end of the eighteenth century leading gradually from the legendarily corrupt colonial "nabobs" of Robert Clive's era to the Indian Civil Service, noted for its professionalism, integrity, and social capital – much of which carried over into the Indian Administrative Service and the Civil Service of Pakistan following the partition of 1947. One could also point to the transformation of British and American national-level bureaucracies from their egregious corruption of the mid- and late nineteenth century to the trustworthy organizations they had become by the early twentieth century. Perhaps a more relevant case would be that of Taiwan. The Nationalist government bureaucracy was notoriously corrupt back on the mainland and in the early days after the flight to Taiwan, but by the beginning of the twenty-first century had attained a ranking above Italy in the Corruption Perception Index. Still shorter in length of time was the experience which Judith Tendler (1997) reports in northeast Brazil, where good leadership and (more importantly, she finds) a combination of decentralization, local civil society, and continuing involvement of higher level government forged a remarkable improvement in civil service dedication and performance. But even here the whole process took almost a decade to show real results. So these were long-term processes, not to be taken up lightly by donors with short program attention spans. However, the inculcation of professional worker norms along with democratic constitutional structures shows the direction in which reform must move. In the end, if some kind of internalized norm cannot be realized within the civil service, external monitoring of whatever severity will not be enough to build integrity within it.

The donor challenge

The strategic challenge facing donors in post-conflict interventions is to gauge how far and how fast it will be possible to move along the axis of Figure 8.5, as donor interest changes from *relief* to *governance*. Before progressing further, however, it should be clarified that the eight positions in Figure 8.5 (and correspondingly the five rows in Table 8.1 and three rows in Table 8.2) are not intended to be strictly sequential, nor are they meant to be hierarchical. For example, devolution does not replace competition, nor is it somehow superior to the latter. Rather, Figure 8.5's gradation moves from easier- to harder-to-implement, so it makes sense for donors to consider taking them up conceptually and to some extent chronologically in the order shown.

Donors and service delivery mechanisms

In the first stages of post-conflict assistance, when donor agencies feel intense pressure both on the ground and from back home to deliver critical services, and also when funding is relatively flush, *foreign outsourcing* will be the obvious choice. The extent to which contractors will be needed will vary greatly, of course, from situations like Afghanistan (where the domestic bureaucracy was shattered after decades of war and misrule) or Timor Leste (where it largely decamped along with the rest of the departing Indonesians) to various Balkan states like Macedonia (where it remained essentially intact). In the first two cases outsourcing was needed for almost everything, while in the latter it was hardly needed at all. Wherever much outsourcing is done, whatever exists of the earlier civil service will feel marginalized by the influx of resource-rich and highly remunerated outsiders. Because they are so expensive, however, the contractors will have to be replaced fairly quickly, thus reducing the threat of a "second civil service."

Domestic NGOs present a very attractive option for donors. Foreign contractors and NGOs can hand over operations smoothly as local NGOs get up to speed, donors can exercise a fair degree of control through their assistance mechanisms, costs become reasonable (at least compared to the foreign contractors), and the work done is generally acceptable in terms of quality. In addition, donors feel comfortable working with NGOs; there is a great deal of experience – much of it quite successful – to draw on.

But the marginalization issue will continue to exist, as civil service personnel feel less favored by donors and resent the higher salaries generally being drawn by their domestic NGO counterparts. There is also likely to be a "creaming" problem, as NGOs use their higher salaries to retain the best qualified people (often raiding the state bureaucracy) and select the best sites for their service delivery activities (urban areas, more progressive villages, marginally poor people as opposed to the truly destitute). The civil service, which will have to be the residual service provider, is left with fewer well-qualified personnel and less favorable places to work. In the short term, though, working with NGOs on a large scale as service delivery mechanisms allows donors to put off the messy and unpleasant prospect of dealing with civil service reform.

Private sector competition is also relatively easy to implement, in addition to fitting nicely within the "Washington consensus" on development policy. Moreover, privatization offers an excellent opportunity to eliminate wasteful subsidies. Finally, some services are likely to operate better in the private sector, such as bus transportation, or perhaps agricultural input provision. But donors and host-country governments will face several serious obstacles in any attempt at privatization. First, consumers will be angry at losing subsidized bus fares or artificially cheap irrigation water. Second, retrenched civil servants are sure to protest, perhaps disruptively. Third, the privatization process itself may be distorted through insider manipulation (as has happened in numerous cases). Fourth, the newly privatized sector will be subject to market failure through collusion and concentration of vendors. Finally, those state sectors charged with monitoring the newly privatized service provision will be sorely tempted to engage in rent-seeking.

But beyond all these problems are the real limitations of any privatization initiative, namely that many state sector activities simply cannot be made competitive. The judiciary (especially including police), roads, and sewage are all labor-intensive activities that cannot be privatized, and even those sectors that can take on a large amount of privatization will have to continue being publicly operated, as in health and education, where private actors cannot gear up to handle demand at all levels. In the end, donors and host country governments cannot avoid the need to build or rebuild a significant civil service capacity by taking a privatization route.

Devolution

Decentralization initiatives are attractive to donors essentially for two reasons. First, as mentioned earlier, devolution promises to bring decision-making about service provision closer to the citizenry, letting localities decide what they want and how much they want to pay for it. In many ways, this flexibility to meet inherently differing local needs is much superior to a "one-size-fits-all" operation that is run from a distant capital city (see, e.g. Beschel 2002). Furthermore, putting local folk in charge of their own governance has a de Tocquevillean appeal that is hard to resist, especially for American donors. Pitfalls abound, as is well known, for civil servants will resist being relegated to the countryside, central managers will try to undermine attempts to steal away their turf, and local elites will endeavor to seize control of whatever largesse comes their way from the center.[20] But the rewards are many as well.

The second reason for devolution's allure is less flattering to donors, namely that decentralization – like privatization – offers a way to avoid coming to grips with the need for fundamental bureaucratic reform that will tackle the abiding corruption and neo-patrimonialism which everyone knows exists and will cause immense problems if challenged. If responsibility can be offloaded on to the rural areas, then there will be no pressing need to face the fracas and turmoil that is sure to occur if a serious initiative is to be undertaken at civil service reconstruction. Moreover, the problems that decentralization will surely create will be out in the countryside and thus safely out of sight, at least in the short term.

Reforming the *line bureaucracy* will seem the most difficult option to anyone having much acquaintance with the country in question. Apart from the few cases like Timor Leste where everything must begin essentially *in vacuo*, there is a civil service that is already in place which can be continued and staffed through emergency recruitment efforts as needed. And speed will be essential, both to get the state machinery running again (especially in sectors such as the police) and in anticipation of donor drawdowns in assistance levels.

But this is where serious trouble begins, often starting with donors themselves, who are likely to have combed every conceivable source for trained people to manage their own relief operations, including the bureaucracy itself. Thus the net will have to be stretched further and lower to pull in enough people to run government operations. But such overhasty recruitment efforts are all too likely to lead to disastrous results. Lateral entry schemes (recruiting people directly to senior positions instead of bringing them up through the system) and quick promotions from within most often pull incompetent people in far over their heads. Overhasty vetting of candidates invites patronage and corruption to become even more salient than usual in filling positions. And these pathologies, added to a donor community that is only too anxious to "move money" in the early days of post-conflict recovery, will function as an open invitation to fraud and venality far in excess of the norm. Moreover, once in place and tied into the patronage systems that preceded them, these poor appointments and malevolent practices quickly become a part of the institutional structure itself, so entrenched that they cannot be removed without doing severe structural damage.

To preclude – or at least to attenuate – these unpleasant scenarios, the moment for planning and beginning a thoroughgoing civil service reform must come right at the outset of post-conflict assistance, at the very time when other more urgent priorities easily crowd such a task off the donor radar screen altogether. Bureaucratic reform will seem to be a challenge that can be deferred until later on after calm has returned, but, as indicated above, this will almost certainly be too late. The place to start should ideally be the creation of an administrative staff training college (or extensive renovation of an existing one) so that it can train higher level civil servants to an adequate degree (which will almost surely be higher than pre-conflict standards) and inculcate an *esprit de corps* that will provide the professional worker norms constituting the last and most difficult step in Figure 8.5.

Donors and accountability mechanisms

Like service delivery NGOs, advocacy *civil society organizations* offer a good option for donors. CSOs are not hugely expensive to create and train, they can draw on a good talent pool, and they accord very well with donor ideals of pluralist democracy.[21] Acting through CSOs, active citizens become the principals exercising the long route to hold service providers accountable. This is an area where Western donors do well, and one they are generally enthusiastic about working in.

So it is not hard to see how donors gravitate to civil society, not only as an addition to the other mechanisms discussed here, but even as a substitute for them. Sponsoring civic advocacy groups, after all, is much more gratifying and immediately rewarding than entering the morass of such efforts as bureaucratic reform or judicial reconstruction. Civil society can have a meretricious attraction in that it is all too easy to support citizen advocacy instead of taking on the more difficult tasks indicated toward the right of Figure 8.5.

A second problem with civil society lies in its connections to the rest of a political system; it is not a stand-alone mechanism. To function properly, or even at all, civil society needs a democratic enabling environment of free speech, right of assembly, and an open media, which in turn all depend on political will at the top. In post-conflict situations, this kind of political will may be hard to find, and even if it does assert itself, its duration may prove brief. Civil society, in short, cannot be depended upon to deliver enough accountability goods that it can substitute for constitutional structures or, in the long run, professional worker norms.

Constitutional structures entail high cost and long gestation as accountability mechanisms supporting the long route, particularly in comparison with civil society. An election or two may not be so difficult to manage, but a system guaranteeing free and fair elections on a regular schedule is much more elusive. Beyond elections, the executive and legislature placed in office by voters usually present deeper challenges for donors to build or rebuild, and judicial systems probably even more so. It is not surprising that success stories in these areas have been few, and that donor enthusiasm has tended to fade before serious reforms could have a chance to take root.

However, it is periodic elections that enable voters to act as principals giving (or withholding) a broad mandate to the executive and legislature as their agents, and these two branches in turn then become principals to monitor and hold accountable the bureaucracy as their agents. An independent judiciary acts in effect as a very remote (i.e. not removable, assuming that it is truly independent) agent for the citizenry, becoming in turn (like the executive and legislature) a system of principals helping to hold the bureaucracy to account. Thus if a post-conflict state is to develop a sustainable governance system, these structures will have to be strengthened, and most likely will need to be pretty thoroughly rebuilt in the process, for in all likelihood it was their failure to manage the state on behalf of the citizenry that was a key factor in initiating the conflict in the first place. In the end, the challenge is for nothing less than state-building. When all is said and done, nothing less will do.

The last mechanism in Figure 8.5, *professional worker norms* in the bureaucracy, is surely the hardest to set into place, for it attempts to change the cultures both of tradition – neo-patrimonialism and extended family kinship networks – and of the modernity portrayed in public choice theory, where individuals seek to maximize their own utility at whatever cost to the collective welfare. But with time and hard work, dedicated leadership and accumulated social capital can produce an organization in which a moral order creates a whole greater than the sum of its parts, where workers consistently exceed what is expected of them. This constitutes the real end game for a post-conflict civil service, and should be a goal donor's plan from the outset of their involvement. It is what makes state-building actually sustainable over time.

Notes

1 This chapter is a revised version of a paper originally written for USAID's Center for Development Information and Evaluation (CDIE), under a contract with the Mitchell Group, of Washington, DC. The views expressed are solely those of the author and should not be attributed to USAID.

2 For instance, see Cutillo (2006). This ambitious research monograph, commissioned by the International Peace Academy, covers fifteen years of post-conflict interventions and runs over sixty-six pages, but does not mention "civil service" or "bureaucracy" even once.

3 At times, depending on context, local government employees will be included as well, but for the most part, "civil service" will include only central government workers.

4 See World Bank (2004). For an excellent summary, see Meagher (2005: 16–19).

5 The discussion here is inspired by Fukuyama (2004: esp. ch. 2), though he does not employ the Bank's concept of long and short routes.

6 In some ways "methodological familism" might be a better term, inspired by Edward Banfield's "amoral familism." See Banfield (1958).

7 And to the extent that they move up in the system, individuals seek to become patrons, building up their position by bestowing favors on their own clients.

8 The basic idea here is taken from Pritchett and Woolcock (2002). Fukuyama (2004) takes a similar approach but, following Israel (1987), uses "specificity" (how specifically can outcomes be gauged) rather than discretion as the vertical axis. For an example of using Israel's concept to analyze development support, see Blair (2001).

9 Taylorism refers to the "scientific management" movement of the early twentieth century that sought to eliminate worker discretion by breaking tasks down into routinized components that specified in advance how to achieve them.

10 See Schwartz *et al.* (2004) for a study of ten countries for which post-conflict data were available over an eight-year period.

11 Except insofar as they can get the providers to become patrons who can be manipulated. See Scott (1985).

12 For the first and third functions, some short-term possibilities exist for external provision. To begin with the political leadership function, the first election or two can be managed by a team of outside consultants cobbled together with local hires given quick training in electoral mechanics, and some immediate security needs can be met at great cost by hiring private foreign contractors, as in Afghanistan or Iraq. It is also possible in at least some instances to fly in a few expert technocrats and set up an operable central banking system that can then be turned over to in-country economists and financial managers who had the good fortune to have been trained at Harvard or MIT and perhaps then put in a stint at the World Bank. But such tasks as managing the state executive branch, running the legislature, and operating the basic legal and criminal justice systems – which require far more personnel – will have to be undertaken by one form or another of civil service. Conducting diplomacy, maintaining the army, administering the court system, fielding a police force, are all examples of government duties that cannot be outsourced. Capacity in these areas will have to be built by investing in the state itself.

13 I have taken the expression from Cliffe and Manning (forthcoming).

14 Even in a country like Bangladesh with its huge NGO presence in the service delivery sector, the most generous estimate speculates that perhaps 80 percent of villages are reached by NGOs and 35 percent of the rural population. This represents an impressively productive record, but still leaves a great deal of work for other (presumably state) agencies. See Thornton *et al.* (2000: 2). Landell-Mills *et al.* (2002: 60), on the other hand, estimate that NGOs "have a strong presence in less than half of all villages" in Bangladesh – still a remarkable achievement, but leaving even more to the public sector civil service.

15 Many other services can be privatized as well, such as health delivery, water systems, waste removal, and electricity. The first would be similar to education and surface transport, while the latter are inherently monopolies in most cases, and so subject to all the problems of monitoring that monopolies entail.

16 Even small-scale operators can combine against the public interest, as with the thousands of independent jitney (small bus) operators in the Philippines, who for years successfully opposed the introduction of more expensive lead-free gasoline.

17 The proviso is critical here. Frequently, decentralization initiatives are incomplete, and while responsibility may be shifted downward, resources (or even the ability to raise resources locally) are not. Stillborn decentralization schemes have a long history. See Manor (1999) and Blair (2000).

18 The term comes from Rauch (1994) and denotes a hardening of democratic arteries, as advocacy organizations plunder the public interest to satisfy their own constituencies.

19 Fukuyama (2004) deals only with the first type of social capital.

20 These difficulties have been abundantly documented in the literature. See Blair (2000) for a discussion.

21 Idealistic recent university graduates, often unable to find work in the post-conflict economy, form an almost perfect recruitment base for CSOs in many post-conflict countries (clearly there are exceptions, such as Cambodia or Afghanistan, where higher education was put on hold altogether for many years). As the economy picks up, many CSO staffers will move on to other careers, but in the meantime they provide an excellent workforce for civil service advocacy.

References

Banfield, E.C. (1958) *The Moral Basis of a Backward Society*, New York: Free Press.

Beschel, R.B. (2002) "Rebuilding the Civil Service in a Post-conflict Setting: Key Issues and Lessons of Experience," Washington, DC: World Bank, Conflict Prevention and Reconstruction Unit, Dissemination Notes No. 1, March.

Blair, H. (2000) "Participation and Accountability at the Periphery: Democratic Local Governance in Six Countries," *World Development* 28(1): 21–39.

—— (2001) "Institutional Pluralism in Public Administration and Politics: Applications in Bolivia and Beyond," *Public Administration and Development* 21(2): 119–129.

Cliffe, S. and N. Manning (forthcoming) *Building Institutions after Conflict*, New York: International Peace Academy.

Cutillo, A. (2006) "International Assistance to Countries Emerging from Conflict: A Review of Fifteen Years of Intervention and the Future of Peacebuilding," Policy Paper, New York: International Peace Academy, February.

Department for International Development, United Kingdom (DFID) (2005) "Why We Need to Work More Effectively in Fragile States," London: DFID, January, available at: www.dfid.gov.uk.

Fukuyama, F. (2004) *State-building: Governance and World Order in the 21st Century*, Ithaca, NY: Cornell University Press.

Israel, A. (1987) *Institutional Development: Incentives to Performance*, Baltimore, MD: Johns Hopkins University Press, for the World Bank.

Landell-Mills, P., K. Alam, J. Barenstein, N. Chowdhury, P. Keefer, R. Messick, S. Pasha, H. Rahman, V. Saghal, R. Schware, and G. Wood (2002) *Taming the Leviathan: Reforming Governance in Bangladesh*, Washington, DC: World Bank.

Mckechnie, A.J. (2003) "Building Capacity in Post-conflict Countries," Washington, DC: World Bank, Social Development Notes, Conflict Prevention and Reconstruction, No. 14, December.

Manor, J. (1999) *The Political Economy of Democratic Decentralization*, Washington, DC: World Bank.

Meagher, P. (2005) "Service Delivery in Fragile States: Framing the Issues," College Park, MD: IRIS Center, Working Papers on Fragile States No. 5.

Pritchett, L. and M. Woolcock (2002) "Solutions When the Solution is the Problem: Arraying the Disarray in Development," Washington, DC: Center for Global Development, Working Paper No. 10, September.

Rauch, J. (1994) *Demosclerosis: The Silent Killer of American Government*, New York: Times Books.

Schwartz, J., S. Hahn, and I. Bannon (2004) "The Private Sector's Role in the Provision of Infrastructure in Post-conflict Countries: Patterns and Policy Options," Washington, DC: World Bank Social Development Papers, Conflict Prevention and Reconstruction, Paper No. 16, August.

Scott, J.C. (1985) *Weapons of the Weak: Everyday Forms of Peasant Resistance*, New Haven, CT: Yale University Press.

Tendler, J. (1997) *Good Government in the Tropics*, Baltimore, MD: Johns Hopkins University Press.

Thornton, P., J. Devine, P. Houtzager, D. Wright, and S. Razario (2000) "Partners in Development: A Review of Big NGOs in Bangladesh," London: DFID, 13 February to 6 April.

World Bank (1999) *Civil Service Reform: A Review of World Bank Assistance*, Washington, DC: World Bank, Operations Evaluation Department, August.

World Bank (2004) *World Development Report 2004: Making Services Work for Poor People*, Washington, DC: World Bank.

9

CONTRIBUTIONS OF DIGITAL DIASPORAS TO GOVERNANCE RECONSTRUCTION IN FRAGILE STATES

Potential and promise

Jennifer M. Brinkerhoff

It is impossible to address what may be new in post-conflict governance reconstruction without addressing the impacts of globalization in the 1990s and 2000s. Globalization has enhanced economic and political interdependence and, at the same time, has afforded opportunities for some countries and communities to advance while leaving others behind. The resulting marginalization and/or conscious social exclusion exacerbate the potential for conflict, on economic, political, and/or social grounds (see Lake and Rothchild 1996; Gissinger and Gleditch 1999). Social tension leading to conflict inside nation states is not new, though the consequences and potential for conflict escalation through external intervention have increased through globalization. This chapter considers the influence of information technology (IT) and migration in societies emerging from or vulnerable to conflict.

In today's world, information and people cross international borders at speeds and in numbers unimagined previously. Some see these movements as cause for alarm, particularly after September 11, 2001. Conventional wisdom holds that IT, especially as it is applied transnationally, poses a threat to nation states' sovereignty and capacity to govern. IT has "exposed the porosity of geographic and political borders and the limited extent of any national jurisdiction" (Montgomery 2002: 26). Recent research on IT and terrorism confirms the Internet's enabling features for terrorist activities, including its ease of access, anonymity, and international character (see Tsfati and Weimann 2002). Some have even claimed that IT has highlighted the marginalization resulting from globalization, promoting despair and hopelessness in the South, and thus contributing to the emergence of terrorism (see, e.g. Elnur 2003).

Migration offers both challenges and opportunities in the search for solutions to conflict. Migration has grown significantly, doubling from 75 million in 1965 to 150 million in 2000 (IOM 2000), and rising to 185 million in 2005 (IOM 2005). Collier and Hoeffler (2001) found that diasporas substantially affect the risk of renewed conflict; after five years of post-conflict peace, the presence of diasporas increases the likelihood of renewed conflict in the home country sixfold. In addition to economic challenges, migrants face the socio-psychological challenges associated with negotiating their way through a new culture and embracing an altered identity, while still maintaining an identity associated with their culture of origin (Friedman 1994; Lavie and Swedenburg 1996). For many, assimilation is a stressful process culturally, socially, and economically (Nelson-Jones 2002). The inability to assimilate may be associated with violence. Galtung (1996) defines the structure of violence as encompassing exclusion, inequality, and indignity. Feelings of marginalization and social exclusion have been shown to lead to violent behavior and to exacerbate existing conflict (see, e.g. Lemarchand 2000; Barber 2001). When the migrant's home country is itself embroiled in conflict, national and homeland identity can become problematic, increasing stress and a sense of marginalization (see, e.g. Esman 1986; Cohen 1996).

Diasporas can also make significant contributions to post-conflict reconstruction and development. The most noticeable and commonly recognized diaspora contributions include repatriation for the purpose of capacity building, economic remittances, and international advocacy. Some diaspora contributions are directly relevant to governance reconstruction: to effectiveness, legitimacy, and security. Repatriation is particularly salient to countries emerging from conflict, such as in Afghanistan and Iraq, where the filling of specific government and development positions is solicited from among diaspora members with the requisite expertise; and in the former Soviet Union and Eastern Europe (see, e.g. King and Melvin 1999–2000). Diaspora communities may be explicitly maintained and mobilized for the purpose of influencing international public opinion and building political support for human rights and political freedoms (see Shain 1999). For better or for worse, home country governments recognize that even settled diasporas "can still advance state consolidation and national development from abroad" (Levitt 2001: 204). Organized diasporas may use IT to facilitate these agendas.

This chapter explores how diasporas, using IT, may contribute to governance reconstruction in post-conflict and fragile states. It begins with a brief literature review on diasporas' identity, mobilization, and use of IT, and then illustrates with examples the contributions to each of the three dimensions of governance. Activities of the Afghan-American diaspora illustrate contributions to effectiveness (effective and sustainable service delivery and policy implementation). The case of the Egyptian Copts reveals how diasporas and local communities can utilize communication networks to enhance government legitimacy (reducing inequities, creating accountability, assuring service delivery, and protecting human rights). And Somalinet.com suggests the potential of cyber-grassroots organizations, specifically digital diasporas (diasporas organized on the Internet), to prevent conflict escalation and re-emergence from within the diaspora, addressing the security dimension (preventing conflict re-emergence, supporting the rule of law). The chapter concludes with policy implications. I do not refute the potential for the destructive impact of diasporas using IT to influence post-conflict societies. The case examples and analysis seek to highlight the potential and promise of digital diasporas' constructive contributions to post-conflict governance reconstruction.

What we know about diasporas, identity, and IT

Diasporas and identity

Several features common to diasporas bind their members and suggest a potential for collective action. Cohen (1997: 515) identifies a range of these, including:

- A collective memory and myth about the homeland.
- An idealization of the putative ancestral home and a collective commitment to its maintenance, restoration, safety and prosperity, even to its creation.
- The development of a return movement which gains collective approbation.
- A strong ethnic group consciousness sustained over a long time and based on a sense of distinctiveness, a common history and the belief in a common fate.
- A sense of empathy and solidarity with co-ethnic members in other countries of settlement.

These features contribute to the development of communities of identity, where members reinforce in each other their links to the home culture and associated values. Allegiance to the home country "provides emotional support and identity resources" (Kastoryano 1999: 198).

The literature on cultural identity in the context of globalization calls for and confirms cultural hybridization (see Friedman 1994; Lavie and Swedenburg 1996). Immigrants neither wholly accept their host country culture, nor do they automatically embrace their traditional ethnic culture to the exclusion of other influences. An important benefit of diaspora organizations, then, is the opportunity to negotiate cultural identity (Brainard and Brinkerhoff 2004; Brinkerhoff 2004) and enact it through communication and collective action. In his research on diasporas in the U.S., Yossi Shain (1999) argues that the US's tolerance for hyphenization – that is, African-American, Asian-American, and Arab-American – affords diasporas a greater opportunity to pursue their cultural identity, within the context of their American selves, as well as their identity-based political agendas. He contends that diasporas can both "humanize" and "Americanize" U.S. foreign policy, combating isolationist tendencies, on the grounds of American values of freedom and democracy. In doing so, they can contribute meaningfully to the quality of life in their home territories (e.g. through lobby-ing for foreign assistance, economic remittances, and/or informing policy and programs).

Mobilizing to help the homeland represents an expression of migrants' iden-tity. For some, the expression of homeland identity is based solely on a sense of belonging, in response to feelings of marginalization in their adopted societies. For others, mobilization is an expression of a hybrid identity which may encompass liberal values. Many migrants to the U.S. embrace American values of pluralism, democracy, and human rights. According to the integrationist plu-ralist model, migrants will protect "*cultural practices that are compatible with liberalism*" [emphasis in the original] (Spinner 1994: 76, quoted in Shain 1999: 26). Liberalism is both an assumption and a prescription. On the one hand, it assumes that "diverse cultures will ... prefer, express, and adhere to the same democratic values when allowed to flourish and attain the best that is in them" (Shain 1999: 26). On the other hand, it expects that citizens "will extend to others the same rights they themselves claim" (ibid.). Even where traditional cultures are less tolerant, Raz (1994) argues that they will face pressure within the American multicultural society to conform to more liberalist tendencies.

Identity is also implicated in mobilization for and against conflict. The culture model of conflict defines it as the breakdown of shared reality (Vayrynen 2001). The cross-categorization of identity can be a means to promote common identities and understanding, where one unifying identity dimension can be priv-ileged over conflicting ones, potentially fostering new perceived identities (Brewer 2000). Cross-cutting cleavages prevent conflict because "they create multiple loyalties, mutual dependencies, and common interests" (Coser 1956, quoted in Leatherman *et al.* 1999: 59). These new identities increase the degree of trust across category boundaries, contributing to both bonding and bridging social capital (see Putnam 1993). Bonding social capital can counter the destabi-lizing forces of social marginalization (Gittel and Vidal 1998); and bridging social capital can foster shared understanding, potentially preventing the dehu-manization of the other (see Northrup 1989; Varshney 2001).

Mobilization and IT

Political activism resulting from cultural identity, whether targeted to home or host country, is likely to be driven by "interests and obligations that result from migrants' simultaneous engagement in countries of origin and destination" (Nyberg-Sorensen *et al.* 2002). The higher the cost to status and security in their adopted country, the greater the likelihood that the diaspora community will split and/or fail to support the homeland (Esman 1986).

Successful mobilization is dependent on a number of factors, ranging from building a shared social identity (Pratkanis and Turner 1996) and providing an organizational or networking base (Klandermans and Oegema 1987) to generat-ing a sense of efficacy and subsequent impact (see, e.g. Kelly and Kelly 1994).

Issues need to be appropriately framed in order to focus individuals' attention and energy and enable effective coordination of their efforts (Snow *et al.* 1986).

Scholars have identified several factors conducive to diaspora participation in home country development. Esman (1986) identifies three: the material, cultural, and organizational resources available; the "opportunity structures" available in host countries; and "their inclination or motivation to maintain their solidarity and exert group influence" (p. 336). Economic resources are especially critical to remittances and sometimes repatriation. Organizational resources impact upon the ability to mobilize for political action and for independent development activities, such as home town associations, and the ability to access host country and international decision-making structures. The most commonly identified factor necessary for effective mobilization is the creation of a sense of solidarity and community identity (see, e.g. King and Melvin 1999–2000; Shain 1999).

These prerequisites to effective mobilization can be facilitated by IT as demonstrated by cyber-grassroots organizations (CGOs) (see Brainard and Brinkerhoff 2004).[1] Despite the digital divide, research demonstrates that the Internet offers hard-to-reach populations access to information beyond their particular location and enables these populations to "bring those resources to bear on real and immediate problems" (Mele 1999: 305). Several studies confirm the importance of the Internet for small, marginalized groups in networking and promoting their political agendas (see, e.g. Bennett and Fielding 1999). Not only does the Internet facilitate the rapid exchange of information for the purpose of coordinating collective action, it also reconfigures networks of communication, reinforcing and extending them, and influencing communication patterns and information access. Finally, Internet technology facilitates the framing of issues, both through established social norms, and through the structuring of interactive components and the rules regulating participation (see Warkentin and Mingst 2000). The Internet provides an organizational and networking base, facilitates information dissemination related to generating a sense of efficacy and impact, and links both like-minded and diverse diaspora members, forming an intense but heterogeneous network of social capital.

The Internet facilitates the expression of liberal values such as individualism and freedom of speech, either through anonymity or access opportunity. Jacobsen and Lawsen (1999) argue that IT may promote cosmopolitanism, or "a universal moral code transcending state boundaries and state interests." The Internet can become a test bed for experimenting with liberal values. In fact, many cyber grassroots organizations are expressly democratic in their functioning (see, e.g. Brainard and Brinkerhoff 2004).

Most of all, the Internet provides important opportunities for creating a sense of identity and solidarity around a shared cultural heritage. That is, it provides a forum for negotiating and reinforcing community identity (see Brainard and Brinkerhoff 2004; Brinkerhoff 2004). Rheingold (1993) demonstrates how the interactive components of the Internet provide forums for the exchange of ideas, debate, and the mobilization of opinion, potentially culminating in strong social bonds and relationships (see also Wellman and Gulia 1999). There is emerging evidence to support McCormick's (2002: 12) hypothesis that "if the Internet can provide a canvas upon which nations can paint their social, linguistic, cultural, and political beliefs, then perhaps the physical struggle for safe cultural havens and borders may no longer be as necessary for their preservation or evolution."

In sum, diasporas adopt hybrid identities that are often inclusive of liberal values. Their mobilization on behalf of the homeland is often an expression of this identity – both the homeland culture ties, and the liberal values acquired or reinforced by the adopted society. The balance among these will vary. When diasporas mobilize around a shared national identity rather than an ethnic group, they foster both bonding and bridging social capital with implications for conflict and conflict prevention. Mobilizing on behalf of the homeland is determined, at least implicitly, by a cost–benefit analysis with respect to the costs and risks to the diaspora member's quality of life in the adopted country. Mobilization is most likely to occur where groups maintain a shared cultural identity, and they have access to an organizational and networking base that facilitates the constructive framing of issues and ideas, fosters a sense of efficacy, and generates impact. IT facilitates this mobilization by providing an organizational base, contributing to issue framing, and providing a dialogical space of identity negotiation inclusive of liberal values. The following three cases illustrate these findings with respect to post-conflict reconstruction of governance effectiveness, legitimacy, and security.

Digital diasporas and governance reconstruction in post-conflict and fragile states: three cases

All of these case descriptions draw on personal interviews with the founders, and a review of empirical data and observation of their web pages, including an analysis of their links and discussion boards where available. With permission from the site founders, the research team registered as a user in order to obtain access to the CGO discussion forums, but did not participate in any discussions or exchanges. Quotes from the web pages and discussion forums include the original stylized language, as well as errors in punctuation and spelling.

Effectiveness: Afghan-Americans' contributions to government capacity and service delivery

Three Afghan diaspora organizations demonstrate varied contributions which diasporas may make to enhancing governance effectiveness.[2] AfghanistanOnline emphasizes solidary member benefits, or associational advantages that flow from feeling connected to others and belonging to a community. It maintains active discussion boards and provides a wealth of information related to Afghanistan. Rebuild Afghanistan is also an information source on Afghanistan and, through information links, facilitates purposive action related to Afghanistan's reconstruction. Afghans4Tomorrow has an explicit purposive mission, with a more traditional cyber-presence (more for information dissemination) and a greater physical world presence.

AfghanistanOnline's extensive links page connects members and visitors to sites and organizations that include those active in promoting purposive goals related to Afghanistan. A subset of these links includes information on specific actions individuals can take in support of development and reconstruction in Afghanistan. Examples include traditional financial donation (e.g. Help the Afghan Children, Inc., The Children of War Organization, and Afghan Women and Education); materials solicitation (e.g. School Supplies for Afghanistan); sponsorship opportunities, for example, of orphans (Sanam Foundation) or minefields (Adopt a Minefield); and volunteer opportunities (e.g. Sanam Foundation, Adopt a Minefield).

AfghanistanOnline also provides a "General Discussion Forum on Afghanistan," where individuals can create and add their own threads. Many threads are concerned with continuing developments in Afghanistan, the future of Afghanistan, and history, culture, and personal memories of Afghanistan. A few threads seek expertise (e.g. a translating company sought Pashto speakers, and an unidentified source sought a range of vocational skills), presumably to staff programs in Afghanistan. Also posted in July 2003 was a questionnaire prepared by the Secretariat of the Constitutional Commission, soliciting Afghan-American feedback on the draft Afghan Constitution it prepared.

Rebuild Afghanistan (www.rebuild-afghanistan.com) was founded in the aftermath of September 11, 2001. Its mission is to "serve as a virtual place and point of contact among all who are willing to participate in rebuilding of Afghanistan." Because of its explicit focus on rebuilding Afghanistan, Rebuild Afghanistan is listed as a "cooperating organization" on the Development Gateway Foundation's web page on Afghanistan Reconstruction (www.developmentgateway.org). The home page includes links to other Afghanistan- and reconstruction-related sites. A prominent feature on the home page is a job and resumédatabase, though the database was not very active during the period of investigation.

Rebuild Afghanistan's home page also provides an opportunity for discussion. The founder created and structured the original discussion topics. The threads pertain to specific challenges related to rebuilding Afghanistan: education, health care, the economy, and government reform. These discussion forums are used primarily to post announcements. However, a few threads have been relatively more active, for example, those related to donating school supplies. Under "Job Openings" an official from the Organization for International Migration advertises its "Return of Qualified Afghans Programme" and indicates where individuals can apply.

Afghans4Tomorrow (A4T) (www.afghans4tomorrow.com) was established in 1999 and formally registered as a 501(c)3 non-profit organization in 2001. It is a "non-political organization dedicated to the reconstruction and development of Afghanistan ... [that] provides essential services to its people through the expertise, knowledge and dedication of Young Afghan Professionals abroad." A4T is a vehicle for members of the Afghan-American diaspora to take leave and vacation time from their jobs in order to go to Afghanistan and make contributions of time, energy, and expertise to the rebuilding effort. Its welcome message clearly targets the Afghan diaspora: "It is time for Afghan Professionals from around the world to *mobilize* and help in the reconstruction effort" [emphasis in the original].

A4T is a purely voluntary organization. Active departments include agriculture, education, and health and human services. A4T seeks affiliate organizations for each of its departments, "in order to build strong networks for the betterment of the Afghan people" and to ensure access to requisite expertise. Approximately thirty volunteers occupy formal roles in the organization, with additional periodic and informal volunteer support from other members of the Afghan-American diaspora. As the number and range of projects has increased, the volunteer staff residing in Afghanistan has also increased, with approximately half now living in Afghanistan. The President of A4T currently resides in Afghanistan. Some of the staff in Afghanistan formally work for other organizations focused on the rebuilding efforts and volunteer for A4T on the side.

Among the projects A4T has implemented in Afghanistan are Ministry of Finance (MOF) training and staffing support, and support to schools. For the MOF, staff of A4T worked directly with the Ministry to provide training in Microsoft Office software, and assisted a USAID contractor in staffing the MOF with qualified diaspora members. Individuals who come to the MOF through the efforts of A4T are asked, once on the ground in Afghanistan, to volunteer for local A4T projects.

One of the most active departments is education. A4T provides basic supplies, books, and teacher salaries, sometimes adopting selected schools. A4T solicits donations for its school programs on its web page. It also supports the building of new schools, for which it has effectively partnered with other organizations, responded to local needs, and introduced innovative technology. For example, working in partnership with Engineers Without Borders International, A4T built a new school in Bustan. The villagers donated the land. A4T worked closely with the Ministry of Education to ensure that the school would be staffed with teachers. In consultation with the villagers, A4T coordinated a system whereby the villagers constructed the school using traditional construction techniques, combined with new roofing technology for which Engineers Without Borders provided training and materials.

These Afghan-American diaspora organizations present potentially significant opportunities for enhancing governance capacity for effective and sustainable service delivery. They do so by linking diaspora expertise to salient capacity needs for service delivery in the context of development industry projects and programs, in cooperation with international and local NGOs and civil society organizations, and directly with governments and communities. To a limited extent in all three cases, representatives of formal development organizations used the organizations' web page infrastructure to seek inputs from the diaspora. These included recruitment of expertise, and participation in repatriation programs. Discussion of programs offered by other organizations and links to other organizations further benefited development actors in terms of potential donations, recruitment, and volunteer efforts.

A4T best illustrates a proactive intermediary role. It acts as an intermediary between: (1) industry programs and diaspora members – soliciting expertise and recruiting for specific positions, such as for staffing the Ministry of Finance; (2) government expertise and capacity needs and the expertise available in the diasporas; and (3) local communities and other development actors, such as international NGOs and contractors working in the education sector. A4T works closely with the government to ensure sustainability of its projects.

Legitimacy: Egyptian Copts, diasporas, and communication networks[3]

The U.S. Copts Association is a dispersed population assembled electronically to debate, discuss, and propose and take action to support advocacy and promotion of human rights for Copts in Egypt. Founded in the mid-1990s, its mission is to promote the "advancement of Copts inside and outside their homeland" (U.S. Copts Association 2003). Copts comprise a majority of the 8 to 10 percent of Christians in Egypt.

The U.S. Copts Association has nineteen key demands connected to its pursuit of equality for all Egyptian Christians. These center on the need to end discrimination against Copts, increase Copts' access to government services and role in the government, and respect the basic human rights of all Copts. According to its mission statement, acts of discrimination and atrocities targeted against the Copts "are perpetuated and perpetrated, intentionally or through denial and neglect, by the Egyptian government as well as some misguided and misinformed Muslim individuals" (U.S. Copts Association 2003). Despite these allegations, the mission statement also confirms: "We firmly believe that what is good for the Copts is good for Egypt and what is good for Egypt is good for the Copts, as their past and future were and shall remain inseparable" (ibid.).

The U.S. State Department (2002) reports that the Government of Egypt (GOE) has continued a trend towards "improvement in the Government's respect for and protection of religious freedom." Nevertheless, there are exceptions to this trend (ibid.). An Ottoman decree from 1856 coupled with Interior Ministry regulations of 1934 require non-Muslims to obtain presidential permission to build places of worship. In carrying out these functions, the government must rule on the location of the site and the composition of the community in which the site is to be located. The President must also approve permits for church repairs. As a result of a December 1999 decree, the permission process for church repairs has been facilitated; however, Copts claim that local permits from security authorities must still be obtained, and the approval process continues to be time-consuming and inefficient.

The U.S. Copts Association relies on a range of communication technologies to educate Egyptian Copts, gather information, expose atrocities and discrimination as they occur, and facilitate individual participation in the organization's goals. It maintains a telephone network, and depends on local-level sharing of information. Some Egyptian villages may have only one computer, but the articles and information available on Copts.com – as well as its e-mail Digest – are shared much more broadly through word of mouth and hard-copy printouts. The founder estimates that for every one to two computers, another thirty or forty people receive the distributed information. The Association also relies on a network of people on the ground in Egypt to funnel out information and documentation of human rights abuses to the U.S.

For example, in November 2002, the founder received a Federal Express package from Egypt with pictures of a church whose renovation had been stopped by local Egyptian authorities. A family from the local village has a member living in Belgium who, following a telephone conversation with them, posted information about the problem to the Digest and e-mailed Meunier the priest's telephone number. The priest gathered information regarding all of the paperwork, permits filed, and photographs, and passed them to a Copt in Cairo, who then sent it to the U.S. Copts Association. The founder subsequently arranged a meeting between the priest and the GOE, resulting in formal permission to resume the renovation.

The interactive components of Copts.com have become a central forum for debate and expression about human rights issues. This is demonstrated in the discussions concerning the El-Kosheh massacre. On December 31, 1999 an argument between a Coptic shopkeeper and a Muslim customer erupted in two days of violence in which twenty-one Copts were killed and 260 Coptic homes and businesses were destroyed. Members of the Copts Digest debated whether to wait for the Egyptian courts to process the case or whether to present the issue to the International Criminal Court (ICC) at The Hague. In February 2003, ninety-three of the ninety-six defendants were acquitted. By March 2003, the listserv was lighting up with members expressing horror at the acquittals and seeking directions from the U.S. Copts Association on how they could take personal action to facilitate the presentation of the case to the ICC.

The efforts of the Association support actions that lead the GOE to take steps that may increase its legitimacy. These actions promote voice and accountability, inclusion, and equity. Arguably, the Association's efforts may assist the GOE in identifying and responding to instances where elements of Egyptian society may be fomenting civil unrest, thus contributing to political stability. More problematic is the GOE's capacity to formulate policy independent from imbalanced pressure from society or special interests. The national constitution defines Egypt as an Islamic state. Some laws/policies have disadvantaged minority religious groups. The U.S. Copts Association focuses attention on mobilizing demand to call for the enactment of legal reforms and their enforcement. By gathering and disseminating information, the Association enables and creates accountability mechanisms. It calls attention to instances where the national government's own policies may not be appropriately implemented at the local level and where that policy and/or its enforcement is inconsistent with international standards, thus potentially damaging the GOE's legitimacy in the international system.

The U.S. Copts Association's approach to promoting transparency and responsiveness is strategically directed. That is, it pursues a behind-the-scenes approach, as in the church repair example above, recognizing political sensitivities, especially as it draws upon the influence of political elites and international pressure. This choice of clandestine networking may reflect a sophisticated awareness of Kalathil's and Boas' (2003) caution: if corruption is widespread, using IT to promote transparency may lead to a crisis of legitimacy. By selectively and unobtrusively addressing policy and enforcement issues, the U.S. Copts Association gives the GOE the opportunity to quietly rectify the problem, and/or build its legitimacy by demonstrating its enforcement will and capacity.

Security: the Somali diaspora and conflict prevention

Somalinet is one of the largest digital diasporas, receiving approximately 3.7 million page views per month, with 126 discussion boards, and an estimated 20,000 members.[4] Its discussion boards are open to anyone and exhibit an extreme penchant for freedom of speech bordering on the chaotic and, sometimes, the offensive. Denigration, inclusive of profanity, of one clan by members of another is quite common.

Occasionally members request that discussants refrain from name-calling. In the research sample, such requests often emerged in the context of substantive debates about Somali identity and options for the reconstruction of Somalia, the subject of approximately one-third of the threads analyzed. The limits and perceptions of personal and clan attacks are continuously re-negotiated in the context of individual threads. For example, in response to accusations of clannism, one member writes, "As far as I can see there is no clanism here but the telling of some harsh and uncomfortable truths. We are not here to give aid and comfort but to get people to think clearly and analyze the situation" (*Entire City of GALCACIO . . . gets TAP water . . . except BARXLEY [habr githir section]*).

Threads related to future prospects and options for Somalia include: *Shall we forgive each other of what?*, *Would non-violent protest work in Somalia?*, *Do you think Somalia needs a foreign HELP?*, and *Reconstructing Somalia: help wanted*. One member initiated and moderated ten threads on topics concerning non-violence. In one of these he writes:

A united Somalia, without distinction of your tribe is where I yearn that I want to live, and I know that many do have similar dreams. How could we make a reality of our dream? A simplistic answer would be that we should approach nation building from the premise of shared customs, such as language, religion, and culture. It has never happened before (from independence to the last regime), and it is time that we should commence it.

(Who we are we Somalis?)

Another member underscores a common Somali identity: "In the end we are Somali. We will get pulled to the side at immigration counters, stopped by Kenyan, Habashi police, continue being passportless ... we look alike and will get the same kind of harsh treatment" (*WE HAVE DONE OUR HOMEWORK*). On several occasions members stressed the importance of Somalis still residing in Somalia determining their future, indicating that "those living abroad do not have the knowledge and understanding to make that decision" (*the former Somalia should be divided!*).

Hybrid identity is confirmed with reference to liberal values. For example, in a thread titled *ABDIQASIM BECOME DISAPOINTED AFTER HE ARRIVED*, members discuss the need to accept a president if that president was legitimately elected. One member writes: "On the whole America is ahead on the individuals rights and freedoms,so instead of knocking it we should be using the possibilities that are opened to those of us who got the chance to live there" (*What is American values*). Another member relies on an American cultural icon, John F. Kennedy's famous statement, "Ask not what your country can do for you. Ask what you can do for your country." This member goes on to encourage hard work, as opposed to looting and welfare, reminiscent of the Protestant work ethic (*the former Somalia should be divided!*).

Some threads garner more attention than others. For example, one thread, *Shall we forgive each other or what?* received no replies and only twenty-eight views, compared to the research sample's average of twenty-three replies and 378 views. Another similarly motivated thread *Would non-violence protest work in Somalia* received four replies and thirty-six views. The initial response was pessimistic, citing the power of warlords, though examples of peace marches in various regions of Somalia were noted. The thread ended with a proposal for every Somali citizen to disarm one "mooryaan" (variously defined as gunman, thug, or marauding youth).

More interest was demonstrated in a purposive discussion of how to rebuild Somalia (*Reconstructing Somalia: help wanted*), with forty-nine replies and 749 views. Here, members focused on problem-solving, reported on visits to Somalia, debated the role of clans in Somalia's future, and expressed guilt for not actively contributing to a solution. Another thread expresses a more instrumental perspective on why the Somali diaspora should help the reconstruction of Somalia, referring to family requests for remittances (*PEACE & Your POCKET: Good for your $$$$*). Members may express despair through angry exchanges, and at the same time confirm a shared interest in future peace. In *The first medical school in Somalia for 12 years* a member responds stating the futility of such efforts since the doctors to be trained will be murdered "for simply wearing a nice shirt." After some angry exchange, the member expresses hope that the initiator may be right in his expressed optimism.

Among the most heated topics are the possible secession of Somaliland and the appropriate role of clans. Debates regarding secession tend to include significant name-calling and graphic language. In one exception, *WE HAVE DONE OUR HOMEWORK*, the discussion was much more amicable, with a focus on practical issues, such as where to draw the border, whether or not refugees would be able to return, the name of Somaliland, and so on. Participants noted the pleasant nature of the debate several times, complimenting the primary debaters. When, after about a month, profanities started to appear, one participant announced his withdrawal from the discussion. Despite the heated discussions regarding the potential secession of Somaliland, the majority of participants appear to support a common future for a unified Somalia. Concern for what would become of southern Somalia is frequently expressed.

One of the most popular threads during the period of investigation (370 replies and 3707 views) concerned clan relations (*Entire City of GALCACIO ... gets TAP water ... except BARXLEY [habr githir section]*). The discussion included personal attacks and some responses in the Somali language. One member contrasts the diaspora's manifestation of clannism with his perception of clannism in Somalia:

> I don't think tribe will solve our problems. Just watch the forum and how some people are violently hateful. I don't think Somalis back home are to the level of doom some people in here talk about other tribes. I have hopes when I talk to people back home, and they seem to understand the futility of tribalism, perhaps they suffered the most while we enjoy driving nice cars in a well taken care of homes, that is why I don't take what people say here seriously. Somalis are Somalis at the end of the day.

That approximately 75 percent of these posts (not including the above quote) were entered anonymously may indicate the sensitivity of the topic.

Somalinet members seem to have a tendency to discourage destructive means of violence and to bridge their differences rather than inflame them. Clearly, Somalinet has not eliminated latent conflict. The tone of the discussions, with their frequent personal attacks and profanity, highlights continued tensions and frustration, and is perhaps indicative of a marginalized subculture. However, these frequently antagonistic assaults occur verbally in cyberspace. There is no evidence to suggest that they occur in the physical world. Nowhere in the period of investigation did members call for violent action with respect to the situation in Somalia. The one instance of an appeal to violence, the call to assassinate the author of a book purported to blaspheme Islam, was quickly quelled with reference to Islam's non-violent nature.

While the discussions of forgiveness and the prospects for non-violent protest demonstrated minimal member interest, the fact that some members initiate these topics and that others do not vilify these attempts suggests that the membership may not be inclined to take or at least condone violent action. The lack of interest in these topics may be due, in part, to members' pessimism and sense of helplessness, as indicated by expressions of frustration and cynicism with regard to the future. Several members call repeatedly for constructing a future around a shared Somali identity, beyond clan loyalty and geographic region. Members may shy away from topics they deem unrealistic, but embrace more feasible activities, such as participating in specific project proposals.

The community's norms enable members to express frustration and despair, even with anger, potentially resulting in healthy venting; and at the same time allow members to self-regulate to encourage respect and rational debate. Arguably this self-regulation may expand the range of actors and skills development for facilitation and democratic practice. Subgroups, such as clans, are limited in their ability to manipulate the framing of issues and needs for their own self-interest or to foment further conflict. These limits derive from a culture of individualism, equality, and active participation. Members hold each other to account by questioning the credibility of perspectives expressed and citing additional information and sources.

Somalinet is unlikely to prevent any single individual determined to engage in violent action from doing so. However, it may change the motivational cost–benefit equation of those who may be on the edge in considering violent engagement by addressing their needs to belong (countering alienation), negotiate their identity, and develop cross-cutting, shared understanding among diverse parties to latent conflict, all the while experiencing first hand the expression and enactment of liberal values.

Hybrid identities, mobilization, and IT

Whether or not contributing consciously to enhancing governance effectiveness, legitimacy, or security, the three examples above demonstrate how diasporas negotiate hybrid identities, and mobilize and use IT in support of these governance components. The Afghan-American diaspora organizations presume an interest on the part of diaspora members in the reconstruction of their homeland post-September 11, 2001. At the same time, A4T acknowledges that opportunities to do so through formal employment or repatriation may be of limited feasibility or interest to diaspora members. The U.S. Copts Association maintains communication networks that bridge the homeland and the adopted societies, enabling diaspora members to participate in governance processes by sharing and mobilizing around information originating in the homeland. Somalinet is probably the best example of how hybrid culture identity is manifested and informs opinions about the future of the homeland. Specific reference is made to both members' Somali and American identities, which are also used to bridge divisive clan identities.

198

Each of the above cases illustrates implicit cost–benefit equations that inform diaspora members' willingness to engage on behalf of the homeland. For example, some Afghan-Americans opt to repatriate or take long-term jobs with the Government of Afghanistan or in the development industry supporting it. Others are keen to contribute but do not choose to forgo their employment in the U.S. The U.S. Copts Association treads carefully in its human rights work so as to not jeopardize the quality of life and security of Copts residing in Egypt. In this instance the costs of engagement are likely greater for the resident Copts than for the diaspora. The degree of interest in particular discussions on Somalinet suggests that diaspora members may view engagement in an issue as threatening to their American quality of life; and/or they may simply view the potential rewards as too uncertain. Their reluctance to engage – for better or for worse – in the physical world on behalf of their homeland is illustrated by their support for the self-determination of Somalis residing in Somalia and by threads exploring the benefits of living in the U.S.

Each of the organizations uses IT in facilitating a shared identity, providing an organizational/networking base, generating a sense of efficacy (as in the case of A4T reporting its successes on its web page), and framing issues to channel energy constructively. Rebuild Afghanistan and A4T are structured to foster diaspora contributions to specific sectors in support of Afghanistan's reconstruction; and the U.S. Copts Association is explicit in its support for a common future for Copts and the Government of Egypt; contradictory submissions to the e-mail Digest are met with reiterations of this orientation. Members of Somalinet negotiate continuously for the norms of their online community; the nature of the large and heterogeneous membership precludes any one clan from framing issues and action agendas for others. Members do not appear to tolerate calls for violent action.

The inclusive nature of these organizations, their horizontal structure, and the hybrid identity of their membership reinforces liberal values which support commonly accepted features of good governance, including democratic practice, responsiveness, equality, and respect for human rights.

Digital diasporas: potential and promise

Post-conflict reconstruction takes place within the boundaries of an individual nation, yet the success in rebuilding is influenced, to varying degrees, by actors and circumstances external to those borders. These external factors can be proximate, as in the impact of a country's neighbors; for example, the interests and actions of Pakistan strongly affect reconstruction prospects in Afghanistan. They can also be more distant, though also important, as in the efforts of diasporas, supported by IT, to insinuate themselves into conflict processes or reconstruction efforts. While much attention has focused on the risks and potential negative impacts of these factors, this chapter illustrates the potential of digital diasporas to contribute meaningfully to governance reconstruction. Specifically, diasporas can use IT to: (1) link homeland expertise and capacity needs to skilled, available, and interested diaspora members in support of governance effectiveness – either through capacity building or direct service delivery; (2) facilitate communication channels in support of accountability and responsiveness to human rights concerns, enhancing governance legitimacy; and (3) potentially prevent the participation of diaspora members in continuing or instigating renewed violence in the homeland.

The physical activities of digital diaspora organizations are generally small-scale, leveraging very limited resources. Most diaspora members face a steep learning curve in terms of skills and experience related to supportive governance activities. On the other hand, while not a panacea, digital diasporas do offer promise in terms of framing governance objectives for interested diaspora members, facilitating diaspora mobilization in support of these objectives, and channeling expertise and resources to those ends. Digital diasporas represent a wealth of information, human resources, skills, and networks that can be mobilized in support of post-conflict governance reconstruction. They are also a ready, structured network for reaching out to dispersed, heterogeneous diaspora groups for information dissemination, public relations, and marketing of governance reconstruction programming.

Diaspora organizations are increasingly active transnational actors. Their scope and activity is likely to increase as these are facilitated by new communications and transportation technologies. Rather than exclusively nefarious forces, threatening political stability and undermining or competing with reconstruction programs, some diaspora organizations are contributing to governance reconstruction in their home countries, and mobilizing latent capacity to supplement and improve upon existing networks and strategies. The activities of digital diasporas suggest that reconstruction program and policy-makers need to expand their conception of diaspora contributions beyond individual repatriation and remittances in order to better coordinate and capitalize on untapped resources for creativity and impact. This research seeks to contribute to a better understanding of the drivers and capacity of diaspora members to contribute – or interfere – with post-conflict governance reconstruction. The less constructive historical experiences of diasporas suggest this imperative, if only to become more aware of the realities and to consider potential strategies for damage control.

Notes

1 CGOs are grassroots organizations that exist only in cyber-space (Brainard and Brinkerhoff 2004).
2 The discussion of AfghanistanOnline draws from Qazi (2002) and an empirical analysis of the web page. Discussion boards were intensely observed for a representative three-month period (August 1 to November 1, 2002); and were subsequently reviewed, less systematically, from June 1 to September 12, 2003. A link analysis was conducted on September 10, 2003. The description of Rebuild Afghanistan builds upon Meraj (2002). The empirical data for Rebuild Afghanistan cover the life of the organization

up to September 12, 2003. The Afghans4Tomorrow case draws from Mayel *et al.* (2003), an analysis of the web page content as of September 12, 2003, and Omar (2003). The case description draws from Brinkerhoff (2004).

3 The case description draws on personal interviews with the founder and CEO of the U.S. Copts Association, Michael Meunier, and secondary reports and literature. Two interviews were conducted: on November 25, 2002, and December 17, 2002 (Meunier, M. President and CEO, U.S. Copts Association). Secondary data sources include U.S. State Department reports, journal articles, and media coverage. Additional information regarding the activities of the U.S. Copts Association is taken from the website, Copts.com. The case description draws from Brinkerhoff (2005). Data collection also included a review of empirical data and observation of its web page, e-mail digest, and discussion boards, covering the three-month period January 1 to April 1, 2003.

4 Data include a personal interview and correspondence with the founder, and a review of empirical data and observation of the Somalinet web page (www.somalinet.com), including an analysis of its links and discussion boards. Selected threads (363, based on the topic's relevance to the research questions) were systematically analyzed during the three-month period May to August 2003. To augment this analysis and partially counter bias selection, additional threads were selected randomly to sample the general climate of the digital diaspora. Approximately 12 percent of the selected threads were not in English, resulting in 318 threads analyzed. The case description draws from Brinkerhoff (2006). The page views per month figure was provided by Abdi Osman and was drawn from his Internet server statistics page; personal interview by Jennifer Brinkerhoff, October 2, 2003.

References

Barber, B. (2001) "Political Violence, Social Integration, and Youth Functioning: Palestinian Youth from the Intifada," *Journal of Community Psychology* 29(3): 259–280.

Bennett, D. and Fielding, P. (1999) *The Net Effect: How Cyberadvocacy Is Changing the Political Landscape*, New York: Capital Advantage.

Brainard, L.A. and Brinkerhoff, J.M. (2004) "Lost in Cyberspace: Shedding Light on the Dark Matter of Grassroots Organizations," *Nonprofit and Voluntary Sector Quarterly* 33(3 Supplement): 32S–53S.

Brewer, M.B. (2000) "Reducing Prejudice Through Cross-categorization: Effects of Multiple Social Identities," in S. Oskamp (ed.) *Reducing Prejudice and Discrimination*, Mahwah, NJ: Erlbaum, pp. 165–184.

Brinkerhoff, J.M. (2004) "Digital Diasporas and International Development: Afghan-Americans and the Reconstruction of Afghanistan," *Public Administration and Development* 24(5): 397–413.

—— (2005) "Digital Diasporas and Governance in Semi-authoritarian States: The Case of the Egyptian Copts," *Public Administration and Development* 25(3): 193–204.

—— (2006) "Digital Diasporas and Conflict Prevention: The Case of Somalinet.com," *Review of International Studies* 32(1): 25–47.

Cohen, R. (1996) "Diasporas and the Nation-state: From Victims to Challengers," *International Affairs* 72(3): 507–520.

—— (1997) *Global Diasporas: An Introduction*, Seattle: University of Washington Press.

Collier, P. and Hoeffler, A. (2001) "Greed and Grievances in Civil War," *Policy Research Working Paper*, No. 2355, Washington, DC: The World Bank.

Coser, L. (1956) *The Functions of Social Conflict*, Glencoe, IL: The Free Press.

Elnur, I. (2003) "11 September and the Widening North–South Gap: Root Causes of Terrorism in the Global Order," *Arab Studies Quarterly* 25(1 and 2): 57–70.

Esman, M.J. (1986) "Diasporas and International Relations," in G. Sheffer (ed.) *Modern Diasporas in International Politics*, London and Sydney: Croom Helm, pp. 333–349.

Friedman, J. (1994) *Cultural Identity and Global Process*, London and Thousand Oaks, CA: Sage.

Galtung, J. (1996) *Peace by Peaceful Means: Peace and Conflict, Development and Civilization*, Thousand Oaks, CA: Sage.

Gissinger, R. and Gleditch, N.P. (1999) "Globalization and Conflict: Welfare, Distribution, and Political Unrest," *Journal of World Systems Research* 5: 274–300.

Gittel, R. and Vidal, A. (1998) *Community Organizing: Building Social Capital as a Development Strategy*, Thousand Oaks, CA: Sage.

International Organization for Migration (2005) *World Migration 2005: Costs and Benefits of International Migration*, Geneva: Author.

—— (2000) *World Migration Report 2000*, Geneva: Author.

Jacobsen, M. and Lawson, S. (1999) "Between Globalization and Localization: A Case Study of Human Rights Versus State Sovereignty," *Global Governance* 5(2): 203–220.

Kalathil, S. and Boas T.C. (2003) *Open Networks, Closed Regimes: The Impact of the Internet on Authoritarian Rule*, Washington, DC: Carnegie Endowment for International Peace.

Kastoryano, R. (1999) "Muslim Diaspora(s) in Western Europe," *South Atlantic Quarterly* 98(1 and 2): 191–202.

Kelly, C. and Kelly, J. (1994) "Who Gets Involved in Collective Action?: Social Psychological Determinants of Individual Participation in Trade Unions," *Human Relations* 47: 63–88.

King, C. and Melvin, N.J. (1999–2000) "Diaspora Politics: Ethnic Linkages, Foreign Policy, and Security in Eurasia," *International Security* 24(3): 108–138.

Klandermans, B. and Oegema, D. (1987) "Potentials, Networks, Motivations, and Barriers: Steps Towards Participation in Social Movements," *American Sociological Review* 52: 519–531.

Lake, D.A. and Rothchild, D. (eds) (1996) *The International Spread of Ethnic Conflict: Fear, Diffusion, and Escalation*, Princeton, NJ: Princeton University Press.

Lavie, S. and Swedenburg, T. (eds) (1996) *Displacement, Diaspora, and Geographies of Identity*, Durham, NC: Duke University Press.

Leatherman, J., DeMars, W., Gaffnew, P.D., and Vayrynen, R. (1999) *Breaking Cycles of Violence: Conflict Prevention in Intrastate Crises*, West Hartford, CT: Kumarian Press.

Lemarchand, R. (2000) "Exclusion, Marginalization and Political Mobilization: The Road to Hell in the Great Lakes," Bonn: Center for Development Research.

Levitt, P. (2001) "Transnational Migration: Taking Stock and Future Directions," *Global Networks* 1(3): 195–216.

Mayel, T. (Acting President and Public Relations Director), Hakim, F. (Financial Director), and Amiryar, H. (Information Technology Director) (2003) Personal interview by L.A. Brainard and J.M. Brinkerhoff, July 28.

McCormick, G.M. (2002) "Stateless Nations: 'I Pledge Allegiance To …?'," in M.J. Mazarr (ed.) *Information Technology and World Politics*, New York: Palgrave MacMillan, pp. 11–23.

Mele, C. (1999) "Cyberspace and Disadvantaged Communities: The Internet as a Tool for Collective Action," in M.A. Smith and P. Kollock (eds) *Communities in Cyberspace*, London: Routledge, pp. 290–310.

Meraj, A. (2002) Personal interview by L.A. Brainard and J.M. Brinkerhoff, 2 October.

Montgomery, J.D. (2002) "Sovereignty in Transition," in J.D. Montgomery and N. Glazer (eds) *How Governments Respond: Sovereignty Under Challenge*, New Brunswick and London: Transaction Publishers, pp. 3–30.

Nelson-Jones, R. (2002) "Diverse Goals for Multicultural Counselling and Therapy," *Counselling Psychology Quarterly* 15(2): 133–143.

Northrup, T. (1989) "The Dynamics of Identity in Personal and Social Conflict," in L. Kriesberg, T. Northrop, and S. Thorson (eds) *Intractable Conflicts and their Transformation*, Syracuse, NY: Syracuse University Press, pp. 55–82.

Nyberg-Sorensen, N., Van Hear, N., and Engberg-Pedersen, P. (2002) *The Migration–Development Nexus: Evidence and Policy Options*, IOM Migration Research Series, No. 8, Geneva: International Organization for Migration, July.

Omar, W. (Director of Education Department, Afghans4Tommorow) (2003) "Department of Education: Report for the Months of March/April," Afghans4Tomorrow, Department of Education. Available online at www.afghans4tomorrow.com (accessed 12 September 2003).

Pratkanis, A.R. and Turner, M.E. (1996) "Persuasion and Democracy: Strategies for Increasing Deliberative Participation and Enacting Social Change," *Journal of Social Issues* 52: 187–205.

Putnam, R. (1993) *Making Democracy Work*, Princeton, NJ: Princeton University Press.

Qazi, A. (2002) Personal interview by L.A. Brainard and J.M. Brinkerhoff, 2 October.

Raz, J. (1994) "Multiculturalism: A Liberal Perspective," *Dissent*: 67–79.

Rheingold, H. (1993) *Virtual Community: Homesteading on the Electronic Frontier*, Reading, MA: Addison-Wesley.

Shain, Y. (1999) *Marketing the American Creed Abroad: Diasporas in the U.S. and Their Homelands*, Cambridge: Cambridge University Press.

Snow, D.A., Rochford, Jr. E.B., and Worden, S.K. (1986) "Frame Alignment Processes, Micro-mobilization, and Movement Participation," *American Sociological Review* 51: 464–481.

Spinner, J. (1994) *The Boundaries of Citizenship*, Baltimore, MD: Johns Hopkins University Press.

Tsfati, Y. and Weimann, G. (2002) "www.terrorism.com: Terror on the Internet," *Studies in Conflict and Terrorism* 25(5): 316–332.

U.S. Copts Association (2003) www.copts.com (accessed 24 May.

U.S. Department of State (2002) "Egypt: International Religious Freedom Report," Washington, DC: Bureau of Democracy, Human Rights, and Labor. Available online at www.state.gov/g/drl/rls/irf/2002/13994.htm (accessed 7 October).

Varshney, A. (2001) "Ethnic Conflict and Civil Society: India and Beyond," *World Politics* 53: 362–398.

Vayrynen, T. (2001) *Culture and International Conflict Resolution: A Critical Analysis of the Work of John Burton*, Manchester and New York: Manchester University Press.

Warkentin, C. and Mingst, K. (2000) "International Institutions, the State, and Global Civil Society in the Age of the World Wide Web," *Global Governance* 6(2): 237–256.

Wellman, B. and Gulia, M. (1999) "Virtual Communities as Communities: Net Surfers Don't Ride Alone," in M.A. Smith and P. Kollock (eds) *Communities in Cyberspace*, London: Routledge, pp. 167–194.

Part III

REFORMING AND REBUILDING GOVERNANCE
Focus on the local

10

DECENTRALIZATION, LOCAL GOVERNANCE, AND CONFLICT MITIGATION IN LATIN AMERICA

Gary Bland

The progress of decentralization and the development of local democratic institutions in Latin America over the past two to three decades has been extraordinary.[1] In some countries, the change has amounted to a fairly quiet promulgation of new norms, as with Costa Rica's 2002 constitutional reform, while in other countries change has been dramatic and drawn wide attention, as in Bolivia with the 1994 Popular Participation Law or in Colombia with the long series of laws transferring extensive political, administrative, and financial resources to the departmental and municipal levels. The local governance resulting from the changes of decentralization has been reinforced in a wide variety of ways; some countries – such as Paraguay and, more recently, Peru – have even created new levels of elected government. Viewed against Latin America's centuries-old tradition of political and socioeconomic centralization (Veliz 1980), decentralization is one of the region's watershed reform movements of the late twentieth and early twenty-first centuries.

Latin America has experienced its share of large-scale conflict during this same period.[2] In fact, beginning in the 1980s and into the 1990s, Central America became the hot-war testing ground for Cold War grievances. The region absorbed record and highly controversial levels of US military and developmental aid and became the focus of world attention, not unlike the Middle East today. Colombia has been plagued by a multifaceted internecine conflict and related drug violence for four decades, with no resolution likely soon. Peru's Shining Path insurgency, which effectively collapsed with the capture of its founder in 1992, as well as various movements created to resist dictatorial regimes, also come to mind. Boundary disputes continue to flare up in the region. The Falklands–Malvinas Islands War (1982) and the brief battle between Peru and Ecuador (1995, and an incident in 1981), for example, remind us that conventional warfare remains a possibility.

The coincident development of both governmental reform and conflict suggests some measure of relationship between violence and the emergence of local governance in Latin America. Indeed, it is fair to assume that the link between the two is fairly strong in some instances, and for this chapter I have chosen three cases: Colombia, Guatemala, and El Salvador. Following decades of reform, Colombia's 1991 constitution affirms that the country is a "unitary, decentralized Republic." Once highly centralized, Colombia has become the most decentralized unitary state and also one of the most decentralized countries of any kind in the region. Yet guerrilla insurgencies and drug-related violence continue like an interminable nightmare. In Guatemala, thirty-six years of varying levels of civil war ended in 1996 with signed peace accords committed to the strengthening of local government. Although El Salvador remains a highly centralized country, its municipal system, ironically, continues to help sustain one of the world's most successful transitions from war to democratic and stable peace.

Given the considerable international interest today in failed and failing states, the relationship between conflict and subnational institutional reform in Latin America gives rise to any number of pointed issues for examination. Three such issues seem to be of central importance. First, what is the nature of the relationship between decentralization or local governance and conflict? Second, what has been the impact of these institutional reform efforts on conflict (and perhaps vice versa); have they fueled or helped resolve the violence? Finally, what does the Latin American experience allow us to conclude about the prospects for resolving conflict through local governance reform?

Decentralization and the development of local governance have long been associated in theory and empirical studies with the mitigation of conflict. The primary argument is that decentralization promotes *inclusion*: reforms to the system improve citizen access and the system becomes more participatory. By distributing power to the local level, the center allows local authorities and their communities to govern more of their own affairs and to take greater charge of their destiny. This can be a powerful message where ethnic and inter-communal conflict is at issue and where populations have long been marginalized by state neglect or absence. Riker (1964), for example, argues that all federal systems emerged following armed conflict. Conflict led to the emergence of a federal solution allowing the subnational jurisdictions, at least formally, to assume an exclusive set of governing functions. The opposing argument, of course, is that under the right conditions, decentralization is a recipe for state fragmentation.

A second argument focuses on the *division of power* that strengthening local government entails. It can break up authoritarian regimes (or democratize nominally democratic systems) and make it much more difficult for them to re-emerge. Decentralization can dilute the zero-sum politics of the center and allows for low-intensity conflict locally around local issues; a national crisis is unlikely to emerge over sewerage delivery. On the other hand, some argue, local elites or armed groups can take advantage of the decentralization of authority to create their own fiefdoms locally. Third, strengthening local government gives it the capacity to *improve performance*, especially service delivery, which in turn gives the community a belief in the state, or a stake in the future, and undermines the rationale for taking up arms. The opposite side of this argument is that the weak capacity of local authorities produces waste and corruption, further public dismay, and increased support for any disloyal opposition. A final argument that decentralization can mitigate conflict is that the local political process allows communities to engage in the resolution of disputes through *discussion and compromise*. One counter-concern, however, is the assumption that societies would actually change attitudes rapidly enough to make a difference, especially in a conflict setting.

Colombia: reforming municipal and departmental governance as conflict endures

Colombia's combination of extensive, multifaceted decentralization and continuing conflict over a lengthy period is surely unrivaled anywhere in the world. Decentralization emerged in earnest in 1983 as a governmental response to the burgeoning crisis of governance. For the following two decades – and arguably to the current day – the long process of strengthening municipal and departmental governance has been inextricably, albeit not exclusively, linked to the following interrelated factors:

- The Colombian government's commitment, to varying degrees, to intergovernmental reform as part of a peace accord.
- A desire by successive governments and a demand by civil society to open up the democratic system and allow Colombians – and guerrilla groups – to participate in public decision making of consequence.
- A belief that strengthening subnational government would undermine the rationale for insurgency and eventually weaken the guerrillas' motivation and support.
- A desire to enhance state legitimacy by reducing clientelism, rationalizing fiscal management, strengthening public service delivery, and otherwise enhancing the state's effectiveness in addressing citizen needs.

Two seminal events define contemporary decentralization in Colombia. The first was a 1986 constitutional amendment providing for, among other important measures, the direct election of mayors as opposed to their appointment by departmental governors. The second event was the creation of a new constitution in 1991. Colombia in 1983 was characterized as a regime facing the pressures of societal change produced by rapid urbanization; deteriorating public order, the emergence of various insurgent movements, drug cartels, and paramilitary death squads; rising civic protest; and strong public dissatisfaction with a centralized, exclusionary two-party system dominated by the Liberals and the Conservatives. This system was the product of the National Front accords of 1958, which were designed to restrict the scope of decision-making to a narrow group of elites.

To preserve the stability of the regime, the government relied increasingly on repression to control both the legitimate political opposition and the insurgents (Chernick 1989: 56–57).

Although intergovernmental fiscal and administrative reform had been pursued in years past, in the second year of his term President Belisario Betancur (1982–1986) turned to a policy of "democratic opening" and linked progress toward reforming the system of government to an extensive, partially successful series of peace negotiations with the insurgents. Opening up the democratic process meant, in practice, amnesty for political prisoners and guerrillas, negotiations with the armed opposition, national dialogue among all actors, and new rules of the game for participatory governance and opposition politics. The concept dramatically altered both the political discourse and the cleavages within Colombian politics into the 1990s (Chernick 1989: 53–54).

Direct elections of mayors, a measure advocated years earlier, became a central issue in the national policy debate and in negotiations with the guerrillas. Viewed as an historic reform – the first movement toward a Colombian *perestroika* – the provision became increasingly popular and gradually overcame the opposition of members of congress who felt they could nonetheless continue to control municipal administrations (Angell *et al.* 2001: 25). The government passed an amnesty law in 1982 and by 1984 signed peace agreements (that would ultimately fail) providing for political reform with four guerrilla groups. During the proposed eighteen-month ceasefire with the Revolutionary Armed Forces of Colombia (FARC), for example, the government pledged to adopt a group of democratic reforms, including the direct election of mayors and departmental governors (Chernick 1989: 71–72). As described by Orjuela, "the popular election of mayors and new forms of popular participation began to be spoken of, which would contribute to opening up the political arena so that political groups would have legal alternatives of political expression upon reincorporating themselves into civilian life" (quoted in Dugas 1994: 18). The proposal finally became law through constitutional amendment (Legislative Act 1 of 1986), and the first elections were held in 1988.

Additional reforms in 1986 provided a strong sense of the degree to which the broadening of participatory, accountable, and democratic local governance was a focus of reform. Although the measures were subject to criticism and their use was in many ways restricted, reforms included: the possibility of a municipal plebiscite petitioned by community members; citizen oversight of service delivery through local administrative boards; mandated local consumer representation on the boards of local public service companies; and permission for non-profit community groups to receive contracts to construct local public works and deliver services. Meanwhile, on the administrative side, the presidential decrees of 1987 under the Barco administration (1986–1990) transferred an array of significant new functions to the municipalities, including, for example, the provision of potable water, construction of schools, and maintenance of ports. State reform continued in the following two years as education and health responsibilities were also transferred to the municipal and departmental levels. Fiscal decentralization was progressing as well, as reforms beginning in 1983 strengthened the potential for local revenue generation, enhanced borrowing capacity, and provided for expanded, albeit conditioned, intergovernmental transfers to the municipal level (Dugas 1994: 25–27, 29–32).

The convening of the 1990 National Constituent Assembly to rewrite the Colombian constitution was the result of the initiative of a student movement that tapped into broad popular dissatisfaction with the continuing crisis. The increasing violence and political pressure from the guerrillas in the late 1980s created demands for change. Indeed, the prospect of participating in the Assembly provided a strong incentive for the M-19 (which would come to hold a 26.4 percent share of the votes in the Assembly) and smaller guerrilla groups that agreed to reincorporate into political life before the Assembly met – a major achievement of the peace process for the Barco government and subsequent 1990 to 1994 presidency of César Gaviria (Angell *et al.* 2001: 27–28). Commenting on the importance of the relationship between the Constituent Assembly and peace, Gaviria himself noted:

> It is enormous. Not only for the possibility that, through this process, new guerrilla groups will disarm themselves and integrate themselves into civil society, but also for the fact that those who continue the armed struggle who do not take advantage of this historic opportunity will find themselves isolated and will have to confront renovated institutions that are stronger and much more legitimate and representative.
>
> (quoted in O'Neill 2005: 115)

Yet it was the political impact of the extraordinary influence and violence of the drug traffickers, particularly the Medellín cartel, that placed the stability of the Colombian state in question. By 1989, the war with the cartels had fueled public discontent with the regime, and the drug barons' influence on congress was seen as partly responsible for the failure of constitutional reform efforts under the Barco administration. This strong and increasing public disillusionment was channeled into a broad-based demand for a more democratic political system (Dugas 1995: 26–27).

The 1991 Constitution and pursuant laws significantly deepened the earlier decentralization reforms and extended the effort to produce more accessible, effective, and accountable subnational governance. The new national charter provided for direct election of departmental governors – a landmark reform for a unitary state – and not only accorded the departments considerable new autonomy, but also identified their role as one of coordination between the national and municipal governments. Among the most important departmental reforms was the allocation of specific functions in health and education, institution of a series of participatory mechanisms akin to those introduced and now strengthened at the municipal level,[3] and dispensation of authority to governors to appoint national agency heads operating in their departments. The new constitution provided for the transfer, by 2002, of 22 percent of the central government current income to municipalities and also guaranteed the continued transfer of a special tax allowance to departments to cover their health and education functions. Meanwhile, reflecting the depth of the shift to subnational control over national fiscal resources, the reform abolished the national budget quotas (*auxilios parlamentarios*) managed by members of congress to bolster their clientele. Major new laws that defined the terms of the new constitutional provisions and further refined the new system were enacted throughout much of the 1990s and into the new century (Dugas 1994: 28; Angell *et al.* 2001: 28–29).

As much of this reform was expected to diminish insurgent activity and the escalating violence associated with drug cartels and paramilitary groups, anyone committed to resolving the conflicts must have been sadly disappointed. The two strongest guerrilla organizations, the ELN and FARC, emerged with even greater force in the 1990s, and violence associated with kidnapping, drug trafficking, and terrorism continues to the present. Four years of peace efforts during the Pastrana government (1998–2002) ended in failure, though the Uribe administration (2002–2006) has made progress in disbanding the paramilitary forces. Political intimidation and violence at the local level has increased. By 1997, guerrilla groups were present in 622 municipalities, and from 1988 (the year of the first directly elected mayors) to 1995, twenty-five mayors were assassinated and 102 kidnapped (cited in Angell *et al.* 2001: 37).

An important debate in Colombia has thus been the question of the impact of decentralization and strengthening local governance on the conflict. By democratizing the old system and improving local public administration, has reform undermined the guerrillas' rationale for continuing the conflict or, to the contrary, has it allowed armed groups of all kinds to capture local resources and institutions and enhanced their capacity to battle the state? Eaton (2005) argues persuasively that the impact on security of decentralization has been highly negative because armed groups have been able to take advantage of decentralized resources to destabilize the state. Others note the progress of institutional reform and expect the situation would have been much worse had decentralization not occurred (Angell *et al.* 2001: 38).

Ultimately, one's view of the role of political decentralization and the democratization of local governance on mitigating conflict in Colombia depends on the extent to which the new local institutions have delivered on the promises of reform. Again, the impact is hardly clear. Early on at least, increased electoral participation, greater local pluralism, and the return of guerrilla groups to legal political activity boded well. In 1988, when the first direct elections were held, more than a hundred mayors were elected from parties other than the Liberals or Conservatives (fourteen were former guerrillas), and voter turnout was higher than in the presidential elections two years later (Eaton 2005: 13). The insurgent groups who returned to political life in the early 1990s all presented candidates in 1988, including the Patriotic Union Party (UP), which was the political arm of the FARC (Eaton 2005: 13–14). Since the late 1980s, however, voter turnout has steadily declined, new parties have not shown much more growth (though the multiple candidates can participate under the banner of two traditional parties), and the UP was virtually exterminated by an assassination campaign against the organization.

Based on experience in other Latin American countries, it is probable that the leadership and professionalism of local administrations has improved because there is more at stake at the local level now. Colombians also increasingly expect their elected leaders to perform, and the old bosses appear to be feeling the pressure. It is unlikely, however, that the introduction of new participatory mechanisms has generated much change in the heavy clientelism of local politics (Bland 2000, 1998; Angell et al. 2001: 36–37, 39).

Striving for peace and participatory local democracy in Guatemala

Like Colombia, Guatemala is intriguing for the extraordinary degree to which the decentralization is associated with the incorporation of civil society, and historically marginalized populations in particular, into the decision-making processes of local government. The Guatemalans' emphasis on participatory, inclusive local democracy is a logical result of an enduring history of oligarchic government, repressive centralism, state neglect, social exclusion, decades of civil war – and consequently a peace process that makes decentralization and the empowerment of civil society a lead priority. What most distinguishes Guatemala from Colombia is the timing of reform. Whereas in Colombia reform efforts have continued in the midst of failed negotiations, partial success, and continuing war, in Guatemala the reform was integral to broad-based peace negotiations that brought the conflict to an end.

Guatemala's transition to democratic government began with the election of Vinicio Cerezo (1986–1990), who under a new constitution (1985) provided relief from the brutal military dictatorship of the early 1980s. Reacting in no small measure to the years of authoritarian rule, a series of important intergovernmental reforms was soon enacted, including regionalization, a development councils law, a municipal code for the re-establishment of municipal autonomy, and an electoral law allowing for the establishment of civic committees at the local level for the purpose of competing in municipal elections. A measure of fiscal, educational, health, and environmental decentralization also occurred over the following ten years.

These early reforms provided the foundation for a long process of achieving peace following thirty-six years of conflict resulting, in large part, from the distrust of the state and the state's exclusion from participation of citizens, indigenous populations, and women especially, in decision-making. These concerns reflected the engagement of civil society in the debate over the accords, through the establishment of the Civil Society Assembly. By the end of 1996 – following a constitutional reform (1994) providing a foundation for decentralization, participation, and respect for indigenous customs – the last of a series of accords dating back two years (negotiations began in 1991) was signed. Reflecting the tremendous desire for change, the agreement on social and economic issues declared:

> This Agreement seeks to create or strengthen mechanisms and conditions to guarantee the effective participation of the people and contains the priority objectives for Government action to lay the foundations of this participatory development. . . . Bearing in mind that the people who live in a department or municipality . . . are the ones who best define the measures that benefit or affect them, a package of instruments must be adopted for institutionalizing the decentralization of social and economic decision making.[4]

Among the many provisions to be implemented under the accords were the following:

- Reform the municipal code to provide for the appointment of deputy mayors based on citizen recommendations in an open town meeting, which allows easier access to local leadership.
- Promote civic participation through decentralization and the development of municipal technical, administrative, and financial capacity.
- Establish as soon as possible a municipal training program.
- Re-establish local development councils, reform the development councils law, and provide adequate funding to support the councils.
- Guarantee women's right to participate in decision-making at all levels.
- Promote administrative decentralization of health services.
- Promote municipal capacity to generate revenue. [5]

In the midst of the negotiations, the unprecedented election in 1995 of an indigenous mayor of Guatemala's second largest city reflected the new promise of democratic change.

Ten years later, a significant body of legislation had been enacted in an attempt to attain the peace objectives. By 2002, despite considerable delay, the Guatemalan congress adopted a reform of the municipal code, decentralization law, and related regulations, and a reform of the development councils law. A national decentralization policy was established in 2004, providing a framework for departmental-level deconcentration and municipal decentralization. The development councils – established at all levels of government, but not entirely functioning, to provide a forum for civil society – are considered a primary access point for citizens looking to engage decision-makers. The municipal code formally provided for or reformed the use of community associations, deputy mayors, indigenous mayoral offices, open town meetings, open municipal sessions, consultation with local authorities, and consultation at the request of indigenous leaders. Although not a product of the peace accords, a positive development is the continued acceptance and growth of local civic committees, which allow for increased pluralism in local elections. In the 1985 elections, civic committees competed in fifty-three of the country's 325 municipalities (16 percent) and a civic-committee mayoral candidate won in eight of them; by 1999, civic committees competed in 174 of 331 municipalities (52 percent) and won twenty-five mayor's races (Puente and Linares 2004: 257).

Actual intergovernmental and local institutional progress has been limited thus far, however (Külwein-ICMA/USAID 2004: 3–8, 28; Neuhoff 2005: 7, 11), by the delays and failures of implementation, and the difficulty of the challenge of achieving change.[6] Although there appears to be greater recognition of the value of participation, citizen involvement remains weak (Külwein-Neuhoff 2005: 7, 11). New mechanisms for public participation are being adopted gradually at best (ICMA/USAID 2004: 3–26), and conflict has emerged locally as a result of land disputes, vigilantism, and some lynchings of local officials viewed as corrupt. Decentralization has made little progress, as the confusion of functions, central control (and local dependence) of municipal fiscal transfers, highly inefficient service delivery, and the lack of municipal capacity to improve revenue collection are serious problems. Professionalization of municipal administrations has hardly progressed at all (Külwein-Neuhoff 2005: 19). Much of the promise of peace in Guatemala lies in the potential for improved local governance that has been generated by the reform movement.

Municipalities emerge in El Salvador's successful post-war transition

In view of the Colombian and Guatemalan experiences, it is perhaps surprising that the peace accords signed by the government of El Salvador and the Farabundo Martí National Liberation Front (FMLN) in January 1992, successfully bringing to an end a violent, twelve-year civil war, essentially had nothing to do with decentralization and municipal or participatory local governance. Yet the nature of the Salvadoran peace process and transition to democracy were very different from what we have seen in Colombia and Guatemala. In El Salvador, the accords amounted to reconciliation among political elites, an exclusive negotiation between the government and the leadership of the FMLN. Civil society played virtually no role. Indeed, the emphasis on input from civil society in the Guatemalan peace process was partly a response to the Salvadoran experience, which suffered from questions of public legitimacy (Arnson 2001: 44). The accords focused on demobilization, establishment of the FMLN as a political party, reform of the military and other human rights protections, creation of a national civilian police force, national electoral and judicial reform, and socioeconomic reform benefiting former combatants and the war zones. Reform was limited to the institutions – the judiciary, military, and national elections body, for example – perceived to be directly responsible for the conditions that led to the conflict: human rights abuse, military impunity, and electoral exclusion.

Moreover, El Salvador was and remains almost fifteen years after the signing of the accords one of the most centralized countries in Latin America. For example, the political parties are highly centralized. El Salvador is the only country in the region without a local property tax; municipal government is dependent on national fiscal transfers, and according to law there can be no political opposition represented in elected municipal councils, a feature also not seen anywhere else in Latin America. Finally, there appears to be no effective political will to promote intergovernmental reform today (Bland 2005).

It is the success of the peace process coupled with the weakness of elite-level interest in the purported benefits of decentralization and improved local governance – inclusion, division of power, and improvement of state performance – that makes El Salvador an intriguing case. El Salvador is atypical because, despite limited intergovernmental reform since 1992, the emergence of a local development movement in the wake of the peace accords has helped ensure the success of the accords and sustain the democratic transition. Municipal elections, sponsored by the U.S. as part of a policy of marginalizing the FMLN, were held during the 1980s under conditions of war and extensive human rights abuse. A measure of political liberalization occurred in the late 1980s, but these efforts were primarily directed for policy reasons toward external audiences (especially the U.S. Congress), rather than at ending the war and building local democratic governance.

The explanation for the emergence of local governance may be found in postwar intergovernmental politics and in the growth of influence of municipal or local development-related organizations.[7] Its impact has been favorable for the democratic transition in several ways. First, local government has provided political space for the major opposition party, the FMLN – a significant development following a civil war caused in part by the exclusion of the legitimate opposition from electoral politics for nearly seventy years. The FMLN candidate has yet to win a presidential election against its nemesis, the party of the far right, the Nationalist Republican Alliance (ARENA). By the end of the current term of President Saca (2004–2009), ARENA will have controlled the executive branch for two decades. ARENA's control of the Legislative Assembly continues, though it has slipped as the FMLM has made gains, including winning a plurality in 2003. At the municipal level, however, the FMLN's presence has grown considerably. Most notably, the FMLN has controlled the municipality of the national capital, San Salvador, since 1997 and won another three-year majority in March 2006. Municipal government has ensured the achievement of political inclusion and provided an outlet for tensions that emerge around the "winner-take-all" politics of the national level.

Second, though it has yet to occur at the national level, local government has provided for alternation in executive power and demonstrated that turnover of government from one party to another is possible without inciting violence. Figure 10.1 illustrates how, in successive elections, ARENA's local government presence has declined, the FMLN's has grown and waned, and the military's old National Conciliation Party (PCN) has increased significantly. In addition, in 2003, 105 municipal governments (40 percent) were won by non-incumbent political parties with new mayors (ECA 2000: 244). Whereas in 1994 ARENA controlled thirteen of fourteen departmental capitals, by 2003 ARENA controlled four and the FMLN (with alliances) eight (ECA 2000: 276 and Supreme Electoral Tribunal [TSE] data). Again, in the post-war Salvadoran context, the demonstration effect is of considerable significance, and the results indicate increasing institutionalization of democratic norms.

Third, municipal government has served as an arena for the incipient emergence of transversal national politics: local leaders are working across political parties with national decision-makers to achieve their common interests. The primary advocate for decentralization, participatory governance, and local economic development has been the Council of Municipalities of the Republic of El Salvador (COMURES), the Salvadoran national municipal association, which grew in stature with its own reorganization, considerable international donor financial support, and the increased interest in municipal development by international donors, non-governmental organizations (NGOs), and other private and public organizations in the immediate post-war period. COMURES' influence is considerable because the organization represents all mayors, who in many ways have common institutional interests despite their political affiliations, and their municipalities. Salvadoran mayors are also known to have that all-important local political base which can deliver votes for an Assembly candidate in the same jurisdiction (mayors and Assembly deputies are elected on the same day).

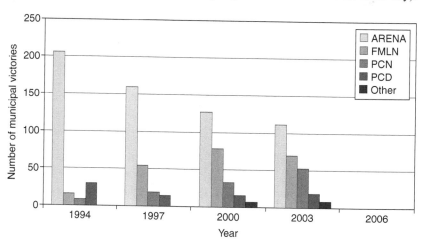

Figure 10.1 El Salvador's municipal elections by party (source: Compiled by author from ECA (2000: 244) and Supreme Electoral tribunal data)).

217

When COMURES lobbies the Assembly for additional fiscal transfers – something all mayors have little trouble agreeing on – the Assembly tends to be responsive. In 1998, COMURES secured an increase in transfers to municipalities from 1 percent to 6 percent of the national budget – arguably the most significant decentralization measure to date – despite the objections of the government, national political party, and a presidential veto.[8] The presidency of COMURES has now shifted from a representative of ARENA, to the FMLN, and to the PCN, a further reflection of cross-party collaboration and acceptance of alternation of leadership.

COMURES' emergence coincided in the early post-war period with the establishment of numerous NGOs dedicated to social and economic development of the country, with a particular emphasis on municipal strengthening. Their emergence was partly inspired by the near absence of concern for such issues or the role of civil society during the peace process, and the support they received from the international community early on was instrumental to their growth. Together, through their research on intergovernmental and municipal reform, training of municipal staff, and technical assistance to municipalities, these groups have become the leading civil society advocates for institutional reform and development expertise.

By 1997, the electoral gains of the political opposition induced the Sol administration (1994–1998) to reassess its governing strategy. ARENA, the governing party, lost eleven national assembly deputies that year, while the FMLN gained six and the PCN gained seven (ECA 2000: 244). In the same year, the ARENA party lost forty-six municipalities, while the FMLN (in alliance with smaller parties) increased its share by thirty-eight, including the capital, San Salvador (ECA 2000: 244). The PCN also increased its total. The Salvadoran president was suddenly faced with concerns about maintaining stable governance and about the prospect of his ARENA party losing its hold on the executive branch. His response was to call for a broad-based national plan of action for the country's development, something that was difficult to oppose. The result was the creation of a National Development Council and a series of consultations with civil society in all fourteen departments, multiple workshops across the country, and coordination with departmental mayoral councils, local and regional leaders, and representatives of various sectors in each department. Departmental facilitating groups provide a mechanism for national public sector and local interaction. The National Plan, based on inputs from hundreds of civil society representatives, followed.

Any effort to implement the plan and the consultative development process that brought it about would fade as the Sol government came to an end, but the momentum of the process pushed decentralization and participatory local development on to the national policy agenda. COMURES developed its proposal in 1998 for decentralization and submitted it for consideration (along with subsequent revisions over several years) to the Legislative Assembly's Municipal Issues Commission, which was established only a year earlier. Meanwhile, five major NGOs[9] founded the Local Development Network aimed at advocating for participatory local and regional development, creating alliances with international donor organizations, and presenting proposals for reform of the municipal code, decentralization, and other legislative initiatives. By the time Calderon Sol left office in 1999, he declared that the new Flores administration (1999–2004) was to inherit "the work of addressing with a long-term vision and vigorous political will problems as serious as territorial disequilibrium and the centralization of the State" (Red de Desarrollo Local 2003: 102).

The Flores administration indicated early on a clear commitment to decentralized governance as essential to the execution of the government's program. The establishment of the Social Investment Fund for Local Development (FISDL) as the leading agency for local development, and giving it the responsibility of developing a plan, as seen below, was significant. FISDL convoked governmental and non-governmental representatives and COMURES – the consultative group – to prepare the National Strategy for Local Development. That strategy included an emphasis on participatory process and decentralization and was adopted as national policy. The administration began to backtrack soon afterwards, however, and the lack of commitment to implementation of the strategy became clear (Red de Desarrollo Local 2003: 106–110). The devastating earthquakes that hit El Salvador in 2001 demonstrated to the public the role the municipalities could play in addressing citizen needs in crisis, and with NGO and international donor support, some were quite successful in areas such as emergency care for children. The Flores government, however, brought no significant movement toward enactment of a decentralization policy for the country. The promises of the previous administration would continue into the Saca administration (2004–2009), which has established the National Commission for Local Development to further address the question of intergovernmental reform.

These developments were the basis for the fourth favorable result of the emergence of a local government movement in El Salvador: considerable use of mechanisms of participatory municipal governance and local consensus-building. Promoted largely by the FISDL, RDL, and international donor support, Salvadoran municipalities use several of the mechanisms defined in the municipal code, including open discussions, public consultations, local development councils, community assemblies, and public hearings. Most notably, the introduction of participatory strategic planning to establish priority municipal investments in collaboration with the community achieved a considerable degree of institutionalization. The establishment of both the Development Fund of El Salvador (FODES) and FISDL during the Saca administration, for example, mandated that a municipality had to establish a participatory development plan with the community to be able to procure project resources. FISDL also decentralized the project cycle, making municipalities responsible for investment, design, and supervision. In one sample of local investment projects, 70 percent had been selected following a participative planning process. Legitimate questions about the sustainability of such efforts have been raised, but Salvadoran local leaders and NGOs have developed an understanding of participatory planning, enacted ordinances requiring participatory processes, and put them to use. Projects developed through medium- and long-term development plans appear to be most sustainable. Moreover, the establishment of *mancomunidades* (associations of adjacent municipalities for service delivery, among other functions), which have become increasingly popular, seems to have some permanence as well (ICMA/USAID 2004: 2–14, 32–33).

Finally, with respect to the favorable developments that have emerged from the municipal movement, it bears noting that municipalities are relatively well regarded in El Salvador, and they carry a level of legitimacy that other major public institutions (e.g. justice system, political parties) lack. As public dissatisfaction with national institutions declines – and it has significantly (Cruz 2003: 31–33) – faith in municipal leadership carries significance, considering the importance of maintaining system support during the democratic transition. Some of the explanation for this lies in the favorable view that Latin Americans, throughout the region, have traditionally held about their municipal governments as compared to major national institutions. In addition, in El Salvador the quality of mayors, councils, and municipal personnel seems to have improved, as has municipal service delivery and investments of the new resources transferred from the central government. Large and broad-based opinion surveys, some sponsored by NGOs, confirm the view that Salvadoran citizens strongly believe that municipal government is more responsive and able to do a better job in areas such as schools and community safety than the center (ICMA/USAID 2004: 2–48–50; USAID 2005: 50). In one poll, 47.4 percent of the respondents reported their belief that municipal service delivery was either "good" or "very good" (33.2 percent were neutral), which is surprising given the degree of centralization (USAID 2005: 126), but it also reflects the time and effort municipal governments spend addressing particularistic needs and favors of their constituents. It is also further support to the argument for some decentralization of basic public services to the local level.

Conclusion

Colombia, Guatemala, and El Salvador demonstrate that decentralization and local governance reforms are viewed by national policy-makers, local officials, and the public alike as one means of reducing or eliminating conflict and preventing it from re-emerging after peace agreements are reached. In Colombia and Guatemala, the armed opposition and former combatant leadership considered the pursuit of decentralization and stronger, participatory local government to be important strategic objectives. Repeatedly, from the early 1980s up until the present, Colombian governments have tied their peace initiatives and other attempts to end the war to the extensive decentralization and local institutional development programs. From the perspective of conflict mitigation, to the extent that the peace effort was successful in helping demobilize some of the armed opposition during the early 1990s, these institutional reforms were helpful. They may have also helped fuel the conflict by allowing the guerrillas and other armed groups access to additional resources.

In Guatemala, progress toward decentralized government and the creation of development councils and other participatory mechanisms demonstrated the government's willingness to reform during the initial stage of democratic trans-itions after 1985, and then served as one of the foundations for the achievement of peace by 1996. Finally, in El Salvador the politics of intergovernmental rela-tions and the efforts of civil society, supported by the international donor community, has placed decentralization and participatory local governance on the national policy agenda during post-war transition. It has also generated basic improvements in municipal governance – and continuing public confidence in the municipal system – despite the limited progress of national reform. In all three cases, the desire to mitigate conflict or sustain a democratic transition was by no means the only motivation for the advance of intergovernmental reform in the three countries, but it was a central objective nonetheless.

In each of the cases, the armed opposition was either seeking to win a share of power or overthrow the government.[10] Decentralization, which by definition amounts to a redistribution of power to the local level, provided a means for the guerrillas to achieve a "share" of power through legitimate political competition and without insisting that the central government directly negotiate away a measure of its authority to an armed opposition group. In Colombia, the promise of decentralization and increased local autonomy, which arguably achieved important successes, was hardly enough to bring an end to the war. In Guatemala, a similar promise was helpful within the larger package of negoti-ated agreements in halting the conflict. In El Salvador, the question of citizen inclusion in governmental decision-making and local autonomy did not come to the fore immediately, but did happen in less than a decade, and promises to remain part of the national debate for some time to come.

The importance of decentralization and local reform to the attempt to achieve peace was linked, to varying degrees, to the imperative of enhancing the legiti-macy and effectiveness of the state. Large protests and other broad-based expressions of public dissatisfaction, including the emergence of several guer-rilla movements, made it clear that a significant segment of the Colombian public had found the state inaccessible and unresponsive or simply uninterested in their demands to participate in decision-making. The system created under the National Front had also become ineffective in addressing the concerns of the population, be they a desire to end the war, poor service delivery, the lack of state presence throughout the country, or something else. A dramatic and lengthy process of intergovernmental reform consequently followed. Likewise, much of the Guatemala population had long been systematically excluded from a substantive role in decision-making, so it is not surprising that the civil society-minded elements of pluralistic representation and participatory governance became the focus of intergovernmental reform. Moreover, in El Salvador, bringing an end to the conflict and the emergence of local governance were not directly linked. However, increased local government legitimacy and effectiveness, the relatively high level of public support municipalities receive, and eroding faith in national government institutions, demonstrate the importance of the local level to a continuation of the relatively successful post-war democratic transition.

It is worth emphasizing, then, that in all three cases – and to a much lesser and delayed extent in El Salvador – as far as decentralization and strengthened local governance are concerned, the classic notions of the benefits of these reforms have predominated. The establishment or improvement of the democratic system was, and remains, the general goal. During these conflicts and/or during the subsequent democratic transitions, leaders at all levels of government and current and former combatants have accepted the beliefs long associated with liberal democracy that decentralization and improved local governance, as noted above, can bring the advantages of political inclusion; the division of centralized, authoritarian power; enhanced local government performance; and increased consensus-building through discussion.

The impact of intergovernmental reform on the conflicts in the three countries, which because of the numerous variables involved is essentially impossible to measure with any certainty, warrants several considerations. Despite all of the problems, expense, and adjustments required and ongoing, it is hard to argue that the reforms in Colombia have not produced favorable progress in local institutional development – improved leadership, for example, more professional administrations, and enhanced functions that are best carried out subnationally. It is also likely that this progress will provide an important foundation for sustaining any future, comprehensive peace agreement. In the area of conflict mitigation, however, it may be that decentralization helped prolong the conflict or fueled the guerrilla opposition – meaning that despite all the reforms, the conflict continues today. In Guatemala and El Salvador, the promise of decentralization and participatory local governance has helped bring the conflict in the former country to an end and sustain the transition to peace in the latter. For the most part, however, especially in El Salvador, where the framework for reform has yet to be enacted, that promise has yet to be fulfilled.

Decentralization and local governance is a lengthy, often controversial process that occurs gradually and requires frequent adjustment. Its impact is best assessed in decades as opposed to every few years with each new national administration. As is often noted, it is also not a panacea. Strengthening local governance is about gradual change in the operation of institutions and attempts to make them more responsive, accountable, and effective. On its own, decentralization will neither cure poverty, restore faith in a democratic system, nor end wars, as we have seen in Colombia. Indeed, it may worsen the violence. As we have seen in Colombia, Guatemala, and El Salvador, in the context of extreme violence, the most important aspect of intergovernmental reform may well be the hope it provides for peace: the idealism surrounding decentralization and the pursuit of improved local governance is impressive in all three cases. If conditions are not ripe for settlement of a conflict – perhaps a military stalemate, international pressure, new leadership, or other developments that could favor resolution – reform may well help, but it will by no means be sufficient.

Notes

1 Throughout this chapter, "local" refers to any level of government below the national level and is synonymous with "subnational." Decentralization is defined as transfer of power from the central government to popularly elected subnational government.
2 I consider "conflict" to be a broad concept encompassing a wide variety of armed activities carried out at varying levels of intensity, the core objective of which is to dispense with the opposition. The three cases addressed in this chapter clearly are/were conflicts.
3 Laws enacted in 1994 provided for citizen legislative initiatives, referenda, public consultations, open town meetings, requiring candidates for executive office to present their government programs, creation of submunicipal councils, and local administrative boards (Angell *et al.* 2001: 28).
4 "Agreement on Social and Economic Aspects and Agrarian Situation concluded on 6 May 1996 between the Presidential Peace Commission of the Government of Guatemala and the *Unidad Revolucionaria Nacional Guatemalteca*," Peace Agreements Digital Collection: Guatemala, United States Institute of Peace, www.usip.org/library/pa/guatemala/guat_960506.html, 1.
5 "Agreement on Social and Economic Aspects," 2, 4, 7.
6 These observations are based in part on the author's field research in May 2002 and February 2004.
7 This following discussion is based on the author's research in El Salvador in May 2003 and April 2005.
8 An effort is currently underway to increase the transfers by an additional 2 percent of the national budget, again over the veto of the president.
9 The five are: Salvadoran Foundation for Integral Support (FUSAI); National Foundation for Development (FUNDE); Advisory and Training System for Local Development (SACDEL); Guillermo Manuel Ungo Foundation (FUNDAUNGO); and the Foundation for Support to Municipalities of El Salvador (FUNDAMUNI).
10 Chernick (1989: 78) refers to the armed opposition in Colombia and Guatemala as "minority armed insurgencies," in which the stability of the regime is less subject to threat, as opposed to the civil war in El Salvador.

References

Angell, A., Lowden, P., and Thorp, R. (2001) *Decentralizing Development: The Political Economy of Institutional Change in Colombia and Chile*, New York: Oxford University Press.
Arnson, C. (2001) "El Salvador and Colombia: Lessons of the Peace Process," in M.S. Studemeister (ed.) *El Salvador: Implementation of the Peace Accords*, Washington, DC: US Institute of Peace.
Artiga-Gonzalé, A. (2004) *Elitismo Competitivo: Dos Décadas de Elecciones en El Salvador (1982–2003)*, San Salvador: UCA Editores.

Bland, G. (1998) "Political Brokers Revisited: Decentralization and Democracy in Chile and Venezuela," Ph.D. Dissertation, Washington, DC: Johns Hopkins University, School of Advanced International Studies.

—— (2000) "The Popular Participation Law and the Emergence of Local Accountability," in *Bolivia: From Patronage to a Professional State: Bolivia Institutional and Governance Review*, Washington, DC: World Bank, Volume 2, pp. 82–110.

—— (2002) "Decentralization in Guatemala: The Search for Participatory Democracy," Woodrow Wilson Center Update on the Americas, No. 3 (March).

—— (forthcoming) "The Transition to Local Democracy in Latin America," paper under review for publication, Washington, DC: RTI International.

Centro de Información, Documentación y Apoyo a la Investigación (CIDAI) (2000) "Las Elecciones del 12 de Marzo: Triunfo del FMLN o Fracaso de ARENA?," Estudios Centroamericanos (ECA) (ed.), San Salvador, LV, 617 (March).

Chernick, M. (1989) "Negotiated Settlement to Armed Conflict: Lessons from the Colombian Peace Process," *Journal of Inter-American Studies and World Affairs* 30(4): 53–88.

Cruz, J.M. (2003) "The Peace Accords Ten Years Later: A Citizens' Perspective," in C. Arnson (ed.) *El Salvador's Democratic Transition Ten Years After the Peace Accord*, Woodrow Wilson Center Reports on the Americas No. 6, Washington, DC: Woodrow Wilson International Center for Scholars.

Dugas, J. (1994) "The Economic Imperative of Decentralization in Colombia: An Inquiry into the Motives for Intergovernmental Reform," paper presented to the Latin American Studies Association, Atlanta, Georgia, March 10–12.

—— (1995) "Structural Theory and Democratization in Colombia: The Role of Social Classes, Civil Society, and the State in the 1991 Constitutional Reform," paper presented to the Latin American Studies Association, Washington, DC, September 28–30.

Eaton, K. (2005) "Armed Clientelism: How Decentralization Complicated Colombia's Civil War," paper prepared for the Naval Postgraduate School, Monterrey, California, June.

Estudios Centroamericanos (ECA) (ed.) (2000) "Descentralización del Estado y Desarrollo Local en El Salvador: Número Monográfico," San Salvador: ECA, LVII, 660 (October).

International City/County Management Association (ICMA) and United States Agency for International Development (USAID) (2004) "Trends in Decentralization, Municipal Strengthening and Citizen Participation in Central America, 1995–2003: Country Reports," Washington, DC: ICMA.

Külwein-Neuhoff, H. (2005) "Desarrollo Local Mediante la Buena Gobernabilidad Municipal en Guatemala," Report of the Planning Mission, German Ministry of Economic Cooperation and Development, ASDI, GTZ, final draft (May).

O'Neill, K. (2005) *Decentralizing the State: Elections, Parties, and Local Power in the Andes*, New York: Cambridge University Press.

Puente Alcarez, J. and Lopez, L.F. Linares (2004) "A General View of the Institutional State of Decentralization in Guatemala," in J.S. Tulchin and A. Selee (eds) *Decentralization and Local Governance in Latin America*, Washington, DC: Woodrow Wilson International, Center for Scholars, pp. 231–275.

Red de Desarrollo Local (2003) *El Salvador, Desarrollo Local y Descentralización del Estado: Situación Actual y Desafíos*, San Salvador: Red de Desarrollo Local.

Riker, W. (1964) *Federalism: Origin, Operation, and Significance*, Boston, MA: Little, Brown.

United States Agency for International Development (2005) *La Cultura Política de la Democracia en El Salvador, 2004: Un Estudio del Proyecto de Opinión Pública en América Latina (OPAL)*, San Salvador: USAID.

Véz, C. (1980) *The Centralist Tradition in Latin America*, Princeton, NJ: Princeton University Press.

11

SUBNATIONALISM AND POST-CONFLICT GOVERNANCE

Lessons from Africa

Joshua B. Forrest

One of the most compelling challenges of governance in war-torn and post-conflict societies is the rise of subnationalist movements, particularly as state fragility increases. In Africa, Asia, the Balkans, and in nations created upon the fall of the Soviet Union, the political assertion of regional autonomy has presented large-scale challenges to national governments that lack the institutional strength, infrastructure, and resources to decisively incorporate peripheral territories. As a result, the consolidation of political authority and sovereignty – a primary foundational assumption of the Weberian theory of nation-building – is in flux in large segments of the developing world. The political legitimacy of the state, overall security, and public management effectiveness on a nation-wide basis – the three central components of post-conflict governance as elaborated in Chapter 1 of this volume – cannot be re-established while mobilized subnationalist movements actively seek wider levels of political autonomy or even complete secession from a state that is unwilling to negotiate on those issues. This is especially the case if movement leaders are successful in capturing the loyalty of large portions of a regional populace.

This governance challenge is especially visible in Africa, where subnationalist movements have proliferated since the beginning of the 1990s, when the end of the Cold War and the distraction of the major powers by other conflicts left African states increasingly challenged to confront the growing tide of intra-country regional self-assertion. In northern Somalia (Somaliland), the Puntland region of Somalia, the Casamance (southern Senegal), Eritrea (part of Ethiopia), the Oromo region (of Ethiopia), the Western Sahara (versus Morocco), and the Caprivi region (of Namibia), these movements evolved into full-fledged secessionist efforts to achieve independent nationhood (Forrest 2004). Two of these movements were successful, resulting in the new states of Eritrea and Somaliland. In other cases, quests for greater levels of autonomy (but not independence) and/or a larger distribution of national economic goods have led to serious and often violent regional autonomy movements. These include movements in the southern Sudan, eastern Congo, northern Cameroon, the delta region of Nigeria, northern Uganda, northern Côte d'Ivoire, and (until recently) Zulu-land/Natal in South Africa (Forrest 2004: 53–76; IRINnews.org: May 1, 2002). Even in states where regional autonomy movements have not turned violent, such as in southern Mozambique, they nonetheless pose significant challenges to national governance.

In the following section I briefly review key aspects of the political and historical context of African subnationalism and discuss key policy errors made in grappling with this governance challenge. This is followed by an overview of major lessons from the Casamance secession movement in Senegal. The chapter concludes with suggestions regarding post-conflict governance in Africa, including a potential redesign of the African state.

Declining state capacity

In the past two decades, the capacity of most African states to impose order in the countryside or strike workable compromises with subregional actors has diminished (Boone 2003). The increasingly tenuous character of state–society relations is highlighted by dramatically declining levels of bureaucratic capacity and nation-state infrastructure breakdown (Bach 1999; Herbst 2000). This, in turn, has helped to open the door to a greater political assertion of regionally based authorities and challengers.

There are exceptions to this general trend. For example, South Africa and Namibia retain relatively well-developed state capacities. In these countries, despite some implementation difficulties, state capacity regarding public policy programs in socially important domains such as health care, housing, pensions for the elderly, job skill training, business support, public education, and funding for municipalities are relatively impressive (Development Bank 1999). This comparative success helps to explain why subnationalist movements in those two nations either failed to gather steam or faltered quickly when they did so. The promise of economic growth and of state largesse helped to parlay territorial grievances into democratic institutional domains (Forrest 1998: 182–189, 201–206; Forrest 2004: 203, 207).

This has not been the case in most African nation states, which have been marked by gradual infrastructure decay and by bankrupt or ineffective service delivery capacities. As a consequence, much of Africa has witnessed a dramatic loss of state authority in many territorial areas. In its place, alternative political structures have arisen, ranging from local spiritual figures to collective decision-making units of clan elders, from restored "traditional" kingships to youth-staffed bands of brigands (Forrest 2003: 227–247; Simons 1995). In a number of African territories, subnationalist movements have managed to merge these alternative authorities into a common front united in their assertion of regional autonomy.

Cameroon, viewed as among Africa's better performing states through much of the post-colonial period, declined in state capacity in the 1980s to 1990s and was challenged in the late 1990s to early 2000s by a movement generated by anglophones seeking regional separation in the northwest and southwest provinces. Niger, one of Africa's poorest and weakest states on the precipice of "failed state" status, has been grappling with a movement by Tuaregs for regional separation. Both the anglophones of Cameroon and the Tuaregs of Niger feel discriminated against in their respective nation states, but what is new about their situations is that, along with other factors, state decline has occurred to such a degree that nation state integrity can be more seriously questioned and challenged (Forrest 2004).

The diffusion of subnationalism is marked furthermore by the de facto secession of Somaliland (formerly northern Somalia), the percolation of a major subnationalist movement in the Oromo province of Ethiopia (the country's most populous region), and by subnationalist ferment in eastern Congo (DRC). In Ghana, Akan chiefs periodically advance an ethno-territorial agenda for political autonomy; Nigeria's delta region has mobilized an inter-ethnic front that is struggling for greater autonomy from the Nigerian state. In addition, significant territories reflect such political disorder or instability that they are ripe for subnationalist mobilization, including parts of northern Uganda, South and North Kivu in the Congo, and eastern and western Nigeria, where non-violent autonomy-seeking regional movements have been reconstituted (Forrest 2004; Kurti 2006).

Policy errors

A major factor behind the spread of subnationalist movements has been a now predictable series of policy errors made by central state leaders. In a context of already existing bureaucratic fragility, the margin for policy error is extremely narrow (Boone 2003). This means that serious strategic planning mistakes and miscalculations are magnified and are likely to result in major social or political crises. In Africa over the past two decades, policy errors regarding subnationalism have helped to weaken the institutional bonds between locality and nation, thereby exacerbating nation state decay.

The most significant policy errors shared by a majority of African countries are:

1   Failure to implement meaningful decentralization reforms in practice. From Ethiopia to Ghana, Mali to Burkina Faso, Benin to the Congo (DRC), ambitious reforms on paper to decentralize power to local authorities have not involved a meaningful allocation of fiscal resources or political power. On the contrary, these reforms tend to provide the central government with a more rigidly enforced, closer-to-the-ground control over local affairs (Boko 2002; Rothchild 1996). This, in turn, has provoked greater alienation

228

between local or community leaders and the government. Local elites often conclude that local economic development and greater local autonomy can only be generated through a separatist movement.

2 A second policy error has been an inadequate level of dialogue and negotiation with local and community representatives. Village elders (both men and women), schoolteachers, heads of age groups, recent high school graduates, community activists and other members of local civil society serve as repositories of local knowledge, cultural wealth, and social influence, and have a large impact on the political leanings of individual communities (Forrest 2003). When national governments ignore civil society institutions and individuals at the village level, discontent may build into what eventually becomes a subnationalist movement. Democratizing reforms may show some initial promise in providing inclusive opportunities for regional activists, but in Africa (Senegal, Nigeria, Cameroon) they have often been carried out in a way that simply reinforces the existing central state-dominant politico-administrative structure, while sometimes even providing new opportunities for subnationalist activists in Africa to articulate their cause (Ottaway 1999).

3 Lopsided regional resource distribution may be considered a third policy error. I suggest below that this is not as primary as the first two factors, but this has certainly contributed to the generalized region-wide dismay that in some circumstances led importantly to subnationalist strife. Regional economic inequity is a long-standing problem in Africa that dates from the colonial period and has too often been ignored in the post-colonial period. In Kenya, the Cameroon, southern Sudan, northern Uganda, and northern Somalia, economic neglect played a noteworthy role in helping to spur secessionist rebellions (Forrest 2004).

Case study: the Casamance

Senegal is not typically considered a failing or conflict-oriented state – on the contrary, it has achieved considerable success with regard to state-building, public management, and, especially, multiparty democratization and the holding of free and fair elections (Gellar 2005). Thus, Freedom House ranked Senegal 2 for Political Rights and 3 for Political Liberties in 2006, using a 1–7 scale with 1 representing most free and 7 least free. These are among the highest democratic rankings in Africa (www.freedomhouse.org.).

Nonetheless, for the past two decades a subnationalist movement in the Casamance region has threatened the country's overall integrity and political stability. This makes Senegal's Casamance uprising a particularly intriguing case study, with important implications for the study of conflict and post-conflict governance in Africa. Here we consider what generated the movement in the first place, what policy errors were made, and what constructive steps may be taken in a post-conflict context that can move the country toward peace-building and political reconstruction.

Historical background

Historically, the Casamance is characterized by highly decentralized, relatively autonomous political leadership structures and by animist, local religious belief systems. State centralizers, first the French colonialists and then the Socialist Party of independent Senegal (perceived by Casamancians to be dominated by northern-based Diola) spent years seeking to undermine and control these self-ruling communities (Diouf 2004). This contributed to Casamancian resentment against the central state-oriented Senegalese, as did the growing feeling of being economically exploited by the national government because the region's natural resources are extracted in large quantities but the state reinvests very little money in the Casamance (Gasser 2000). Moreover, in the 1970s to 1980s, the central state allocated unregistered lands – many of which were considered to be traditional Diola or Mancanha territories – to northern political elites (often Wolof), which exacerbated the region-wide growth of resentment against the national government (Evans 2004).

Policy errors and conflict evolution

Overtly exploitive economic policies such as land confiscations and failure to redistribute regional profits to the Casamance represented an important policy error. A second policy error was failure to provide political support to locally autonomous communities in order to obtain their allegiance to the Senegalese nation state. Instead, political domination was simply reinforced through the appointment of local authorities who remained subservient to the Dakar-based national government (Gasser 2000).

A third error proved to be the use of unnecessary repression against a group of rebels in 1982 who used primitive weapons to attack a local police station. This was the first organized, violent attack on Senegalese authority, but it was poorly executed and the rebels were easily dispersed. Afterward, the Senegalese state carried out a large-scale troop mobilization, used tanks to roam through Diola villages to pursue activists, and arrested (and reputedly tortured) hundreds of young men. This state overreach and excessive violence ignited widespread hostility among erstwhile non-activist villagers and helped to provoke a wide political breach between ordinary Casamancians and central state officials (Gasser 2000).

Through the remainder of the 1980s and 1990s, the state pursued a two-track strategy focused on political reform at the regional level, including administrative redistricting, and violent repression at the grassroots level in the Casamance. Political reform revolved around a "decentralization" program instituted in 1996 through which the Casamance was effectively divided into two new regions: Ziguinchor in the west, and Kolda in the east. For the first time, Casamancians were appointed in large numbers to local administrative positions. However, this was not combined with an increase in autonomy. On the contrary, the changes merely facilitated Dakar's direct control over the local political system. Moreover, this program was combined with a continuity of outright military repression in the villages (Amnesty International 1998).

For these reasons, the two-track policy of decentralization (deconcentration in practice) plus repression was popularly viewed as illegitimate state-perpetrated violence masked by showpiece administrative changes. The absence of major increases in economic redistribution added to the popular outrage. Through the 1990s, the rebellion became better organized and was led by skilled mobilizers under the banner of the "Mouvement des Forces Démocratiques de la Casamance" (Movement of Democratic Forces of the Casamance). The conflagration progressively widened into most territories in the Casamance (Gasser 2000: ch. 6).

In the 2000s, newly elected President Abdoulaye Wade added two elements to Senegal's anti-rebel strategy: the pursuit of direct negotiations, with the government offering amnesty in return for a stoppage of the fighting; and the initiation of a development project scheme wherein demobilized MFDC fighters were provided with lodging, provisions, business training and start-up funds for micro-enterprises such as shops, millet mills, rice-husking or chicken rearing, each of which was typically affiliated with a local NGO. Some MFDC fighters did agree to demobilize, with a number of them in fact emerging as rural development project initiators. However, the majority of MFDC fighters turned down the offer of amnesty and economic incentive, making clear their distrust of the government and their adherence to the separatist movement (Evans 2004).

While Wade's administration should be praised for its efforts at peacemaking, the political stand-off between the government and the rebels did not end. This primarily reflects the fact that the gap between the MFDC's autonomy-seeking goal and the Senegalese state's "no-compromise-on-autonomy" position remains unbridged. In the long run, this hard-line stance on the part of the government may prove to be a policy error, considering the extent of civil violence that has engulfed those African nations whose central governments failed to demonstrate flexibility regarding regional autonomy.

However, there are promising signs of the potential for a peaceful resolution of the conflict. Most, although not all of the leaders of the MFDC backed away from open violence in the early to mid-2000s, which made possible the return of thousands of refugees and the reconstruction of houses and agricultural infrastructure that had been destroyed in previous fighting. Furthermore, negotiations between MFDC leaders and government officials produced a peace accord in December 2004, with most MFDC political leaders re-confirming that accord in February 2005 (Colombant 2005). Nonetheless, demobilization remains an unresolved issue, and there is concern that some MFDC fighters intend to use funds they receive for the purpose of post-accord development to finance the rebuilding of rebel troop squadrons (Evans 2004). Furthermore, an important military wing of the MFDC did not sign the accord, and its leader appeared in an October 2005 interview (along with a corps of armed rebels) insisting on the legitimacy of the violent separatist struggle. The Senegalese police forcefully shut down the radio station that had aired that interview, indicating a return to the repressive tactics which the central state pursued in the 1990s and representing a potential provocation of further violence despite the recent accord (IRINnews.org: October 17, 2005).

Toward post-conflict governance

This recounting of the separatist movement's evolution and durability, combined with policy errors committed by the Senegalese state, has important implications for post-conflict governance. In the first place, beyond its impressive guerrilla military capacity, one of the Casamance separatist movement's greatest strengths is its multi-ethnic inclusivity, with non-Diola minority groups participating strongly in predominantly Diola MFDC units (Gasser 2000; ch. 2). If MFDC unit heads and political leaders are given significant political and administrative roles in a post-conflict context, this ethnic inclusivity may well serve to encourage stability and a sense of region-wide unity. Second, the MFDC has learned how to effectively exploit the region's natural resources, including timber, fishing, and cashew-nut marketing (Evans 2004). Surely this is an organizational strength that can contribute to the Casamance's economic prosperity if the Senegalese state provides the region with sufficient political and economic autonomy and, again, if MFDC leaders are accorded a responsible role in managing the region.

Third, it is clear that administrative deconcentration masking as decentralization is an inadequate response to a deep-rooted quest for regional autonomy, even when accompanied by an infusion of local development-oriented projects. Reform efforts need to be combined with a genuine empowerment of locally entrenched political forces, including the MFDC, as part of a creative redesign of the local political authority framework. That framework may include central state representatives, but a post-conflict creative redesign of the Casamancian political structure should prioritize local and regional control over Casamancian politics and resources.

Fourth, the central government ought to serve mainly as facilitator of such a creative redesign, rather than would-be hegemonic manager. Adopting a more bargaining-oriented attitude in the redesign of regional administration would benefit Senegalese leaders by increasing the likelihood of achieving a permanent peace, which would bring the Senegalese government international political praise and recognition as a peacemaker. This would be of great value to President Wade in particular because it would increase Wade's standing regionally (in the Economic Commission of West African States, for example) as well as internationally (in the African Union, the European Union, and the United Nations), while also boosting his prestige as an effective president at home. Furthermore, a permanent peace would help generate increased resources for the Senegalese nation by re-establishing tourism as a major industry in Casamance and by assuring that no further blockages to center–periphery trade flows occur.

232

Subnationalist movements and post-conflict governance

There are a number of lessons that may be gleaned from the Casamance case, and from the dynamics of subnationalist movements in other parts of Africa, that have implications for peace-building and for the establishment of effective post-conflict governance. First, from a policy perspective – "How should the national state deal with subnationalist movements?" – it is clear from the above discussion that state strategies focused on either military suppression or administrative domination are unlikely to prove successful, and may simply exacerbate subnationalist resistance. Subnationalist rebels may be open to negotiation if central governments are willing to seriously consider allowing a degree of regional autonomy and the inclusion into local administrative structures of true representatives of local civil society institutions. Rebel leaders have made that clear in the Casamance as well as in southern Sudan, where a 2004 accord that appears to have ended thirty years of secessionist warfare was reached once the central government finally agreed to cede a wide latitude of political autonomy to the region (Agence France-Presse 2005).

The most politically astute choice of nation state leaders dealing with regionalist uprisings is to arrive at the bargaining table with a flexible attitude regarding regional self-rule. Incentives for adopting such an attitude include: (1) the avoidance of a widening of the conflagration that might threaten the long-term political stability, democratization, and development of Senegal as a nation state, (2) the likely increase in international development aid and donor support that would flow into the Casamance region should a permanent peace be achieved, and (3) an increased potential for improving the effectiveness of local public service delivery that would accompany the incorporation of genuine representatives of rural civil society into local administrative frameworks. This, in turn, would help generate increased popular legitimacy for those local frameworks and, by extension, for the integrity of the nation state.

Second, some subnationalist movements have characteristics that are not only favorable to long-term peace-building but can facilitate the implementation of decentralization approaches to post-conflict governance. Relatively successful movements in the Casamance, Eritrea, and northern Somalia (Somaliland) initially gained popular support due, in part, to the respect they demonstrated for village and community-level autonomy (Forrest 2004). It is rarely the case, in most of Africa, that regional movement leaders simply impose their authority on hostile local cultures. More typically, movement organizers spend years building up relationships at the human level with villagers in communities throughout the region, and tend to abide by the predominant mores of the local culture (ibid.). The ability to retain community-based autonomy often spurs villagers to support a subnationalist movement; in the post-conflict phase, a new mode of governance ought to be predicated on a decentralization strategy that takes full advantage of this already-existing self-administered decision-making at the community level.

Third, contrary to popular belief, most subnationalist movements are similar to the Casamance rebellion in that they are inter-ethnic in character, based on region-wide alliances among a broad variety of social actors and community leaders (ibid.). The multi-ethnic, territorially based movement supporting the secessionist struggle in the Western Sahara represents a compelling example (Antil 2002). The alliance-based political foundation of political order is already there, as it is in other rebellious regions. Empowering inter-ethnic movements at the regional level by giving movement leaders responsibility for administrative management and adjudication roles would enable governments to not only reduce the potential for further violent conflict, but would also preserve the inclusive character of regional politics. This, in turn, would facilitate the post-conflict political reconstruction of authority systems on a more locally legitimate, alliance-oriented, peace-generating basis.

Fourth, even if rebels use violent means to pursue their political ends, they may well prove positively disposed to electoral democratization in the post-conflict period. Somaliland (formerly northern Somalia) provides a stellar example, with regularly held elections (three times in the past ten years), the most recent being September 2005, when eighty-two parliamentarians were elected from among 346 candidates in balloting declared free and fair by international observers (IRINnews.org: September 29, October 4, October 10, 2005). For the past decade, this separatist state has had a popularly chosen president and an effective Parliament that includes a broad variety of elected representatives from across the region (Forrest 2004). The Oromo rebel movement in Ethiopia has extensive electoral experience and the rebels claim a democratic commitment. And in Southern Sudan, the 2004 treaty signed by the rebels commits the new regional government in the south to a political reform process that is aimed at electoral governance (Agence France-Presse 2005; Blunt 2003). The establishment of a multi-ethnic legislative assembly in September 2005 represented a noteworthy step in that direction (IRINnews.org: September 30, 2005).

Finally, the movements that endure over time tend to produce viable organizational structures, such as intra-movement communication networks, that can potentially serve as a basis for governance-building and the creation of political and administrative infrastructure in the post-conflict period. The organizational competence of the Eritrean People's Liberation Front was demonstrated not only in their effective management of the secessionist war against Ethiopia but also in their construction of new nation-wide political, economic, and educational institutions following Eritrea's independence. These post-independence institutions were, at least in part, based on the infrastructure and inter-village networks established by the liberation movement (Pool 2001).

In this regard, in addition to the Southern Sudanese legislature (mentioned above), in October 2005 an autonomous regional Cabinet was created in large part with former rebel leaders from various political factions (IRINnews.org: October 24, 2005). This means that the Southern Sudanese government now has the opportunity to construct region-wide governance institutions at least in part on the basis of the organizational infrastructures established by the former rebel groups (AP News 2004). It is likely that should a similar agreement be reached in the Casamance, post-conflict governance would benefit from the incorporation of rebel organizational and communications networks into a new, more regionally autonomous political-administrative framework.

Post-conflict governance and redesigning the African state

This discussion of subnationalism and post-conflict governance allows us to respond to the important query raised in Chapter 1 regarding the sequences of post-conflict priorities: economics first, then politics? Or vice versa? Or should other issues take priority in post-conflict governance? It is clear from our analysis that political issues trump economics when it comes to restoring nation state legitimacy. While it was the case that economic underdevelopment in the Casamance region (compared to Dakar and other areas) contributed to regional dissatisfaction, it was principally the government's insistence on political domination, the lack of meaningful decentralization, and military repression that increased popular support for the Casamancian separatist movement.

Economic development is crucial to assuring successful long-term governance, but the first-order-of-priority factors in constructing a workable post-conflict governance framework are political in nature: the restoration of political legitimacy, assuring inclusivity, carrying out a substantive decentralization program, and meaningful bargaining between central state and regional actors. This, in turn, would require a major redesign of most African states, especially those grappling with subnationalist discontent. Legitimacy, inclusivity, decentralization, and bargaining would be best promoted in a flexible, innovative politico-administrative context that builds on the positive features of subnationalist movements.

A redesign of the African state system would involve a more dispersed system of locally idiosyncratic political rule than the centralized model which the current state system embraces. An innovative, inclusive decentralization program would respect regionally specific political traditions and would ensure that legitimate local leaders are based in their home territories – rather than being directly incorporated into an administrative-political hierarchy whose summit is the center of national power in the capital city. Meaningful decentralization would contrast with the typical African governance strategy in which states deconcentrate their administrative structures without relaxing centrally controlled bureaucratic and fiscal constraints (Boko 2002).

Broadly speaking, center–periphery political relations in a redesigned African state model ought to reflect a cooperative, bargaining-oriented sharing of decentralized political authority, rather than a struggle for control over regional authority and resources. The historical evidence for such a negotiation-based model is compelling; it characterized a number of power-sharing and polyarchical regimes in West, East, and Southern Africa in the 1960s to 1990s (Rothchild 1997). A contemporary version of a decentralized shared authority political system could be viable given appropriate incentives provided to regional political leaders by the state (such as de facto autonomy), and to central state leaders by the international community (such as providing increased development aid to states that adopt and employ shared authority models).

Shared political authority systems at the regional level ought to prove more flexible and politically manageable than more rigidly defined constitutional structures. A looser political design that focuses on the *process* of informal bargaining was a key factor in the success of pre-colonial African state-building (Vansina 1990), and was important in the early post-colonial period in establishing a balance between local and central power (Rothchild and Olorunsola 1983).

Informal, flexible shared authority systems can again prove valuable in a post-conflict political context if adequate incentives are provided to key stakeholders. Regional rebels are more likely to abandon an armed struggle if agreements are fashioned that focus on an increase in regional autonomy. Rebel leaders are more likely to accept peace agreements if they are given an important leadership role within newly autonomized regional institutions. International authorities on decentralization in Africa such as Dele Olowu, James Wunsch, and Donald Rothchild have pointed to newly decentralized public administrative structures as a possible conflict resolution strategy, already used in such nations as South Africa and Ethiopia (to variable effect) (Olowu and Wunsch 2004: 51; Rothchild 1997: 56–58). Decentralization that incorporates former rebels (as in southern Sudan) could appeal to state leaders as a mechanism for holding on to the broad reigns of political power in a disputed territory without the use of state violence, while also serving as an incentive for regional elites (and regional rebels) to enter into peacemaking negotiations because doing so would provide them with greater local and international legitimation.

As new decentralization programs are forged and implemented, state leaders could be offered rewards from external donors for adhering to newly crafted regional administrative structures that in fact allow for greater levels of regional autonomy. Those rewards could include economic investments in the newly decentralized regions, combined with budgetary support to national ministries that demonstrate a sustained commitment to broadening the autonomous fiscal and political powers of local governments. Rothchild refers to the use of economic incentives to state leaders as "purchase" to be employed as a domestic conflict-reducing strategy (Rothchild 1997: 99–100), but here I extend the concept by applying it specifically to the international support for the implementation of a meaningful decentralization program. Rewards provided by international donors could include, in addition to those mentioned above, a separate stream of development aid to support infrastructural development (modern water piping, road-building, railroad improvements) and social development (rural health care, agricultural technical supports) to regions in those nations that adopt a power-sharing form of decentralization. The specific choice of program to be internationally financed would depend on the priorities of each particular region, as articulated by a newly decentralized local or regional government.

It was indicated above that many subnationalist movements in part represent multi-level constructions of political authority and include locally generated authority systems at the grassroots level. The decline of the central state in Nigeria, Uganda, Ghana, and elsewhere in contemporary Africa has enabled many traditional authority systems to be reinvented in a politically legitimate (often electoral) way that has restored the influence of kings or elders (Forrest 2004). In a newly decentralized polity, traditional leaders and respected elders could play a key role by providing a substantial degree of political security and stability, especially in rural areas. However, over-reliance on rural chiefs in some contexts could prove problematic, considering that many traditional authorities in fragile states such as Sierra Leone base their power on personally controlled police forces and unregulated taxation, and do not seek electoral confirmation (Jackson 2005). Furthermore, locally legitimate leaders may be entrenched within collective, egalitarian decision-making structures that are independent of any chieftaincy authority system.

Because of these complexities, post-conflict decentralized governance systems – especially those where there is no region-wide former rebel organization on which to base the system – ought to reflect preliminary investigations of the micro-level structure of authority in the rural areas of fragile nation states. Here, external donors could seek out professional anthropologists to provide an objective analysis of the allocation of political power at the micro-level, and who would pass along their findings to the general public and to the national government. The information garnered from those investigations could help to assure that negotiations held between regional political leaders and central state representatives are informed by an accurate understanding of local power arrangements. This does not mean to suggest that regional leaders currently lack information about grassroots politics in their respective regions; the contrary is typically the case. But central state officials often are, in fact, unfamiliar with the history of local political structures, and improving their understanding of those structures could in turn improve the quality and outcome of center–regional bargaining processes (once such processes are in place) as well as the construction of a post-conflict administrative system with high levels of decentralized authority.

The incorporation of the results of an objective investigation of village-level political arrangements would likely prove beneficial to the viability and authenticity of newly empowered local governments. In their recent study of decentralization in Africa, Olowu and Wunsch (2004) emphasize the importance of including a broad variety of community-level representatives and indigenous leaders with conflict resolution experience into restructured local government frameworks. Here I would suggest that the aforementioned anthropological-level investigations could contribute substantially to crafting new institutions that accurately reflect the existing power structure at the local level. Actors in rural Africa who could also play a helpful role in building knowledge about the history of authentic local political institutions into governance arrangements include, especially, schoolteachers (as they are educated and able to articulate to state officials the local histories of their communities), representatives of peasant organizations (considering the key economic role of peasant producers), local religious leaders (as they have often played local conflict resolution roles), a geographically dispersed representation of older women (as they are aware of local power structures but are often omitted from them), and a territorially dispersed representation of older men (as they often have the wisdom and insight of having observed local political arrangements over the course of decades and can therefore contribute usefully to deciding what may and may not prove workable).

Redesigned political-administrative frameworks necessitate a commitment on the part of national authorities to long-term change that empowers local communities; this has not been Africa's recent history, and it will be difficult and challenging to generate a commitment by government leaders to strongly decentralized intergovernmental arrangements. However, African states' interest in conflict avoidance and in receiving higher levels of external aid represent incentives that could generate movement toward a broad administrative restructuring, especially in countries where regional violence has already flared. Inclusion of schoolteachers, religious leaders, peasant organizations, respected elderly women and men from geographically disparate areas, as well as professional anthropologists, could represent a helpful step toward a locally informed redesign of the local state. The representational character of newly decentralized authority structures is vital both to their short-term political legitimacy and to their long-term public service effectiveness (Olowu and Wunsch 2004).

The goal of a restructured public management framework would be to create an inclusive, shared authority decentralization program wherein regional and local authority structures that are locally regarded as politically legitimate are fiscally supported by the central state, as well as by international donor funding. Such a system is more likely to generate bargaining-oriented politics, political stability, and effective governance over the long term than more commonplace approaches that rely on de facto re-centralization and inflexible policies toward politically assertive regions.

References

Agence France-Presse (2005) "Highlights of the Sudan Peace Accord," Paris: Agence France-Presse, January 9, available at: www.reliefweb.int/rw/rwb.nsf/AllDocsByU-NID/.

Amnesty International (1998) "Senegal: Climate of Terror in Casamance," Amnesty International.

Antil, A. (2002) "Une dimension mal connue du Sahara occidental," *Afrique contemporaine* 201: 83–88.

Associated Press News (2004) "Juba, South Sudan Sees Signs of Peace," New York: AP News, February 21, available at: mathaba.net/0_index.shtml?x=38308.

Bach, D.C. (ed.) (1999) *Regionalisation in Africa: Integration and Disintegration*, Oxford: James Currey.

Blunt, P. (2003) "Governance Conditions, Roles and Capacity-building Needs in the Rebel-held Areas of Southern Sudan," *Public Administration and Development* 23: 125–139.

Boko, S.H. (2002) *Decentralization and Reform in Africa*, New York: Kluwer/Springer.

Boone, C. (2003) *Political Topographies of the African State*, Cambridge: Cambridge University Press.

Colombant, N. (2005) "Senegal's Casamance Separatists Agree to Peace Agenda," Voice of America, February 2, available at: www.VOANews.com.

Development Bank (1999) *Review of the South African Government's Grant-funded Municipal Infrastructure Programs*, Johannesburg: Development Bank of South Africa.

Diouf, M. (2004), "Between Ethnic Memories and Colonial History in Senegal: The MFDC and the Struggle for Independence in Casamance," in B. Berman, D. Eyoh and W. Kymlicka (eds) *Ethnicity and Democracy in Africa*, Athens: Ohio University Press, pp. 218–239.

Evans, M. (2004) *Senegal: Mouvement des Forces Démocratiques de la Casamance (MFDC)*, Briefing Paper, London: Chatham House.

Forrest, J.B. (1998) *Namibia's Post-Apartheid Regional Institutions*, Rochester, NY: University of Rochester Press.

—— (2003) *Lineages of State Fragility. Rural Civil Society in Guinea Bissau*, Athens: Ohio University Press.

—— (2004) *Subnationalism in Africa. Ethnicity, Alliances, Politics*, Boulder, CO: Lynne Rienner.

Gasser, G. (2000) "Manger ou s'en aller: le conflit ethnorégional casamançais et l'état sénégalais," Ph.D. Thesis, Montreal: University of Montreal.

Gellar, S. (2005) *Democracy in Senegal. Toquevillian Analysis in Africa*, Toronto: Playwrights Canada Press.

Herbst, J. (2000) *States and Power in Africa*, Princeton, NJ: Princeton University Press.

IRINnews.org (May 1, 2002) "Somalia: Puntland Mediation Efforts Fail," United Nations Integrated Information Network.

—— (October 17, 2002) "Authorities Close Radios, Detain Staff Over Interview of Separatist Leader," United Nations Integrated Information Network.

—— (September 29, 2005) "Somaliland Voters Go to the Polls," United Nations Integrated Information Network.

—— (September 30, 2005) "Sudan: Southerners get New Assembly," United Nations Integrated Information Network.

—— (October 4, 2005) "US Commends Somaliland on Poll," United Nations Integrated Information Network.

—— (October 10, 2005) "Interview with Mark Bradbury, Somaliland Poll Observer," United Nations Integrated Information Network.

—— (October 17, 2005) "Senegal: Authorities Close Radios, Detain Staff Over Interview of Separatist Leader," United Nations Integrated Information Network.

—— (October 24, 2005) "Sudan: Kiir names Southern Cabinet," United Nations Integrated Information Network.

Jackson, P. (2005) "Chiefs, Money and Politicians: Rebuilding Local Government in Sierra Leone," *Public Administration and Development* 25(1): 49–58.

Kurti, D.B. (2006) "New Militia is Potent Force in Nigeria's Oil-rich Delta Region," *Christian Science Monitor*, March 7.

Olowu, D. and Wunsch, J.S. (2004) *Local Governance in Africa: The Challenge of Democratic Decentralization*, Boulder, CO: Lynne Rienner.

Ottaway, M. (1999) "Nation-building and State Disintegration," in K. Mengisteab and C. Daddieh (eds) *State Building and Democratization in Africa*, Westport, CT: Praeger, pp. 83–97.

Pool, D. (2001) *From Guerrillas to Government: The Eritrean People's Liberation Front*, Athens: Ohio University Press.

Rothchild, D. (1996) *Strengthening African Local Initiative: Local Self-governance, Decentralization, and Accountability*, Hamburg: Institut fü Afrika-Kunde.

—— (1997) *Managing Ethnic Conflict in Africa: Pressures and Incentives for Cooperation*, Washington, DC: Brookings Institution.

Rothchild, D. and Olorunsola, V.A. (1983) "Managing Competing State and Ethnic Claims," in D. Rothchild and V.A. Olorunsola (eds) *State Versus Ethnic Claims: African Policy Dilemmas*, Boulder, CO: Westview Press, pp. 1–24.

Simons, A. (1995) *Networks of Dissolution: Somalia Undone*, Boulder, CO: Westview Press.

Vansina, J. (1990) *Paths in the Rainforests: Towards a History of Political Tradition in Equatorial Africa*, Madison: University of Wisconsin Press.

12

SUBNATIONAL ADMINISTRATION AND STATE BUILDING

Lessons from Afghanistan

Sarah Lister and Andrew Wilder

In post-conflict contexts, multilateral and other donors have emphasized the importance of building or restoring the administrative and fiscal structures of government. In recent years, the World Bank, in particular, has focused on reconstructing civil services and public administrations – prioritizing this above the rebuilding of human resources, the repairing of infrastructure, and developing of private enterprises (World Bank 2003). It has allocated increasing resources to funding programs in this area, focusing especially on revising the legal frameworks under which civil services function, management issues, revision of salary structures and grades, and personnel issues including promotion and recruitment. Specific activities have often involved equipment purchases and management training (World Bank 2002, 2003).

This chapter discusses aspects of the reform of public administration, particularly subnational administration, which are often overlooked or neglected by donors in post-conflict contexts.[1] It assesses the role of subnational administration in state-building in Afghanistan in the first three years after the fall of the Taliban, during the period in which the Bonn Agreement provided the overall framework for political development. Primarily it analyzes findings of research conducted in Afghanistan in six provinces (Badakhshan, Bamyan, Faryab, Herat, Kandahar, and Wardak) between December 2002 and July 2003. It also draws on ongoing research conducted in the same provinces as part of a larger governance research program, as well as a specific assessment of progress in provincial public administration reform conducted between November 2004 and January 2005.

We argue that the functioning of subnational administration both shapes and is shaped by complex political dynamics and is part of broader political processes. Interventions to strengthen subnational administration in post-conflict contexts should therefore not only focus on mechanisms and structures designed to increase the collection of revenues and facilitate the more efficient delivery of services. Instead, it should be recognized that reform processes are affected by the distribution of power in a country and have political effects on the establishment of legitimate authority throughout the territory. The reform of subnational administration should therefore be seen as part of an overarching political strategy of state-building, even in immediate post-conflict contexts.

We first provide a brief discussion of the context in Afghanistan, highlighting key political issues, including the disparity between the *de jure* state and de facto states. The subsequent section discusses the control of de facto states by commanders. The fourth section identifies the mechanisms through which commanders control subnational administration and the bases of their power. The final section revisits issues around strengthening subnational administration and the need for an extension of the control of the *de jure* state. It also provides an assessment of prospects for the future in Afghanistan.

The political context

After twenty-three years of civil conflict, the fall of the Taliban in November 2001 was widely seen as a moment of great potential for Afghanistan. The Bonn Agreement signed in December 2001 laid out a series of steps to be taken toward the establishment of a peaceful, democratic state. An interim administration was appointed for six months, until an Emergency *Loya Jirga* (grand council) was convened in July 2002. The *Loya Jirga* appointed the Afghan Transitional Administration (ATA) headed by President Hamid Karzai to oversee the drafting and approval of a new constitution and to govern until elections could be held. After several delays, a presidential election was held in October 2004, which was won by Hamid Karzai. Parliamentary and provincial council elections were held in October 2005, and with the inauguration of the National Assembly on December 19, 2005, as well as the completion of other provisions laid out in the Bonn Agreement, the so-called "Bonn era" was considered to have come to an end.

However, despite completing the steps laid out in the Bonn Agreement, there remain today many constraints to the establishment of a peaceful and democratic state in Afghanistan. Insecurity reigns through much of the country, the disarmament of warlords and militias in Kabul and elsewhere has been impeded by internal and external politics (Bennett *et al.* 2003), and there is a renewed Taliban insurgency in the south. By June 2004, the end of the original time frame of the Bonn Agreement, the security situation was worse than it was in January 2002 (Bhatia *et al.* 2004). Since then it has continued to deteriorate, with figures showing that 2005 was "the bloodiest year since the end of the Taliban."[2] In February 2006 the Head of the U.S. Defense Intelligence Agency, Lieutenant General Michael Maples, told the U.S. Congress, "We judge insurgents now represent a greater threat to the expansion of Afghan government authority than at any point since late 2001."[3] Many blame these difficulties on the nature of the Bonn Agreement itself, which was agreed with one particular faction of the Afghan political scene, and established a government that rested on a power base of warlords, which subsequent political developments have served to consolidate rather than challenge (Rubin 2004). Moreover, some of these power holders have aggressively continued to strengthen their political and economic positions, generating resources through criminal activity such as smuggling, involvement in the trafficking of opium, and the imposition of illegal taxes (Lister and Pain 2004; Sedra 2002).

Understanding states in Afghanistan

To understand the current political situation in Afghanistan in the context of state-building, it is helpful to appreciate the difference between *de jure* and de facto states (Jackson 1990, developed by Ottaway 2002). *De jure* states are those that exist by fiat of the international community which recognizes them as sovereign entities whether or not they have a government which can effectively control or administer the territory. De facto states are those that actually administer a territory. States that enjoy international recognition and exercise control through strong institutions are both *de jure* and de facto.

Centralized state institutions in Afghanistan have always co-existed uneasily with fragmented, decentralized traditional society since attempts at state-building began in Afghanistan (Rubin 1995). However, twenty-three years of conflict undoubtedly changed the nature of politics both at the local level and between local and national levels. Decentralized power, which in pre-war years had rested largely on the structures of customary institutions (primarily tribal and religious), by 2001 rested on control of military and financial resources generated by participation in the conflict and the war economy of the previous twenty-three years (Cramer and Goodhand 2002). There are indications that this has been changing, not however towards centralized state control, but in favor of those benefiting from the illegal cultivation and trafficking of opium poppy (Byrd and Ward 2004).

In Afghanistan today, the *de jure* state, headed by President Karzai, has very weak institutions, and a lack of both military and administrative control in many parts of the country, particularly, but not exclusively, in the south and southeast. The de facto states in most areas outside Kabul are operated by regional warlords, local commanders, and drug traffickers. Their make-up and operation vary from province to province, but they are built on power which is clustered according to factional and personal grounds, and based on financial and military strength as well as historical loyalties, supported by the current political economy of Afghanistan.

It is, however, worth noting that the boundaries between the *de jure* and de facto states are not always clear. As will be discussed below, some individuals are influential within both the *de jure* and the de facto states. Indeed, they owe their *de jure* positions to their de facto power. Moreover, they use their de facto powers to influence the *de jure* structures according to their interests at both central and local levels.

Who controls subnational administration?

It is only in name that we have a system of government – it doesn't exist in reality. I'm the Acting Governor but I have no authority. I can only sign but have no feeling of responsibility – I don't have the power to say "no".

(Acting Provincial Governor)

The weakness of the *de jure* state at the subnational level was a consistent finding in all of the provinces in which research was conducted. At the time of the research in 2002 to 2003, the most extreme example of this was in Herat, which provides a useful illustration of the complex dynamics of *de jure* and de facto power in Afghanistan.

In the province of Herat, Commander Ismail Khan claimed significant political and fiscal autonomy, and controlled both military and civil administration. This control was supported by large amounts of customs revenues from trade with Iran and Turkmenistan, and the reverse traffic from Kandahar and Pakistan. The central government worked hard to reduce Khan's power by pressuring him to remit customs revenues to the center, publicly rejecting his self-appointment as "Amir of Western Afghanistan," and acknowledging only his control over civil administration as Governor, and not over the military. However, his strong financial position meant that he was largely in a position to ignore demands from Kabul. In a surprising and unanticipated move in September 2004, President Karzai removed Khan from his position as Governor of Herat. Khan publicly accepted this removal, but initially refused to accept a ministerial appointment and go to Kabul, before eventually accepting the position of Minister of Energy and Water. It is not clear as to the exact extent to which he maintains control and influence in his former de facto state, or the extent to which he or his family and supporters are still benefiting from customs revenue. However, ongoing research in Herat suggests that there are many expectations locally that he will return to the seat of his de facto power, and this is a significant hindrance to reform. Moreover, the *de jure* state seems happy to reinforce this local perception with certain actions – for example, he was sent to investigate the causes of the disturbances in Herat City in February 2006.

Herat was different from most other provinces covered in this research in that, while the structures of the central state were not subject to political control by central government but were instead dependent on the patronage of Ismail Khan, he did use them to provide services to residents of the province (especially in urban areas), and ensured that the residents received far more than their entitlement of what should have been national revenues. As a result of Khan's position and activities, Herat City was one of the few places in the country in which infrastructure was maintained, power was consistently available, and businesses could operate with some measure of confidence. In the transport industry, for example, although all trucking and transport in the province was centrally controlled by the Ministry of Transport (answerable to Khan) to which fees had to be paid by operators, truck drivers preferred to work in this province than in any other, due to the security provided for their shipments (Lister and Karaev 2004).

In other provinces, the divorce between de facto and *de jure* states rendered subnational government structures largely irrelevant in the important decisions that affected the province. In Faryab province, for example, in 2002 to 2003, the Governor only dealt with day-to-day civil affairs. Major issues, particularly those related to security, were referred first to the regional commander, General Dostum, or his representatives rather than directly to Kabul. According to the former Deputy Governor of that province, Dostum's "Special Representative" title bestowed on him by President Karzai legitimized his involvement in civil affairs and his title of "Deputy Defense Minister" legitimized his involvement in military affairs. The weakest of the local government structures were in Wardak, largely because of that province's close proximity to Kabul, the fact that it generated virtually no local resources and was therefore dependent on the center and the lack of domination by any one political faction. This meant that no particular grouping was able to exert sufficient control to ensure some minimal measure of functioning.

However, in contrast to the actual situation, there was a strong desire for centralized authority. Interviewees from local government in all six provinces were virtually unanimous in their support for the restoration of central political authority over provincial administration. Interestingly, this sentiment was often expressed most passionately by those who owed their appointments to warlords and commanders, suggesting that these loyalties may not be strong. It was also surprising to find that state administrative structures had proven to be remarkably resilient through the years of conflict. Administrative and fiscal mechanisms which had been standardized before the war had continued in use throughout the country, despite the lack of an ongoing relationship with Kabul. This suggests a strong commitment to the idea and processes of centralized government. Other poll-based research has also provided evidence that there is a strong attachment to the idea of central government – for many it would be their first port of call, even though citizens are all too aware of its limited capacity (Human Rights Research and Advocacy Forum 2003).

Mechanisms of control by de facto powers

Commanders still try to influence appointments and transfers. If Kabul appoints someone they should insist that that person get appointed – not give in to commanders who are resisting these appointments. We need support from our departments to resist the influence of commanders. If people thought I wasn't supported by the Governor and [the local commander] they could maybe replace me. I am trying to cut my close relations with [the local commander] and get my support from the

Governor, but still if people think I don't have the support of [the local commander] they might start disobeying me.

(District Chief of Police)

The primary mechanism through which regional and district commanders controlled subnational administration was through the appointments system, as well as by the manipulation of other administrative systems. However, this control was both facilitated by, and reinforced, their military control of physical territory, which in turn was supported by their access to financial resources.

Control of the appointments system

Not only were security positions such as the head of police and head of intelligence determined by the dominant commanders in a province, civil administration positions were too. In provinces dominated by warlords and commanders, most mid- and upper-level government employees owed their employment, and therefore their loyalties, to local and regional power holders rather than to the central government. Some political factions provided subsidies to their representatives in local government, which further reinforced loyalty to regional and local power holders. In Herat, for example, all district governors were reported to be in their positions because they had fought in the *jihad* (the holy war against the Soviets) with Ismail Khan. In other areas where overall command was less clear, those in authority tried to maintain stability by keeping a balance between opposing factions, playing a delicate balancing game, and splitting major appointments between rival factions. The control of commanders over appointment systems was also strengthened by the weaknesses of the formal process for granting appointments from the center, which was slow and lacked clarity. This made it easier for regional and local commanders to ensure that their favored candidates were appointed.

The control of civilian appointments by commanders had a number of detrimental effects in terms of the administration. In particular, it limited the influence of civilian administrators, who may not have wished to be tied to any particular faction, but nonetheless felt forced to abide by the decisions of local and regional commanders. In addition, it prevented the appointment of qualified and competent bureaucrats and technical staff, which further weakened the administration, both in practice and in legitimacy. Informants described how local commanders often rejected the appointments made by the central government and refused to let those individuals take up their positions. Attempts had been made to transfer government employees away from their home areas, thus cutting their ties to their networks and supporters. However, these were only partially successful. In Badakhshan, for example, when a policy was announced to transfer all district governors to different districts, only ten of the twenty-seven district governors – those without strong commander connections – were transferred.

Low salaries and lack of non-salary allocation

The control by regional warlords and local commanders over appointment systems was strengthened by other administrative weaknesses. Not surprisingly, low salaries were a universal complaint of all government employees who were interviewed, and the point was made that this not only weakened their loyalty to the *de jure* state, it also forced people into engaging in corrupt practices which further weakened the authority of central government. In some areas, for example, the ability to tax the drugs trade at all stages was considered to be payment in lieu of a reasonable government salary. When the first research was carried out in 2002 to 2003, not only were salaries low (deputy governors, for example, earned about US$35 per month), they were often received three to five months late. Due to measures taken to centralize payroll management in Kabul, in many regions someone (usually the head of the provincial finance department) had to travel to Kabul to collect the payroll. Employee representatives from districts, in turn, had to travel to the provincial capital to collect salaries. The travel costs were deducted from the employees' salaries. Many of these administrative issues have now been improved. For example, by early 2005, pay was in most cases received monthly and on time. However, low pay continued to be a major complaint (Evans and Osmani 2005).

Low salaries were also a factor in the failure to transfer administrators away from their home areas, because government staff could not afford to live away from home without the added income provided by land or other sources of livelihoods (for example, shops, livestock). Indeed, it seems likely that in some areas the only reasons there were government employees at all was because government jobs required relatively few hours, and were therefore perceived as a bonus on top of other income sources.

The lack of non-salary allocation to provincial administration units also weakened the influence of the central government. Administrators had no option but to look elsewhere for sources of revenue, including from commanders. In addition, the legitimacy of the *de jure* state was called into question when it had no resources to do anything. Meetings with provincial and district governors always began with a long list of problems that local authorities had no resources to address. Indeed, the role of local administrators had become that of intermediaries, able to refer difficulties to NGOs or commanders, but without the resources to tackle the problems themselves. Deprived of resources as they were, civilian administrators had little with which they could demonstrate the relevance and importance of central government. As one District Governor argued:

> The poorer government is at the district level, the bigger the gap between central government and the people. *Wuluswal* [district administrator] offices are ninety times less than NGO or commander offices, so the prestige of the *wuluswal* is going down while that of commanders and NGOs increases. Either get rid of *wuluswals* or strengthen them – it's better to have no government than a weak government that ruins the reputation of government.

The rule of the gun

Disarmament is the top priority – the administrative system can't function as long as people are armed because you have to do what the armed people tell you to do, not what the rules tell you to do.

(Provincial Deputy Governor)

The strongest and most consistently articulated issue raised in interviews in all provinces was that, for the effectiveness and authority of the *de jure* state to be restored, disarmament of commanders and their armed groups was the top priority. There was considerable criticism of the international community and the Karzai government for being so slow to do anything about an issue of such great importance. This was especially the case as many felt that disarmament would not be that difficult to achieve in the immediate post-Taliban period due to the strong public support and demand for disarmament, combined with the fact that the vast majority of commanders were not very strong and were so unpopular.

Many provincial and district level government staff emphasized that until disarmament put an end to the "rule of the Kalashnikov," the rule of law and authority of the central government could not be restored. In Badakhshan, in particular, the difference between the quality of local administration in the districts where disarmament had taken place and those districts still dominated by local factional commanders was striking. In one district, where two commanders had been fighting each other, the new district governor was able to get troops from Kunduz who disarmed the two commanders in three days. The result was that the district became one of the most peaceful districts in the province. In the words of the District Governor:

Before I came to [this district] there was no district administration. All NGO assistance and humanitarian assistance – about where to build schools, clinics, etc. – used to go through commanders. Land disputes went to commanders to be solved. Since I've been here and commanders were disarmed, people now come to the administration to resolve their problems. When I came, no one thought the administration could make a difference. People really want a powerful administration system and a reduced role for commanders.

While the security sector reform strategy for Afghanistan included a disarmament, demobilization and reintegration (DDR) component – the Afghan New Beginnings Programme (ANBP) – it was notably unsuccessful, especially at the beginning of its implementation, and its impact has been variable (Dennys 2005). The original ANBP plan announced in early 2003 was to disarm and reintegrate an estimated 100,000 members of the Afghan Militia Forces (AMF) prior to the elections originally scheduled for June 2004. By June 2004, however, the number of disarmed had exceeded 10,000, and the target figure of disarming

100,000 was subsequently reduced to 40,000. Resistance from the unreformed Ministry of Defense (MoD) was one of the major obstacles to successful DDR. In addition, the DDR program only aimed to disarm AMF members who come under the authority of the MoD (Bhatia *et al.* 2004). Even after the end of the DDR process in July 2005 there were still an estimated 1800 armed bands consisting of more than 80,000 individuals in Afghanistan. A subsequent process – the Disbandment of Illegally Armed Groups (DIAG) – aimed to disarm and demobilize militias that fell outside the former military forces. However, this process started so late that many such groups had already tightened their grip on their territories, and public confidence in central government and its willingness and ability to disarm had been shaken. To strengthen the authority of the *de jure* state at the subnational level, more thought, effort, and resources should have been devoted to achieving successful disarmament much earlier.

The military control of commanders has been further strengthened by the weakness of police forces. Civil administrators could not rely on a loyal and competent force to maintain security in their regions. Unqualified, poorly paid, and ill-equipped forces were unable to carry out basic law-and-order missions, and tended to be under the command of those with close links to numerous political factions, supported by illicit revenues:

> Most heads of police departments used to be commanders and are mostly illiterate. When the center has tried appointing more qualified heads of police they are not accepted. These positions have been occupied by force. For example, the Head of Police in this district received a transfer letter [from the Ministry of Interior]. Another person was appointed who had no *jihadi* background so he hasn't been able to take up his new position.
>
> (District Governor)

The research also suggested that the current policy of incorporating commanders and their armed men into the army or police force was working to strengthen, not weaken, commanders by giving them official positions in their areas of influence, and hence legitimizing their roles.

The political economy of subnational power

> We warned people we would punish them if they grew poppy but in some areas local commanders encouraged farmers to grow saying central government is weak and won't do anything. They have their own self-interest in mind as they tax the poppy. There's now no war on so commanders are looking for alternative livelihoods.
>
> (Provincial Governor)

While broader political economy issues were not explicitly explored in this research, interviewees frequently commented on them as factors that contributed to the weakness of the central government's authority at the subnational level, and other research has also confirmed their importance (Lister and Pain 2004). The financial resources that underpin control by regional and local commanders come from a variety of sources including the narcotics trade, customs revenues, revenues from mines in some regions, and unofficial taxation. Not only do these financial resources provide the commanders with the opportunity to arm themselves and resist the authority of the *de jure* state, they also enable them to engage in more "legitimate" activities designed to win support, such as providing equipment or salary supplements to government employees.

One of the most serious threats to the *de jure* state in Afghanistan, and one of the biggest challenges it faces in increasing its authority at the subnational level, is the dramatic spread of the opium economy. In 2004, poppy cultivation increased to the highest recorded figure for the Afghanistan, covering 131,000 hectares and present to some extent in most provinces of the country (Byrd and Ward 2004). In 2003, the United Nations Office on Drugs and Crime had estimated that the $2.3 billion opium economy amounted to about half of Afghanistan's GDP, and the UNODC Director made a point of highlighting that "Out of this drug chest, some provincial administrators and military commanders take a considerable share."[4] The World Bank too recognizes the links between a weak state, subnational power brokers, and the drug economy, referring to a "self-reinforcing 'vicious circle' that would keep Afghanistan insecure, fragmented politically, weakly governed, poor, dominated by the informal/illicit economy, and a hostage to the drug industry" (Byrd and Ward 2004: 1).

Indeed, the researchers for this study heard of the alleged involvement in the narcotics trade by elites at all levels, including government ministers, commanders, police, and provincial and district governors. For example:

> Poppy cultivation and processing is strongly supported by commanders and police. They are very involved and take their share. No one could produce poppy if they did not allow it . . . opium/heroin is transported . . . in vehicles with official plates.
>
> (District Administrator)

> The poppy business is linked to important people in Kabul and there is no support from Kabul to fight with commanders – they have more money than we do.
>
> (General of provincial garrison)

Such comments have been confirmed by other, subsequent research (Pain 2006). The narcotics trade not only provided financial resources to warlords and commanders to support their de facto power, the failure of central government to control both the growth of poppy and the processing and transportation of opium was a visible sign of the weakness of the central administration and its inability to reinforce its edicts. To quote one District Administrator:

> We received a letter from Kabul about not growing poppy which we announced to the people but we can't stop farmers from growing poppy with forty soldiers.... If smuggling continues the prestige of the administration will be reduced – both at the national and international levels, as well as the local level. Smugglers always try to hurt and weaken the administration system.

It is not just the illicit economy, however, that is supporting the de facto decentralized states in Afghanistan. As mentioned, in Herat and also in Kandahar, revenues from customs duties were considerable, and the process of revenue remittance to Kabul at the start of this period was regarded as one of "negotiation." Through the period of this research that situation improved, but it is still widely acknowledged that not all custom revenues from border posts are remitted to Kabul. Furthermore, there is some "semi-official" revenue collection, apparently with the knowledge and assent of senior figures both nationally and locally (Evans and Osmani 2005). Other potentially licit revenues that were not remitted to the center also continued to provide resources for commanders. For example, research suggested that revenues from the Daulatabad salt-mines in Faryab were a source of income for one of General Dostum's commanders, and revenues from the lapis lazuli mines in Badakhshan were captured by local commanders. There were also many other sources of unofficial taxation by commanders at all levels, including taxes on productive and transport activities, although there is some evidence that this is decreasing. Furthermore, some regional warlords are reportedly still funded by neighboring states seeking to increase their influence in the country.

Power holders have often manipulated the structures of subnational government to ensure the continued access to resources that underpin their control. For example, four northern districts of Faryab province were taken over by the neighboring province of Jowzjan. The Deputy Governor politely explained that while these four districts were "administratively" still part of Faryab province, they were "operationally" part of Jowzjan province. While geographical considerations could be used to justify this change, as these districts are more accessible from the provincial capital of Jowzjan than Faryab, political economy factors were behind the change. The four northern districts include the major carpet-trading town of Andkhoi and, more importantly, the Turkmenistan border customs post at Aqina. Whenever General Abdul Rashid Dostum was in a position of power, these districts along with their carpet and customs revenues unofficially come under the control of Dostum's home province of Jowzjan, whereas historically and when he was out of power during the Taliban period, they belonged to Faryab province. When the remittance of customs revenue to Kabul improved and the districts' attractiveness therefore decreased, they were quietly returned to Faryab's jurisdiction.

Conclusions: subnational administration and the state-building agenda

This chapter has considered the continuing control of subnational administration in Afghanistan by de facto power holders during the period 2001 to 2005, and has examined the mechanisms through which these power holders exerted their control. In the period during which the Bonn Agreement provided the overall political framework for activities, the Government of Afghanistan failed to extend its control over subnational government in all parts of the country. Ongoing research shows that in many places district police and administrators continue to respond to local power holders rather than to central control. In addition, allegedly corrupt or criminal provincial and district governors continue to be appointed to some provinces. The assertion of control by the *de jure* state over the structures of local government in this period was an important goal, not just for the efficient delivery of services, but also as part of the establishment of the power of the *de jure* state throughout the territory, and the wider state-building agenda in Afghanistan. The failure in this area has significantly hampered reconstruction and development processes, as well as reduced public confidence in formal government.

The World Bank and other donors have supported and continue to support a number of public administration reforms in Afghanistan designed to increase central control of local government. These include pay and pension reform, the establishment of an independent civil service commission, and measures to increase the authority and oversight of the Ministry of Finance over payroll and budgets. They have also attempted to build provincial loyalty to Kabul by removing delays in processing payroll, approving staff appointments, updating staffing lists, increasing the flow of non-salary cash to the provinces, and improving Kabul presence in the provinces (Evans *et al.* 2004b). In addition, they are supporting the restoration of provincial dignity and capacity through improving the physical reconstruction of provincial infrastructure. As discussed above, some of these approaches have been successful in improving bureaucratic processes and efficiency (Evans and Osmani 2005).

However, such measures were not sufficient alone to extend the reach of the state into all areas and the consensus is that the so-called "Bonn period" saw, at best, mixed performance on public administration reform and broader reform of subnational governance. This has also been exacerbated by tremendous confusion and duplication of reform efforts at the subnational level (Lister 2005). The above discussion has shown how control of provincial civil administration in Afghanistan during the period under consideration was closely linked to the military control of an area, which, in turn, was closely linked to issues of political economy. While the structures of the *de jure* state were more resilient than had been anticipated, these structures were often controlled by the de facto power holders at the local level. In some cases, technocratic interventions to strengthen subnational administration that failed to understand the political context were not only ineffective; they actually resulted in strengthening de facto power holders rather than the *de jure* state.

The precondition for strengthening subnational administration should have been an overarching political strategy to rebuild and strengthen the *de jure* state, rather than an emphasis on bureaucratic reform. The wresting of control from regional and local commanders through disarmament, security reform, and reform of the political economy would have weakened their ability to influence the structures of subnational administration. It would also have provided revenues that could have been used to link the provinces and districts more strongly to the center, and enable local government to carry out activities that would have increased its influence and legitimacy with local populations. The staffing of provincial and district governments with trained administrators appointed according to their competence would also have had this dual effect of weakening local power holders and increasing the legitimacy of local government structures.

What next for subnational administration in Afghanistan?

Assessments from officials, commentators and the media of the situation in Afghanistan at the end of the "Bonn period" are almost without exception bleaker than those at any other time since the fall of the Taliban. One respected commentator noted:

> Grim phrases are on the lips of diplomats, government officials, and aid workers in Kabul when describing Afghanistan these days. Narco state, political disillusionment, military stalemate, donor fatigue, American military pullout. Tie it all together, and it's a picture that suggests Afghanistan could be reverting back to a failed state.
>
> (Baldauf 2006)

Despite such widespread pessimism, it is not all bad news. In January 2006, the government and the international community signed a new agreement, the Afghanistan Compact, which will act as the overall framework to guide political development and reconstruction efforts. The Compact is closely tied to the Interim Afghanistan National Development Strategy (I-ANDS), which lays out the government's strategy for improving governance and security, as well as its approach to economic and social development.[5] The Compact and the I-ANDS explicitly recognize the current weakness of public administration, especially at the subnational level, and highlight the importance of subnational governance for the achievement of political and development goals. These documents, and the complex processes through which they were agreed, have encouraged government ownership of the issues, and focused donor attention on the problems. There is now, for the first time since the fall of the Taliban, a consensus between the government and the donors that the issues of subnational governance must be tackled, and there is a stated commitment from all actors to tackle it.

Putting this commitment into action and seeing results will require long-term involvement in Afghanistan from the international community, as well as the continued presence of international military. Experience to date in Afghanistan suggests that most donors shrink from addressing the political realities of the country, and there has been an over-reliance on reconstruction projects to try to legitimize and strengthen the *de jure* state. Due, in part, to the shortsighted communications strategies of the government, donors, and assistance agencies, the expectations of Afghans for reconstruction assistance have been raised to unrealistic levels. The inevitable perception of the majority of Afghans that they are not receiving enough assistance means that reconstruction projects, while critically important, should not be the main strategy relied upon to strengthen the legitimacy and authority of the *de jure* state. Instead, a broader political strategy of state-building must integrate the critical need for security sector reform, the need for the *de jure* state to control most state revenues and limit illicit revenues, with reconstruction strategies and the building of institutions of democratic governance at all levels.

Such a strategy will also require international actors in Afghanistan to consider the integrated nature of their policy objectives and interests in the country – drug control, the "war on terror," regional stability, poverty reduction, to name a few – and stop pursuing potentially conflictive and mutually undermining approaches. As one interviewee in this study argued:

> There is currently a paradoxical situation where the international community and government of Afghanistan want to bring security to Afghanistan through those people who don't want security and have been the greatest cause of insecurity. How can the government be successful with this strategy?
>
> (District Governor)

According to many of the interviewees for this research, expectations of the current central government were greatest at the time of the Emergency *Loya Jirga*, as people anticipated that the rule of central government would be restored, that commanders would be disarmed, and that qualified people would be brought into government positions. However, following the Emergency *Loya Jirga*, which brought little change in terms of the make-up of the government, and confirmed rather than undermined the status of warlords, people's expectations began to diminish and disillusionment set in. There was a strong feeling that a space for change had been created, but that significant opportunities to assert central control had so far been squandered. The parliamentary elections held in October 2005 unfortunately reinforced the perception of many Afghans that those with records of human rights abuses and criminal behavior would continue to be accommodated rather than confronted (Wilder 2005). Research has consistently shown that Afghans consider that the window of opportunity to reassert central authority will not remain open indefinitely, and recent events suggest that that window is now closing. It is important that the opportunity presented by the recent commitments between the government and the international community is fully grasped, that difficult political decisions are taken, and that the control of the *de jure* state is now extended throughout the country. The reform of subnational administration will be an integral part of that process.

Beyond Afghanistan

The experience of Afghanistan also, undoubtedly, holds lessons for other post-conflict contexts, but they are not new lessons. As former World Bank employees comment, "The sequencing of post-conflict reconstruction is an art form, best informed by clear analysis of the political economy ... followed by a sustained, consistent and aligned support over many years" (Middlebrook and Miller 2006: 5). This is not new. The consensus that has now been reached on the importance of reforming subnational administration and the political nature of the reform required was identified several years ago in Afghanistan, and was identified before that in other post-conflict contexts. Unfortunately, in the time it has taken to reach that consensus, opportunities for action have been lost, and the task in Afghanistan is now much, much harder. The experience in Afghanistan shows us (again) the importance of a strong internal political commitment to reform, the centrality of disarmament (particularly before elections), and the weaknesses in certain contexts of a "light footprint" approach to international military intervention. It highlights the complexity and interrelated nature of the issues we are dealing with, most notably that reform of government structures is related to different constellations of power, which are underpinned by political economy issues. It also reminds us of the critical importance of a long-term international commitment, with funding linked to absorptive capacity.

However, what really needs to be understood is why these lessons that have been identified time and again in different contexts are not learned. Why is it that when large-scale international reconstruction and development efforts swing into action the voices of political analysts are either drowned out by those clamoring for bureaucratic reform, or simply ignored by those pursuing different foreign policy objectives? When will it be recognized that, however distasteful or inconvenient it may be to some, state-building is an essential task, and one that is not only complex and time-consuming, but primarily a political, and not just a technocratic, endeavor?

Notes

1 This chapter is based on research undertaken by the Afghanistan Research and Evaluation Unit (AREU) from 2002 to 2006. It particularly draws on a research project conducted jointly by AREU and the World Bank and funded by the European Commission, with additional support from the governments of Switzerland and Sweden, and the United Nations Assistance Mission in Afghanistan (UNAMA). Major findings from that research were published in two volumes, Evans *et al.* (2004a and

2004b). An earlier version of this chapter was included in ch. 1 of Evans *et al.* (2004a), and in Lister and Wilder (2005), but it has been substantially revised and updated, drawing on subsequent research funded by the World Bank and by the U.K. Department for International Development (DFID). However, the views expressed in this chapter are those of the authors alone.

2 United Nations Integrated Regional Information Network (IRIN), Kabul, January 11, 2006.

3 Reported on BBC "Bush Praises Afghanistan Progress," March 1, 2006, news.bbc.co.uk/2/hi/south_asia/4761432.stm.

4 Reported on BBC "Opium 'Threatens' Afghan Future," October 29, 2003, news.bbc.co.uk/1/hi/world/south_asia/3224319.stm.

5 See Middlebrook and Miller (2006) for a discussion of the significance of these documents.

References

Baldauf, S. (2006) "Mounting Concern Over Afghanistan," *Christian Science Monitor*, February 14.

Bennett, C., Wakefield, S., and Wilder, A. (2003) *Afghan Elections: The Great Gamble*, Briefing paper, Kabul: AREU, November, available at: www.areu.org.af.

Bhatia, M., Lanigan, K., and Wilkinson, P. (2004) *Minimal Investments, Minimal Results: The Failure of Security Policy in Afghanistan*, Briefing paper, Kabul: AREU, June, available at: www.areu.org.af.

Byrd, W. and Ward, C. (2004) *Drugs and Development in Afghanistan*, Social Development Papers No. 18, Washington, DC: World Bank.

Cramer, C. and Goodhand, J. (2002) "Try Again, Fail Again, Fail Better? War, the State and the 'Post-Conflict' Challenge in Afghanistan," *Development and Change* 33(5): 885–909.

Dennys, C. (2005) *Disarmament, Demobilisation and Rearmament? The Effects of Disarmament in Afghanistan*, Kabul: Japan Afghan NGO Network (JANN).

Evans, A. and Osmani, Y. (2005) *Assessing Progress: Update Report on Subnational Administration in Afghanistan*, Kabul: AREU, available at: www.areu.org.af.

Evans, A., Manning, N., Osmani, Y., Tully, A., and Wilder, A. (2004a) *A Guide to Government in Afghanistan*, Washington, DC, and Kabul: World Bank and AREU.

Evans, A., Manning, N., Osmani, Y., Tully, A., and Wilder, A. (2004b) *Subnational Administration in Afghanistan: Assessment and Recommendations for Action*, Washington, DC, and Kabul: World Bank and AREU.

Human Rights Research and Advocacy Forum (2003) *Speaking Out: Afghan Opinions on Rights and Responsibilities*, Kabul: Author, November, available at: www.reliefweb.int/library/documents/2003/care-afg-19nov.pdf.

Jackson, R. (1990) *Quasi-states: Sovereignty, International Relations and the Third World*, Cambridge: Cambridge University Press.

Lister, S. (2005) *Caught in Confusion: Local Governance Structures in Afghanistan*, Briefing paper, Kabul: AREU, available at: www.areu.org.af.

Lister, S. and Karaev, Z. (2004) *Understanding Markets in Afghanistan: A Case Study of the Markets in Construction Materials*, Kabul: AREU, available at: www.areu.org.af.

Lister, S. and Pain, A. (2004) *Trading in Power: The Politics of "free" Markets in Afghanistan*, Kabul: AREU, available at: www.areu.org.af.

Lister, S. and Wilder, A. (2005) "Strengthening Subnational Administration in

Afghanistan: Technical Reform or State-building?," *Public Administration and Development* 25(1): 39–48.

Middlebrook, P.J. and Miller, S.M. (2006) "Lessons in Post Conflict Reconstruction from the New Afghanistan Compact," Foreign Policy in Focus Policy Report, January 27, available at: www.fpif.org.

Ottaway, M. (2002) "Rebuilding State Institutions in Collapsed States," *Development and Change* 33(5): 1001–1023.

Pain, A. (2006) *Opium Trading Systems in Helmand and Ghor*, Kabul: AREU, available at: www.areu.org.af.

Reynolds, A. and Wilder, A. (2004) *Free, Fair or Flawed: Challenges for Legitimate Elections in Afghanistan*, Kabul: AREU, September, available at: www.areu.org.af.

Rubin, B. (1995) *The Fragmentation of Afghanistan: State Formation and Collapse in the International System*, New Haven, CT: Yale University Press.

—— (2004) "(Re)building Afghanistan: The Folly of Stateless Democracy," *Current History* April: 165–170.

Sedra, M. (2002) *Challenging the Warlord Culture: Security Sector Reform in Post-Taliban Afghanistan*, Bonn, Germany: Bonn International Center for Conversion (BICC).

Wilder, A. (2005) *A House Divided? Analysing the 2005 Afghan Elections*, Kabul: AREU, available at: www.areu.org.af.

World Bank (2002) *Rebuilding the Civil Service in a Post-conflict Setting: Key Issues and Lessons of Experience*, Washington, DC: World Bank, Conflict Prevention and Reconstruction Unit, Dissemination Notes No. 1.

—— (2003) *Recent Bank Support for Civil Service Reconstruction in Post-conflict Countries*, Washington, DC: World Bank, PREM Notes No. 79.

—— (2004) *Afghanistan: State-building, Sustaining Growth and Reducing Poverty*, Washington, DC: World Bank.

INDEX

258

An environmentally friendly book printed and bound in England by www.printondemand-worldwide.com

PEFC Certified

This product is
from sustainably
managed forests
and controlled
sources

PEFC

www.pefc.org

PEFC/16-33-415

FSC

www.fsc.org

MIX

Paper from
responsible sources

FSC® C004959

This book is made entirely of chain-of-custody materials

#0459 - - C0 - 234/156/15 - PB